Visions of Love

Compilation and introductions copyright © William Sykes 1992

The author acknowledges the moral right
to be identified as the author of this work

Published by
The Bible Reading Fellowship
Peter's Way, Sandy Lane West
Oxford, OX4 5HG
England
ISBN 0 7459 2522 7
Albatross Books Pty Ltd
PO Box 320, Sutherland, NSW 2232, Australia
ISBN 0 7324 0634 X

First edition 1992
Reprinted 1993, 1996

A catalogue record for this book is available
from the British Library

Printed and bound in Malta
by Interprint Ltd

VISIONS
of LOVE

An Anthology of Reflections

Compiled by William Sykes

●》 the bible reading fellowship

Contents

Preface

A READER'S VIEW

Steve Sheppard practises and teaches law in Mississippi in the United States. He was at University College, Oxford, pursuing his D.Phil. from 1989–1992. This is what he writes about *Visions of Love:*

"Here is something different. The stuff of these pages won't fit easily into a librarian's category, which is unsurprising as it seems to be drawn from them all. But there is a common thread running through it, a compelling story without a plot. I still find myself drawn to it, even after I think 'I've reflected enough for now, thank you so much.'

"A quick flip through these pages gives their skeleton: a collection of aphorisms, sayings, witticisms and Biblical bits, arranged into a host of topics. It looks from a distance like a dozen or so reference works already on my shelf.

"But Bill Sykes is not the son of Bartlett,* and there is much more than that here. It is a bit like a travelogue by a good tracker with an unknown destination. The beauty of such a journal is rarely in where the traveller is, but in what he notices and how he sees it. Here, our sturdy pilgrim has set himself a task to search for nothing less than the Holy Spirit. The paths he has chosen are the writings of Mankind, and the journey's wake is littered with brilliant artifacts. He strikes me as not unlike Ralph Emerson, learning of God through God's creations and their creations.

"I was in one of Bill's reflection groups for years, watching readers choose their topic (an easy way of focussing the worry *du jour*), digest the material (this material), and then gently prodding the discussion forward. Was it ministry, study, or just group therapy? I couldn't care less! It was at worst a study of human nature. It was at best an exciting and enlightening hour in which I and my friends faced our demons and found them tamed. In the cynical world of an Oxford college, these groups remained terrifically popular throughout my tenure there.

"You are lucky to have this book. Hopefully, it will be one of a set of three. Between them is a compendium of knowledge. It reflects a rare sort of wisdom: the insight of humanity struggling at its most enlightened."

Steve Sheppard

---

* *Bartlett* is the compiler of a well-known American anthology

HOW A SCHOOLMASTER USES AN ANTHOLOGY
OF REFLECTIONS

Robert Aldred is a housemaster at St Edward's School, a boys' boarding school in Oxford. A few years ago his wife, Alison, was the nurse at University College, and working closely in that capacity with the Chaplain of the College, Bill Sykes. Through that contact Robert discovered Bill Sykes' first anthology, Visions of Faith (now out of print) and from the moment he read it he realised what an invaluable resource it was. He has been using it for various groups in the school ever since and I asked him how.

"I use it in just one way", he told me. "We have copies of the book for the boys. We had a set of about forty at one stage, but over the years they have diminished. It is a very stimulating book, and sometimes a boy will say 'Can I borrow it?' And he will take it away for a while and then bring it back—but not always!

"What I do is to give them just one section of quotations to look at in one period, which usually lasts for forty minutes. They stay in the class room and I ask them just to go through the quotations, to think about them, and to make notes. Then the following week they come back and we discuss them. I use the book two or three times a year, and I try to choose subjects which the boys themselves are interested in pursuing.

"Basically, I use the same method that Bill uses himself, in order to get people to think about whatever subject it is, and to meditate upon it. I actually use the word meditate, and I say to them, 'To meditate means to chew it over and to thrash it through: to ask yourself whether you agree with it, and to ask yourself "What is it actually saying? What does it mean by this phrase, and that phrase?"' I find that it raises the intellectual level of discussion to a much more serious one.

"Quite often a group will tend to treat things at the level where they are, which can be rather shallow. But I have found that this book forces them to go to a level which is more mature and more demanding, and there is a greater level of seriousness in the discussion. This year I have got four groups. Three of them are fine, but one is rather hard work, because of the level of input (or the lack of it) from the various members. There is a group within the group who are somewhat immature, and they tend to be flippant and a bit silly. But using Bill's book has forced them to be more thoughtful.

"It is enormously stimulating, and it provides a broad spectrum of types of writing. To give you an example, I wanted to do something with the sixth form on marriage and sexuality, and when I was looking through those sections I found this marvellous quotation from The Prophet, by Kahlil Gibran:

But let there be spaces in your togetherness,
and let the winds of heaven dance between you.

"Brilliant! First of all I found it strange to see that juxtaposed against the Christian view of marriage. But then I thought, 'Well, there's nothing much wrong with that!' And it made me realise how good it was to read people who were writing from all backgrounds, and from all walks of life and all the Church traditions. It's an enlarging experience.

"It is interesting how the pupils invariably pick out that passage from *The Prophet.* And when we are looking at the theme of suffering they almost always pick out the passage said to have been written by a young cancer patient (and often known as Footprints):

> One night a man had a dream. He dreamt he was walking along the beach with his Lord. Across the sky flashed scenes from his life. For each scene he noticed two sets of footprints in the sand, one belonging to him, the other to the Lord. When the last scene in his life flashed before him he looked back at the footprints on the sand. He noticed that many times along the path of his life there was only one set of footprints. He also noticed that it happened at the very lowest and saddest times of his life. This really bothered him, and he questioned the Lord about it. 'Lord, you said that, once I decided to follow you, you would walk with me all the way. But I've noticed that during the most difficult times in my life there is only one set of footprints. I don't understand why, in times when I needed you most, you would leave me.' The Lord replied, 'My precious child, I love you and would never leave you during your trials and sufferings; when you see only one set of footprints, it was then that I carried you.'"

The Reverend Shelagh Brown
Bible Reading Fellowship

The story behind Visions of Love
HOW IT CAME INTO BEING AND HOW TO USE IT

A priest who lost his faith
What happens when a priest thinks he has lost his faith? I was thirty years old and, faced with this situation, saw three options: leave the Church; stay put in the Church and go through the motions; or stand my ground and fight. I had one thing on my side in making the choice—fresh memories from being a Gurkha officer. I had to fight.

Where he started the fight to find it
I started anew in the book of Genesis. In the story of the creation of man God is depicted as fashioning and shaping man in his own image. He breathed into man and man became a living being. I was fascinated by this simple story. I took it to mean that God breathed something of his own nature into man, giving a divine potential to life.

Then I turned to the Gospels and found this "something of God in man" worked out in the man—Jesus Christ. He found the Father in the depths of himself. He tried to explain this to the disciples: "Do you not believe that I am in the Father and the Father in me? ... the Father who dwells in me does His works" (John 14.10). As I struggled with what these words meant, I began to understand Jesus as the image of the invisible God.

Starting to see the way of love
This understanding brought me a new insight. Jesus discovered not only the presence of "the Father" in Himself, but also discovered that this presence is *love*, not just as an abstraction, but for people individually: "As the Father loved me, so have I loved you; abide in my love" (John 15.9) This is the basis for the two great commandments: "You shall love the Lord your God with all your heart, and with all your soul, and with all your mind, and with all your strength... and you shall love your neighbour as yourself" (Matthew 22.37-39). He made this simpler: "A new commandment I give to you, that you love one another; even as I have loved you" (John 13.34). The vision of love was beginning to take shape.

I went back to the Epistles. Paul discovered that what Christ had experienced in his life, we can all experience in some measure. Some time after his conversion on the Damascus road, Paul wrote: "It is no longer I who live, but Christ who lives in me..." (Galatians 2.20). "In Him the whole fullness of deity dwells bodily and you have come to fullness of life in Him" (Colossians 2.9-10). I knew this meant much to me, that the whole power of the Trinity could be found in each of us: Life, Light, Truth, Joy. I held fast to these and thought of Christ's words, "I came that they might have life, and have it abundantly" (John 10.10). But I still felt that I was missing some part of his vision for me.

Dust and Divinity
Then something in Genesis clicked into place: *that which was fashioned and shaped in the image and likeness of God was taken from the dust of the earth.* I saw then that in addition to being born with a "divine" potential, we are still earthy and creaturely. This was no news to me, but now I saw that if either side was repressed or allowed too much sway the consequences would be negative and destructive.

But how could I make such a balance? I went back again to the Gospels. What do we find in the life of Christ? An integration of the divine and the earthy, the godly and the creaturely—"very God and very Man"—a perfect combination of the divine and the human. I now began to understand why he was called "the second Adam". By his life, death and resurrection he had pioneered a way of integrating both sides of his nature, and so became the prototype of a new humanity. The vision of love underlying this anthology finally made sense.

In many people over many years
Granted this Vision of Love, I thought I might find evidence of it in the experience of men and women in the last two thousand years. I started searching for signs of this vision in the thoughts and words of others. Firstly I sought it in the recorded experience of saints and theologians. Secondly from poets, novelists, playwrights, musicians and artists. Thirdly, of philosophers, scientists, statesmen, historians, politicians, economists and psychologists.

The material I found has been set out in seventy-six topics. These contain many aspects of Love, and their opposites—with some related topics.

How to grow in the Vision
The aim of the Anthology is to provide a means to grow in this Vision of Love. This is done primarily through the practice of Reflection. Hence the subtitle, *An Anthology of Reflections.*

The Concise Oxford Dictionary defines "Reflection" as to "go back in thought, meditate, or consult with oneself, remind oneself, or consider." Reflection indicates a way of thinking with the mind, the imagination, intuition and feelings. It includes "lateral thinking" and "vertical thinking"—thinking which takes into account the spiritual dimension. A good description comes from the Collect for the Second Sunday in Advent (a prayer for the study of the Scriptures) . . . "Grant that we may in such wise hear them, read, mark, learn and inwardly digest them." Reflection can have a devotional aspect, and merge into meditation and contemplation. I hope *Visions of Love* can be used in many ways—as a book to dip into from time to time—as a bedside book—as a guide in time of need—as an aid to keeping a Journal—as a personal book of devotion.

How to run a reflection group
As Chaplain and Fellow of an Oxford College, I have used the material for "reflection groups". These have been very popular, and in term-time at least thirty groups of up to five students meet each week.

I have been asked to describe in detail how these groups function. We meet for an hour a week at a mutually convenient time. We begin with a cup of tea, coffee or hot chocolate and briefly catch up on news. A list of topics is circulated and after two or three minutes a topic is chosen by consensus. Each topic consists of an introduction and some twenty quotations, two from the Old Testament, two from the New Testament, and the remaining sixteen from a wide variety of sources. Each person in the group is then given a copy of this material and the reflection group gets under way.

We then have about half an hour of silence. We look through the quotations, thinking them through, and working out what they mean to us individually. Some of our participants are not used to being quiet and find silence difficult at first, so I make available a clipboard, pen and paper. We have found that writing down thoughts and insights has eased this period of silence and been a useful way of developing ideas.

As convenor of the group, I use this half-hour period to go through the quotations in the same way as the others, but in addition to formulate some questions. These can be useful for stimulating discussion in the second half of the reflection group.

At the half-way stage, I ask if everyone has completed the material. I then ask, "Was there any particular reason for choosing this topic?" Someone usually comes forward with a reason. My next question is: "Did you find anything helpful?" The person who has chosen the topic responds, and then the other members of the group join in. Having reflected on the same material, conversation comes fairly easily. As convenor, my role is mainly to listen and make sure everyone has an opportunity to contribute. Sometimes the questions formulated by me earlier are a help; often they are not needed. The group ends promptly on the hour. (Time is precious in an eight week term).

How a reflection group begins

I usually start a new group with one person. Before long he or she usually suggests a person to join. Sometimes the addition is actually uninterested in religion but a good thinker. Sometimes it is someone committed to a particular creed, often not that of the first in the group. The two of them then invite a third member and so on. So the groups are based on trust and friendship, not orthodoxy. In the groups we have Roman Catholics, Methodists, members of the Church of England, the United Reformed Church, and the Christian Union, and the occasional Jew, Hindu, Muslim, Buddhist, atheist and agnostic.

Sometimes a group doesn't grow. Some people are shy, and are not ready for the group experience. Others want to go forward slowly. A few need individual attention. Some function quite happily in twos and threes. I reckon four or five is the best working number. Trust can still be maintained, and everyone can fully participate. Above this number, communication tends to break down.

I see Visions of Love as a skeleton (or framework) of Love—and I leave it to the individual to put upon it (to clothe it with) his or her own flesh and blood.

Bill Sykes

ADORATION

"Adore" in the Concise Oxford Dictionary means "regard with the utmost respect and affection."

As a teenager I found adoration very difficult. "God" was somehow depicted as high and lifted up—many thousands of miles away—and consequently very difficult to adore. Later I came to see that first and foremost God is a "presence" in the depths of our being—something of the Father, the Son, and the Holy Spirit—and close enough to be valued and adored. Reflection, using one's mind, feelings and imagination on other people's insights on adoration, became a way of experiencing the glory, wonder and love of God.

O come, let us worship and bow down, let us kneel before the Lord, our Maker!
Psalm 95.6.

Not to us, O Lord, not to us, but to thy name give glory,
for the sake of thy steadfast love and thy faithfulness!
Psalm 115.1.

To the only God, our Saviour through Jesus Christ our Lord, be glory, majesty, dominion, and authority, before all time and now and for ever.
Jude 25.

Day and night they never cease to sing, "Holy, holy, holy, is the Lord God Almighty, who was and is and is to come!"
Revelation 4.8.

We adore in order to love, to absorb into our own beings the being of God.
Kenneth Leech, *True Prayer*, Sheldon Press, 1980, p.119.

This is adoration: not a difficult religious exercise, but an attitude of the soul.
Evelyn Underhill, *The Love of God*, Mowbray, 1953, p.136.

If we would understand Divine things, we must cultivate an attitude of humble adoration. Whoever does not begin by kneeling down, runs every possible risk.
Ernest Hello, *Life, Science, and Art*, R. & T. Washbourne Ltd., 1913, p.158.

Nothing is more needed by humanity today, and by the church in particular, than the recovery of a sense of "beyondness" in the whole of life to revive the springs of wonder and adoration.
John V. Taylor, *The Go-Between God*, SCM Press Ltd., 1973, p.45.

But "to adore" (Lat: *ad-orare*) is "to pray toward..." It is to go out of oneself, to commune with a Reality larger, deeper, purer than one's own being. Adoration is an enhancement of one's being, though paradoxically this comes about through going out of oneself.

John Macquarrie, *Paths in Spirituality*, SCM Press Ltd., 1972, p.6.

What I cry out for, like every being, with my whole life and all my earthly passions, is something very different from an equal to cherish: it is for a God to adore...

The more man becomes man, the more will he become prey to a need, a need that is always more explicit, more subtle and more magnificent, the need to adore.

Pierre Teilhard de Chardin, *Le Milieu Divin*, William Collins Sons & Co. Ltd., 1960, p.117.

They (monastics) have only one destiny: to bear the same kind of witness to God that is borne by martyrs: to praise Him at no less cost than that of the wild, perfect, supreme love that transcends every other love, every other work, every other desire; to lose itself entirely from the eyes of men in that profound abyss which is known as adoration.

Thomas Merton, *The Waters of Silence*, Hollis & Carter, 1950, p.266.

"Glory to the Father and to the Son and to the Holy Spirit."

The "content" of our adoration is self-giving love, made possible by God's having first so loved us (1 John). Like love among humans, our adoration of God expresses itself in gestures, words and silence. The "sacrifice of praise" (Heb. 13.15) is not meant to flatter God but to enact our responsive self-surrender to him.

Geoffrey Wainwright, in *A New Dictionary of Christian Theology*, edited by Alan Richardson and John Bowden, SCM Press Ltd., 1985, p.6.

Adoration leads naturally to the other responses which must always be present in worship—confession, dedication, thanksgiving and intercession... A clear awareness of failure and unworthiness must always follow a vision of the highest, and it is a sure sign that our worship has been a failure if we have not known afresh a deep need of God's forgiveness... To reaffirm our loyalty, renew our vows, and re-dedicate ourselves as instruments of His will is surely pleasing to God.

Thomas F. Green, *Preparation for Worship, (Swarthmore Lecture)*, George Allen & Unwin Publishers Ltd., 1952, p.17.

Adoration is a rejoicing in what we believe God is in himself, in the more that he must be that we cannot understand; it is a reaching out to this in love and longing, wanting to know and prove as much of this as is permitted here on earth, going to that rim of experience where something tells you to turn back to life because this is as far as you can go in wonder at the devastating richness of life. The rest we may hope to know after death, but it is not for now.

J. Neville Ward, *The Use of Praying*, Epworth Press, 1967, p.28.

Adoration and thanksgiving should be the chief part of our prayer. Our relationship to God when we come to pray is the relationship of those who adore Him because He is what He is. As we are filled with joy when we look upon some exquisite scene, so we adore God because of His transcendent and unutterable beauty. We adore Him because He has loved us, because He is Love; because He has revealed Himself to us in a human life of unspeakable beauty and tenderness; because when we treated Him worst, He treated us best; because when we rejected Him, He did not reject us; because His Holy Spirit is ever healing, restoring, and following us with mercy. We adore His unutterable love and His awful holiness.

Father Andrew, SDC, *Meditations for Every Day*, A.R. Mowbray & Co. Ltd., 1941, p.171.

Adoration can never exempt the Christian from this-world action; and this-world action, however beneficial, will fail of effect if its foundations are not based upon the life of adoration. To go back to Brother Giles's parable, the sparrow must go to the mountain; but it must also live the common sparrow life, build its nest, and feed its young. The awed sense of the mystery in which we live, and which enfolds and penetrates us, must not stultify our small human activities, but improve them. It is by this alternation of the transcendent and the homely, the interaction of lofty thought and concrete living—all the fiction and effort consequent on our two-levelled human life—that true growth of human personality is achieved.

Evelyn Underhill, *The Spiritual and the Secular*, in *Politics and the Faith*, edited by Maurice B. Reckitt, Church Literature Association, 1953, p.17.

Prayer is both the natural expression of Christian faith and its vitalizer. The adoration of the glorified Christ and the contemplation of his oneness with the Father inevitably arouse hope and joy. It is not the function of adoration to produce joy because, so understood, the multitudinous beauty of Christian praise becomes a mere pattern of incantatory formulae without reference to what is in fact the state of things. The purpose of adoration is to express faith, to say with utmost joy what we believe to be true, that as we open ourselves to Christ we become receptive to that ultimate power and love who is working continually to bring all things to fulfillment and lead all men and women out of their hates and prejudices and grievances into happiness.

J. Neville Ward, *Five for Sorrow, Ten for Joy*, Epworth Press, 1971, p.110.

Adoration is "love and worship". St Augustine closes his great work, *The City of God*, by picturing the "eternal felicity" of heaven, "where we shall have leisure to utter forth the praises of God, which shall be all things in all!... There we shall rest and see, we shall see and love, we shall love and we shall praise!" In another place he says: "The blessedness of the dwellers in God's house is to be always praising Him... The praise of God is man's highest work... the voice of praise is never silent but when we fall from righteousness."

The essence of adoration, however, is something far deeper and more demanding than the most ardent praise. It asks for our whole being; and it is rooted in the will. In the words of a French writer: "You must be convinced that you go to adoration not to receive but to give, and, further, to give often without seeing what you are giving. You go to this act of worship to give your whole being to God in the dark. And you need to realize what these words mean of obscure faith, sometimes of suffering, and always of love. Adoration is not primarily a sentiment or a thought, it is the recognition of the fact that God has laid His hand upon us... in the very depths of our being: it is a work which is greater and more absolute than we can ever imagine."

Olive Wyon, *On the Way*, SCM Press Ltd., 1958, p.101.

Adoration is a form of prayer which lies at the very heart of religion. The word which seems to characterize adoration most aptly is "absolute." On the one hand, there is the sense of the absolute claim of God. It is indeed this claim which initiates and calls forth the prayer of adoration. God is unique in his absoluteness, and so he is different from everything created and finite. That is why adoration may be offered to God alone...

It is important not to think of adoration as a kind of homage such as might be paid to an earthly ruler. That again would be to overlook the uniqueness of God's absolute being and the unique character of adoration. Homage is a bad analogy. We do not adore God for his power or even for his goodness but as the limit which surpasses everything that is admirable in our finite experience. God is the supremely Holy One, and the adjective "holy", as Otto showed, not only includes the perfection of power and goodness and mercy and so on, but the mystery of the "numinous" which surpasses all our powers of comprehension. Mystical writers have declared God to be more than power, more than goodness, more than beauty, and this is their way of saying that although these qualities do point us to God, when they are raised to the absolute they transcend our understanding. The vision of God infinitely surpasses the most beautiful and most impressive sights upon earth...

Intense adoration brings a kind of ecstasy in which the person who adores is taken out of himself and set in the context of a reality which so transcends his own in love and beauty and every perfection that he is filled with wonder and thanksgiving.

John Macquarrie, in *A Dictionary of Christian Spirituality*, edited by Gordon S. Wakefield, SCM Press Ltd., 1986, p.307.

ANGER

"Anger"— "rage, hot displeasure."

I first came across anger at school. A contemporary of mine used to go into tantrums whenever he was unable to get his own way. This used to amuse me, once I could stand outside his rage and observe it unperturbed. More serious was the Housemaster, who used to vent his wrath on us each evening, as a way of exercising power over us.

These early experiences of anger gave me some insight into the nature of anger. This "hot displeasure" can be used selfishly (as outlined above), or as a great source of energy and dynamism to be channelled in so many different and positive ways. For instance, in developing our gifts and talents and in being actively engaged in bringing about useful changes in the world around us.

Refrain from anger, and forsake wrath! Fret not yourself; it tends only to evil.

Psalm 37.8.

A soft answer turns away wrath, but a harsh word stirs up anger.

Proverbs 15.1.

But I say to you that every one who is angry with his brother shall be liable to judgment; whoever insults his brother shall be liable to the council, and whoever says, "You fool!" shall be liable to the hell of fire.

Matthew 5.22.

Let all bitterness and wrath and anger and clamour and slander be put away from you, with all malice.

Ephesians 4.31.

Anger punishes itself.

Thomas Fuller, *Gnomologia*, Stearne Brock, 1773, p.30.

Touch me with noble anger.

William Shakespeare, *King Lear*, Act II. sc.iv. l.274.

The best answer to anger is silence.

German Proverb.

Beware of the Fury of a Patient man.

John Dryden, *The Poems and Fables of John Dryden*, edited by James Kinsley, Oxford University Press, 1970, *Absalom and Achitophel*, l.1005, p.215.

Anger is never without a Reason, but seldom with a good one.

Benjamin Franklin, *Poor Richard's Almanack*, Taurus Press, 1962, p.13.

For there was never an angry man that thought his anger unjust.

St. Francis de Sales, *Introduction to the Devout Life*, translated and edited by John K. Ryan, Longmans, Green & Co. Ltd., 1962, p.141.

To be angry, is to revenge the fault of others upon our selves.

Alexander Pope, *The Prose Works of Alexander Pope*, Shakespeare Head Press, 1986, Volume II, The Major Works 1725-1744, *Thoughts on Various Subjects*, xiii, p.152.

Anger and hatred are negative emotions only when they are misdirected. Never fear to hate the odious.

A.R. Orage, *On Love*, The Janus Press, 1957, p.60.

Selfish anger is always a sin; selfless anger can be one of the great moral dynamics of the world.

William Barclay, *The Gospel of Matthew*, The Saint Andrew Press, 1987, Volume 1, p.96.

Anger is sometimes good. The world needs anger. The world often continues to allow evil because it isn't angry enough.

Bede Jarrett, OP, *The House of Gold*, Blackfriars Publications, 1954, p.19.

A man that does not know how to be angry does not know how to be good. Now and then a man should be shaken to the core with indignation over things evil.

Henry Ward Beecher, *Proverbs from Plymouth Pulpit*, Charles Burnet & Co., 1887, p.19.

There is perhaps no phenomenon which contains so much destructive feeling as "moral indignation," which permits envy or hate to be acted out under the guise of virtue.

Erich Fromm, *Man for Himself*, Routledge & Kegan Paul, 1975, p.235.

Never forget what a man has said to you when he was angry. If he has charged you with any thing, you had better look it up. Anger is a bow that will shoot sometimes where another feeling will not.

Henry Ward Beecher, *Life Thoughts*, Ward, Lock, and Tyler, 1874, p.198.

Call for the grandest of all earthly spectacles, what is *that*? It is the sun going to his rest. Call for the grandest of all human sentiments, what is *that*? It is that man should forget his anger before he lies down to sleep.

Thomas De Quincey, *Confessions of an English Opium-Eater*, A. & C. Black, 1897, p.292.

To be angry... is what any man can do and easy: but to do these to the right person, in due proportion, at the right time, with a right object, and in the right manner, this is not as before what any man can do nor is it easy.

Aristotle, *The Nicomachean Ethics of Aristotle*, translated by D.P. Chase, James Thornton, Oxford, 1877, Bk.ii, ch.9, p.52.

The intoxication of anger, like that of the grape, shows us to others, but hides us from ourselves; and we injure our own cause, in the opinion of the world, when we too passionately and eagerly defend it...

Neither will all men be disposed to view our quarrels precisely in the same light that we do; and a man's blindness to his own defects will ever increase in proportion as he is angry with others, or pleased with himself.

Charles Caleb Colton, *Lacon*, William Tegg, 1866, p.15.

Anger is natural to man. It is part of our instinctive inheritance. It is the immediate reaction of our nature to intentional injury, to militant opposition, to thwarting and injustice. Even so, it needs to be controlled. One mark of maturity is the ability to control anger. People who act instantly and violently at the impulse of anger go berserk. They say more than they mean, misrepresent their own better nature, give bitter expression to the darker moods of the soul and prove themselves incapable of balanced judgment...

W.E. Sangster, *The Secret of Radiant Life*, Hodder & Stoughton Ltd., 1957, p.153.

Anger is an offshoot of pride. When one person will react to another's dominance with envy, another person will react with anger. Anger, which sometimes explodes like a hand grenade or erupts like a volcano, is an emotion inherited from our animal ancestors whose ability on occasion to fight with fury was necessary to their survival. As everyone has observed it is one of the normal ways in which a baby reacts to the many frustrations of infant life. If a child learns from experience that to fly into a rage is an effective way of obtaining what he wants he loses the incentive to control his anger despite the unpopularity it incurs. He may grow up with a habit hard to break of losing his temper when frustrated.

Anger when it possesses a man is apt to deprive him of judgement; it leads him to speak and act unfairly, and to inflict pain recklessly. In the heat of the moment a man is provoked into words and actions which he bitterly regrets when he has cooled down. Openly expressed anger may do less harm than anger felt but unexpressed, which creates a hostile atmosphere or spreads a measure of gloom. All the same, despite the destructiveness of uncontrolled anger, when under control it can play a creative part in enabling a person to fulfil a demanding task. Controlled anger can give a teacher the inner force to maintain order in a difficult and unruly class, it can lend fire and steel to a speaker advocating an unpopular cause, it can infuse iron into a man's determination to fight some piece of injustice.

Christopher Bryant, SSJE, *The Heart in Pilgrimage*, Darton, Longman & Todd Ltd., 1980, p.39.

Anger is one of the basic emotions. For the most part it is unpleasant in its feeling tone, creates a great deal of physical tension which seeks release in action, and tends to engender both impulsiveness and a sense of power and self-assurance. It has a wide variety of causes. Its destructive potential is well known, both when it is turned outward toward others (especially when it results in violent or aggressive behaviour) and also when it is turned inward (as in bitterness, resentment, guilt, or depression). Theologically, anger has traditionally been regarded as one of the seven deadly sins, and there are many biblical passages which acknowledge its dangers and the difficulties it creates in human affairs (e.g., Gen. 4.4-8; Matt. 5.22; Gal. 5.20-21). Both Platonism and Stoicism saw anger as an irrational, and therefore unworthy passion.

The negative view of anger in Western Christian piety is currently undergoing reappraisal. In part this is a response to developing psychological awareness of the creative as well as the destructive possibilities of anger and of its importance both to survival and to quality of life... Pastoral care has recognized the importance of acknowledging what anger we have (including any we may feel toward God) and learning how to express it appropriately—for the sake of minimizing its destructive potential and of enhancing its creative possibilities...

Much of our everyday anger is petty and selfishly oriented, but if we had no capacity for anger we would equally have no capacity for genuine love and little or no motivation to attack what is evil and false in our own lives or in the life of our world. Anger is an emotion which commonly only arises when we care sufficiently about someone or something and we see that person or thing under threat. The ethical ambiguities surrounding anger are neatly summed up in Eph. 4.26: "Be angry, but do not sin."

Graeme M. Griffin, in *A New Dictionary of Christian Ethics*, edited by James F. Childress and John Macquarrie, SCM Press Ltd., 1986, p.22.

APATHY

"Apathy"—"insensibility to suffering; passionless existence; indolence of mind."

W hilst doing National Service in the Army, I came across someone suffering from apathy during basic training. He lacked motivation and had very little energy, except when the Corporal's boot was behind him. His favourite occupation was to sit on his bed and smoke. With eyes half shut, just knocking off the ash of his cigarette required a superhuman effort!

The reasons why we are apathetic can be complex. In some cases it is sheer laziness. More often it is due to a host of contributory factors—heredity, environment, bad experiences, and a consequent inability to find a sense of purpose and meaning in life. Somehow we need to find "an upwelling spring of life" in ourselves, and then to use it in furthering life around us, in activity.

When will you arise from your sleep? A little sleep, a little slumber, a little folding of the hands to rest, and poverty will come upon you like a vagabond, and want like an armed man.

Proverbs 6.9–11.

The soul of the sluggard craves, and gets nothing.

Proverbs 13.4.

Do you want to be shown... that faith apart from works is barren?
James 2.20.

Would that you were cold or hot! So, because you are lukewarm, and neither cold nor hot, I will spew you out of my mouth.
Revelation 3.15-16.

To live a life half dead, a living death.
John Milton, *The Poetical Works of John Milton*, Oxford University Press, 1950, *Samson Agonistes*, l.100, p.551.

Indolence is a delightful but distressing state: we must be doing something to be happy.
William Hazlitt, *The Collected Works of William Hazlitt*, J.M. Dent & Sons Ltd.., 1903, Vol. VI, *Table Talk*, p.11.

It is the just doom of laziness and gluttony, to be inactive without ease, and drowsy without tranquillity.
Samuel Johnson, *The Yale Edition of the Works of Samuel Johnson*, Yale University Press, 1963, Volume II, *The Idler and The Adventurer, The Adventurer*, No.39, p.351.

There is in man an upwelling spring of life, energy, love, whatever you like to call it. If a course is not cut for it, it turns the ground round it into a swamp.
Mark Rutherford, *More Pages From a Journal*, Oxford University Press, 1910, p.246.

Ennui, perhaps, has made more gamblers than avarice, more drunkards than thirst, and perhaps, as many suicides as despair. Its only cure is the pursuit of some desirable object.
Charles Caleb Colton, *Lacon*, William Tegg, 1866, p.85.

Most persons have died before they expire—died to all earthly longings, so that the last breath is only, as it were, the locking of the door of the already deserted mansion.
Oliver Wendell Holmes, *The Breakfast-Table Series*, The Professor at the Breakfast Table, Thomas Nelson & Sons, Ltd., 1906, p.227.

Most people go on living their every-day life: half-frightened, half indifferent, they behold the ghostly tragi-comedy that is being performed on the international stage before the eyes and ears of the world.
Albert Einstein, *Out of My Later Years*, Thames and Hudson Ltd., 1950, p.204.

And boredom, ennui, depression
are long slow vibrations of pain
that possess the whole body
and cannot be localised.
D.H. Lawrence, *The Complete Poems of D.H. Lawrence*, William Heinemann Ltd., edited by Vivian de Sola Pinto and Warren Roberts, 1967, Volume Two, *Boredom, Ennui, Depression*, p.627.

There is the sheer *inertia of human nature*. It is true of so many people that the only thing they desire is to be left alone. They automatically shrink away from anything which is disturbing, and even choice is a disturbance.
William Barclay, *The Gospel of Matthew*, The Saint Andrew Press, 1975, Volume 2, p.44.

It's extraordinary how we go through life with eyes half shut, with dull ears, with dormant thoughts. Perhaps it's just as well; and it may be that it is this very dullness that makes life to the incalculable majority so supportable and so welcome.

Joseph Conrad, *Lord Jim*, J.M. Dent & Sons Ltd., 1946, p.143.

The characteristic modern disease is boredom; and boredom is the direct result of selfishness. So long as a man lives on the principle of, "Why should I do it? Let someone else do it," he is bound to be bored. The interest of life lies in service.

William Barclay, *The Letters to Timothy, Titus & Philemon*, The Saint Andrew Press, 1987, p.259.

It is appalling to reflect that there are enormous masses of human energy which can find no proper outlet. The consequence is mischief either through expression in any direction and at any cost, or through suppression. We want an organization of energy, one of the noblest offices of a true Church.

Mark Rutherford, *More Pages From a Journal*, Oxford University Press, 1910, p.227.

If we were to live in a covenant with this passionate God, we would not become apathetic. Our whole life would be shaped by sympathy, by compassion. We would suffer with God's suffering in the world, and rejoice with God's rejoicing over the world. We would do both at the same time and with the highest intensity because we would love, and with the love of God we would go outside ourselves.

Jürgen Moltmann, *The Open Church*, SCM Press Ltd., 1978, p.23.

Perhaps what's wrong is simply lack of vitality.
The frame of things has grown so heavy, it's just too heavy for men altogether.
So, the poor male has succumbed under it.
And a boy, as he reaches the age of fourteen, when he should become manly and tackle the outside world
Caves inward, knowing the outside world
The wild gods send vitality, they put the lightning into the hand
Of those that can use it, smite with it.

D.H. Lawrence, *The Complete Poems of D.H. Lawrence*, edited by Vivian de Sola Pinto and Warren Roberts, William Heinemann Ltd., 1967, Volume II, *What's Wrong*, p.842.

For a physician apathy is a symptom of illness. The apathetic patient appears exhausted. He no longer participates in what is going on about him. His perceptions decline and his feelings die away. He no longer reacts to visits and conversation addressed to him. To me such apathy seems to be a characteristic sign of the illness of our society and of many individuals in it. Interest in life is crippled. The "courage to be" is weakened. One withdraws into a cell, boxes oneself in, locks oneself up in order not to be exposed to suffering, and so passes life by. One really doesn't live anymore but grows stiff in a living body.

Jürgen Moltmann, *The Open Church*, SCM Press Ltd., 1978, p.20.

Apathy is a state, sometimes found in a distressed person, where all emotion and feeling appears to be absent. It presents as coldness, and can be mistaken for indifference, but should be understood as psychological protection against feeling rather than as lack of feeling...

Apathy is often seen as a state of despair; an apparent indifference to possible future events or to the consequences of intended action; a sense that nothing matters, that nothing has meaning...

Apathy shows itself in a lack of motivation; absence of energy; inability to carry out necessary tasks; and, generally, incapacity to function in an effective way. There is an absence of emotion of any kind towards others, a sense of lassitude, and often of helplessness.

Barbara K. Fowles, in *A Dictionary of Pastoral Care*, edited by Alastair V. Campbell, SPCK, 1987, p.17.

Sloth or accidie, to give it its ancient name, is the last of the seven capital sins. It refers to something more than mere physical self-indulgence; it is lethargy of the spirit, a weariness of life, a boredom in which nothing seems worth while. Frank Lake has shown the close resemblance between the symptoms of accidie as outlined by the old ascetic writers and those which the modern psychotherapist associates with depression. Doctors now recognise that depression can be a disease which requires medical treatment. But there is a normal depression which often succeeds a burst of activity in which much nervous energy has been expended, or some big disappointment or painful bereavement. It is as though a black dog lurks within some people waiting its opportunity to leap out and occupy the centre of the mental stage. The old writers recognised that underneath accidie there lived the demon of bottled-up rage. When a person who has for long restrained his anger under severe provocation of a sudden completely loses his temper he often experiences a wild lifting of his spirits. It is often the inability to express anger openly that is the prime cause of depression. If sloth is often linked with bottled-up anger, it can also be allied with pride. So long as I maintain a masterly inactivity I can cling to my picture of myself as a person of great talents.

If I were to act, this picture might be shattered; therefore better do nothing. By inactivity I can keep up my sense of superiority to all the people who run around trying to make themselves important. Many evils have been tolerated because those who could have put an end to them were too lazy to act. All the same, sloth is not wholly evil, or rather, it is the corruption of an attitude potentially good. The world is not merely something to be exploited and used; it is something to be appreciated and delighted in; to those whose ears are open it can speak of the Creator who made it. It is good sometimes just to stand and stare. There is a creative leisure out of which is born the vision which makes action fruitful. Perhaps this creative, contemplative leisure is what the world above all needs today. It is the true answer to the boredom which has been called public enemy number one in the contemporary world.

Christopher Bryant, SSJE, *The Heart in Pilgrimage*, Darton, Longman & Todd Ltd., 1980, p.41.

AWARENESS

"Awareness"—"a condition of conscious knowing."

In the latter reaches of a nine year period as Chaplain to University College, London, I was invited to join a group consisting of the Director of the Health Centre (a psychiatrist), two G.P. doctors from the Health Centre, and the Student Counsellor.

We met once a fortnight. We took it in turns to present a student problem. If it was my turn I would put before the others all the material facts about the student and the problem, except his or her name—observing confidentiality. We would then try to solve the problem. The psychiatrist would make one or two observations arising out of his background and training, and bring his analytical skills to bear on the problem. The two G.P.s would then join in, looking to the medical side, and drawing on their practical experience. They in turn were followed by the Student Counsellor who tackled the problem from a different angle and invariably came out with something previously not considered. We would then discuss the problem afresh in the light of what had been forthcoming in the meeting. At the end of the hour's session, I would leave the Health Centre, feeling that my awareness and brain-power had increased four-fold. As a consequence there was now a real possibility of solving the problem. In addition the increased knowledge and awareness could be brought to bear on other problems in the future.

Reflection Groups, and using this Anthology on an individual basis, work on the same principle, with the aim of increasing our awareness in many different areas of life.

Only take heed, and keep your soul diligently, lest you forget the things which your eyes have seen, and lest they depart from your heart.
Deuteronomy 4.9.

Consider what you do, for you judge not for man but for the Lord.
2 Chronicles 19.6.

But watch at all times.
Luke 21.36.

I desire you to insist on these things, so that those who have believed in God may be careful to apply themselves to good deeds; these are excellent and profitable to men.
Titus 3.8.

Lack of sensitivity is perhaps an unawareness of ourselves.
Eric Hoffer, *The Passionate State of Mind*, Martin Secker & Warburg Ltd., 1956, p.76.

All true intercession is a deepening of awareness towards others rather than a request.
John V. Taylor, *The Go-Between God*, SCM Press Ltd., 1973, p.232.

He that would live in peace and at ease, must not speak all he knows, nor judge all he sees.
Benjamin Franklin, *Poor Richard's Almanack*, Taurus Press, 1962, p.4.

The inability to see into ourselves often manifests itself in a certain coarseness and clumsiness. One can be brazen, rude and even dishonest without being aware of it.
Eric Hoffer, *The Passionate State of Mind*, Martin Secker & Warburg Ltd., 1956, p.76.

Be quite sure that you will never have the unclouded vision of God here in this life. But you may have the awareness of him, if he is willing by his grace to give it you.
The Cloud of Unknowing, translated by Clifton Wolters, Penguin Books Ltd., 1971, p.66.

He (Jesus) was not concerned with advice about conduct, but with the exposure of motive, penetrating the inner heart's secrets with the two-edged sword of his inescapable insight.
F.R. Barry, *The Relevance of Christianity*, James Nisbet & Co. Ltd., 1932, p.75.

When thou lookest upon the Imperfections of others, allow one Eye for what is Laudable in them, and the balance they have from some excellency, which may render them considerable.

Sir Thomas Browne, *The Works of Sir Thomas Browne*, edited in 4 volumes by Geoffrey Keynes, Faber & Faber Ltd., 1964, Volume 1, *Christian Morals*, p.254.

We can then have an excellent knowledge of God without that of our own wretchedness, and of our own wretchedness without that of God. But we cannot know Jesus Christ without knowing at the same time both God and our own wretchedness.

Blaise Pascal, *Pensées*, translated by W.F. Trotter, Random House, Inc., 1941, p.181.

If we had a keen vision and feeling of all ordinary human life, it would be like hearing the grass grow and the squirrel's heart beat, and we should die of that roar which lies on the other side of silence. As it is, the quickest of us walk about well wadded with stupidity.

George Eliot, *Middlemarch*, Penguin Books Ltd., 1985, p.226.

We must so heed God all our days that our sensitivity is never blunted, that our awareness is never dimmed, that our spiritual hearing never becomes spiritual deafness. It is a law of life that we will only hear what we are listening for, and that we will only hear what we have fitted ourselves to hear.

William Barclay, *The Gospel of Matthew*, The Saint Andrew Press, 1975, Volume 2, p.50.

If we do not understand our fellow-creatures we shall never love them. And it is equally true, that if we do not love them we shall never understand them. Want of charity, want of sympathy, want of good feeling and fellow-feeling—what does it, what can it breed but endless mistakes and ignorances, both of men's characters and men's circumstances?

Charles Kingsley, *Daily Thoughts*, Macmillan Publishers Ltd., 1884, p.103.

The person who never notices the person next to him can never move beyond and see the "incognito" Christ in him. Busyness can lead pastors to miss seeing those they meet: people can be a hindrance in a carefully-planned schedule for the day, since they are so unpredictable and time-consuming. And simply to be noticed, recognized as a person, transforms the day for many people.

Frank Wright, *The Pastoral Nature of the Ministry*, SCM Press Ltd., 1980, p.34.

In order to understand the signs that you see and perceive their significance you must be small and humble of heart.

It is essential!

It seems absurd but it is precisely for this reason that many people remain outside the truth. "Seeing they do not see, and hearing they do not hear..." (Matthew 13.13).

And God passes them by.

Carlo Carretto, *The Desert in the City*, translated by Barbara Wall, William Collins Sons & Co. Ltd., 1983, p.40.

Whoever really loves will use a magnifying glass to see the small and hidden details of another's need. I will be able to see that he has cold feet and I can move him nearer the fire; that he is deaf and I must speak closer to his ear; that a secret anxiety torments him; that he longs for a good word; and many more such things which usually lie, seemingly hidden, under the surface of our lives.

Helmut Thielicke, *I Believe—The Christian's Creed*, translated by John W. Doberstein and M. George Anderson, William Collins Sons & Co. Ltd., 1969, p.35.

While we are immersed in our own thoughts we cannot recognise the reality of other people's needs, we do not see the other person at all as he is; all we see is a being who is or is not meeting our requirements. For this reason most domestic dissension is a battle between ghosts. Neither husband nor wife is loving or hating the real other, only an illusion, a projection of his or her personal wishes or resentments.

J. Neville Ward, *The Use of Praying*, Epworth Press, 1967, p.25.

Study the human figure, both as intrinsically beautiful and as expressing mind. It only expresses the broad natural childish emotions, which are just what we want to return to from our over subtlety. Study "natural language"—I mean the language of attitude. It is an inexhaustible source of knowledge and delight, and enables one human being to understand another so perfectly. Therefore learn to draw and paint figures.

Charles Kingsley, *Daily Thoughts*, Macmillan Publishers Ltd., 1884, p.155.

To become different from what we are, we must have some awareness of what we are. Whether this being different results in dissimulation or a real change of heart—it cannot be realized without self-awareness.

Yet it is remarkable that the very people who are most self-dissatisfied and crave most for a new identity have the least self-awareness. They have turned away from an unwanted self and hence never had a good look at it. The result is that the most dissatisfied can neither dissimulate nor attain a real change of heart. They are transparent, and their unwanted qualities persist through all attempts at self-dramatization and self-transformation.

Eric Hoffer, *The Passionate State of Mind*, Martin Secker & Warburg Ltd., 1956, p.75.

There is a long story by Henry James... titled "The Beast in the Jungle." It is about a man who confides in a woman, over the years, that something important is meant to happen to him in life and when it does, he will seize the event to live life to the fullest. Years pass and the event never appears to occur. The woman dies, and it is only then that he realizes that *she* was the event—her selfless love was what he should have seized upon in order to return it as fully as he could. However, in his self-centredness he could not recognize the truth of their association. How true that may be of each of us in our relationship with Jesus? Are we in danger of passing through life virtually unaware that Christ is already present to us and in us? Awareness is, after all, an important aspect to Christian virtue.

Harry James Cargas, *Encountering Myself*, SPCK, 1978, p.8.

With regard to the world around one, there should be a conscious willed period of attentiveness each day. It is the will that has to be used to raise the consciousness from the depths of the self to the world outside. It is important to notice positively the objects in one's environment, the things in the familiar street, the flowers and trees in the garden and park, and above all the people one passes to and from one's work. Each is complete in itself, but it needs our recognition, just as we need the recognition of others to be fully human. If we do not trouble to recognise others because of inner preoccupation, no one will trouble to recognise us. It is important not only to recognise and acknowledge the uniqueness of each object and each person but also to flow out to them in silent gratitude for being what they are. All life in awareness is a blessing, and we show this by blessing those around us. This does not require a formula or an articulated statement; it is essentially an inner attitude.

This awareness of the meaningfulness of the surroundings and our gratitude that it should be so is the precursor of the prayer of thanksgiving and praise.

Martin Israel, M.B., *An Approach to Spirituality*, published under the auspices of the Mysticism Committee of the Churches Fellowship for Psychical and Spiritual Studies, 1971, p.28.

BLESSINGS

"Blessings"—"happiness; enjoyment of divine favours."

I t took me some thirty-six years to understand the mystery of blessings. The insight came through a re-reading of the Genesis story of the creation of man. In that story God is depicted as fashioning and shaping man in His own image and likeness, and the last thing He did was to breathe into man for man to become a living being. I've taken that to mean that all of us have an enormous source of life in the depths of ourselves. If we want to see this fully worked out in a life we can go to the person of Jesus Christ—recognized in Scripture as "the image of the invisible God." During His life He found something of the "Father's" presence in the depths of Himself—as well as the Holy Spirit, and such attributes as Life, Light, Truth, Joy and Love. In this He experienced Blessings and discovered true "happiness; enjoyment of divine favours."

The Good News of the Gospel is that we too can find this source of happiness and divine favour in the depths of ourselves. Reflection on these passages might well trigger it off, so that we can live our lives in love and compassion, and experience blessings for ourselves.

For thou dost meet him with goodly blessings; thou dost set a crown of fine gold upon his head. He asked life of thee; thou gavest it to him.

Psalm 21.3-4.

The blessing of the Lord makes rich, and he adds no sorrow with it.

Proverbs 10.22.

For to every one who has will more be given, and he will have abundance.

Matthew 25.29.

Every good endowment and every perfect gift is from above, coming down from the Father of lights with whom there is no variation or shadow due to change.

James 1.17.

But blessedness comes to the man who, in spite of failures and failings, still clutches to him the passionate love of the highest.

William Barclay, *The Gospel of Matthew*, The Saint Andrew Press, 1987, Volume 1, p.100.

The soul of man can by recognizing God draw Him into its narrow boundaries, but also by love to Him itself expand into the Infinite—and this is blessedness on earth.

Jacob Burchhardt, *The Civilization of the Renaissance in Italy*, Harper & Brothers, Publishers, 1958, p.516.

Grant to them, too, Lord, eternal rest, and may your perpetual light shine on them as on us. May it shine upon them now as the light of faith, and then in eternity, as the light of the blessed life.

Karl Rahner, S.J, *The Eternal Year*, translated by John Shea, Burns & Oates Ltd., 1964, p.144.

Bless to me, O God, my body and my soul;
Bless to me, O God, belief, condition whole;
Bless to me, O God, my heart, my speaking too,
And bless to me, O God, the things my hands do.

Catherine Maclennan, in *God in our midst*, Martin Reith, Triangle/SPCK., 1989, p.19.

There is nothing that is a greater blessing in a community than a man who is known to be an honest, truth-speaking man, and who is kind and genial and cheerful everywhere and at all times.

Henry Ward Beecher, *Proverbs from Plymouth Pulpit*, Charles Burnet & Co., 1887, p.170.

God is present in a silent way always. A certain hidden element or hiding element then is in the Divine mind. God's blessings steal into life noiselessly. They are neither self-proclaiming nor even self-announcing.

Henry Ward Beecher, *Proverbs from Plymouth Pulpit*, Charles Burnet & Co., 1887, p.136.

When God at first made man,
Having a glass of blessings standing by;
Let us (said he) pour on him all we can:
Let the world's riches, which dispersed lie,
Contract into a span.

George Herbert, *The Poems of George Herbert*, Oxford University Press, 1967, *The Pulley*, p.150.

All the great works and wonders that God has ever wrought or shall ever work in or through the creatures, or even God Himself with all His goodness, so far as these things exist or are done outside of me, can never make me blessed, but only in so far as they exist and are done and loved, known, tasted and felt within me.

Theologia Germanica, translated by Susanna Winkworth, Stuart & Watkins, 1966, p.48.

Neither evil tongues,
Rash judgements, nor the sneers of selfish men,
Nor greetings where no kindness is, nor all
The dreary intercourse of daily life,
Shall e'er prevail against us, or disturb
Our cheerful faith, that all which we behold
Is full of blessings.

William Wordsworth, *Lines Composed a Few Miles above Tintern Abbey*, l.128.

Blessings and thanks for ever for the sweet rain; blessings for the fresh fresh air blowing, and the meadows illimitable and the grass and clouds;
Blessings and thanks for you, you wild waters eternally flowing: O come flowing, encroaching, over me, in my ears: I salute you who are pure and sweet (ah! what designs, what love, are hid within you!)—
I praise you for your faithfulness for ever.

Edward Carpenter, *Towards Democracy*, George Allen & Unwin Publishers Ltd., 1931, p.27.

The first Beatitude is very properly first. "Blessed are the poor in spirit." This means: Blessed is he who knows that he is not wise and good and strong enough to make himself good, and who therefore relies wholly upon God to give him that positive righteousness which alone is sufficient. The man in Christ is not distinguished by the absence of evil in him, but by the dominant and overmastering presence in him of the good which comes from God.

Carroll E. Simcox, *The Promises of God*, Dacre Press: A. & C. Black, 1958, p.91.

The Spirit of Love, wherever it is, is its own Blessing and Happiness, because it is the Truth and Reality of God in the Soul; and therefore is in the same Joy of Life, and is the same Good to itself, everywhere, and on every Occasion...

Would you know the Blessing of all Blessings, it is this God of Love dwelling in your Soul, and killing every Root of Bitterness, which is the Pain and Torment of every earthly selfish Love. For all Wants are satisfied, all Disorders of Nature are removed, no Life is any longer a Burden, every Day is a Day of Peace, everything you meet becomes a Help to you, because everything you see or do is all done in the sweet gentle Element of Love.

William Law, *The Spirit of Prayer and The Spirit of Love*, edited by Sidney Spencer, James Clarke & Co. Ltd., 1969, p.165.

Life indeed must be measured by thought and action, not by time. It certainly may be, and ought to be, bright, interesting, and happy; and, according to the Italian proverb, "if all cannot live on the Piazza, everyone may yet feel the sun."

If we do our best; if we do not magnify trifling troubles; if we look resolutely, I do not say at the bright side of things, but at things as they really are; if we avail ourselves of the manifold blessings which surround us; we cannot but feel that life is indeed a glorious inheritance. Few of us, however, realise the wonderful privilege of living, or the blessings we inherit; the glories and beauties of the Universe, which is our own if we choose to have it so; the extent to which we can make ourselves what we wish to be; or the power we possess of securing peace, of triumphing over pain and sorrow.

Sir John Lubbock, *The Pleasures of Life*, Macmillan Publishers Ltd., 1891, p.5.

O man... whoever you are, stand still for a moment, and think earnestly of the high dignity for which you were created and sent into the world by God. You were not made for time and for passing things, but for God and eternity, and to have your heart filled with God and with things eternal.

You are here for a while that you may seek the blessed face of God, from which sin has turned you away, so that you fix your eyes only on the things below, whereas if you turned to Him, you would be filled through and through with light and holiness, and God would have in you His pleasure, His joy, His peace, and His contentment, and you would have yours in Him.

In this one thing all your gladness and blessedness consist, in time and in eternity, which nothing beside God can give you. The outside things of this world can scarcely bring you any pleasure, even for the short time of your weary life. You have within you an eye that is not satisfied with seeing, a mind that can find no rest except in that which is all-sufficient, and of endless loveliness, and this is in God alone.

Gerhard Tersteegen, in *Sketches of the Quiet in the Land*, Frances Bevan, John F. Shaw and Co., 1891, p.398.

One great cause of our insensibility to the goodness of the Creator is the very *extensiveness* of His bounty. We prize but little what we share only in common with the rest, or with the generality of our species. When we hear of blessings, we think forthwith of successes, of prosperous fortunes, of honours, riches, preferments, i.e., of those advantages and superiorities over others which we happen either to possess, or to be in pursuit of, or to covet. The common benefits of our nature entirely escape us. Yet these are the great things. These constitute what most properly ought to be accounted blessings of Providence; what alone, if we might so speak, are worthy of its care. Nightly rest and daily bread, the ordinary use of our limbs and senses, and understandings, are gifts which admit of no comparison with any other. Yet, because almost every man we meet with possesses these, we leave them out of our enumeration. They raise no sentiments; they move no gratitude. Now, herein is our judgment perverted by our selfishness. A blessing ought in truth to be the *more* satisfactory—the bounty at least of the donor is rendered more conspicuous—by its very diffusion, its commonness, its cheapness: by its falling to the lot and forming the happiness of the great bulk and body of our species, as well as of ourselves. Nay, even when we do not possess it, it ought to be matter of thankfulness that others do. But we have a different way of thinking. We court distinction. That is not the worst; we *see* nothing but what has distinction to recommend it. This necessarily contracts our views of the Creator's beneficence within a narrow compass; and most unjustly. It is in those things which are so common as to be no distinction that the amplitude of the Divine benignity is perceived.

William Paley, *Natural Theology*, Ward Lock, 1879, p.233.

BROTHERHOOD

"Brotherhood"—"fraternal tie; companionship; community of feeling."

One of the happiest periods of my life was spent in Singapore during National Service, in which I was commissioned into a Gurkha Battalion. During that short time with them I learnt a great deal about brotherhood. Four characteristics were particularly prominent—courage and bravery—a pride in their job—an infectious sense of humour—and a great capacity for friendship and brotherhood.

Several years later I went to their country, Nepal, as interpreter on an Oxford University Expedition. Towards the end of our stay, we were camped at 10,000 feet on the slopes of Annapurna, and the local village decided to put on a party for us. I remember leaving the party at about 1.00am. The moonlight on the shining peaks of the main Himalayan range was breathtakingly beautiful. I was joined by an ex-Gurkha soldier and for a few moments we gazed in silence at the magnificent spectacle. After a while he said quietly, "Do you know why we Gurkhas and the British get on so well with each other? It's because we both believe in the same God." Now the Gurkhas are Hindus, but when I later became conscious of what is meant by man being made in the image and likeness of God, I began to understand the simplicity and profundity of his observation. All men are made in the image and likeness of God, no matter what race, colour or creed. And a consequence of this should be—brotherhood.

For the poor will never cease out of the land; therefore I command you, You shall open wide your hand to your brother, to the needy and to the poor, in the land.
Deuteronomy 15.11.

Have we not all one father? Has not one God created us?
Malachi 2.10.

Love one another with brotherly affection; outdo one another in showing honour. Never flag in zeal, be aglow with the Spirit, serve the Lord. Rejoice in your hope, be patient in tribulation, be constant in prayer. Contribute to the needs of the saints, practise hospitality.
Romans 12.10-13.

For he who sanctifies and those who are sanctified have all one origin. That is why he is not ashamed to call them brethren.
Hebrews 2.11.

We cannot possibly let ourselves get frozen into regarding everyone we do not know as an absolute stranger.
Albert Schweitzer, *Memories of Childhood and Youth*, translated by C.T. Campion, George Allen & Unwin Publishers Ltd., 1924, p.95.

Admiration for ourselves and our institutions is too often measured by our contempt and dislike for foreigners.
W.R. Inge, *Outspoken Essays*, Longmans, Green & Co. Ltd., 1933, p.36.

Men need brotherhood and sympathy as much as they need the loaf. The soul is often hungrier than the body, and no shops can sell it food.
Henry Ward Beecher, *Proverbs from Plymouth Pulpit*, Charles Burnet & Co., 1887, p.15.

The brotherhood of man is evoked by particular men according to their circumstances. But it seldom extends to all men. In the name of freedom and our brotherhood we are prepared to blow up the other half of mankind and to be blown up in turn.
R.D. Laing, *The Politics of Experience*, Penguin Books Ltd., 1967, p.79.

Make a rule, and pray to God to help you to keep it, never, if possible, to lie down at night without being able to say, I have made one human being at least a little wiser, a little happier, or a little better this day. You will find it easier than you think, and pleasanter.
Charles Kingsley, *Daily Thoughts*, Macmillan Publishers Ltd., 1884, p.83.

I understand the origin of brotherhood among men. Men were brothers in God. One can be a brother only *in* something. Where there is no tie that binds men, men are not united but merely lined up. One cannot be a brother to nobody...
  As the inheritors of God, my civilization made men to be brothers in Man.
Antoine de Saint-Exupéry, *Flight to Arras*, translated by Lewis Galantière, William Heinemann Ltd., 1942, p.147.

You mustn't just tolerate yourself. You must also *love* yourself. If you don't love yourself, how could you possibly love your brother? The Lord asks you to love him as yourself. Loving yourself means first accepting your limitations and weaknesses.

Then, *believing in yourself,* that is, being confident in the knowledge that the Lord has given you all you need to do what you must do, wherever you find yourself.

Michel Quoist, *With Open Heart*, translated by Colette Copeland, Gill and Macmillan Ltd., 1983, p.183.

So this commandment of the love of our brethren is the supreme wish of Christ: it is so much His desire that He makes of it, not a counsel, but a commandment, *His* commandment, and He makes the fulfilment of it the infallible sign by which His disciples shall be recognised ... It is a sign all can understand, none other is given: no one can be mistaken as to it: the supernatural love you have for one another will be the unequivocal proof that you truly belong to Me. And, in fact, in the first centuries, the pagans recognised the Christians by this sign: "See," they would say, "how they love one another".

D. Columba Marmion, *Christ: the Life of the Soul*, Sands & Company, 1922, p.353.

The next thing to the love of God is the love of our neighbour, and that is attested by the most mystical saints. S. John says, "If a man say, I love God, and hateth his brother, he is a liar: for he that loveth not his brother whom he hath seen, how can he love God Whom he hath not seen?" "I should not love my neighbour," says S. Teresa, "unless the love of God were in me." The love of our brother is the test of our love of God.

We are called to a discipleship in fellowship. There is great joy in the comradeship of disciples and good men, but fellowship with others is to have in it something much more rich and sacramental than just the comfort that we get from their company. We are bound together in mystic reality with other people; and our failures help them to fall, and our triumphs help them to win. The rich joy of fellowship with one's brothers and sisters in life is in this, that our service to them, if it is true, is inseparably bound up with our loyalty to God. If my friendship is to be valuable, I as a friend must be valuable, and my value depends really on my own degree of union with God. Each time we look forward to meeting a friend again, we should look forward to bringing to that friend a worthier personality and so a richer friendship.

Father Andrew, SDC, *The Way of Victory*, Mowbray, 1938, p.97.

His standard of human life is the highest yet conceived, and brotherhood is its central and abiding element. He gives a religion which takes up and absorbs all the truths in other religions, including the law and the prophets, and He adds the factors which make it ultimate, and will in due course, render it universal; and in every line of it it is the religion of brotherhood; and its unique characteristic and strong commendation is, that He who founds it, *is* Himself what He taught. He achieved the life He prescribed. He was the Brother every man should be. Action preceded and led the way for speech. He did, and then, said. The "Mountain Sermon" astonished those who heard it, partly because of its contents but also because in fact it was backed up by His deeds, was autobiographic and charged with the mighty forces of His personality. The Beatitudes were lived first; and then fell from His lips in their native simplicity and beauty. The seemingly impossible ethics He preached as principles of living were counsels He had followed. He had loved His enemies; prayed for those who despitefully used Him; and enjoyed the blessing of those who were persecuted for the sake of the right and the true and the good; displaced anxiety by trust, and low aims by the most determined search for the Kingdom of God. He is the supreme authority on brotherhood because He lived the brother's life; not only without a solitary flaw, but with a splendid fulness and strength. So we sit at His feet with unlimited confidence, and bow to His authority with glad reverence and unstinted homage.

John Clifford, *The Gospel of World Brotherhood According to Jesus*, Hodder & Stoughton Ltd.\, 1919, p.12.

CHARITY

"Charity"—"Christian love of fellow men, kindness, natural affection."

J ust outside Pokhara in Western Nepal there used to be a Tibetan Refugee Camp. It was run, almost single-handedly, by a Swiss nurse from the Red Cross—Sister Matilde. She held a surgery each day in a makeshift dispensary, but her duties didn't end there. She had set up a school for the children, who enthusiastically went about their studies. We were taken round the workshops—a hive of cheerful activity. Cotton was being spun, clothes made, rugs woven, and Tibetan boots manufactured, all under her careful supervision. We were led out to an area of land, supposedly impossible to cultivate, where several varieties of vegetables and crops were growing. The Camp was almost self-sufficient, mainly due to her tireless efforts and inspiration. She had adopted a two year old Tibetan boy, Dowa, whose parents had been killed. Whenever he saw her his face lit up and was radiant, and this in turn was reciprocated. Deep inside her was a certain sympathy and feeling for these people, matched with costly sacrificial activity—charity in action.

If there is among you a poor man ... you shall not harden your heart or shut your hand against your poor brother, but you shall open your hand to him, and lend him sufficient for his need, whatever it may be.

Deuteronomy 15.7-8.

I was eyes to the blind, and feet to the lame. I was a father to the poor, and I searched out the cause of him whom I did not know.

Job 29.15-16.

He said also to the man who had invited him, "When you give a dinner or a banquet, do not invite your friends or your brothers or your kinsmen or rich neighbours, lest they also invite you in return, and you be repaid. But when you give a feast, invite the poor, the maimed, the lame, the blind, and you will be blessed, because they cannot repay you. You will be repaid at the resurrection of the just."

Luke 14.12-14.

And above all things have fervent charity among yourselves: for charity shall cover the multitude of sins.

1 Peter 4.8 (A.V.).

For I believe there is no sentiment he has such faith in as that "Charity begins at home."

R.B. Sheridan, *The Dramatic Works of Sheridan*, Oxford University Press, 1946, *The School for Scandal*, Act 5. sc.1. p.259.

In Faith and Hope the world will disagree,
But all Mankind's concern is Charity.

Alexander Pope, *The Poems of Alexander Pope*, edited by Maynard Mack, Methuen & Co. Ltd., 1950, Volume III, *An Essay on Man*, l.307, p.125.

Zeal dropt in charity, is good; without it, good for nothing: for it devours all it comes near.

William Penn, *Fruits of Solitude*, A.W. Bennett, 1863, p.65.

When love is merely a decision of the will and not also a venture of the heart, it lacks genuine humanity. It lacks depth, warmth, intimacy, tenderness, cordiality. Christian charity often made little impression just because it had so little humanity.

Hans Küng, *On Being a Christian*, translated by Edward Quinn, William Collins Sons & Co. Ltd., 1977, p.262.

And this is that *charity* I named as the second branch of religion, and under which all the parts of justice, all the duties we owe to our neighbour, are eminently comprehended: for he who doth truly love all the world, will be nearly concerned in the interest of every one; and so far from wrongdoing or injuring any person, that he will resent any evil that befalls others, as if it happened to himself.

Henry Scougal, *The Life of God in the Soul of Man*, C.J.G. & F. Rivington, 1829, p.16.

The fire of Charity, lit in the soul, needs careful tending. The first tiny flame must not be allowed to lie down for lack of fuel; and we may have to feed it with things we should prefer to keep for ourselves. It will only be developed and kept burning in a life informed by prayer—faithful, steady, mortified, self-oblivious prayer, the humble aspiration of the spirit to its Source: indeed, the very object of prayer is to increase and maintain Charity, the loving friendship of the soul with God.

Evelyn Underhill, in *The Wisdom of Evelyn Underhill*, edited by John Stobbart, Mowbray, 1951, p.20.

For the creative Charity of God, as experienced by man, is a redemptive force. It comes into human life in Christ, His Spirit, His Church, His sacraments, and His saints, not to inform, but to transform; to rescue from the downward pull which is felt throughout the natural order, to reform, energize, and at last to sanctify the souls of men, making those rescued souls in their turn part of the redeeming organism through which the salvation of the world shall be achieved.

Evelyn Underhill, in *The Wisdom of Evelyn Underhill*, edited by John Stobbart, Mowbray., 1951, p.20.

Rise above your difficulties—be sorry for *them* through whom your difficulties come to you. In refusing to be put out or annoyed, you are taking God's hand in yours, and once you feel God's hand, or the hand of anyone who loves good, in yours—let pity take the place of irritation, let silence take the place of a hasty answer, let the longing to suffer in ever so small a way take the place of a longing to rest. Overcome evil with good ... Charity suffereth long and is kind, especially to the unkind.

Edward Wilson, in *Edward Wilson of the Antarctic*, George Seaver, John Murray Ltd., 1935, p.72.

Charity is the great channel through which God passes all His mercy upon mankind. For we receive absolution of our sins in proportion to our forgiving our brother. This is the rule of our hopes, and the measure of our desire in this world; and in the day of death and judgment the great sentence upon mankind shall be transacted according to our alms, which is the other part of charity. Certain it is that God cannot, will not, never did, reject a charitable man in his greatest needs, and in his most passionate prayers; for God Himself is Love, and every degree of charity that dwells in us is the participation of the Divine nature.

Jeremy Taylor, *Holy Living and Holy Dying*, George Routledge and Sons, Limited, 1894, *Holy Dying*, p.33.

In the economy of divine charity we have only as much as we give. But we are called upon to give as much as we have, and more: as much as we are. So the measure of our love is theoretically without limit. The more we desire to give ourselves in charity, the more charity we will have to give. And the more we give the more truly we shall be. For our Lord endows us with a being proportionate to the giving for which we are destined.

Charity is the life and the riches of His Kingdom, and those are greatest in it who are least: that is, who have kept nothing for themselves, retaining nothing but their desire to give.

He who tries to retain what he is and what he has, and keep it for himself, buries his talent. When the Lord comes in judgment, this servant is found to have no more than he had at the beginning. But those who have made themselves less, by giving away what they had, shall be found both to be and to have more than they had. And to him who has most shall be given that which the unprofitable servant kept for himself.

Thomas Merton, *No Man is an Island*, Burns & Oates Ltd., 1974, p.145.

Charity does not demand of us that we should not see the faults of others; we must, in that case, shut our eyes. But it commands us to avoid attending unnecessarily to them, and that we be not blind to the good, while we are so clear-sighted to the evil, that exists. We must remember, too, God's continual kindness to the most worthless creature, and think how many causes we have to think ill of ourselves; and, finally, we must consider that charity embraces the very lowest human being. It acknowledges that, in the sight of God, the contempt that we indulge for others has, in its very nature, a harshness and arrogance opposed to the spirit of Jesus Christ. The true Christian is not insensible to what is contemptible—but he bears with it.

Because others are weak, should we be less careful to give them their due? You who complain so much of what others make you suffer, do you think that you cause others no pain? You who are so annoyed at your neighbour's defects, are you perfect?

How astonished you would be, if those whom you cavil at should make all the comments that they might upon you. But even if the whole world were to bear testimony in your favour, God, who knows all, who has seen all your faults, could confound you with a word; and does it never come into your mind to fear, lest he should demand of you, why you had not exercised towards your brother a little of that mercy which he who is your master so abundantly bestows upon you?

François de la M. Fénelon, *Selections from the writings of Fénelon*, Mrs Follen, Edward T. Whitfield, 1850, p.232.

Charity has various senses, but is excellent in all of them. It imports, first, the commiserations of the poor and unhappy of mankind, and extends an helping hand to mend their condition. They that feel nothing of this, are, at best, not above half of kin to human race ... Nor can we expect to be heard of God in our prayers, that turn the deaf ear to the petition of the distressed amongst our fellow-creatures. God sends the poor to try us; as well as he tries them by being such: and he that refuses them a little, out of the great deal that God has given him, lays up poverty in store for his own posterity. I will not say these works are meritorious, but I dare say they are acceptable, and go not without their reward; though, to humble us in our fulness, and liberality too, we only give what is given us to give, as well as to use: for if we ourselves are not our own, less is that so which God has entrusted us with. Next, charity makes the best construction of things and persons; and is so far from being an evil spy, a back-biter, or a detractor, that it excuses weakness, extenuates miscarriages, makes the best of everything, forgives everybody, serves all, and hopes to the end. It moderates extremes, is always for expedients, labours to accommodate differences, and had rather suffer than revenge: and is so far from exacting the utmost farthing, that it had rather lose than seek its own violently. As it acts freely, so zealously too, but it is always to do good, for it hurts nobody. An universal remedy against discord, and an holy cement for mankind. And lastly, it is to love God and the brethren, which raises the soul above all worldly considerations; and as it gives a taste of heaven upon earth, so it is heaven, in the fulness of it, to the truly charitable here. This is the noblest sense charity has: after which all should press, as that "more excellent way." Nay, most excellent: for as faith, hope, and charity, were the more excellent way that the great apostle discovered to the Christians; (too apt to stick in outward gifts and church performances) so, of that better way, he preferred charity as the best part, because it would out-last the rest, and abide for ever. Wherefore a man can never be a true and good Christian without charity, even in the lowest sense of it; and yet he may have that part thereof, and still be none of the apostle's true Christian: since he tells us, "That though we should give all our goods to the poor, and want charity (in her other and higher senses) it would profit us nothing." Nay, "Though we had all tongues, all knowledge, and even gifts of prophecy, and were preachers to others, aye, and had zeal enough to give our bodies to be burned; yet if we wanted charity, it would not avail us for salvation." It seems it was his (and indeed ought to be ours) "One thing needful", which our Saviour attributed to Mary, in preference to her sister Martha, that seems not to have wanted the lesser parts of charity. Would to God this divine virtue were more implanted and diffused among mankind, the pretenders of Christianity especially: and we should certainly mind piety more than controversy: and excite love and compassion, instead of censuring and persecuting one another, in any manner whatsoever.

William Penn, *Fruits of Solitude*, A.W. Bennett, 1863, p.97.

CHEERFULNESS

"Cheerfulness"—"contented, in good spirits, hopeful, animating, pleasant; willing, not reluctant."

For four years I was a part-time Hospital Chaplain in Bradford, West Yorkshire. This involved visiting about a hundred patients a week, mainly in three wards. I remember coming across a man suffering from multiple sclerosis. He was in hospital for three weeks and in that time we got to know each other well. When he was discharged, he asked me to visit him at home. I did so, and was very impressed with his wife. She was one of those good Yorkshire types—inevitably good humoured and cheerful. She fed him and nursed him, without complaint. She reassured him and devoted all her time and energy in making him as comfortable as possible. When he died, she was heart-broken, but after a few weeks her cheerful good spirits returned. She decided it was time to get out of the house and do something for the local community. So she went to the local Primary School and volunteered her services.

She started helping with lunches, and soon got to know the children. Her exuberance for life made her a great favourite with the boys and girls. Before long the Headmistress invited her to help in the classrooms, where she was a great success. Her next exploit was to accompany the Headmistress and a group of the children on a day trip to London. And what an adventure that was. She later asked me to prepare her for Confirmation so that she could contribute something to the community through the local Church. I learnt through her (as did others) the value of cheerfulness.

A glad heart makes a cheerful countenance.
Proverbs 15.13.

A cheerful heart is a good medicine, but a downcast spirit dries up the bones.
Proverbs 17.22.

Be of good cheer.
Matthew 14.27 (A.V.).

I have said this to you, that in me you may have peace. In the world you have tribulation; but be of good cheer, I have overcome the world.
John 16.33.

Continual cheerfulness is a sign of wisdom.
Thomas Fuller, *Gnomologia*, Stearn Brock, 1733, p.43.

A merry heart goes all the day,
Your sad in a mile-a.
William Shakespeare, *The Winter's Tale*, Act IV. sc.iii. l.125.

A happy, joyful spirit spreads joy everywhere; a fretful spirit is a trouble to ourselves and to all around us.
Anon.

I have tried too in my time to be a philosopher; but, I don't know how, cheerfulness was always breaking in.
Oliver Edwards, in Boswell's, *Life of Samuel Johnson*, edited by G.B. Hill, Clarendon Press, 1934, 17 April 1778, p.305.

Cheerfulness, it would appear, is a matter which depends fully as much on the state of things within, as on the state of things without, and around us.
Charlotte Brontë, *Shirley*, Clarendon Press, 1979, p.43.

In my long illness, the people who helped me most were those who took for granted that I should behave with apparent cheerfulness and courage.
A.C. Benson, *Extracts from the Letters of Dr. A.C. Benson to M.E.A.*, Jarrold Publishing, 1927, p.19.

What then remains, but well our Pow'r to use,
And keep good Humour still whate'er we lose?
And trust me, Dear! good Humour can prevail,
When Airs, and Flights, and Screams, and Scolding fail.
Alexander Pope, *The Poems of Alexander Pope*, Methuen & Co. Ltd., 1966, Volume 2, *The Rape of the Lock*, Canto V, l.29, p.201.

Cheered by the presence of God, I will do at the moment, without anxiety, according to the strength which he shall give me, the work that his providence assigns me. I will leave the rest; it is not my affair.

François de la M. Fénelon, *Selections from the Writings of Fénelon*, Mrs Follen, Edward T. Whitfield, 1850, p.233.

> Thy soul was like a Star, and dwelt apart:
> Thou hadst a voice whose sound was like the sea:
> Pure as the naked heavens, majestic, free,
> So didst thou travel on life's common way,
> In cheerful godliness.

William Wordsworth, *London*, 1802, l.9.

The men whom I have seen succeed best in life have always been cheerful and hopeful men, who went about their business with a smile on their faces, and took the changes and chances of this mortal life like men, facing rough and smooth alike as it came, and so found the truth of the old proverb that "good times and bad times and all times pass over."

Charles Kingsley, *Daily Thoughts*, Macmillan Publishers Ltd., 1884, p.227.

I believe that God will help us to forget things, the memory of which would do us harm, or rather that He will enable us to remember only so much of them as will be for our good, and we, ourselves, not emotionally overwhelmed...

The pain endured. The lesson learned. Let it now be forgotten! Face the future with courage, cheerfulness, and hope. Give God the chance and He will make you forget all that it would be harmful to remember.

W.E. Sangster, *Westminster Sermons*, Epworth Press, 1960, Volume One, *At Morning Worship*, p.4.

> Let me play the fool,
> With mirth and laughter let old wrinkles come,
> And let my liver rather heat with wine
> Than my heart cool with mortifying groans.
> Why should a man whose blood is warm within,
> Sit like his grandsire, cut in alabaster?
> Sleep when he wakes? and creep into the jaundice
> By being peevish?

William Shakespeare, *The Merchant of Venice*, Act I. sc.i. l.79.

Be brave! Let us remain aware of our task and not grumble, a solution will come... I know what I want, I have a goal, an opinion, I have a religion and love. Let me be myself, and then I am satisfied. I know that I'm a woman, a woman with inward strength and plenty of courage.

If God lets me live... I shall not remain insignificant, I shall work in the world and for mankind!

And now I know that first and foremost I shall require courage and cheerfulness!

Anne Frank, *The Diary of Anne Frank*, Pan Books Ltd., 1954, p.175.

COMMUNITY

*"Community"—defined as a "body of people living in the same
locality; a body of people having religion in common."*

My first real experience of community, in terms of this definition, happened in my
Curacy at Bradford Cathedral. I was asked to run the Youth Fellowship. The "lay
reader" was pure gold, and had got together a group of lively and interesting young
people. They came together from all parts of the city two or three times a week. We
had a study group on a Monday evening, and discussed many topics, thinking things
through together. On a Sunday, we worshipped in the Family Eucharist, and after
Evensong, would meet in the Cathedral Hall for a talk of a more general nature. In the
Summer, about a dozen of us went on holiday together, under canvas in Wales, and
did some horse-riding. The following year, by way of change, we had a House Party in
the Yorkshire Dales. In addition to a guest speaker, we went hiking and caving.
Towards the end of the Curacy we concocted a Revue. I still laugh when recalling the
sketches. I learnt more about "Community" and the Christian life in general with the
Youth Fellowship, than all my time at Theological College. In retrospect it was a
formative period of my life—a debt I owe to the members of that community.

And I will make my abode among you, and my soul shall not abhor you. And I will
walk among you, and will be your God, and you shall be my people.

Leviticus 26.11-12.

For my brethren and companions' sake I will say, "Peace be within you!" For the
sake of the house of the Lord our God, I will seek your good.

Psalm 122.8-9.

But God has so composed the body... that there may be no discord in the body, but
that the members may have the same care for one another. If one member suffers, all
suffer together; if one member is honoured, all rejoice together.

1 Corinthians 12.24-26.

So if there is any encouragement in Christ, any incentive of love, any participation in
the Spirit, any affection and sympathy, complete my joy by being of the same mind,
having the same love, being in full accord and of one mind.

Philippians 2.1-2.

We expect a theophany of which we know nothing but the place, and the place is
called community.

Martin Buber, *Between Man and Man*, William Collins Sons & Co. Ltd., 1974, p.24.

Let him who cannot be alone beware of community.
Let him who is not in community beware of being alone.

Dietrich Bonhoeffer, *Life Together*, SCM Press Ltd., 1955, p.67.

The land is mark'd for desolation & unless we plant
The seeds of Cities & of Villages in the Human bosom
Albion must be a rock of blood.

William Blake, *Complete Poems*, edited by Geoffrey Keynes, Oxford University Press, 1974, *Jerusalem*, plate 83, p.728.

What life have you if you have not life together?
There is no life that is not in community,
And no community not lived in praise of GOD.

T.S. Eliot, *The Complete Poems and Plays of T.S. Eliot*, Faber & Faber Ltd., 1975, *Choruses from "The Rock", 1934*, 11, p.152.

Poverty of heart creates community since it is not in self-sufficiency but in a creative interdependency that the mystery of life unfolds itself to us.

Henri J.M. Nouwen, *Reaching Out*, William Collins Sons & Co. Ltd., 1980, p.100.

The children of God should not have any other country here below but the universe itself, with the totality of all the reasoning creatures it ever has contained, contains, or ever will contain. That is the native city to which we owe our love.

Simone Weil, *Waiting on God*, translated by Emma Craufurd, William Collins Sons & Co. Ltd., 1974, p.60.

The Church as community of faith… In these days it must not be concerned primarily with the observance of ritual, disciplinary and moral regulations, but with men being able to live and receive from one another what they need in order to live.

Hans Küng, *On Being a Christian*, translated by Edward Quinn, William Collins Sons & Co. Ltd., 1977, p.508.

It is the lower classes which do the really creative work, forming communities on a genuine religious basis. They alone unite imagination and simplicity of feeling with a non-reflective habit of mind, a primitive energy, and an urgent sense of need.

Ernst Troeltsch, *The Social Teaching of the Christian Churches*, translated by Olive Wyon, The University of Chicago Press, 1981, p.44.

In a culture increasingly dependent on visual parables and signs for its orientation to the world, the conduct of the Christian community, its visible behaviour, will become a much more significant "word" than the pronouncements of the pulpit.

Harvey Cox, *On Not Leaving It To The Snake*, SCM Press Ltd., 1968, p.28.

We forget that there is no hope of joy except in human relations. If I summon up those memories that have left with me an enduring savour, if I draw up the balance sheet of the hours in my life that have truly counted, surely I find only those that no wealth could have procured me. True riches cannot be bought.

Antoine de Saint-Exupéry, *Wind, Sand and Stars*, William Heinemann Ltd., 1939, p.35.

Sometimes it seems as if the Christian community is "so busy" with its projects and plans that there is neither the time or mood to pray. But when prayer is no longer its primary concern, and when its many activities are no longer seen and experienced as part of prayer itself, the community quickly degenerates into a club with a common cause but no common vocation.

Henri J.M. Nouwen, *Reaching Out*, William Collins Sons & Co. Ltd., 1980, p.143.

"The aim of God in history is the creation of an all-inclusive community of loving persons, with Himself included in that community as its prime sustainer and most glorious inhabitant." (Dallas Willard). Such a community would live under the immediate and total rulership of the Holy Spirit. They would be a people blinded to all other loyalties by the splendour of God, a compassionate community embodying the law of love as seen in Jesus Christ.

Richard J. Foster, *Celebration of Discipline*, Hodder & Stoughton Ltd., 1982, p.162.

Much that has been said about prayer might create the false impression that prayer is a private, individualistic and nearly secret affair, so personal and so deeply hidden in our inner life that it can hardly be talked about, even less be shared. The opposite is true. Just because prayer is so personal and arises from the centre of our life, it is to be shared with others. Just because prayer is the most precious expression of being human, it needs the constant support and protection of the community to grow and flower. Just because prayer is our highest vocation needing careful attention and faithful perseverance, we cannot allow it to be a private affair. Just because prayer asks for a patient waiting in expectation, it should never become the most individualistic expression of the most individualistic emotion, but should always remain embedded in the life of the community of which we are part.

Henri J.M. Nouwen, *Seeds of Hope*, edited by Robert Durback, Darton, Longman & Todd Ltd., 1989, p.80.

The paradox of the Christian community is that people are gathered together in voluntary displacement. The togetherness of those who form a Christian community is a being-gathered-in-displacement. According to Webster's dictionary, displacement means to move or to shift from the ordinary or proper place. This becomes a telling definition when we realize the extent to which we are preoccupied with adapting ourselves to the prevalent norms and values of our milieu. We want to be ordinary and proper people who live ordinary and proper lives. There is an enormous pressure on us to do what is ordinary and proper—even the attempt to excel is ordinary and proper—and thus find the satisfaction of general acceptance. This is quite understandable since the ordinary and proper behaviour that gives shape to an ordinary and proper life offers us the comforting illusion that things are under control and that everything extraordinary and improper can be kept outside the walls of our self-created fortress.

Henri J.M. Nouwen, *Seeds of Hope*, edited by Robert Durback, Darton, Longman & Todd Ltd., 1989, p.90.

Baptism is the sacrament which gives entry into the Christian community. The promises made at the baptism service are for a deep commitment in return for a great gift (bought at a great price). They are expected to be taken seriously. In an age of divided families and broken relationships, the Church, as the community of Christ's followers, is here to help integrate lives and whole families into the warmth of Christian love.

Love cannot be given or shared in isolation. A parent or child who never sees the family is no more than a nominal member. The same is true of the Christian family. Sharing, caring, laughing, worship and expressing thankfulness, are best done together.

Rivers enable water to flow. Roads enable traffic to reach its destination. Sacraments are channels for enabling God's power to flow into and direct our lives. The sacrament of baptism is the outward sign by which God, in his great love for us, calls us to be his own. In receiving this sacrament we become his and part of life eternal. In his giving us this sacrament our lives are enhanced by his strength and guidance uniquely revealed through Jesus Christ. As with Christ and his disciples we become part of a fellowship which shows us how to be grateful for what we have been given, and how to share what we have. That thankfulness and sharing is done through a life-of-sharing in the community of those who love in this particular way. Through this sign, we are saved from the consequences of living only for ourselves.

At baptism we promise that we or our children will live and grow up in this unself-centred context. We cannot grow as Christians unless we honestly try to love our fellow Christians and neighbours, and receive instruction from the Church in how we can grow as Christians. A child, teenager, or adult has to be part of the Christian community if he or she is to receive the insights of sharing, tolerance, kindness, understanding, compassion and forgiveness which the loving Christian community can give.

The sharing community or Church is a collection of people in any area who stand by the values of Christ which they have tested against experience and therefore believe to be important. They say, in effect, our first allegiance is to God through the on-going life and example of Jesus Christ; we admit that we need help in living; and we also need the support and encouragement of the sharing community.

Of course you can believe in God outside the Christian community; the Jews, Muslims, Hindus and others do so devoutly. But for the insights of Christian understanding you have to live in a Christian context—not only for what you can receive but also for what you can share and encourage for the benefit of all.

It is because the beauty and strength of Christ's promises touch the deepest roots in our lives that we should take the sacrament of baptism sincerely as well as with joy.

Giles Harcourt, *Dawn through our Darkness*, William Collins Sons & Co. Ltd., 1985, p.34.

COMPASSION

"Compassion"—"pity inclining one to spare or help."

I was in my Chaplain's office in London. The phone rang one Sunday morning— after the early Service. It was a student asking for help. He had come across a young man in a semi-conscious state suffering from drug abuse. Could I come over and lend a hand?

I drove over to where he was—in Holborn. Initial fears were quickly confirmed. We were both out of our depth! Fortunately I knew of an Anglican priest nearby, an unusual man—a qualified psychiatric nurse, with a specialized knowledge of drugs. He was free to come and lend a hand.

From the moment he arrived I saw "compassion" in action. The young man quickly realized he was in the presence of an expert. Communication immediately took place. The names and quantities of drugs were taken and noted. An atmosphere of pity and sympathy predominated. We took him to a hospital in South London, where he was registered as a drug addict. He was refused admission. The priest then showed the depth of his compassion by taking him to his home and looking after him there.

I had a strange sensation at the time that I was experiencing "Christ" in action.

The Lord, a God merciful and gracious, slow to anger, and abounding in steadfast love and faithfulness, keeping steadfast love for thousands, forgiving iniquity and transgression and sin.

Exodus 34.6-7.

The Lord is good to all, and his compassion is over all he has made.

Psalm 145.9.

Go home to thy friends, and tell them how great things the Lord hath done for thee, and hath had compassion on thee.

Mark 5.19 (A.V.).

Put on then, as God's chosen ones, holy and beloved, compassion, kindness, lowliness, meekness, and patience, forbearing one another and, if one has a complaint against another, forgiving each other; as the Lord has forgiven you, so you also must forgive.

Colossians 3.12-13.

Christianity taught us to care. Caring is the greatest thing, caring matters most.

Baron Friedrich von Hügel, *Letters to a Niece*, J.M. Dent & Sons Ltd., 1929, p.xlv.

What value has compassion that does not take its object in its arms?

Antoine de Saint-Exupéry, *The Wisdom of the Sands*, translated by Stuart Gilbert, Hollis & Carter, 1952, p.98.

Love is more just than justice; compassion will cure more sins than condemnation.

Henry Ward Beecher, *Proverbs from Plymouth Pulpit*, Charles Burnet & Co., 1887, p.202.

Jesus does not regard in Judas his enmity, but the order of God, which He loves, and admits, since He calls him friend.

Blaise Pascal, *Pensées*, translated by W.F. Trotter, Random House, Inc., 1941, p.176.

By compassion we make anothers misery our own, & so by relieving them, we relieve our selves also.

Sir Thomas Browne, *The Works of Sir Thomas Browne*, edited by Geoffrey Keynes, Faber & Faber Ltd., 1964, Volume 1, *Religio Medici*, Part II, sec.2, p.72.

Our tragedy is not that we suffer but that we waste suffering. We waste the opportunity of growing into compassion.

Mary Craig, *Blessings*, Hodder & Stoughton Ltd., 1979, p.61.

Compassion is born when we discover in the centre of our own existence not only that God is God and man is man, but also that our neighbour is really our fellow man.

Henri J.M. Nouwen, *The Wounded Healer*, Doubleday, 1979, p.41.

The Son of God was seen
Most glorious, in him all his Father shone
Substantially express'd, and in his face
Divine compassion visibly appear'd.
Love without end, and without measure Grace.

John Milton, *The Poems of John Milton*, Clarendon Press, 1900, *Paradise Lost*, Bk.III, l.138, p.231.

Compassion is not a simple feeling-state but a complex emotional attitude toward another, characteristically involving imaginative dwelling on the condition of the other person, an active regard for his good, a view of him as a fellow human being, and emotional responses of a certain degree of intensity.

L. Blum, in *A New Dictionary of Christian Ethics*, James F. Childress and John Macquarrie, SCM Press Ltd., 1986, p.109.

Compassion is one of the emotions, or attitudes with an emotional component, that are altruistic or other-regarding. Compassion presupposes sympathy, is close to both pity and mercy, and leads to acts of beneficence—the Samaritan "showed mercy on" the victim and "took care of him." Compassion presupposes sympathy, is often an expression of love, or *agape*.

James F. Childress, in *A New Dictionary of Christian Theology*, James F. Childress and John Macquarrie, SCM Press Ltd., 1986, p.109.

Let us not underestimate how hard it is to be compassionate. Compassion is hard because it requires the inner disposition to go with others to the place where they are weak, vulnerable, lonely, and broken. But this is not our spontaneous response to suffering. What we desire most is to do away with suffering by fleeing from it or finding a quick cure for it.

Henri J.M. Nouwen, *The Way of the Heart*, Darton, Longman & Todd Ltd., 1981, p.34.

The root of the matter is a very simple and old-fashioned thing, a thing so simple that I am almost ashamed to mention it, for fear of the derisive smile with which wise cynics will greet my words. The thing I mean—please forgive me for mentioning it— is love, Christian love, or compassion. If you feel this, you have a motive for existence, a guide in action, a reason for courage, an imperative necessity for intellectual honesty.

Bertrand Russell, *The Impact of Science on Society*, George Allen & Unwin Publishers Ltd., 1968, p.84.

> Poor naked wretches, whereso'er you are,
> That bide the pelting of this pitiless storm,
> How shall your houseless heads and unfed sides,
> Your loop'd and window'd raggedness, defend you
> From seasons such as these? O! I have ta'en
> Too little care of this! Take physic, Pomp;
> Expose thyself to feel what wretches feel,
> That thou mayst shake the superflux to them,
> And show the heavens more just.

William Shakespeare, *King Lear*, Act III. sc.iv. l.28.

Compassion is probably the only antitoxin of the soul. Where there is compassion even the most poisonous impulses are relatively harmless. One would rather see the world run by men who set their hearts on toys but are accessible to pity than by men animated by lofty ideals whose dedication makes them ruthless. In the chemistry of man's soul, almost all noble attributes—courage, honour, hope, faith, duty, loyalty, etc.—can be transmuted into ruthlessness. Compassion alone stands apart from the continuous traffic between good and evil proceeding within us.

Eric Hoffer, *The Passionate State of Mind*, Martin Secker & Warburg Ltd., 1956, p.69.

But once God has called you to solitude, everything you touch leads you further into solitude. Everything that affects you builds you into a hermit, as long as you do not insist on doing the work yourself and building your own kind of hermitage.

What is my new desert? The name of it is *compassion*. There is no wilderness so terrible, so beautiful, so arid and so fruitful as the wilderness of compassion. It is the only desert that shall truly flourish like the lily. It shall become a pool, it shall bud forth and blossom and rejoice with joy. It is in the desert of compassion that the thirsty land turns into springs of water, that the poor possess all things.

Thomas Merton, *The Sign of Jonas*, Sheldon Press, 1976, p.333.

I don't know what has caused me to read so many articles lately on the subject of "compassion", but I think we, as Co-workers, are faced with compassion when we are with the poor and the lonely and the dying. Compassion asks us to go where it hurts, to enter into places of pain, to share in brokenness, fear, confusion and anguish. Compassion challenges us to cry out with those in misery, to mourn with those who are lonely, to weep with those in tears. Compassion requires us to be weak with the weak, vulnerable with the vulnerable, and powerless with the powerless. Compassion means full immersion in the conditions of being human. When we look at compassion in this way, it becomes clear that something more is involved than a general kindness.

A Co-worker, in *A Chain of Love*, Kathryn Spink, SPCK, 1984, p.113.

Often I have said to people, "I will pray for you," but how often did I really enter into the full reality of what that means? When I really bring my friends and the many I pray for into my innermost being and feel their pains, their struggles, their cries in my own soul, then I leave myself, so to speak, and become them, then I have compassion.

Compassion lies at the heart of our prayer for our fellow human beings. When I pray for the world, I become the world; when I pray for the endless needs of the millions, my soul expands and wants to embrace them all and bring them into the presence of God. But in the midst of that experience I realize that compassion is not mine but God's gift to me. I cannot embrace the world, but God can. I cannot pray, but God can pray in me. When God became as we are, that is, when God allowed all of us to enter into the intimacy of the divine life, it became possible for us to share in God's infinite compassion.

In praying for others, I lose myself and become the other, only to be found by the divine love which holds the whole of humanity in a compassionate embrace.

Henri J.M. Nouwen, *Seeds of Hope*, edited by Robert Durback, Darton, Longman & Todd Ltd., 1989, p.72.

CONSCIENCE

"Conscience"—"a moral sense of right and wrong."

O ne of the difficulties of a College Chaplain is how to make contact with students. One way I did this was to follow up one of my natural interests— sport.

I used to play squash on a regular basis with one of the students, in London House. After our first match, whilst in the shower, I noticed a big scar round one of his lungs. "What happened there?" I asked. "Oh," he quietly replied, "some time ago I was on my way to a tube station in North London. It was late one Saturday night, and I came across someone being mugged. No one else was around so I went to help and before I knew what was happening, got stabbed. It was a painful experience, but it's all right now." I was very impressed, and made a mental note not to give him a rough ride in our next match.

Several weeks later he nervously came to see me in my room. Something was clearly troubling him. "Bill," he blurted out, "I'm afraid I told you a lie about that mugging. There was no such thing. The truth is, I had actually tried to kill myself. My conscience has been troubling me ever since. I thought I ought to come and tell you the truth."

The origin of conscience is a mystery. Some of the quotations which follow suggest it has to do with the voice of God in the depths of our being.

Far be it from me to say that you are right; till I die I will not put away my integrity from me. I hold fast my righteousness, and will not let it go; my heart does not reproach me for any of my days.

Job 27.5-6.

The spirit of man is the lamp of the Lord, searching all his innermost parts.

Proverbs 20.27.

So I always take pains to have a clear conscience toward God and toward men.

Acts 24.16.

Whereas the aim of our charge is love that issues from a pure heart and a good conscience and sincere faith.

1 Timothy 1.5.

He that loses his conscience has nothing left that is worth keeping.

Izaak Walton, *The Compleat Angler*, The Nonesuch Press Ltd., 1929, p.193.

The world's fight is between conscience and moral purity and the animal that is in man.

Henry Ward Beecher, *Proverbs from Plymouth Pulpit*, Charles Burnet & Co., 1887, p.93.

From what innate principle does this arise, but from the *God within the mind!*

W.H. Brown, *The Power of Sympathy*, Columbia University Press, 1937, Volume II, p.64.

Give me the liberty to know, to utter, and to argue freely according to conscience, above all liberties.

John Milton, *Complete Prose Works of John Milton*, Volume II, Oxford University Press, 1959, *Areopagitica*, p.560.

There is no more sensitive conscience than that of a person who loves God. It registers every shadow that passes over the heart of God.

Helmut Thielicke, *I Believe—The Christian's Creed*, translated by John W. Doberstein and H.George Anderson, William Collins Sons & Co. Ltd., 1969, p.7.

I know myself now, and
I feel within me
A peace above all earthly dignities,
A still and quiet conscience.

William Shakespeare, *Henry VIII*, Act III. sc.ii. l.378.

There is an agent in my soul which is perfectly sensitive to God. I am as sure of this as I am that I am alive: nothing is as near to me as God is. God is nearer to me than I am to myself.

Meister Eckhart, *Meister Eckhart*, translated by Raymond B. Blakney, Harper & Row, Publishers, 1941, p.129.

Fear, shame, self-respect, and self-interest hold in check cruelty and cunning, and all forms of passion, and all gross and sensual appetites, and in so far are the auxiliaries of conscience.

Henry Ward Beecher, *Proverbs from Plymouth Pulpit*, Charles Burnet & Co., 1887, p.29.

Oh! Conscience! Conscience! Man's most faithful friend,
Him canst thou comfort, ease, relieve, defend:
But if he will thy friendly checks forego,
Thou art, oh! woe for me, his deadliest foe!

George Crabbe, *The Complete Poetical Works*, Clarendon Press, Oxford, 1988, Volume 11, *The Struggles of Conscience*, l.492, p.196.

He that has light within his own clear breast
May sit i' the centre and enjoy bright day,
But he that hides a dark soul and foul thoughts
Benighted walks under the mid-day sun—
Himself is his own dungeon.

John Milton, *Comus and other Poems*, edited by F.T. Prince, Oxford University Press, *Comus*, l.381, p.56.

Conscience, also is an experience of God. It is said that conscience is the voice of the repressed good in us, which is not very different from saying it is the voice of the repressed God. It is true that ideas of what is right and wrong vary from age to age and from place to place, but the significant thing is the abiding conviction that there *is* a distinction between right and wrong. The inner compulsion to do right and the shame we feel when we are aware of having done wrong are an experience of God.

Leslie J. Tizard, *Facing Life and Death*, George Allen & Unwin Publishers Ltd., 1959, p.64.

Conscience in man is a God-given thing. The operations of conscience can be perverted, and its findings can be distorted by wrong assumptions. Yet it is always a phenomenon to be reverenced because it is God-given, and the Christian duty of educating consciences in the light of Christian truth goes with this reverence for them.

Not seldom has it happened that Christians have found themselves corrected by the consciences of pagans, and the will to admit this need not weaken the claims made for Christian revelation.

Michael Ramsey, *Through the Year with Michael Ramsey*, edited by Margaret Duggan, Hodder & Stoughton Ltd., 1975, p.93.

The complex human capacity, utilizing people's understanding of moral life and their decision-making ability, to live in conformity with those principles it deems acceptable and good. In a morally informed and psychologically balanced person, the conscience serves as a guide or a monitor of life, enabling the individual to evaluate and choose potential courses of action and thought in the light of his or her values and commitments. Though the Bible does not contain a fully developed theory of conscience, the New Testament implies that this capacity is an integral part of the human personality and that its volition results in great harm to the individual's innermost being. For Christians, the conscience is not the sole guide to moral life; rather, informed by scripture, nurtured by grace, inspired by the Holy Spirit, and enacted in love for others, the conscience serves as a flexible and fallible evaluator of one's own actions in light of one's understanding of God's will. Thus, the "good conscience" in Christian terms is continually open to new information and leads one's actions to exhibit love and compassion for others and respect for one's own dignity as a creature of God.

Lewis R. Rambo, in *A New Dictionary of Christian Theology*, edited by Alan Richardson and John Bowden, SCM Press Ltd., 1985, p.119.

The traditional Christian teaching is that one must always obey one's conscience... This is not meant to bolster prejudices or to assert that conscience is infallible. Far from it. Conscience can err because our judgments can be corrupted by personal, social, and economic interests; it can err because it makes errors of factual judgment, and because of ignorance; it can err by not being sensitive enough to the personal and social factors involved in the issues at stake; and it can err by wrongly estimating the possible consequences of possible actions in deciding what to do (and there can rarely be practical certainty in advance about these). Yet the traditional teaching is that an erring conscience (objectively considered) must be followed. We must take responsibility as adults before God for our decisions; no one can live my life for me. Even if we take, e.g., a vow of obedience, the decision to do so must be a conscientious one, and even then if we are ordered to do something against our conscientious judgment we should disobey, whatever anguish or possible danger this causes. The Allies also took this view of German military personnel in the Nuremberg trials after World War II; it was held that on certain points they should have disobeyed their military oath to Hitler. It is a solemn and hard doctrine, which applies all around.

All this means that reasonable care must be taken to consider relevant factors in arriving at a moral judgment. We have therefore a duty to educate our conscience. As Christians we are to allow the mind of Christ to be formed in us (1 Cor. 2.16) so that we grow in sensitivity, in the art of moral discernment. The right environment for the education of conscience is life in the fellowship of the church. Here we shall draw on the resources of prayer, sacramental participation in Christ, and Bible study. Here we shall learn from the practical wisdom the church has acquired over nearly two thousand years, as well as from its mistakes, and be prepared to face the unknowns of the future unafraid. Here we may receive corporate and personal counsel from our fellow Christians in general and from clergy and ministers in particular. But these Christian aids do not exhaust the sources for the education of conscience. We cannot afford to ignore the whole sweep of human knowledge wherever it is relevant, and our sources for this are not peculiarly Christian ones but such as are available to the public at large.

Ronald Preston, in *A New Dictionary of Christian Ethics*, edited by James F. Childress and John Macquarrie, SCM Press Ltd., 1986, p.116.

CONTEMPLATION

"Contemplation"—"gaze upon; view mentally."

I met a medical student who was a natural contemplative. After his pre-clinical training, the two of us formed a contemplative prayer group. We would meet in my rooms for an hour a week, in the evenings. The curtains would be drawn; a candle lit and placed on a small table; the light switched off; and then we would sit down in armchairs close by, and start our contemplation.

We lapsed into silence. Our practice was to repeat the Jesus Prayer quietly to ourselves, either with eyes closed, or gazing at the candle. For those unfamiliar with the Jesus Prayer, it goes as follows: "Jesus Christ, Son of God, have mercy on me, a sinner."

My companion preferred to close his eyes, and before long developed a regular breathing pattern. I was tempted to think he had fallen asleep, but no, he always opened his eyes on the hour. I chose to gaze at the candle. The flame of a candle is very beautiful and observing the beauty of the flame, I was able to concentrate on the words of the Jesus Prayer, to the exclusion of everything else. In the gaps of silence in between, profound truths would come to the surface. When the hour was up, we were both wonderfully refreshed.

Commune with your hearts on your beds and be silent.
Psalm 4.4.

With my whole heart I seek thee; let me not wander from thy commandments! I have laid up thy word in my heart.
Psalm 119.10-11.

The Spirit helps us in our weakness; for we do not know how to pray as we ought, but the Spirit intercedes for us with sighs too deep for words.
Romans 8.26.

Pray at all times in the Spirit.
Ephesians 6.18.

The peace of the contemplative is at once the most beautiful and the most fruitful act of man.
Stephen MacKenna, *Journal and Letters*, Constable & Co. Ltd., 1936, p.120.

Mystical theology, the secret science of God, which spiritual men call contemplation.
St. John of the Cross, *The Complete Works of Saint John of the Cross*, translated and edited by E. Allison Peers, Burns Oates & Washbourne Ltd., 1953, Volume II, *Spiritual Canticle, Poems*, 27,5, p.326.

A Church which starves itself and its members in the contemplative life deserves whatever spiritual leanness it may experience.
Michael Ramsey, *Canterbury Pilgrim*, SPCK, 1974, p.60.

In contemplation a soul dries up the root and ground of sin that is always there, even after one's confession, and however busy one is in holy things.
The Cloud of Unknowing, translated by Clifton Wolters, Penguin Books Ltd., 1978, p.96.

When Contemplation, like the night-calm felt
Through earth and sky, spreads widely, and sends deep
Into the soul its tranquillizing power.
William Wordsworth, *Prelude*, Book Fifth, l.3.

It is hard work and no mistake for the would-be contemplative; very hard work indeed, unless it is made easier by a special grace of God, by the fact that one has got used to it over a long period.
The Cloud of Unknowing, translated by Clifton Wolters, Penguin Books Ltd., 1978, p.94.

More than anything else, it is the loving contemplation of its Maker that causes the soul to realize its own insignificance, and fills it with holy fear and true humility, and with abundant love to our fellow Christians.
Julian of Norwich, *Revelations of Divine Love*, Penguin Books Ltd., 1976, p.71.

In popular usage the word can indicate either thinking about some object or gazing upon some object. In Christian spirituality it is the latter meaning that is uppermost: thinking about God gives place to a simple, loving, looking towards him, and this is contemplation.

Richard Harries, in *A New Dictionary of Christian Theology*, edited by Alan Richardson and John Bowden, SCM Press Ltd., 1985, p.121.

The only goodness worthy of a human soul, or a human Best, is the quiet fruit of a ceaseless contemplation: beautiful thought left ever in the sun ripens surely; it is only the apple fallen from the bough, unkissed by light, untossed by high-blowing winds, that unripened rots.

Stephen MacKenna, *Journal and Letters*, Constable & Co. Ltd., 1936, p.115.

Contemplation means rest, suspension of activity, withdrawal into the mysterious interior solitude in which the soul is absorbed in the immense and fruitful silence of God and learns something of the secret of His perfections less by seeing than by fruitful love.

Thomas Merton, *Elected Silence*, Hollis & Carter, 1949, p.368.

All contemplative life on earth implies penance as well as prayer, because in contempla-tion there are always two aspects: the positive one, by which we are united to God in love, and the negative one, by which we are detached and separated from everything that is not God. Without both these elements there is no real contemplation.

Thomas Merton, *The Waters of Silence*, Hollis & Carter, 1950, p.14.

The contemplation of Christ, friend of man, should accustom us to look at others as Jesus looked at them—that is, in the perspective of their eternity. This all-embracing look of love reaches into the void which is in each one of us and which only God can fill. There is a way of loving men which reveals them in all their mystery. To know and to love men in this way, far from turning us away from the contemplation of God, brings us back to it unfailingly. And so friendship for men fans the flame of contemplation the measure of which is love; provided, that is, we know how to guard against the illusions and deceptions of a friendship turned in upon itself or confined within the horizons of life on earth.

René Voillaume, *The Need for Contemplation*, translated by Elizabeth Hamilton, Darton, Longman & Todd Ltd., 1972, p.69.

But if above all things we would taste God, and feel eternal life in ourselves, we must go forth into God with our feeling, above reason; and there we must abide, onefold, empty of ourselves, and free from images, lifted up by love into the simple bareness of our intelligence. For when we go out in love beyond and above all things, and die to all observation in ignorance and in darkness, then we are wrought and trans-formed through the Eternal Word, who is the Image of the Father. In this idleness of our spirit, we receive the Incomprehensible Light, which enwraps us and penetrates us, as the air is penetrated by the light of the sun. And this Light is nothing else than a fathomless staring and seeing.

What we are, that we behold; and what we behold, that we are: for our thought, our life and our being are uplifted in simplicity, and made one with the Truth which is God. And therefore in this simple staring we are one life and one spirit with God: and this I call a contemplative life.

John of Ruysbroeck, *The Adornment of the Spiritual Marriage*, The Sparkling Stone, The Book of Supreme Truth, translated by C.A. Wynschenk Dom, J.M. Dent & Sons Ltd., 1916, p.203.

Contemplation is the highest expression of man's intellectual and spiritual life. It is that life itself, fully awake, fully active, fully aware that it is alive. It is spiritual wonder. It is spontaneous awe at the sacredness of life, of being. It is gratitude for life, for awareness and for being. It is a vivid realization of the fact that life and being in us proceed from an invisible, transcendent and infinitely abundant Source. Contemplation is, above all, awareness of the reality of that Source. It *knows* the Source, obscurely, inexplicably, but with a certitude that goes both beyond reason and beyond simple faith. For contemplation is a kind of spiritual vision to which both reason and faith aspire, by their very nature, because without it they must always remain incomplete. Yet contemplation is not vision because it sees "without seeing" and knows "without knowing". It is a more profound depth of faith, a knowledge too deep to be grasped in images, in words or even in clear concepts. It can be suggested by words, by symbols, but in the very moment of trying to indicate what it knows the contemplative mind takes back what it has said, and denies what it has affirmed. For in contemplation we know by "unknowing". Or, better, we know *beyond* all knowing or "unknowing".

Poetry, music and art have something in common with the contemplative experience. But contemplation is beyond aesthetic intuition, beyond art, beyond poetry. Indeed, it is beyond philosophy, beyond speculative theology. It resumes, transcends and fulfils them all, and yet at the same time it seems, in a certain way, to supersede and to deny them all. Contemplation is always beyond our own knowledge, beyond our own light, beyond systems, beyond explanations, beyond discourse, beyond dialogue, beyond our own self. To enter into the realm of contemplation one must in a certain sense die: but this death is in fact the entrance into a higher life. It is a death for the sake of life, which leaves behind all that we can know or treasure as life, as thought, as experience, as joy, as being.

Thomas Merton, *New Seeds of Contemplation*, Burns & Oates Ltd., 1962, p.1.

In its Christian use this word normally denotes the kind of prayer in which the mind does not function discursively but is arrested in a simple attention and one-pointedness. In meditation the mind reflects on some Christian truth or passage of scripture or personal experience, using words and ideas in more or less logical progression, with the aim of reaching fuller understanding and personal appropriation of the truth considered, or working through some experience in the light of Christian faith in order to come to some decision, awareness of God's will or re-affirmation of faith. In contemplation the mind functions in the opposite way. Words and thoughts in logical progression, reflections with the aim of coming to fresh insight or decision, are exactly what the mind does not want, and indeed it finds them a hindrance. What is desired is the opportunity simply to express to God one's loving, hoping, trusting, thanking, in as few words as possible. These few words tend to be repeated many times. The repetition has the effect of steadily reducing their meaning and serviceableness. A time comes when a deeper desire is revealed to the person praying. What began as fragmentarily verbalized loving or thanking becomes more than anything else an offering, though without this self-giving being mentally considered or understood...

A more flexible and less doctrinaire understanding of contemplation than that which characterizes traditional ascetic theology is probably more congenial to our time. It is possible that some people are naturally disposed to contemplate at the beginning of their Christian life. The teaching of prayer at local church level could well make room for this and be released from the obsession with petition and intercession, unimaginatively interpreted, that has unfortunately dominated it for too long. It is increasingly being suggested now that intercession itself, when better understood, is constructively seen as a form of contemplation.

Christian contemplation needs Christian meditation, in some sense of reflection on the great Christian image which is Christ himself, his truth, and all that has been well thought and said and done in his name under the guidance of the Spirit. Without this, contemplation could eventually become a not particularly Christian exercise, not necessarily objectionable for that reason but simply a very different matter and perhaps nearer to Transcendental Meditation which seems to be associated with no system of belief, seldom leads to increased awareness of spiritual reality, and has a rather loose relation to the intellectual and emotional life of the practitioner.

J. Neville Ward, in *A Dictionary of Christian Spirituality*, edited by Gordon S. Wakefield, SCM Press Ltd., 1986, p.95.

CONTENTMENT

"Contentment"—"being in a state of satisfaction, well pleased— originally it meant, bounded (in desires by what one has)."

I had the good fortune to go to Kenya to stay with some friends during a summer vacation. We went to stay on a farm on the slopes of Mount Kenya. The farm was vast, specializing in the cultivation of wheat. The farmhouse, built to overlook the farm, included a magnificent view of Mount Kenya. This alone was impressive. What was more striking was the farmer, his wife and family. They all had about them an air of contentment. Here they were, living in the heart of Africa, at an altitude of 8,000 feet. The climate was well-nigh perfect. All the time they were close to nature, living an outdoor life. It was easy to see why they were content.

We were shown round the farm. We looked into barns, full of grain. The recent yield had been particularly good. We met the members of the work-force, just in from the fields. They had returned to their village situated in the middle of the farm. They were expressing joy in being back with their wives and families, after a tiring but satisfying day's work. Here again was contentment—a feeling of trust between employer and employee, a feeling of achievement and of a job well done. Here was a contentment rarely to be found elsewhere.

How do we find contentment?

Be content with your glory.
2 Kings 14.10.

The lines have fallen for me in pleasant places;
yea, I have a goodly heritage.
Psalm 16.6.

I have learned, in whatever state I am, to be content. I know how to be abased, and I know how to abound; in any and all circumstances I have learned the secret of facing plenty and hunger, abundance and want. I can do all things in him who strengthens me.

Philippians 4.11-13.

There is great gain in godliness with contentment; for we brought nothing into the world, and we cannot take anything out of the world; but if we have food and clothing, with these we shall be content.

1 Timothy 6.6-8.

Great wealth and content seldom live together.

Thomas Fuller, *Gnomologia*, Stearne Brock, 1733, p.68.

Content will never dwell but in a meek and quiet soul.

Izaak Walton, *The Compleat Angler*, The Nonesuch Press Ltd., 1929, p.191.

How seldom a face in repose is a face of serene content.

W.E. Sangster, *The Secret of Radiant Life*, Hodder & Stoughton Ltd., 1957, p.19.

The rarest feeling that ever lights the human face is the contentment of a loving soul.

Henry Ward Beecher, *Proverbs from Plymouth Pulpit*, Charles Burnet & Co., 1887, p.26.

We only see in a lifetime a dozen faces marked with the peace of a contented spirit.

Henry Ward Beecher, *Proverbs from Plymouth Pulpit*, Charles Burnet & Co., 1887, p.178.

Content thy self to be obscurely good.
When vice prevails, and impious men bear sway,
The post of honour is a private station.

Joseph Addison, *Miscellaneous Works*, edited by A.C. Guthkelch, George Bell & Sons, Volume 1, *Cato*, Act IV. sc.iv. l.140, p.410.

In order to be content men must also have the possibility of developing their intellectual and artistic powers to whatever extent accord with their personal characteristics and abilities.

Albert Einstein, *Out of my Later Years*, Thames and Hudson Ltd., 1950, p.12.

Nothing is more dangerous than a mass of discontent which does not know what remedy is to be sought. All sorts of cures will be tried, many of them quackery, and their failure will make matters worse.

Mark Rutherford, *More Pages From a Journal*, Oxford University Press, 1910, p.219.

I swear, 'tis better to be lowly born,
And range with humble livers in content,
Than to be perked up in a glistering grief
And wear a golden sorrow.

William Shakespeare, *Henry VIII*, Act II. sc.iii. l.19.

To be content with a little is greater than to possess the world; which a man may possess without being so. Lay up my treasure! what matters where a man's treasure is whose heart is in the Scriptures? there is the treasure of a Christian.

Henry Fielding, *Joseph Andrews*, J.M. Dent & Sons Ltd., 1910, p.173.

Content and discontent should run in and out of each other in every true man's life. Every man should have a generous discontent with what he has attained, and strive to go upward; and yet every one should be so much the master of himself as to refuse to be disquieted by his environments.

Henry Ward Beecher, *Proverbs from Plymouth Pulpit*, Charles Burnet & Co., 1887, p.224.

> Hail blest estate of lowliness!
> Happy enjoyments of such minds,
> As rich in self-contentedness,
> Can, like the reed in roughest winds
> By yielding make that blow but small
> At which proud Oaks and Cedars fall.

Izaak Walton, *The Compleat Angler*, The Nonesuch Press Ltd., 1929, p.147.

One of the very most surprising things in life is the contented aimlessness with which it is so often, almost always, lived. Few live for joy in life, fewer still for something to be done with their life: most live, and apparently in content, not as free animals live who must be doing something, but as tram-horses or trees or as monotonously flowing waters... and without the beauty or dignity of trees or of flowing waters. No doubt there is use in what most are doing, keeping shop or building bridges or spending money idly, but there is not aim, or the aim is merely personal and wholly bounded within time.

Stephen MacKenna, *Journal and Letters*, Constable & Co. Ltd., 1936, p.93.

My friends, whether you will be happier for any knowledge of physical science, or for any other knowledge whatsoever, I cannot tell. That lies in the decision of a higher Power than I; and, indeed, to speak honestly, I do not think that any branch of physical science is likely, at first at least, to make you happy. Neither is the study of your fellow-men. Neither is religion itself. We were not sent into the world to be happy, but to be right—at least, poor creatures that we are—as right as we can be, and we must be content with being right, and not happy... And we shall be made truly wise if we be made content; content, too, not only with what we can understand, but content with what we do not understand—the habit of mind which theologians call (and rightly) faith in God, true and solid faith, which comes out of sadness and out of doubt.

Charles Kingsley, *Daily Thoughts*, Macmillan Publishers Ltd., 1884, p.59.

Spiritual maturity shows itself in the ability to transcend not only repeated frustrations but the mood of despair which repeated frustrations can engender. The spiritually mature are not impervious to disappointment, but are perhaps more keenly sensitive to it than most. The point is that they are not governed by it, do not sink into self-pity because of it, are not fatalistic about it. They accept the cross and even, without being morbid or superstitious about it, expect the cross; they do not make it their whole preoccupation. With an awareness of Christ's promise about the yoke being sweet and the burden light when endured with him, Christian sufferers aim as far as possible at self-forgetfulness in their sufferings. The protesting self, the resentful and potentially embittered self, will be sickened. The reaction to every trial will be St. Paul's "I have learned in whatsoever state I am to be content therewith." Such an attitude is a degree of personal fulfilment not often attained by men and women of considerable ability and position. In any age when achievement counts far more than motive, efficiency is often mistaken for maturity.

Achievement is not the lot of all, so the Christian would be wise to cultivate the disposition of being content to do without it.

Hubert van Zeller, *Leave Your Life Alone*, Sheed and Ward Ltd., 1973, p.101.

The noble inclination whereby man thirsteth after riches and dominion, is his highest virtue, when rightly guided; and carries him as in a triumphant chariot, to his sovereign happiness. Men are made miserable only by abusing it. Taking a false way to satisfy it, they pursue the wind: nay, labour in the very fire, and after all reap but vanity. Whereas, as God's love, which is the fountain of all, did cost us nothing: so were all other things prepared by it to satisfy our inclinations in the best of manners, freely, without any cost of ours. Seeing therefore all satisfactions are near at hand, by going further we do but leave them; and wearying ourselves in a long way round about, like a blind man, forsake them. They are immediately near to the very gates of our senses. It becometh the bounty of God to prepare them freely: to make them glorious, and their enjoyment easy. For because His love is free, so are His treasures. He therefore that will despise them because he hath them is marvellously irrational: the way to possess them is to esteem them. And the true way of reigning over them, is to break the world all into parts, to examine them asunder: And if we find them so excellent that better could not possibly be made, and so made they could not be more ours, to rejoice in all with pleasure answerable to the merit of their Goodness. We being then Kings over the whole world, when we restore the pieces to their proper places, being perfectly pleased with the whole composure. This shall give you a thorough grounded contentment, far beyond what troublesome wars or conquests can acquire.

Is it not a sweet thing to have all covetousness and ambition satisfied, suspicion and infidelity removed, courage and joy infused? Yet is all this in the fruition of the World attained. For thereby God is seen in all His wisdom, power, goodness, and glory.

Thomas Traherne, *Centuries*, The Faith Press Ltd., 1969, p.12.

CYNICISM

"Cynicism"— "sneering fault-finding; churlish, incredulous of human goodness."

S ome years ago, a highly intelligent undergraduate arrived in College. He had come from a caring background and a good school, but he had one fatal flaw— cynicism.

He began by finding fault with his fellow-undergraduates. He tended to sneer at those who had been to Public Schools, and was patronizing to those from Comprehensives. His attitude towards women students was scornful and manipulative. As soon as he settled down he started to find fault with the College. The administration was put under merciless scrutiny, and found to be wanting. His academic course of study was found to be boring and lacking in stimulation. Tutors were the next object of his scathing invective. They were heavily criticized for being uninspired and for not being particularly bright. The Governing Body was condemned out of hand. They were quite definitely exploiting the Junior Members of the College. As for finding any meaning in the universe, the attitude was "eat, drink and be merry, for tomorrow we die."

The impression that came over was a gloomy negativity, and a complete lack of sparkle and enjoyment. Whilst here, his considerable talents were thwarted. He failed to fulfil his early promise and ended up a victim of his own cynicism.

They say to God, "Depart from us! We do not desire the knowledge of thy ways. What is the Almighty, that we should serve him? And what profit do we get if we pray to him?"

Job 21.14-15.

If you scoff, you alone will bear it.

Proverbs 9.12.

He who is not with me is against me, and he who does not gather with me scatters.

Matthew 12.30.

Why do you pass judgment on your brother? Or you, why do you despise your brother?

Romans 14.10.

But a cynic can chill and dishearten with a single word.

Ralph Waldo Emerson, *Society and Solitude*, Success, J.M. Dent & Sons Ltd., 1912, p.145.

Bitterness does not help oneself or weigh with others.

A.C. Benson, *Extracts from the Letters of Dr. A.C. Benson to M.E.A.*, Jarrold Publishing, 1927, p.46.

I often wonder why men are so full of bitterness towards each other. It is one of those things I shall never live to understand.

Norman Douglas, *An Almanac*, Chatto & Windus in association with Martin Secker & Warburg Ltd., 1945, p.43.

The sweetest and most generous natures are the ones in greatest danger of becoming soured through the ingratitude of the world.

Henry Ward Beecher, *Proverbs from Plymouth Pulpit*, Charles Burnet & Co., 1887, p.48.

By letting themselves be cynical, unhappy people aggravate their melancholy. They are like a dog which tears at its wounded paw so as to hurt the pain.

Hubert van Zeller, *Considerations*, Sheed and Ward Ltd., 1974, p.101.

Such ugly-quilled dispositions as obstinacy, arrogance, self-opinioned ways, sneering, critical, cynical, teasing, disputative dispositions are hateful and produce hate.

Henry Ward Beecher, *Proverbs from Plymouth Pulpit*, Charles Burnet & Co., 1887, p.192.

Cynicism is intellectual dandyism without the coxcomb's feathers; and it seems to me that cynics are only happy in making the world as barren to others as they have made it for themselves.

George Meredith, *The Egoist*, The Times Book Club, 1912, Volume 1, p.75.

The cynic is one who never sees a good quality in a man, and never fails to see a bad one. He is the human owl, vigilant in darkness, and blind to light, mousing for vermin, and never seeing noble game.

Henry Ward Beecher, *Proverbs from Plymouth Pulpit*, Charles Burnet & Co., 1887, p.43.

While the executive part of some men grows sharper and more effective as they advance in life, those things which constitute noble traits grow worse and worse, till nothing seems left in old age but teeth and claws.

Henry Ward Beecher, *Proverbs from Plymouth Pulpit*, Charles Burnet & Co., 1887, p.23.

Worldly cynicism is less nauseating than pious humbug! But the course of honest testimony to principle in this tangled world is very difficult and only possible where faith in God has really exorcised self-centredness and self-concern.

William Temple, *Citizen and Churchman*, Eyre & Spottiswoode Publishers, 1941, p.53.

Cynic. More common to men than women. The cynic coats himself round by saying all the world is a bad place and all people are bad; so is he; but he is superior to other people in that he knows he is bad and does not pretend.

G.A. Studdert Kennedy, *The New Man in Christ*, Hodder & Stoughton Ltd., 1916, p.53.

Cynicism such as one finds very frequently among the most highly educated young men and women of the West results from the combination of comfort with power-lessness. Powerlessness makes people feel that nothing is worth doing, and comfort makes the painfulness of this feeling just endurable.

Bertrand Russell, *The Conquest of Happiness*, Unwin Paperbacks, 1984, p.115.

Our cynics and railers are mere egotists, who stand aloof from the common duty, and in their indolent remoteness are of no service to society against any ill which may attack it.

Their cultivation consists in having got rid of feeling. And thus they fall farther and farther away from true humanity.

Henri Frédéric Amiel, *Amiel's Journal*, translated by Mrs. Humphry Ward, Macmillan & Co. Ltd., 1918, p.178.

> Turn cynic if you will. Curse God and die.
> You've ample reason for it. There's enough
> Of bitterness, God knows, to answer why.
> The road of life is rough,
> But then there is the glory of the sky.

G.A. Studdert Kennedy, *The Unutterable Beauty*, Hodder and Stoughton, 1964, p.95.

The man who does not know where he is going or what kind of world he is heading toward, who wonders if bringing forth children into this chaotic world is not an act of cruelty rather than love, will often be tempted to become sarcastic or even cynical. He laughs at busy friends, but offers nothing in place of their activity. He protests against many things, but does not know what to witness for.

Henri J.M. Nouwen, *The Wounded Healer*, Doubleday, 1979, p.43.

Clever boys are often cynics because their desire for truth is thwarted, and because, in consequence, they value nothing but the activity of the intellect. They do not know what ails them, nor do their elders know. The parent and the teacher are often impatient of the perversities of the starved spirit; but it is their business not to starve it in any of its proper desires. It is their business to make the universe seem intelligible, not unintelligible.

A. Clutton-Brock, *The Ultimate Belief*, Constable & Co. Ltd., 1916, p.57.

Be sure that no one knows so little of his fellow-men as the cynical, misanthropic man, who walks in darkness because he hates his brother. Be sure that the truly wise and understanding man is he who by sympathy puts himself in his neighbours' place; feels with them and for them; sees with their eyes, hears with their ears, and therefore understands them, makes allowances for them, and is merciful to them, even as his Father in heaven is merciful.

Charles Kingsley, *Daily Thoughts*, Macmillan Publishers Ltd., 1884, p.191.

Modern cynics are not ready to follow anybody. They have no belief in reason, no criterion of truth, no set values, no answer to the question of meaning. They try to undermine every norm put before them. Their courage is expressed not creatively but in their form of life. They courageously reject any solution which would deprive them of their freedom of rejecting whatever they want to reject. The cynics are lonely although they need company in order to show their loneliness. They are empty of both preliminary meanings and an ultimate meaning, and therefore easy victims of neurotic anxiety.

Paul Tillich, *The Courage to Be*, James Nisbet & Co. Ltd., 1952, p.143.

What does the glittering tumult of human history, the glory and tragedy of the human centuries all come to? The cynic has answered that life is a comedy to him who thinks, and a tragedy to him who feels. The religious man answers that it is victory for him who believes. Believes what? What may we believe about the problem which has vexed thought and tried faith in every generation, namely, the problem of Death? It is no mere play upon word to say that man's life is only to be evaluated in terms of its end. Making sense of life means, ultimately, and always, making sense of Death.

J.S. Whale, *Christian Doctrine*, Cambridge University Press, 1942, p.171.

The great thing *now* to avoid is having a grudge against the way life has treated you and against the world, because if this is allowed the least scope it ends up with a grudge against God. Then the whole process, which was designed to be so purifying, is wasted. You may expect great things of life, but it is of the first importance not to think that life *owes* you anything. Life owes you nothing but what you can give yourself. Half the convicted criminals, and probably all suicides, are those who imagine that they have claims which life has not met. With some it is a grudge against society, with others against individuals, with others against themselves. In one way or another life has cheated them and they mean to compensate. Even taking your own life is an assertion of rights—a last slap in the face of life for having denied what was thought to be owing.

Hubert van Zeller, *Leave Your Life Alone*, Sheed and Ward Ltd., 1973, p.112.

The Cynic in society becomes the Pessimist in religion. The large embrace of sympathy which fails him as interpreter of human life, will no less be wanting when he reads the meaning of the universe. The harmony of the great whole escapes him in his hunt for little discords here and there. He is blind to the august balance of nature, in his preoccupation with some creaking show of defect. He misses the comprehensive march of advancing purpose, because, while he himself is in it, he has found some halting member that seems to lag behind. He picks holes in the universal order; he winds through its tracks as a detective; and makes scandals of all that is not to his mind. He trusts nothing that he cannot see; and he sees chiefly the exceptional, the dubious, the harsh. The glory of the midnight heavens affects him not, for thinking of a shattered planet or the uninhabitable moon. He makes more of the flood which sweeps the crop away, than of the perpetual river that feeds it year by year. For him the purple bloom upon the hills, peering through the young green woods, does but dress up a stony desert with deceitful beauty; and in the new birth of summer, he cannot yield himself to the exuberance of glad existence for wonder why insects tease and nettles sting. Nothing is so fair, nothing imposing, as to beguile him into faith and hope... in selfish minds the same temper takes a meaner turn, and resorts to the pettiest reasons for the most desolating thoughts: "If God were good, why should I be born with a club-foot? If the world were justly governed, how could my merits be so long overlooked?"

James Martineau, *Hours of Thoughts on Sacred Things*, Longmans, Green, Reader and Dyer, 1880, Volume 1, p.97.

DEPRESSION

"Depression"—"A psychological state of extreme low spirits characterized by a sense of hopelessness and despair."

A medical student dropped in to see me. I knew him well. He was normally a bright and cheerful person, competent in his studies and a gifted musician. He was going through a period of depression. He complained of a heavy work load. In common with all medical students he had enormous amounts of Anatomy, Physiology and Biochemistry to learn. He said he felt like a piece of blotting paper, soaking up facts like ink. He had long since reached saturation point, and was in extremely low spirits, close to despair.

I gave him a short quotation, and suggested he get a pen and paper, and write down all his thoughts as he pondered over these words. He was then to come and see me again in an hour's time.

He failed to return. Two hours went by and I was beginning to get concerned. Suddenly there was a loud knock on the door and there he was, back to his usual cheerful self. "Do you know," he explained, "I've just had my very first thoughts ever! Up to now I've always been concerned with other people's thoughts and for years I've been learning facts and more facts. I reckon that is what has been depressing me. But today, for the very first time in my life, I've discovered I have a mind that can think. I got so absorbed I forgot about the time. What enormous resources we have inside us. Now at least I can live!"

How often external pressures depress us, and dampen down our precious inner resources.

Why are you cast down, O my soul, and why are you disquieted within me? Hope in God; for I shall again praise him, my help and my God.
Psalm 43.5.

The sacrifice acceptable to God is a broken spirit; a broken and contrite heart, O God, thou wilt not despise.
Psalm 51.17.

Truly, truly, I say to you, you will weep and lament, but the world will rejoice; you will be sorrowful, but your sorrow will turn into joy.
John 16.20.

God, who comforts the downcast.
2 Corinthians 7.6.

Half the spiritual difficulties that men and women suffer arise from a morbid state of health.
Henry Ward Beecher, *Proverbs from Plymouth Pulpit,* Charles Burnet & Co., 1887, p.163.

More people are destroyed by unhappiness than by drink, drugs, disease, or even failure. There must be something about sadness which attracts or people would not accept it so readily into their lives.

Hubert van Zeller, *Considerations*, Sheed & Ward Ltd., 1974, p.25.

An unhappy man is nearly always one who is at the mercy of some greed or some fear. Weighed down by selfish desire or dread, or both, he is not giving himself room to lead the life he is meant to live. The wish to escape occupies him to the exclusion of all else.

Hubert van Zeller, *Considerations*, Sheed & Ward Ltd., 1974, p.26.

It is one of the secrets of Nature in its mood of mockery that fine weather lays a heavier weight on the mind and hearts of the depressed and the inwardly tormented than does a really bad day with dark rain snivelling continuously and sympathetically from a dirty sky.

Muriel Spark, *Territorial Rights*, Macmillan Publishers Ltd., 1979, p.51.

He wandered aimlessly. The sun was setting. A special form of misery had begun to oppress him of late. There was nothing poignant, nothing acute about it; but there was a feeling of permanence, of eternity about it; it brought a foretaste of hopeless years of this cold leaden misery, a foretaste of an eternity "on a square yard of space."

Fyodor Dostoyevsky, *Crime and Punishment*, translated by Constance Garnett, Folio Society, 1957, p.353.

I can enjoy feeling melancholy, and there is a good deal of satisfaction about being thoroughly miserable; but nobody likes a fit of the blues. Nevertheless, everybody has them; notwithstanding which, nobody can tell why. There is no accounting for them. You are just as likely to have one on the day after you have come into a large fortune, as on the day after you have left your new silk umbrella in the train.

Jerome K. Jerome, *Idle Thoughts of an Idle Fellow*, J.M. Dent & Sons Ltd., 1983, p.21.

For the rest, I was utterly derelict. I felt myself banished from life and from God. And I was quite hopeless; not approximately, not in the sense people often intend when they play with this terrible word, but in the sense that to have had the very tiniest of hopes, for the very briefest of instants, would have been wholly inconceivable. The doom that I lived with in eternity was the doom that I must live in eternity with a self I detested, and must live with it alone.

Victor Gollancz, *More For Timothy*, Victor Gollancz Ltd., 1953, p.92.

The value of solitude—one of its values—is, of course, that there is nothing to *cushion* against attacks from within, just as there is nothing to help balance at times of particular stress or depression. A few moments of desultory conversation... may calm an inner storm. But the storm, painful as it is, might have had some truth in it. So sometimes one has simply to endure a period of depression for what it may hold of illumination if one can live through it, attentive to what it exposes or demands.

May Sarton, *Journal of a Solitude*, The Women's Press, 1985, p.6.

We human beings so often complain that of good days there are so few and of evil days so many, and, as I think, without warrant for the most part. If we always had an open heart to enjoy the good things that God prepares for us every day, we would then have strength enough too to bear affliction when it comes...

With ill humour it is just as with indolence, for it is a kind of indolence. Our nature leans very much that way, and yet, once we muster the strength to shake it off, work goes smoothly and we find a real delight in activity.

Johann Wolfgang von Goethe, *Wisdom and Experience*, selected by Ludwig Curtius, translated by Hermann J. Weigand, Routledge & Kegan Paul Ltd., 1949, p.209.

Sometimes I battle with depression. I never know all the reasons for this "dark pit", as it seems to me. Some of it may be hurt pride. Sometimes it is obviously exhaustion, physical, mental, emotional and spiritual. At times, when I am tired and strained, I can get angry over an incident that may be quite trivial in itself; and then I get angry with myself for getting angry. As I suppress both forms of anger, depression is the result. I am then even more difficult to live with than usual. I do not want people to get too near to me, but I hope very much that they will not go too far away either.

David Watson, *You are My God*, Hodder & Stoughton Ltd., 1983, p.190.

When the heart is hard and parched up, come upon me with a shower of mercy.

When grace is lost from life, come with a burst of song. When tumultuous work raises its din on all sides shutting me out from beyond, come to me, my lord of silence, with thy peace and rest.

When my beggarly heart sits crouched, shut up in a corner, break open the door, my king, and come with the ceremony of a king.

When desire blinds the mind with delusion and dust, O thou holy one, thou wakeful, come with thy light and thy thunder.

Rabindranath Tagore, *Gitanjali*, Macmillan Publishers Ltd., 1971, p.30.

I used to imagine that as one got rid of neurosis so depression would gradually disappear, leaving one in a state of serene cheerfulness. On the contrary, depression when it comes, grows deeper, though the joy which balances it is also more intense. When we have lost our major neuroses, the depression gets less personal—it is no longer principally about ourselves and our problems, nor even of those we love. We seem to go behind and beneath these manifestations of pain and evil until we arrive at a root of suffering, wrestling in terror and darkness with what we do not understand. And then, inevitably, joy follows.

Monica Furlong, *Travelling In*, Hodder & Stoughton Ltd., 1971, p.76.

A vague feeling of anguish is prowling around in me like a caged beast, immobilising my energies and concentration. The feeling has no shape and I don't know what to call it. I am its prisoner. I've got to shake it off. I need all my energy at the moment, at every moment, if I'm to live my life in its fullness. But I won't be free of it until I've let the bad feeling wash over me, then faced it without fear, grabbed it with both hands and offered it to God who can bring new life out of sin.

I can understand the awful pain of those who are suffering from depression. It's a paralysing of one's whole being, while others whisper: He should pull up his socks! Control himself! But the trouble is *he can't*. It's an ordeal, one of the worst. He needs drugs, perhaps. But he also needs someone always to be there, patient, sensitive, to help him set free the little pieces of life which are stagnating in him, polluting his source. And if he is a believer, he must also be helped to offer it all to God.

Michel Quoist, *With Open Heart*, translated by Colette Copeland, Gill and Macmillan Ltd., 1983, p.173.

Nobody has suffered more from low spirits than I have done, so I feel for you. 1. Live as well and drink as much wine as you dare. 2. Go into the shower-bath with a small quantity of water at a temperature low enough to give you a *slight sensation* of cold—75 or 80 degrees. 3. Amusing books. 4. Short views on human life not farther than dinner or tea. 5. Be as busy as you can. 6. See as much as you can of those friends who respect and like you; 7. and of those acquaintances who amuse you. 8. Make no secret of low spirits to your friends but talk to them fully: they are always the worse for dignified concealment. 9. Attend to the effects tea and coffee produce upon you. 10. Compare your lot with that of other people. 11. Don't expect too much of human life, a sorry business at the best. 12. Avoid poetry, dramatic representations (except comedy), music, serious novels, melancholy sentimental people, and everything likely to excite feel or emotion not ending in active benevolence. 13. Do good and endeavour to please everybody of every degree. 14. Be as much as you can in the open air without fatigue. 15. Make the room where you commonly sit gay and pleasant. 16. Struggle by little and little against idleness. 17. Don't be too severe upon yourself, or underrate yourself, but do yourself justice. 18. Keep good blazing fires. 19. Be firm and constant in the exercise of natural religion.

Sydney Smith, in *Sidney Smith, A Biography*, Alan Bell, Clarendon Press, 1980, p.137.

DESPAIR

"Despair"— "Loss, utter want, of hope; thing that causes this, whether by badness or unapproachable excellence."

A postgraduate came to see me, out of the blue. He was working in a research team, designing a computer to go into a space capsule. The project itself was exciting and progressing well, but he himself was going through a period of despair and found that his Astro-Physics, on which he set so much store, had nothing to say to him as a person.

I listened to him for some time. It seemed to me he was on a spiritual quest. I lent him a copy of the book which had changed the course of my life—*The Choice is Always Ours*, by Dorothy Berkley Phillips. I suggested he dip into this and come and see me in a week's time.

On his next visit I noticed a considerable change. It looked as though he had been completely transformed in the space of a few days. He excitedly exclaimed *The Choice* was just what he had been looking for. I listened to him carefully, and we met regularly for an hour a week for the next couple of months.

One day he turned up with a gloomy expression on his face. He was back in despair again. He was unable to open *The Choice* for fear of what it might reveal. We agreed he should obey his feelings and not open the book until he felt like it. We continued to meet but there was no change for several weeks. Then he went down with flu. On the last night of his flu he had a dream. He couldn't remember the contents but was aware of some kind of unity, of things falling into place. The next day he awoke fit and well, and into *The Choice* again.

He was later ordained and has for many years served as a priest in the East End.

And among these nations you shall find no ease, and there shall be no rest for the sole of your foot; but the Lord will give you there a trembling heart, and failing eyes, and a languishing soul; your life shall hang in doubt before you; night and day you shall be in dread, and have no assurance of your life.

Deuteronomy 28.65-66.

The Lord is near to the brokenhearted, and saves the crushed in spirit.

Psalm 34.18.

And he said to them, "My soul is very sorrowful, even to death; remain here, and watch." And going a little farther, he fell on the ground and prayed that, if it were possible, the hour might pass from him. And he said, "Abba, Father, all things are possible to thee; remove this cup from me; yet not what I will, but what thou wilt."

Mark 14.34-36.

We are afflicted in every way, but not crushed; perplexed, but not driven to despair; persecuted, but not forsaken; struck down, but not destroyed.

2 Corinthians 4.8.

Despair gives courage.

Sir Walter Scott, The Heart of Midlothian, Oxford University Press, 1912, p.581.

I am driven
Into a desperate strait, and cannot steer
A middle course.

Philip Massinger, The Great Duke of Florence, Vizetelly & Co., 1889, Act III, sc.i, p.244.

Then black despair,
The shadow of a starless night, was thrown
Over the world in which I moved alone.

Percy Bysshe Shelley, The Complete Poetical Works of Percy Bysshe Shelley, edited by Thomas Hutchinson, Oxford University Press, 1935, Revolt of Islam: Dedication, st.6, p.39.

There are moments so cruel that they would make us regard the brevity of life as the greatest boon, to keep intolerable torment from being interminable.

Johann Wolfgang von Goethe, Wisdom and Experience, selected by Ludwig Curtius, translated and edited by Hermann J. Weigand, Routledge & Kegan Paul, 1949, p.219.

For there is no despair so absolute as that which comes with the first moments of our first great sorrow, when we have not yet known what it is to have suffered and be healed, to have despaired and to have recovered hope.

George Eliot, Adam Bede, Virtue & Co., 1908, Volume II, p.68.

The severely self-rejecting adolescent is his own enemy. He has taken unto himself all the unkindness of his heredity and all the harshness of his environment, and then has added something more: everything is his fault and he is no good.

Arthur T. Jersild, The Psychology of Adolescence, Macmillan Publishers Ltd., 1963, p.35.

Despair is not a durable situation. We shall have to build a moral city without God, without an immortality of the soul, without hope. Buddhism and Stoicism present themselves as possible alternatives.

Henri Frédéric Amiel, Amiel's Journal, translated by Mrs. Humphry Ward, Macmillan Publishers Ltd., 1918, p.214.

The human being cannot live in a condition of emptiness for very long: if he is not growing *toward* something, he does not merely stagnate; the pent-up potentialities turn into morbidity and despair, and eventually into destructive activities.

Rollo May, *Man's Search For Himself*, Souvenir Press Ltd., 1975, p.24.

This, then is our desert: to live facing despair, but not to consent. To trample it down under hope in the Cross. To wage war against despair unceasingly. That war is our wilderness. If we wage it courageously, we will find Christ at our side. If we cannot face it, we will never find him.

Thomas Merton, *Thoughts in Solitude*, Burns & Oates Ltd., 1958, p.20.

Despair is the price one pays for setting oneself an impossible aim. It is, one is told, the unforgivable sin, but it is a sin the corrupt or evil man never practises. He always has hope. He never reaches the freezing-point of knowing absolute failure. Only the man of goodwill carries always in his heart this capacity for damnation.

Graham Greene, *The Heart of the Matter*, William Heinemann Ltd., 1959, p.67.

That Jesus fought despair and triumphed we know from his prayers on the cross which began with "My God, why have you forsaken me?" and ended with "Into your hand, Lord, I commend my spirit." However near we come to despair, we have this precedent to refer to.

Hubert van Zeller, *Considerations*, Sheed & Ward Ltd., 1974, p.76.

Rabbi Nachman of Bratzlav taught me the commandment: "Never despair! Before we can achieve greatness", he used to say, "we must first descend to smallness, to a state of simplicity. Even in the deepest sinking there is the hidden purpose of an ultimate rising. So that the most important thing during the time of smallness is not to despair."

Martin Buber, in *Encounter with Martin Buber*, Aubrey Hodes, Allen Lane The Penguin Press, 1972, p.150.

Quiet desperation, despair, and active desperation are stages in a journey through hell. While one is going through them one could well see oneself as living in a hell. What is happening, though, in all this dark journey is that the self is becoming capable of soul. Living without the life of soul, then finding it in another person and losing it, and then seeking desperately to regain it, one is becoming capable of actually living it.

John S. Dunne, *The Reasons of the Heart*, SCM Press Ltd., 1978, p.99.

I remember a despairing White Father in the Belgian Congo saying to me, "There is another great age of darkness closing in on the life of man and all that we can do is to create little fortresses wherein the authentic light of the spirit can be kept burning. Then, one day, when men wish to reach out for the light they will have places in which to find it. But for the rest, we must just accept the inevitability of disaster."

"Perhaps you're right, and disaster may have to come," I had replied. "But as a matter of honour I believe we must go on working to prevent disaster, if only to make certain that if it ultimately has to come, it is the right kind of disaster life needs."

Laurens van der Post, *Jung and the Story of our Time*, Hogarth Press, 1976, p.41.

Despair is the absolute extreme of self-love. It is reached when a man deliberately turns his back on all help from anyone else in order to taste the rotten luxury of knowing himself to be lost.

In every man there is hidden some root of despair because in every man there is pride that vegetates and springs weeds and rank flowers of self pity as soon as our own resources fail us. But because our own resources inevitably fail us, we are all more or less subject to discouragement and to despair.

Despair is the ultimate development of a pride so great and so stiff-necked that it selects the absolute misery of damnation rather than accept happiness from the hands of God and thereby acknowledge that He is above us and that we are not capable of fulfilling our destiny by ourselves.

Thomas Merton, *New Seeds of Contemplation*, Burns & Oates Ltd., 1962, p.140.

There is in us an organ of malevolence and discontent, just as there is one of contradiction and skepticism. The more we foster it and give it play, the more powerful it becomes until it develops from an organ into a festering cancer that keeps on expanding, consuming, and infecting all healthy tissues. Then it gets incrusted with remorse, self-reproach, and other absurdities. We become unjust toward others and toward ourselves. We lose pleasure in the success and achievements of ourselves and of others. In despair we finally look for the root of all evil outside ourselves instead of finding it in our own contrariness. If we could only take each individual and each event for what it is worth and emerge from the confines of the self to return to it with a new sense of expansion.

Johann Wolfgang von Goethe, *Wisdom and Experience*, selected by Ludwig Curtius, translated and edited by Hermann J. Weigand, Routledge & Kegan Paul, 1949, p.218.

> I am: yet what I am none cares or knows
> My friends forsake me like a memory lost,
> I am the self-consumer of my woes—
> They rise and vanish in oblivious host,
> Like shadows in love's frenzied, stifled throes:—
> And yet I am, and live—like vapours tost
>
> Into the nothingness of scorn and noise,
> Into the living sea of waking dreams,
> Where there is neither sense of life or joys,
> But the vast shipwreck of my life's esteems;
> Even the dearest, that I love the best,
> Are strange—nay, rather stranger than the rest.
>
> I long for scenes, where man hath never trod,
> A place where woman never smiled or wept—
> There to abide with my Creator, God,
> And sleep as I in childhood sweetly slept,
> Untroubling, and untroubled where I lie,
> The grass below—above the vaulted sky.

John Clare, *Poems of John Clare's Madness*, Routledge & Kegan Paul, 1949, *I Am*, p.132.

I can picture one teacher there—I can't recall her name. She was short and spare, and I can remember her eager jutting chin. Quite unexpectedly one day (in the middle, I think, of an arithmetic lesson) she suddenly launched forth on a speech on life and religion. "All of you," she said, "every *one* of you—will pass through a time when you will face despair. If you never face despair, you will never have faced, or become, a Christian, or known a Christian life. To be a Christian, you must face and accept the life that Christ faced and lived; you must enjoy things as he enjoyed things; be as happy as he was at the marriage of Cana, know the peace and happiness that it means to be in harmony with God and with God's will. But you must also know, as he did, what it means to be alone in the Garden of Gethsemane, to feel that all your friends have forsaken you, that those you love and trust have turned away from you, and that *God Himself* has forsaken you. Hold on then to the belief that that is *not* the end. If you love, you will suffer, and if you do not love, you do not know the meaning of a Christian life."

She then returned to the problems of compound interest with her usual vigour, but it is odd that those few words, more than any sermon I have ever heard, remained with me, and years later they were to come back to me and give me hope at a time when despair had me in its grip. She was a dynamic figure, and also, I think, a *fine* teacher; I wish I could have been taught by her longer.

Agatha Christie, *An Autobiography*, William Collins Sons & Co. Ltd., 1977, p.150.

DISCIPLESHIP

"Discipleship"—"one who attends upon another for the purpose of learning from him/her—includes practice as well as theory, learning by doing."

W e had a bright law undergraduate in the new intake. A promising future was predicted—either as a top solicitor in a City firm, or as a barrister.

He became committed in his faith whilst at College. As a way of testing his vocation, he worked in a London hostel for down and outs, during a summer vacation. His "mentor" was the Warden. In those few weeks he learnt a tremendous amount about himself, about other people, about faith and of putting it into practice. He was involved in discipleship—learning by doing.

The problems he faced were enormous—alcoholism, physical and mental sickness, psychological disorders of every kind, discharged prisoners unable to cope with life, sexual perversion, and so on. He was at the receiving end of much verbal abuse and of carrying out many distasteful tasks. At the end of the vacation he came back to College, a much chastened man.

Eventually the predicted First was forthcoming, but much to the dismay of his tutors he went back to the hostel on a full-time basis. He had reached the conclusion that working with people with enormous personal problems was much more demanding and challenging than working for the Law, and for him, more fulfilling too.

Bind up the testimony, seal the teaching among my disciples.
Isaiah 8.16.

The Lord God has given me the tongue of those who are taught, that I may know how to sustain with a word him that is weary. Morning by morning he wakens, he wakens my ear to hear as those who are taught.
Isaiah 50.4.

Come to me, all who labour and are heavy laden, and I will give you rest. Take my yoke upon you, and learn from me; for I am gentle and lowly in heart, and you will find rest for your souls. For my yoke is easy, and my burden is light.
Matthew 11.28-30.

A new commandment I give to you, that you love one another; even as I have loved you, that you also love one another. By this all men will know that you are my disciples, if you have love for one another.
John 13.34-35.

We are meant to be continually encouraged and discouraged, and to hope in God.
J. Neville Ward, *The Use of Praying*, Epworth Press, 1967, p.258.

When the body is most disciplined, the mental and the spiritual faculties are most alert.
William Barclay, *The Gospel of Matthew*, The Saint Andrew Press, 1987, Volume 1, p.234.

The commandment of absolute truthfulness is really only another name for the fulness of discipleship.
Dietrich Bonhoeffer, *The Cost of Discipleship*, translated by R.H. Fuller, SCM Press Ltd., 1956, p.119.

Christ cannot be followed unless a man gives the benefit of his gifts and attainments to the whole community.
Henry Ward Beecher, *Proverbs from Plymouth Pulpit*, Charles Burnet & Co., 1887, p.161.

There is a danger of resting in God's favour. There must be a return; the circuit of giving and receiving must be kept intact to carry the current of love.
J. Neville Ward, *The Use of Praying*, Epworth Press, 1967, p.157.

We are called to represent Christ spontaneously and with incalculable consequences in the pedestrian obscurity of everyday life.
Hans Jürgen Schultz, *Conversion to the World*, SCM Press Ltd., 1967, p.100.

In dealing with ourselves inner genuineness, with our fellows utter goodwill, with God perfect confidence—that, in brief, is discipleship to Jesus.
Harry Emerson Fosdick, *The Hope of a New World*, SCM Press Ltd., 1933, p.179.

For though our Saviour's passion is over, his compassion is not. That never fails his humble sincere disciples. In him they find more than all they lose in the world.
William Penn, *Fruits of Solitude*, A.W. Bennett, 1863, p.13.

We know by doing. Take up thy cross, lift it up yourself on your own shoulder, stagger under it, go on with it, and your intellect will be enriched with what no books could give.
Mark Rutherford, *Last Pages From a Journal*, Oxford University Press, 1915, p.303.

God in Jesus Christ enters the human battles for existence and wholeness, and exerts his power to redeem men. The disciple is called to enter into this decisive issue—not merely "decide" about it, but participate in it.
John J. Vincent, *Secular Christ*, Lutterworth Press, 1968, p.77.

The following that Jesus wanted was not that of men drawn by personal devotion to himself, or of those who were concerned about their own salvation, but of those who would share with him in his devotion to the finding and doing of the Father's will.

Leonard Hodgson, *Sex and Christian Freedom*, SCM Press Ltd., 1967, p.29.

Now it is well enough known that Christ constantly uses the expression "follower"; He never says anything about wanting admirers, admiring worshippers, adherents; and when he uses the expression "disciples", He always so explains it that we can perceive that followers are meant.

Søren Kierkegaard, *Training in Christianity*, translated by Walter Lowrie, Princeton University Press, 1957, p.231.

Your own experience convinces you that our life is in all respects a continual warfare, that everywhere and in all estates we must be proved and tried both from without and within.

This is the lot of a true disciple, and I'm sure 'tis a happy one when improved according to our Lord's intention. Nothing then that happens must disturb or disquiet us...

May it please him to increase our faith and strengthen our dependence on him.

James Keith, in *God in our midst*, Martin Reith, Triangle/SPCK, 1989, p.37.

Congregations and fellowships are all too often aggregations of people who never get any nearer to speaking a common language growing in a common mind, acting with common purpose and praying in one spirit. Their members are just as exposed to depersonalisation as those who remain outside them and make no professions of faith in a unifying Spirit and a Body of Christ. Priority in discipleship must lie in deliberate seeking of ways to assemble such bodies of people to find out together what personal relationships mean. Only so does the great inheritance of Trinitarian faith become for each member of them a truly liberating and energising force.

Alan Ecclestone, *Yet to God*, Darton, Longman & Todd Ltd., 1975, p.113.

We are summoned to a new level of identification. We are summoned to be disciples, and so to a discipline. A disciple is a learner and his discipline is the training whereby he learns. To learn the way of the cross is the hardest thing of all, and the training by which we are to advance in this learning is provided for us by the discipline of prayer and worship. Those who disparage prayer and worship and imagine that without these one can achieve some kind of instant Christianity do not know what they are talking about. They understand neither the weakness of our humanity nor the depth of the richness of the spiritual maturity into which Christ is calling us.

Those who have advanced far along the road of discipleship toward maturity and proficiency are the saints.

John Macquarrie, *Paths in Spirituality*, SCM Press Ltd., 1972, p.116.

We must regard ourselves always as men engaged upon a campaign, as men pressing onwards to a goal.

To win the fight and to be victorious in the race demands discipline. We have to discipline our bodies; it is one of the neglected facts of the spiritual life that very often spiritual depression springs from nothing else than physical unfitness. If a man is going to do his best work in anything he must bring to it a body as fit as he can make it. We have to discipline our minds; it is one of the tragedies of life that men may refuse to think until they become incapable of thinking. We can never solve problems by refusing to see them or by running away from them. We must discipline our souls; we can do so by facing life's sorrows with calm endurance, its temptations with the strength God gives, its disappointments with courage.

William Barclay, *The Letters to the Corinthians,* The Saint Andrew Press, 1988, p.85.

The path of discipleship is narrow, and it is fatally easy to miss one's way and stray from the path, even after years of discipleship. And it is hard to find. On either side of the narrow path deep chasms yawn. To be called to a life of extraordinary quality, to live up to it, and yet to be unconscious of it is indeed a narrow way. To confess and testify to the truth as it is in Jesus, and at the same time to love the enemies of that truth, His enemies and ours, and to love them with the infinite love of Jesus Christ, is indeed a narrow way. To believe the promise of Jesus that His followers shall possess the earth, and at the same time to face our enemies unarmed and defenceless, preferring to incur injustice rather than to do wrong ourselves, is indeed a narrow way. To see the weakness and wrong in others, and at the same time refrain from judging them; to deliver the gospel message without casting pearls before swine, is indeed a narrow way. The way is unutterably hard, and at every moment we are in danger of straying from it. If we regard this way as one we follow in obedience to an external command, if we are afraid of ourselves all the time, it is indeed an impossible way. But if we behold Jesus Christ going on before step by step, if we only look to Him and follow Him, step by step, we shall not go astray. But if we worry about the dangers that beset us, if we gaze at the road instead of at Him who goes before, we are already straying from the path. For He is Himself the way, the narrow way and the strait gate. He, and He alone, is our journey's end. When we know that, we are able to proceed along the narrow way through the strait gate of the cross, and on to eternal life, and the very narrowness of the road will increase our certainty.

Dietrich Bonhoeffer, *The Cost of Discipleship,* translated by R.H. Fuller, SCM Press Ltd., 1956, p.162.

ENVIRONMENT

"Environment"—"the conditions or influences under which any person or thing lives or is developed."

In the weeks following ordination I began to visit the occupants of high-rise flats near the Cathedral, in Bradford, West Yorkshire. For me, this was a real eye-opener.

What struck me first was the large number of tragedies I came across. Some of these were physical handicaps resulting from a mixture of birth, illness and accident. Others were personal, resulting from the break-up of family relationships. But what was more disturbing was the realization that most of the occupants were trapped by their environment. They were restricted and limited by the surroundings and conditions in which they lived and worked—victims of economic factors beyond their control. In addition they were almost all hard hit by loneliness, brought about by the very structure of high-rise flats. This really came home to me one Christmas Eve. I was doing some visiting. I knocked on the door of an elderly gentleman. No reply. I knocked again—a distant groan. I gently opened the door and went into the sitting-room. There he was—almost unconscious. His only way of coping with isolation at Christmas was to get hopelessly drunk. He gazed at me with a mixture of shame and embarrassment. I gave him a small gift of food and fruit, and tried to exercise what compassion and understanding I could muster in the circumstances.

The immediate surroundings of these people were bad enough. Add to this, noisy traffic, an industrial setting with a polluted atmosphere, unemployment, the fear and threat of nuclear war, and the evils of the environment become all too apparent.

You shall not defile the land in which you live, in the midst of which I dwell.
Numbers 35.34.

The earth mourns and withers, the world languishes and withers... The earth lies polluted under its inhabitants; for they have transgressed the laws, violated the statutes, broken the everlasting covenant. Therefore a curse devours the earth, and its inhabitants suffer for their guilt; therefore the inhabitants of the earth are scorched, and few men are left... The city of chaos is broken down... Desolation is left in the city.
Isaiah 24.4-6,10,12.

Thy kingdom come, Thy will be done, On earth as it is in heaven.
Matthew 6.10.

Put on the new nature, created after the likeness of God in true righteousness and holiness.
Ephesians 4.24.

Environment is the nursery of personality.

J.B. Yeats, *Letters to his son, W.B.Yeats and others*, Faber & Faber Ltd., 1944, p.151.

I'm very sensitive to noise. Noise is the curse of the modern world, another form of pollution. We're going to need an awful lot of work to clean it up and I for one, don't know how we're going to manage it.

Michel Quoist, *With Open Heart*, translated by Colette Copeland, Gill and Macmillan Ltd., 1983, p.100.

I want to preach to artists a new doctrine which I will call the doctrine *of the environment* as more important than all. A man of genius is not only divine. There is also the child's heart within the man's, *and the child's heart is all for the environment.*

J.B. Yeats, *Letters to his son, W.B. Yeats and others*, Faber & Faber Ltd., 1944, p.151.

Man is endowed with intellect and creative powers so that he may multiply what is given to him; but up to now he has not created, he has destroyed. Forests are fewer and fewer, rivers dry up, game becomes extinct, the climate is ruined, and every day the earth gets poorer and uglier.

Anton Chekhov, *Uncle Vanya*, translated by Stark Young, Samuel French, Inc., 1955, Act 1, p.14.

We live in a world full of problems; evil and suffering, divisions and hatred (between classes and races, and sexes), the very rich and the very poor. There are problems of the environment, problems of power, even the power to annihilate whole peoples through nuclear war. How does the idea of God fit into this modern world?

Hugh Montefiore, *Confirmation Notebook*, Fifth Edition, SPCK, 1985, p.7.

Pollution of air, water, and land; world human population levels and the rate of reproduction; increased demands for food and shrinking supplies of arable land, energy, and nonrenewable resources; the disappearance of whole species of animal and plant life; economic development and appropriate life-styles on a finite globe; and the threat of nuclear holocaust are some of the issues engaged by environmental ethics over the last two decades.

Terence R. Anderson, in *A New Dictionary of Christian Ethics*, edited by James F. Childress and John Macquarrie, SCM Press Ltd., 1986, p.196.

Vandalism may often be a protest against the inhumanity of the environment and an attempt to soften some of its harshness. In some places this aspect of vandalism has been channelled into positive directions through community arts programmes... Our experience suggests that where a community is constructed on a small scale enough for human relations to be conducted, and for the environment to be cared for by people who live within it, the destructiveness diminishes.

The Family Welfare Association, in *Faith in the City*, Church Publishing House, 1985, p.333.

The growth in material goods available in modern society has increased the opportunities for theft and damage, particularly when goods are very accessible, like cars on the streets and goods in self-service shops... Since our society encourages consumerism and exposes all its members to attractive life-styles through the mass media, yet severely restricts real opportunities for many, particularly if they are black, female, poor or handicapped, it is not surprising that respect for the law should be weakened.

Faith in the City, Church Publishing House, 1985, p.337.

The environment is subject to particular stress at the present time. A whole network of ecological problems is caused by population increases, by affluence, by technology, by capitalism and by economic growth. Species are threatened and extinguished, non-renewable resources are becoming very greatly reduced, widespread pollution is caused, fertility of the soil is threatened or eroded. God gave human beings dominion over nature (Gen. 1.26). According to the story of the Garden of Eden, Adam was placed in the garden to co-operate with nature, which was both intrinsicially good and useful for men (Gen.2.9,15). God intended man to exercise proper stewardship over nature.

Hugh Montefiore, *Confirmation Notebook*, Fifth Edition, 1985, p.8.

The law of uncontrolled economic growth... creates a continually widening gap between rich and poor countries and strengthens among the underprivileged part of mankind feelings of envy, resentment, deadly hatred, but also of sheer despair and helplessness. And... it is turned in the end against the well-to-do themselves. We are suffering increasingly from the apparently endless growth of cities, proliferating traffic, noise on all sides, pollution of rivers and lakes, bad air; we are worried about the disposal of butter and meat mountains, we are crushed under the waste and lumber of our own prosperity. The world's raw materials, ruthlessly and more and more extensively exploited, are becoming increasingly scarce; the problem of an ever more widely expanding world economy is becoming incomprehensible. But what is to be done?

Hans Küng, *On Being a Christian*, translated by Edward Quinn, William Collins Sons & Co. Ltd., 1977, p.596.

I do not minimize the complexity of the problems that need to be faced in achieving disarmament and peace. But I am convinced that we shall not have the will, the courage, and the insight to deal with such matters unless in this field we are prepared to undergo a mental and spiritual reevaluation, a change of focus which will enable us to see that the things that seem most real and powerful are indeed now unreal and have come under the sentence of death.

It is not enough to say, "We must not wage war." It is necessary to love peace and sacrifice for it. We must concentrate not merely on the eradication of war but on the affirmation of peace.

So we must see that peace represents a sweeter music, a cosmic melody that is far superior to the discords of war. Somehow we must transform the dynamics of the world power struggle from the nuclear arms race, which no one can win, to a creative contest to harness man's genius for the purpose of making peace and prosperity a reality for all the nations of the world. In short, we must shift the arms race into a "peace race." If we have the will and determination to mount such a peace offensive, we will unlock hitherto tightly sealed doors of hope and bring new light into the dark chambers of pessimism.

Martin Luther King, *The Words of Martin Luther King*, selected by Coretta Scott King, William Collins Sons & Co. Ltd., 1986, p.85.

"Unemployment", said Archbishop William Temple in the 1930s, "is the most hideous of our social evils." The effects of unemployment in the 1980s have been all too clear to us on our visits to Britain's Urban Priority Areas. We have been confronted time and time again with the deep human misery—coupled in some cases with resentment, in others with apathy and hopelessness—that is its result. The absence of regular paid work has eroded self-respect. "Give me back my dignity" was the heartfelt plea from one man—made redundant, and with no prospect of a job...

Unemployment for most people is not a liberating experience. Although unemployed people clearly have more time for leisure pursuits, their financial position makes it more difficult or impossible for them to indulge in leisure activities. The cheapest form of entertainment available—television—can be a constant and painful reminder of the opportunities of a consumer society that is beyond their reach.

What has most astonished (and depressed) us has been a widespread feeling among those we have talked to in the Urban Priority Areas that "nothing can be done" about unemployment. Not, however, that nothing *should* be done—the feeling is more that the "social evil" is so widespread and unchanging, the problem so baffling, and the authorities apparently so unresponsive, that hope has been abandoned. We wonder whether some politicians really understand the despair which has become so widespread in many areas of the country.

Faith in the City, Church Publishing House, 1985, p.207.

ENVY

"Envy"—"grudging contemplation—of more fortunate persons."

We had an undergraduate who was very unhappy. Everything was wrong— home, College, people, the world—and nothing was right. Life was very unfair to him. Listening to him carefully it suddenly struck me he was suffering acutely from envy.

He was extremely self-critical of his powers of reasoning, and then would point to one of his contemporaries and say how clever he or she was. He would complain of his parents, his home and upbringing, and then would name a wealthy Etonian and observe how fortunate he had been. Next he would be consumed with self-pity and state he had no friends, and with a sigh would observe the popularity of the Captain of Boats. He admitted to a slight streak of talent as an actor, but was no match for the woman undergraduate at the top of his staircase, who had just landed a leading role in a major production.

I encouraged him to audition for a play and was delighted when he succeeded in getting the part. He invited me to come to the opening performance. He was playing the role of a priest, and with obvious relish managed to play back to me all my mannerisms. He certainly got a thrill out of his performance and so did I. For an hour or so he was actually enjoying himself and was happy.

The sad thing was that in his envy he concentrated so much on other people and their gifts that he failed to develop his own unique talents (which were consider-able) and was unable to find fulfilment in himself.

He is not alone.

A sound heart is the life of the flesh: but envy the rottenness of the bones.

Proverbs 14.30 (A.V.)

Then I saw that all toil and all skill in work come from a man's envy of his neighbour.

Ecclesiastes 4.4.

If we live by the Spirit, let us also walk by the Spirit. Let us have no self-conceit, no provoking of one another, no envy of one another.

Galatians 5.25-26.

So put away all malice and all guile and insincerity and envy and all slander.

1 Peter 2.1.

The green sickness.

William Shakespeare, *Anthony and Cleopatra*, Act III. sc.ii. l.6.

Envy slays itself by its own arrows.

Anon.

Envy makes strange bed-fellows.

Norman Douglas, *An Almanac*, Chatto & Windus in association with Martin Secker & Warburg Ltd., 1945, p.57.

Envy and covetousness are never satisfied.

Thomas Fuller, *Gnomologia*, Stearne Brock, 1733, p.52.

Let Age, not Envy, draw wrinkles on thy cheeks; be content to be envy'd, but envy not.

Sir Thomas Browne, *The Works of Sir Thomas Browne*, edited by Geoffrey Keynes, Faber & Faber Ltd., 1964, Volume 1, *Christian Morals*, Pt.1, sec.13, p.247.

Sadness, sorrow, or grief about another's goods insofar as they surpass, or are thought to surpass, one's own.

James F. Childress, in *A New Dictionary of Christian Ethics*, edited by James F. Childress and John Macquarrie, SCM Press Ltd., 1986, p.198.

Has your learning taught you that Envy is the most corroding of the vices and also the greatest power in any land?

J.M. Barrie, *The Entrancing Life*, Hodder & Stoughton Ltd., 1930, p.17.

Envie not greatnesse: for thou mak'st thereby
Thy self the worse, and so the distance greater.

George Herbert, *The Poems of George Herbert*, Oxford University Press, 1979, *The Church Porch*, 44, p.13.

A little grit in the eye destroyeth the sight of the very heavens, and a little malice or envy, a world of joys.

Thomas Traherne, *Centuries*, The Faith Press Ltd., 1969, p.175.

In a consumer society there are inevitably two kinds of slaves: the prisoners of addiction and the prisoners of envy.

Ivan D. Illich, *Tools for Conviviality*, Calder & Boyars, 1973, p.46.

I am a true labourer: I earn that I eat, get that I wear, owe no man hate, envy no man's happiness; glad of other men's good, content with my harm.

William Shakespeare, *As You Like It*, Act III. sc.ii. l.65.

Envy is everywhere.
Who is without envy? And most people
Are unaware or unashamed of being envious.

T.S. Eliot, *The Complete Poems and Plays of T.S. Eliot*, Faber & Faber Ltd., 1975, *The Elder Statesman*, Act 1, p.529.

If a man is for ever envying another his success, grudging another his happiness, shutting his heart against another's need, he becomes that most pitiable of creatures —a man with a grudge. There grows within him a bitterness and a resentment which robs him of his happiness, steals away his peace, and destroys his content.

William Barclay, *The Gospel of Matthew*, The Saint Andrew Press, 1987, Volume 1, p.247.

We may define this vice or pain, grief, or annoyance felt at the happiness, success or fortune of another; dis-pleasure or regret aroused by the superiority of another; plus a certain degree of malice, or malignity, and a desire to depreciate the person envied. It is a vice to which few are entirely strange and from which some people suffer all their lives.

W.E. Sangster, *The Secret of Radiant Life*, Hodder & Stoughton Ltd., 1957, p.118.

The essence of (envy) is that it does not describe the spirit which desires, nobly or ignobly, to have what someone else has; it describes the spirit which grudges the fact that the other person has these things at all. It does not so much want the things for itself; it merely wants to take them from the other person... It is the quality, not so much of the jealous, but rather of the embittered mind.

William Barclay, *The Letters to the Galatians and Ephesians*, The Saint Andrew Press, 1958, p.53.

Envy can be met at all levels of life, but it is more common among professional people and those who are competing for popular favour in the world of entertainment and of sport. But no one is free from the possibility of it.

It is not normally directed against the people who would seem most to incite it: those who vastly outsoar us in ability and who, as strangers, might seem to have no particular claim on our regard. It is directed rather on those who *just* outsoar us; who compete in the same circle and for the same esteem we covet, and who are judged by others to be better than we are (though we positively know they are not!).

W.E. Sangster, *The Secret of Radiant Life*, Hodder & Stoughton Ltd., 1957, p.119.

I envy no quality of mind or intellect in others—not genius, power, wit, or fancy: but if I could choose what would be most delightful, and I believe most useful to me, I should prefer a firm religious belief to any other blessing; for it makes life a discipline of goodness, creates new hopes when all earthly hopes vanish; and throws over the decay, the destruction of existence, the most gorgeous of all lights; awakens life even in death, and from corruption and decay calls up beauty and divinity; makes an instrument of torture and shame the ladder of ascent to Paradise; and far above all combinations of earthly hopes, calls up the most delightful visions of palms and amaranths, the gardens of the blest, the security of everlasting joys, where the sensualist and the sceptic view only gloom, decay, annihilation, and despair.

Sir Humphry Davy, in *My Religion*, Helen Keller, Hodder & Stoughton Ltd., 1927, p.140.

Envy is the child of pride. The envious are less able than the proud to repress their sense of inadequacy by building up a self-image of superiority to others. The realisation that others are or seem to be more fortunate, abler, richer, happier than they is painful to the envious and makes them feel dejected. The failure or misfortune of others gives them a secret pleasure. On the other hand the success or good luck of others depresses them. Envy is sometimes unwittingly encouraged by parents and others who urge children to aim at achievement which is beyond the reach of their limited ability and talent. The competitive structure of modern society is apt to breed envy in the less able or the handicapped. Some people go through life haunted by the feeling that people, circumstances or life itself have not been fair to them.

Christopher Bryant, SSJE, *The Heart in Pilgimage*, Darton, Longman & Todd Ltd., 1980, p.38.

Envy: this is the sin which affects those who hate to see others better, or more handsome, or abler, or more successful than themselves. This shows itself in jealousy. It is a very subtle fault and one to which religious people are often prone. Envious people are often snobbish, jealous and possessive. At bottom they do not respect other people. They do not like thanking anyone for a gift or a service. Envy leads to tale-bearing, spiteful gossip, and detraction. This means "running a person down", sometimes to the extent of taking away a person's reputation with a word or a look, or by means of a "whispering campaign". In spite of these obvious signs, envy is often a "hidden" sin, which may be disguised under fair words and pleasant manners. Thus envy begins out of sight, deep down in the heart, but it is finally expressed by the tongue. The words of St James on these sins of the tongue are not too strong. "The tongue is a fire... it infects the whole body... it is a pest that is never allayed, all deadly poison."

Olive Wyon, *On the Way*, SCM Press Ltd., 1958, p.50.

It is said in the Gospels that Pilate knew the chief priests had delivered Jesus up for trial out of envy (Matt.27.18; Mark 15.10). They had many reasons for their envy, particularly on account of his authority and his refusal to dictate or be dictated to; his power over the people whom he would neither exploit nor flatter; his refusal to bribe or be bribed; and his disregard for his own safety. Like all envious men the chief priests set out to destroy what they could not possess. Some people are as envious of spiritual qualities such as wisdom, truthfulness, courage or sanctity as of riches, power and the prestige of high office. They would find less reason to envy Pilate than to envy his prisoner.

Preachers and pastors unknowingly tempt people to envy by frequent exhortation to have more faith and more courage, giving vivid examples of men and women in every generation who live with the virtues that most people lack. Envy of material things is much easier to detect in oneself than envy of others' spiritual qualities such as faithfulness or devoutness. Parents often, without knowing it, produce conditions which help to make children envy one another, for example, by stressing the cleverness of one and the kindness of another. The members of any group can encourage one another to be envious without knowing what they do.

The Anglican litany groups envy, hatred and malice in that order, perhaps because envy leads to hatred and hatred, together with envy, gives birth to malice. The familiar table of the seven deadly sins (pride, envy, anger, sloth, avarice, gluttony, lust) indicates that pride gives rise to envy—the proud man wants to be rich and adorned with all qualities and honours; when he fails to achieve this his envy kindles anger.

There is no single virtue which can be pitted against envy: rather it is the whole quality of devout living which enables a man to rejoice in the good fortune, sanctity and abilities of others instead of being envious.

R.E.C. Browne, in *A Dictionary of Christian Ethics*, edited by John Macquarrie, SCM Press Ltd., 1967, p.107.

EUCHARIST

*"Eucharist"—"the sacrament of the Lord's Supper, the
Communion, essential elements being remembrance and
thanksgiving."*

W hilst in London, I had to celebrate the Eucharist once a week at 1.00pm in the
Lady Chapel of the University Church of Christ the King. The Chapel was small
and the participants few in number. On one occasion I noticed a man off the streets
fast asleep in a corner of the Chapel. He seemed to be comfortable enough so I let
him be and made a start.

He woke up half-way through the service and looked at me curiously. He perked
up during the Thanksgiving prayer, particularly the part recalling our Lord's Death
and Resurrection. When it came to the distribution, I was suddenly seized by an
impulse to offer him the elements. After all, he was present and appeared to be
involved. He opened his hands reverently to receive "the Body of Christ" and quietly
took a sip of "the Blood of Christ" from the chalice.

When the service was over and the regular participants had departed, I made my
way back to the Lady Chapel to clear up. I got to the door and cautiously looked in.
There he was, kneeling at the alter steps, deep in prayer. I withdrew and let him
continue undisturbed.

Sometimes the Eucharist speaks louder than words and proves to be a real
channel of the love of God.

Now as they were eating, Jesus took bread, and blessed, and broke it, and gave it to
the disciples and said, "Take, eat; this is my body." And he took a cup, and when he
had given thanks he gave it to them, saying, "Drink of it, all of you; for this is my
blood of the covenant, which is poured out for many for the forgiveness of sins.
Matthew 26.26-28.

I am the bread of life; he who comes to me shall not hunger.
John 6.35.

He who eats my flesh and drinks my blood abides in me, and I in him.
John 6.56.

Thanks be to God for his inexpressible gift!
2 Corinthians 9.15.

The Eucharist... is the celebration of, the dramatic reliving of, the great and saving
mystery of Christ's work of deliverance.
Kenneth Leech, *True Prayer*, Sheldon Press, 1980, p.100.

Communion, the sacred act in which the Eucharistic sacrifice finds its consumma
tion, reminds us above all of the completeness of our dependence on God.
Evelyn Underhill, in *The Wisdom of Evelyn Underhill*, edited by John Stobbart, Mowbray, 1951, p.28.

Look upon me till Thou art formed in me, that I may be a mirror of Thy brightness,
an habitation of Thy love, and a temple of Thy glory.
Thomas Traherne, *Centuries*, The Faith Press Ltd., 1969, p.44.

The reception of Christ's body and blood does nothing less than transform us into that which we consume, and henceforth we bear in soul and body him in whose fellowship we died, were buried, and are risen again.

St Leo, in *Readings from Pope John XXIII*, edited by Vincent A. Yzermans, Mowbray, 1968, p.70.

> "I am your life," says the Lord.
> "Your bread
> Your source
> If you drink of this water you'll never thirst.
> If you eat of this bread you will live for ever."
> I suffer from spiritual malnutrition.

Michel Quoist, *With Open Heart*, translated by Colette Copeland, Gill and Macmillan Ltd., 1983, p.35.

The Eucharist is an action which binds visible and invisible in one service. It takes natural and ordinary things, the food of our temporal existence, won by our own labour from the natural world, and makes these things holy by offering them with thanksgiving to God; that He may consecrate them, change their substantial character, translate them to His order, and give them back to us as the very food of our eternal life.

Evelyn Underhill, in *The Wisdom of Evelyn Underhill*, edited by John Stobbart, Mowbray, 1951, p.28.

For in the holy Eucharist the Son of God, in His overflowing mercy, was not content with having made Himself the Son of Man and a Brother as a sharer in our humanity. So he founded a wonderful way of communicating Himself to each one of us in particular. It is in this way he incorporates Himself in us and us in Him. He dwells in us and makes us dwell in Him, becoming our food, flesh of our flesh and bone of our bone, by a grace which surpasses every other grace, since it contains in itself the author of all grace.

Jean Pierre Camus, *The Spirit of St François de Sales*, Harper & Brothers, Publishers, 1952, p.48.

The Eucharist is the centre and norm of all worship. There the Divine Word is revealed in the lections and propers for the nourishment of our souls. But at the climax of the rite, through the consecration prayer, the whole mystery of Christ as priest, victim, and victor, is present.

In the eucharistic canon, gift and response find fullness of expression, and both are inseparable from Christ himself. The divine gift to us is Christ, and so too, the response from man is Christ, himself our sacrifice. Our own response is made only as we are ourselves "in Christ". In the words of an Anglican eucharistic hymn, we say

> Look, Father, look on his anointed face,
> And only look on us as found in him.

Michael Ramsey, *Through the Year with Michael Ramsey*, edited by Margaret Duggan, Hodder & Stoughton Ltd., 1975, p.195.

In the Eucharist... we bring familiar forms of economic wealth, which is always the product of man's labour exercised upon God's gifts, and offer them as symbols of our earthly life. If God had not given to the seed its life and to the soil the quality to nurture it, there would be neither harvest nor bread. Equally, if man had not ploughed the soil and scattered the seed, there would be neither harvest nor bread. Bread is the product of man's labour exercised upon God's gift for the satisfaction of man's need. So is wine.

These are our "oblations" at the "offertory"—often also accompanied by "alms" expressing the charity which seeks to share with others the good things which God has given to us.

William Temple, *Citizen and Churchman*, Eyre & Spottiswoode Publishers, 1941, p.102.

Even the Lord's Supper is not a cultic act, some sort of "high point of the worship service" or communion of the "nucleus of the congregation" (what is that anyway?). It should still be today what it was originally, namely, a strengthening for our departure, when we must go out again to the battle and the work and the testing, when we shall be sent as sheep among the wolves. That is no cultic celebration; it is the assurance that the Lord remains with us when the worship *comes to an end* and when the world of the deadline, the telephone, and the motor surrounds us with its curtains of noise. It is to give us the certainty that he rules this world, too; that he gives us tasks of love in waiting rooms, in laboratories, and in our own homes, and that he has a greeting ready for us along every road, assuring us that he remembers us.

Helmut Thielicke, *I Believe: The Christian's Creed*, translated by John W. Doberstein and H. George Anderson, William Collins Sons & Co. Ltd., 1969, p.234.

So too the priest is the *man of the Eucharist*. The liturgy indeed belongs to all the people. We being many are one bread, one body. We take, we break, we offer, we receive; and the more vivid realization of this has been one of the exciting marks of liturgical renewal in our time. Where then, and why then, the priest? As celebrant he is more than the people's representative. In taking, breaking, and consecrating he acts in Christ's name and in the name not only of the particular congregation but of the Holy Catholic Church down the ages. By his office as celebrant he symbolizes the focusing of the Eucharist and the givenness of the historic gospel and the continuing life of the Church as rooted in that gospel. He finds that at the altar he is drawn terribly and wonderfully near not only to the benefits of Christ's redemption but to the redemptive act itself.

Michael Ramsey, *The Christian Priest Today*, SPCK, 1972, p.9.

The eucharist is *the* action by which God-in-Christ sanctifies us in the world. All our actions and thoughts are related to and flow from this thanksgiving celebration. Each time we participate fully we obey our Lord's command, and share completely with his universal Church as we, and Christians all down the ages, enter simultaneously, Christ's gift and dying on the Cross.

In so doing we are—like the bread—taken, blessed, broken and shared so that re-formed and strengthened we may become yet more lovingly agents for Christ, fulfilled in his service. The entire liturgy is presented by the use of outward signs which point to and flow from the hidden truth, that Christ is really present in the assembly itself, in ministry and word, in the celebrant and more particularly the sacraments themselves.

Giles Harcourt, *Dawn Through our Darkness*, William Collins Sons & Co. Ltd., 1985, p.116.

But when he has led the initiate to the table and has given him His Body to eat He entirely changes him, and transforms him into His own state. The clay is no longer clay when it has received the royal likeness but is already the Body of the King. (By receiving Christ's sacramental Body we are incorporated into His mystical Body, and thus become His Body). It is impossible to conceive of anything more blessed than this. It is therefore the final Mystery as well, since it is not possible to go beyond it or to add anything to it...

"This is a great mystery" said blessed Paul (Eph. 5.32), referring to this union. This is the celebrated marriage by which the most holy Bridegroom espouses the Church as His Bride. It is here that Christ feeds the choir that surrounds Him; by this Mystery alone we become "flesh of His flesh, and bone of His bones" (Gen. 2.21)...

While natural food is changed into him who feeds on it, and fish and bread and any other kind of food become human blood, here it is entirely opposite. The Bread of Life Himself changes him who feeds on Him and transforms and assimilates him into Himself...

This, then, is the account of how the kingdom of heaven is within us.

Nicolas Cabasilas, *The Life of Christ*, translated by Carmino J. de Catanzaro, St. Vladimir's Seminary Press, 1974, p.113.

FAMILY

"Family"—"members of a household, parents, children, etc."

I have had the enormous privilege of belonging to a large family and owe an enormous debt to my parents and four long-suffering sisters. In many ways it has been a world of its own in miniature.

Earliest recollections go back to the Second World War, to the black-out, rationing, air raid sirens, and a time of anxiety and fear. But it was not all doom and gloom. In spite of the War, we had lots of fun and laughter, playing all sorts of games, indoors and outdoors, making the most of a large spacious garden, and a big house. This was a valuable time of life, especially having a natural playmate in my twin sister, Margaret.

When the War was over my father resumed his work as a solicitor and life became more settled. As a family we had our fair share of ups and downs. Quite early on my mother's health broke, and we had to move to a smaller house. Bringing up five children had put pressure on her, and had taken its toll.

School for most of us was a mixed experience with successes and failures. My four sisters went on to High School, and in turn became Queen's Guides, and then went on to careers and marriage. I had a hiccup with the Eleven Plus and went away to school, finally getting to university.

There were times of stress and strain, the usual illnesses, the occasional operation, holidays by the sea, practical jokes, and generally learning to live together as a family—an invaluable arena for the outworking of love which one looks back on with an immense amount of gratitude.

God blessed them, and God said to them, "Be fruitful and multiply, and fill the earth."
Genesis 1.28.

He raises up the needy out of affliction,
and makes their families like flocks.
Psalm 107.41.

While he was still speaking to the people, behold, his mother and his brothers stood outside, asking to speak to him. But he replied to the man who told him, "Who is my mother, and who are my brothers?" And stretching out his hand toward his disciples, he said, "Here are my mother and my brothers! For whoever does the will of my Father in heaven is my brother, and sister, and mother."
Matthew 12.46-50.

The Father, from whom every family in heaven and on earth is named.
Ephesians 3.15.

Nobody's family can hang out the sign "Nothing the matter here."
Chinese Proverb.

The family is the true church; the best expounder of the truths of Christianity.
Henry Ward Beecher, *Proverbs from Plymouth Pulpit*, Charles Burnet & Co., 1887, p.82.

Happy will that house be in which the relations are formed from character, after the highest, and not after the lowest order.
Ralph Waldo Emerson, *Society and Solitude: Domestic Life*, J.M. Dent & Sons Ltd., 1912, p.60.

Parentage is a very important profession; but no test of fitness for it is ever imposed in the interests of the children.
George Bernard Shaw, *Everybody's Political What's What*, Constable & Co. Ltd., 1944, p.74.

The joys of parents are secret, and so are their griefs and fears; they cannot utter the one, nor they will not utter the other.
Francis Bacon, *The Moral and Historical Works of Lord Bacon, Of Parents and Children*, Henry G. Born, 1852, p.18.

Children are on a different plane, belong to a generation and way of feeling properly their own; there is seldom complete understanding between them and their parents, so that affection here suffers from some strain and uncertainty, all the more painful the greater the affection is.
George Santayana, *The Letters of George Santayana*, Constable & Co. Ltd., 1956, p.336.

I don't believe there is any such thing as an ideal social unit. The nuclear family is not large enough to give sufficient variation of experience to children, and should be supplemented. But it does form a solid base of concern and affection where it is integrated into a wider community or kinship.
Elizabeth Janeway, in *Open Secrets*, Barbaralee D. Diamonstein, The Viking Press, 1973, p.200.

Poverty, unemployment, poor housing and social stress in the urban priority areas put severe pressures on families, and can trigger family crises and breakdown. The multiple deprivation of such areas makes it particularly difficult for elderly and handicapped people to maintain their independence. Young children may suffer from stressed family life, and from poor environmental conditions. These and other groups in the Urban Priority Areas need the support and help of skilled services. In urban priority areas there are heavy burdens on those who offer care: individual carers, the voluntary organisations and, especially, the personal social services.
Faith in the City, Church Publishing House, 1985, p.272.

The family is the natural God-given unit in which human beings can find fulfilment and in which children can grow up in security to reach proper maturity. Today the family is under threat. Cheap contraceptives encourage premarital and extramarital intercourse, permissiveness often results in single-parent families, lack of parental discipline can result in lack of security on the part of children. Lowering the age of consent often means premature and hasty marriage. Mothers who are at work may not be able to give time to their children, and conditions of work may impede family life; while unrealistic expectations and easy divorce mean that one out of every three or four marriages dies. Mobility, the break-up of the extended family, and longer expectation of life increase the strain on the family. Jesus taught that the claims of God were greater than those of the family (Mark 3.35), but he took for granted the family unit, and spoke of God as his Father.

Hugh Montefiore, *Confirmation Notebook*, Fifth Edition, SPCK, 1985, p.8.

Generally speaking, the family is a deplorable educational *milieu* for modern parents know nothing about the psychology of childhood and youth. They are too naive, too neurotic, too weak or too stern. One could almost say that the majority of them cultivate the art of producing defects in their children. They are occupied, above all, with their own work and their own pleasures. Too many children witness bad manners, quarrels, selfishness and even drunkenness in their own families. If they are not initiated into such aspects of life by their parents, they will inevitably be so by their companions.

To sum up, neither the school nor the family is capable nowadays of teaching the young how to behave. Consequently, modern youth reflects the mediocrity of its educators like a mirror. Education which limits itself to preparation for examina- tions, to a mere exercise of memory, instead of forming the mind produces only "donkeys loaded with books". Young people brought up in this way are incapable of understanding reality and of playing their natural part in society.

Alexis Carrel, *Reflections on Life*, Hamish Hamilton Ltd., 1952, p.171.

What adolescents fail to realize is that the parents often find them unpleasing and difficult to live with, and for a time at any rate have little sympathy with them. Indeed the parents' sympathy is largely for themselves. They regret the fact that their children have to grow up and lose their baby charms. It is always something of a shock to find the formerly dependent and loving child asserting itself and demand- ing independence. They may feel unwanted and rejected when the adolescents wish to go out all the time and to spend their holidays with their own friends. Many parents are resentful and even hostile to their adolescents, especially to their daughters.

A typical lament is: "We used to have such happy family holidays at the seaside or in the country. The children were quite satisfied with our company then, but now we are no longer interesting enough for them. They seem completely bored by us and are so sulky and moody that they quite spoil the day if we all go out together."

Another mother complained that she had always looked forward to the day when her daughter would be a companion to her; but now it was obvious that the girl did not want her, and resented having to go out with her or to spend an evening at home.

Fathers are often deeply affronted when their sons stand up to them and oppose their views, and even sometimes get the better of an argument.

Dr. Doris Odlum, *Journey Through Adolescence*, Delisle Ltd., 1965, p.59.

The family is a feature of human society that precedes Christian ethical reflection upon it. It is both a social institution and a special relationship. As a social institution the family regulates sexual intercourse, assigns responsibility for children, conserves lines of descent, and orders wealth and inheritance. It assigns roles for the division of labour for everyday living, supports the roles of its members in the external economy, participates with other institutions in the socialization of the coming generation, and plays a role in the physical and psychological welfare of family members. Christian theology and ethics reflect on how to exercise these functions in ways appropriate to Christian conviction and experience.

As a special relationship the family constitutes a moral arena unlike most others formed in the public sphere. The family both forms and expresses the identity and character of its members. Members of one family are not interchangeable with those of another, as each is a part of the formation of others within the family unit. Families also contain voluntary members (parents) and involuntary members (children), and can grow or decrease both naturally (birth and death) and socially (adoption, divorce, remarriage). The family is subject to inescapable tensions between its personal and institutional aspects, whether these are visible within the family or between the family and other institutions such as the state, church, or economy. Indeed, one important task in ethical reflection is distinguishing the special relations of "marriage," "family," and "parenthood" and their corresponding social settings today.

Richard Bondi, in *A New Dictionary of Christian Ethics*, edited by James F. Childress and John Macquarrie, SCM Press Ltd., 1986, p.224.

"A propaganda that at times goes beyond all control makes use of the powerful means of the press, shows, and entertainment to spread the wicked seeds of corruption, especially among young people. It is necessary for the family to defend itself, for women to take their places in this work with courage and with a keen sense of responsibility and to be tireless in keeping on the watch, in correcting, in teaching others to distinguish good from evil; taking advantage, where necessary, of the protection provided by the civil law."

We wanted to repeat this invitation, for the dangerous situations that we complained of before unfortunately have not been eliminated, and in addition there are more and more new attacks being launched on the sanctity of the family. Those who have responsibility and a proper outlook as Christians and as human beings should neglect no means or effort that will help us to succeed in getting back to conditions that are healthier for the development and defence of the family.

The family is a gift of God: it involves a vocation that comes from on high and that does not admit of any ready substitute. It is the basis for good, true education; the family is everything, or almost everything for a human being. For example: for the infant who comes into contact with life in his first unforgettable experiences within it; for the adolescent and the young man, to whom it offers a model for emulation as well as a bulwark against the wicked spirit of evil; for the married couple themselves, whom it defends from the crises and loss of direction that sometimes face them; finally, for old people, who can enjoy in it the hard earned fruits of long fidelity and constancy.

In this picture of the family, there is an irreplaceable role that belongs to women. There is a voice in the home that everyone will listen to, if it knows how to make itself heard, if it has always made itself respected: it is the watchful and prudent voice of the woman, wife and mother. She can claim the testament of the dying Moses as her own and say to her children, and through them to future generations: "I call heaven and earth to witness this day that I have set before you life and death ... choose therefore life, that both thou and thy seed may live; and that thou mayest love the Lord thy God, and obey his voice, and adhere to him."

Pope John XXIII, *Readings from Pope John*, edited by Vincent A. Yzermans, Mowbray, 1968, p.41.

FEAR

*"Fear"—"powerful emotion caused by an impending danger or
evil—or revere (God)."*

I shall never forget a certain pot-holing expedition in the Yorkshire Dales. I went
with a group of Bradford Cathedral choirboys. We were following an under-
ground map of a system and by mistake took a wrong turning. We went down a small
dried-up water course, and got to a very narrow section. One of the boys, much
smaller than me, went ahead and got through to a wider space. It was so narrow I
had to resort to going on my back, and tried edging my way forwards slowly. Even so
I got stuck, somewhere in the region of hips and stomach. Lying there in the dark, I
suddenly became conscious of the tremendous weight of rock above me, and fear
set in. Who would preach in the Cathedral tomorrow morning instead of me? That
was my immediate panic-stricken thought.

The important thing was not to panic, but to remain cool, calm and collected.
After about ten minutes, I gradually moved ahead, and managed to get through to the
wider section. At that point we called a halt, and addressed ourselves to the problem
as to how to get back through this narrow section. In the end I removed most of my
clothes and came through semi-naked. I have never been down a pot-hole since!

Fear in the sense of revering God is rather different. We sometimes get an
awareness of the presence of God, rather like Moses before the Burning Bush, and
we experience feelings of fear and awe, which are rather exciting and reassuring. In
it we experience something of the love of God.

> I sought the Lord, and he answered me,
> and delivered me from all my fears.
>
> Psalm 34.4.

> He who listens to me will dwell secure
> and will be at ease, without dread of evil.
>
> Proverbs 1.33.

> Do not fear those who kill the body but cannot kill the soul; rather fear him who can
> destroy both soul and body in hell.
>
> Matthew 10.28.

> My peace I give to you; not as the world gives do I give to you. Let not your hearts be
> troubled, neither let them be afraid.
>
> John 14.27.

> Fear is the greatest of all inventions.
>
> French Proverb.

> He fears God, why then needs he fear the world?
>
> Robert Browning, *The Complete Works of Robert Browning*, Oxford University Press, 1988, Volume VIII, *The Ring and the Book*, Book VI, l.822, p.110.

> Nothing easier than to say, Have no fear! Nothing more difficult. How does one kill
> fear, I wonder?
>
> Joseph Conrad, *Lord Jim*, J.M. Dent & Sons Ltd., 1946, p.316.

The love that dare not look at life's dark potentiality is not love at all, it is fear.

J. Neville Ward, *The Use of Praying*, Epworth Press, 1967, p.65.

And if it is a fear you would dispel, the seat of that fear is in your heart and not in the hand of the feared.

Kahlil Gibran, *The Prophet*, William Heinemann Ltd., 1970, p.58.

I have been full of fears all my life—always seeing something or other hanging over me that I couldn't bear to happen.

George Eliot, *Felix Holt*, J.M. Dent & Sons Ltd., 1909, p.24.

Fear is the most self-centred of all emotions, and the use of it as a constant moral appeal can make us more self-centred, and therefore must defeat the very object it is desired to attain.

William Temple, *Christian Faith and Life*, SCM Press Ltd., 1963, p.87.

No coward soul is mine
No trembler in the world's storm-troubled sphere
I see Heaven's glories shine
And Faith shines equal arming me from Fear.

Emily Brontë, *The Complete Poems of Emily Jane Brontë*, Oxford University Press, 1952, *No coward soul is mine*, p.243.

There is the natural *cowardice of human nature*. Many a man refuses the way of Christ, because in his heart of hearts he is afraid to take the stand which Christianity demands. The basic thing that stops him is the thought of what other people will think and say. The voice of his neighbours is louder in his ears than the voice of God.

William Barclay, *The Gospel of Matthew*, The Saint Andrew Press, 1975, Volume 2, p.44.

When people feel threatened and anxious they become more rigid, and when in doubt they tend to become dogmatic; and then they lose their own vitality. They use the remnants of traditional values to build a protective encasement and then shrink behind it; or they make an outright panicky retreat into the past.

Rollo May, *Man's Search for Himself*, Souvenir Press Ltd., 1975, p.178.

The fear of failure is a realistic one because, in general, the chances of failing are much greater than those of succeeding, and because failures in a competitive society entail a realistic frustration of needs. They mean not only economic insecurity, but also loss of prestige and all kinds of emotional frustrations.

Karen Horney, *The Neurotic Personality of Our Time*, Kegan Paul, Trench, Trubner & Co. Ltd., 1937, p.285.

Fear always remains. A man may destroy everything within himself, love and hate and belief, and even doubt; but as long as he clings to life he cannot destroy fear: the fear, subtle, indestructible, and terrible, that pervades his being; that tinges his thoughts; that lurks in his heart; that watches on his lips the struggle of his last breath.

Joseph Conrad, *Tales of Unrest*, J.M. Dent & Sons Ltd., 1947, p.107.

Perhaps men and women were born to love one another, simply and genuinely, rather than to this travesty that we can call love. If we can stop destroying ourselves we may stop destroying others. We have to begin by admitting and even accepting our violence, rather than blindly destroying ourselves with it, and therewith we have to realize that we are as deeply afraid to live and to love as we are to die.

R.D. Laing, *The Politics of Experience*, Penguin Books Ltd., 1967, p.64.

Deep within every man there lies the dread of being alone in the world, forgotten by God, overlooked among the tremendous household of millions upon millions. That fear is kept away by looking upon all those about one who are bound to one as friends or family; but the dread is nevertheless there and one hardly dares think of what would happen to one if all the rest were taken away.

Søren Kierkegaard, *The Journals of Kierkegaard*, Harper & Row, Publishers1959, p.129.

Many people fear nothing more terribly than to take a position which stands out sharply and clearly from the prevailing opinion. The tendency of most is to adopt a view that is so ambiguous that it will include everything and so popular that it will include everybody. Not a few men who cherish lofty and noble ideals hide them under a bushel for fear of being called different.

Martin Luther King, *The Words of Martin Luther King*, selected by Coretta Scott King, William Collins Sons & Co. Ltd., 1986, p.24.

Often in my life I have found that the one thing that can save is the thing which appears most to threaten. In peace and war I have found that frequently, naked and unashamed, one has to go down into what one most fears and in that process, from somewhere beyond all conscious expectation, comes a saving flicker of light and energy that even if it does not produce the courage of a hero at any rate enables a trembling mortal to take one step further.

Laurens van der Post, *The Lost World of the Kalahari*, Penguin Books Ltd., 1983, p.171.

Our response to that Gospel will be joyous, but also reverent. We shall run to our Father with cheerful cries, but we shall none the less approach the Eternal Majesty with trembling awe. His greatness and our littleness must always fill us with that feeling of insignificance and helplessness for which the only name is fear: and in that sense the fear of the Lord is not only the beginning of wisdom, but a permanent characteristic of all true religion.

William Temple, *Thoughts on Some Problems of the Day*, Macmillan Publishers Ltd., 1931, p.202.

I was a man who had lived with fear for nearly forty years. To say this is not to suggest that I had lived in a permanent sweat of terror... To live one's life in fear is something much less spectacular and much more commonplace in everyone's experience, I believe, than most of us are prepared to admit or even able to identify.

It is to act, for a great deal of the time, from negative rather than positive motives... We hesitate to speak to strangers for fear of a rebuff, a small humiliation. We are loath to act generously because we fear that more may be taken from us than we really wish to give. We will not stand up and be counted in some small but important matter because it may cost us a security or, more frequently perhaps, an advancement. Gradually we become stultified, incapable of giving to each other, waiting instead for the next hostile move from another fearful man, which must be countered with all the craft at our disposal, for the sake of self-preservation. We are reduced in our ability to go forward and meet, recognise warmly and embrace, Life itself and all who share it with us.

Fear can thus be seen as the most corrosive element attacking the goodness of the human spirit, which, untouched by fear, finds itself always in a natural movement towards its fellows... The most insiduous form of fear, which is certainly the fear of being afraid, is the most potent force of all against this movement, for it does not simply arrest that movement, it does not allow it to begin.

Geoffrey Moorhouse, *The Fearful Void*, Hodder & Stoughton Ltd., 1974, p.16.

FEELINGS

"Feelings"—"readiness to feel, tenderness for others' sufferings, conviction not based solely on reason, sympathy."

L ooking back, I realized my education had been very one-sided and defective. At school, university and theological college, the emphasis was mainly on acquiring objective knowledge to get through exams. The result was inadequate preparation for parish life.

So my "further education" began with my very first visit to Bradford Royal Infirmary as a part-time Hospital Chaplain. Instead of asking patients the question "What do you think about this?" there was a radical change of approach to—"What do you feel about this?" That used to get us talking and sharing our feelings. This change was later confirmed, working with the Student Counsellor at University College, London, and with members of the Health Centre. It's been an invaluable approach to students with problems, especially as the main emphasis in our universities is still on developing critical and analytical faculties of the mind and in acquiring objective knowledge.

Our feelings are most important. I can remember visiting my parents in a nursing home, and returning to Oxford very depressed about their condition. Early next morning I went on an outing with an Eight on the river. It was a beautiful morning in May, and the sun was shining brightly. We came across some ducks and ducklings, and in such company and scenery who could feel depressed? I came back greatly refreshed and my feelings were now positive, making my outlook on life entirely different. Feelings are crucially important.

Man looks on the outward appearance, but the Lord looks on the heart.
1 Samuel 16.7.

In overflowing wrath for a moment I hid my face from you, but with everlasting love I will have compassion on you.
Isaiah 54.8.

That they should seek God, in the hope that they might feel after him and find him.
Acts 17.27.

I am he who searches mind and heart.
Revelations 2.23.

Formulate your feelings as well as your thoughts.
A.R. Orage, *On Love*, The Janus Press, 1957, p.62.

What we feel matters much more than what we know.

George Moore, *Evelyn Innes*, Bernhard Tauchnitz, 1898, Volume II, p.115.

There are some feelings Time can not benumb.

Lord Byron, *The Complete Poetical Works*, edited by Jerome J. McGann, Clarendon Press, Volume II, *Childe Harold's Pilgrimage*, Canto IV, st.19, p.130.

It isn't notions sets people doing the right thing—it's feelings.

George Eliot, *Adam Bede*, Virtue & Co., 1908, Volume 1, p.272.

What an instrument is the human voice! How wonderfully responsive to every emotion of the human soul!

Nathaniel Hawthorne, *House of the Seven Gables*, Harper & Row, Publishers, 1965, p.80.

There is no more grievous sight, as there is no greater perversion, than a wise man at the mercy of his feelings.

George Meredith, *The Ordeal of Richard Feverel*, The Times Book Club, 1912, p.537.

Some are more strongly affected by the facts of human life, others by the beauty of earth and sky.

John Keble, *Lectures on Poetry*, Clarendon Press, 1912, Volume II, Lecture 31, p.277.

Sensations sweet,
Felt in the blood, and felt along the heart.

William Wordsworth, *Lines Composed a Few Miles Above Tintern Abbey*, l.27.

As men are cultivated, the feelings carry with them intellect, and the intellect carries feelings; they are not separated.

Henry Ward Beecher, *Proverbs from Plymouth Pulpit*, Charles Burnet & Co., 1887, p.31.

Pity is feeling sorry for someone; empathy is feeling sorry with someone. Empathy is fellow feeling for the person in need—his pain, agony, and burdens.

Martin Luther King, *The Words of Martin Luther King*, selected by Coretta Scott King, William Collins Sons & Co. Ltd., 1986, p.22.

A perfect feeling eventuates in some form of action. Unfruitful feelings, even if they are not spurious, are likely to become morbid, irregular, mischievous. Action is the right outlet of emotion.

Henry Ward Beecher, *Proverbs from Plymouth Pulpit*, Charles Burnet & Co., 1887, p.31.

No one can make clear to another who has never had a certain feeling, in what the quality or worth of it consists. One must have musical ears to know the value of a symphony; one must have been in love one's self to understand a lover's state of mind.

William James, *The Varieties of Religious Experience*, William Collins Sons & Co. Ltd., 1974, p.367.

Ordinary man is at the mercy of his organism: of the instinctive centre—impressions received by the senses, of appetites, inertia, disease; of the feelings—associations connected with people and places past and present, likes and dislikes, fear and anxiety; of the mind—imagination, day-dreaming, suggestibility.

A.R. Orage, *On Love*, The Janus Press, 1957, p.47.

Feelings indicate more frankly what is going on in the depths of a man's being than his carefully controlled thoughts and words. While some feelings may need to be examined and radically changed, they also need to be recognized as the expression of character and regarded as an integral part of a man's inner nature.

George Appleton, *Journey for a Soul*, William Collins Sons & Co. Ltd., 1976, p.22.

Beware of depending on your own *emotions*, which are often but the fallings and risings of the frail flesh, and mistaking them for spiritual feelings and affections!

Think less of what you *feel*—even of trying *to be* anything.

Look out of yourself at God. Pray and praise, and God will give you His Spirit often when you feel most dull.

Charles Kingsley, *Daily Thoughts*, Macmillan Publishers Ltd., 1884, p.279.

Live a life of *feeling*, not of *excitement*. Let your religion, your duties, every thought and word, be ruled by the *affections*, not by the *emotions*, which are the expressions of them. Do not consider whether you are glad, sorry, dull, or spiritual at any moment, but be yourself—what God makes you.

Charles Kingsley, *Daily Thoughts*, Macmillan Publishers Ltd., 1884, p.79.

Personal life is made up of thinking, feeling and willing, and all those need due recognition and expression. Most of us were taught to control and sometimes repress our emotions, to give more emphasis to the other two partners of mind and will. But if feeling is starved, our inner life becomes unbalanced and unsatisfied. The trinity of the human personality is of co-equals held together in unity.

George Appleton, *Journey for a Soul*, William Collins Sons & Co. Ltd., 1976, p.21.

Life and human relationships are full of subtleties. I know that there is nothing absolute or objectively valid, that knowledge must seep into your blood, into your self, not just into your head, that you must live it, and here I always come back to what one should strive after with all one's might: one must marry one's feelings to one's beliefs and ideas. That is probably the only way to achieve a measure of harmony in one's life.

Etty Hillesum, *Etty, A Diary*, 1941-43, translated by Arnold J. Pomerans, Jonathan Cape Ltd., 1983, p.48.

The doctrines of Christianity that mean most to men are those which concern their emotions, and where our emotions are concerned the external, imposed authority of the Church is not enough; the inner light must shine as well. And the reason why religion for so many does not seem to possess the power it ought to have is that they have accepted the external authority of the Church, but never made the inner response of the heart. So, in the hour of calamity the comfort does not flow, the assurance is not given, the power is not released. They have assented as one assents to astronomical facts, but truth has not become what Shelley called, "a truth of the emotions" *as well*.

Leslie Weatherhead, *The Christian Agnostic*, Hodder & Stoughton Ltd., 1965, p.29.

I hope you will never become scrupulous. It is a bad thing all round, a morbid conscientiousness and brooding. Never brood, brooding is a waste of growth. How I have found this myself! It puts back all my work if I brood. Die without a breath of grievance: religion makes this possible, men have less the spirit of grievance.

Drop things; always keep on dropping and dropping. My religion, my illness, and life have taught me that. Always drop things. Don't chatter to yourself—you can't hear God if you do . . . Drop, then, all these things, these miseries; not by straining, or making or getting strength; but genially, gently; while attending, as you must, to these things, drop them—these flies that bother your nose, God nowhere visible. Resign yourself. That is God's plan—faithfully, wisely, resign yourself.

Baron Friedrich von Hügel, *Letters to a Niece*, edited with an introduction by Gwendolen Greene, J.M. Dent & Sons Ltd., 1928, p.xx.

I am planning a series of sermons on "Educating the Emotions." Why not? We teach people how to think, but not how to feel. We take it for granted that the mental life of man needs to be trained, but we assume that his feelings can look after themselves. As a result, one is constantly meeting people who are sensitive to ideas and quick to detect a false syllogism, but whose emotional life is crude, and chaotic. Many a man would wince at a weak argument who would accept an unreal feeling without protest. Our response to beauty, our use of the senses, our life in the imagination are poor and unregulated compared with our intellectual grasp of things . . .

Our educational practice . . . grows more and more rational and mechanical, designed to produce that never-ending stream of technicians and machine-minders which our society demands if it is to keep up its standard of living. The emphasis is almost all on "useful knowledge", on sharpening the speculative and critical intellect. Consequently, we are turning out people who are quick-witted and slow of heart, mentally full and emotionally empty, their heads stuffed with information and their hearts starved. It is this that partly accounts for the upsurge of violence . . . of our sprawling cities, and the . . . appetite for violence at second hand through films and fiction.

By "educating the emotions", I do not mean educating them out of existence. What is wanted is not a technique for repressing, taming and throttling the rich instinctive life within, but teaching concerning its use and enjoyment. We have heard too much talk about controlling the feelings, and not enough about deepening and purifying them, so that they might suffuse and energise our thinking and raise it to a loftier power.

W.B.J. Martin, *Five Minutes to Twelve*, William Collins Sons & Co. Ltd., 1957, p.105.

FEMINISM

"Feminism"—"advocacy, extended recognition of the claims of women."

T his is an important topic and frequently chosen by Reflection Groups, particularly the women members. What they are keen to investigate is an outlet for their natural gifts and talents. They rightly want a career, and naturally wish to marry and have a family. And yet the highly competitive nature of society continues to favour the somewhat aggressive male. The result is our women nearly always face difficulties entering the job market and later experience added frustration in the places of their work.

Some areas of work are still a closed shop. Take, for instance, the ordination of women. I remember listening to a Diocesan Director of Ordinands. "Do you know, Bill," he said, "we have some really good women coming forward, who want to be ordained. They know exactly what the role of a priest is, whereas most of the men who come before me haven't much clue."

I wonder if our whole way of life is defective, and one-sided. We denigrate the feminine side of life—feelings, compassion, sympathy—at the cost of the quality and value of life. A much-needed balance is urgently required.

Two by two, male and female, went into the ark with Noah, as God had commanded Noah.

Genesis 7.9.

Who can find a virtuous woman? for her price is far above rubies.

Proverbs 31.10 (A.V.).

There is neither Jew nor Greek, there is neither slave nor free, there is neither male nor female; for you are all one in Christ Jesus.

Galatians 3.28.

The most sympathetic of men never fully comprehend woman's concrete situation.

Simone de Beauvoir, *The Second Sex*, Penguin Books Ltd., 1982, p.26.

I shall be interested to discover what proportion of unsatisfactory marriages is due to the bare fact that the male partner does not know his business.

Norman Douglas, *An Almanac*, Chatto & Windus in association with Martin Secker & Warburg Ltd., 1945, p.2.

It is a curious fact that the all-male religions have produced no religious imagery—in most cases have positively forbidden it. The great religious art of the world is deeply involved with the female principle.

Kenneth Clark, *Civilisation*, British Broadcasting Corporation, 1969, p.177.

A pompous gentleman once asked the sharp-tongued British actress, Mrs. Patrick Campbell, "Why do you suppose it is that women are so utterly lacking in a sense of humour?"

"God did it on purpose," Mrs. Campbell answered without batting an eyelash, "so that we may love you men instead of laughing at you."

Bennett Cerf, in *The Home Book of Humorous Quotations*, selected and arranged by A.K. Adams, Dodd, Mead & Company, 1969, p.173.

Why should a woman not break through conventional restraints that enervate her mind and dwarf her body, and enjoy a wild, free, true life, as a man may?—and wander the green world over by the help of hands and feet, and lead a free, rough life in bondage to no man?—forget the old morbid loves and longings?—live and enjoy and learn as much as may before the silence comes?

Olive Schreiner, *Undine*, Ernest Benn Ltd., 1929, p.169.

The bodily experience of a woman is intrinsic to understanding her response to the divine. Biologically, a woman is determined by her role as bearer and deliverer of life. Thus, her entire life is a preparation for the birthing experience and the subsequent nurturing of the life to which she has given birth. There is no woman, whether she has actually given biological birth or not, whose psyche, soul and spirit remain outside the influence of these bodily imperatives.

Nancy C. Ring, in *A Dictionary of Christian Spirituality*, edited by Gordon S. Wakefield, SCM Press Ltd., 1986, p.149.

Can a woman have enough physical and mental energy to pursue a professional career up to the male standard of professionalism, side by side with being a mother? Will her children suffer, even if she does all that the best mother can do for them? Will her children not be jealous of their mother's professional work? Will they not demand to have the first call on their mother? Or is this perhaps a wholesome and useful part of their education? May it not be a means of teaching them, at an early stage in their lives, that in truth the universe does not centre on them?

Arnold Toynbee, *Surviving the Future*, Oxford University Press, 1971, p.128.

The feminist revolution of this century has provided the most powerful challenge to traditional patterns of marriage. Yet, paradoxically, it may also have strengthened the institution by giving greater freedom to both partners, and by allowing men to accept some of the traditionally female values, which rate success in personal relationships as highly as conventional worldly success. While it has been difficult to find appropriate passages about marriage in contemporary feminist writing, I have been struck by the many feminist sentiments to be found in books by eighteenth- and nineteenth-century writers, men as well as women.

Helge Rubinstein, *The Oxford Book of Marriage*, Oxford University Press, 1990, Introduction.

A sexual theology . . . is the awareness of a variety of needs:—the need to recognize that in the very midst of our current sexual chaos and floundering there exists an immense amount of longing for more meaningful and more human sexual relationship;—the need to wrestle with the vastly important insights of recent feminist theology concerning the sexist limitations of much in Christian thought and life; the need to grapple with the possibility that sexual meanings are more socially-created than biologically-given; the need for a sexual theology which positively affirms the wholeness of embodied selves, the goodness of sexual pleasure, and the creative significance of sexual self-affirmation in an incarnational theology; in short, the need to move beyond the traditional confines of "sexual ethics" into sexual theology which takes seriously the human sexual experience in our time and place as an arena for God's continuing self-disclosure, at the same time that it takes seriously the implications of Christian faith for our sexual lives.

J.B. Nelson, *Embodiment, An Approach to Sexuality and Christian Theology*, SPCK, 1979, p.15.

Yet another barrier awaiting destruction is that which divides the sexes and consigns women to a subordinate role in society. The Women's Liberation Movement— sometimes driven by frustration to extreme tactics—is always good for a joke or a wisecrack, yet represents a necessary rebellion against a social structure which has for centuries dehumanized one half of society. This is not the place to discuss the implications of discrimination against women, or the future role of women, but if the church exists to be a reconciling agency in which there is neither Jew nor Gentile, male nor female, bond or free, we cannot avoid asking why the church has not been in the forefront of the movement for the emancipation of women? And, having asked that question, one is obliged to face the unpleasant truth that, far from leading the way, the church has in fact been a powerful force in restricting the sphere of female activity and may well be the last social institution in which they are permitted to exercise responsibility.

Trevor Beeson, *An Eye for an Ear*, SCM Press Ltd., 1972, p.118.

There have been women who have excelled in creative genius as highly as any eminent men. I am thinking for instance, of a whole series of nineteenth-century

English women novelists, who were certainly the equals of the also famous male English novelists of their time. I can think of many other cases; Greek women poets are a notable example. But there have been far fewer women than men who have actually succeeded in coming to the top in any walk of life, in politics or religion or whatever it may be, and this raises a question. Is this because creative genius is in truth rarer among women than among men? Or is it because, since the invention of ploughing and of war, society has been organized for the convenience and for the advantage of men, and women have been under the handicap of having to make their way, when once they get out of the narrow field of conceiving and bearing and bringing up children, in a world that has been organized as a man's world?

This man's world is a social structure, and all social structures can be changed.

Arnold Toynbee, *Surviving the Future*, Oxford University Press, 1971, p.127.

Women... did not count in society at that time and had to avoid men's company in public. Contemporary Jewish sources are full of animosity toward women who, according to Josephus, are in every respect inferior to men. Men are advised to talk very little even with their own wives, still less with other women. Women lived as far as possible withdrawn from public view; in the temple they had access only to the women's forecourt and in regard to the obligation of prayer they were in the same category as slaves. Whatever may be the historical status of the biographical details, the evangelists have no inhibitions about speaking of Jesus's relationships with women. According to them, Jesus had got away from the custom of having no contact with women. Not only does he display no contempt for women, he is surprisingly at ease with them: women accompanied him and his disciples from Galilee to Jerusalem, personal affection for women came naturally to him; women attended him as he was dying and saw to his burial. The legally and humanly weak position of women in the society of that time was considerably upgraded by his prohibition of divorce, which had hitherto been possible if the husband alone simply issued a writ of divorce.

Hans Küng, *On Being a Christian*, translated by Edward Quinn, William Collins Sons & Co. Ltd., 1977, p.266.

I am an ordinary 27-year-old girl and I, too, am filled with love for all mankind, but for all I know I shall always continue to be in search of my one man. And I wonder to what extent that is a handicap, a woman's handicap. Whether it is an ancient tradition from which she must liberate herself, or whether it is so much part of her very essence that she would be doing violence to herself if she bestowed her love on all mankind instead of one single man. (I don't yet see how the two can be combined.) Perhaps that's why there are so few famous women scientists and artists: a woman always looks for the one man on whom she can bestow all her wisdom, warmth, love and creative powers. She longs for a man, not mankind.

It's not at all simple, the role of women. Sometimes, when I pass a woman in the street, a beautiful, well-groomed, wholly feminine, albeit dull woman, I completely lose my poise. Then I feel that my intellect, my struggle, my suffering, are oppressive, ugly, unwomanly; then I, too, want to be beautiful and dull, a desirable plaything for a man. It's typical that I always do end up wanting to be desired by a man, but in fact it is only a primitive instinct. Feelings of friendship, respect and love for us as human beings, these are all very well, but don't we ultimately want men to desire us as women? It is almost too difficult for me to write down all I feel; the subject is infinitely complex, but it is altogether too important not to be discussed.

Perhaps the true, the essential emancipation of women still has to come. We are not yet full human beings; we are the "weaker sex". We are still tied down and enmeshed in centuries-old traditions. We still have to be born as human beings, that is the great task that lies before us.

Etty Hillesum, *A Diary, 1941-43*, translated by Arnold Pomerans, Jonathan Cape Ltd., 1983, p.27.

Feminist theology is not to be understood primarily as theological reflection on separate "feminine" themes. Feminist theology takes as its first agenda the criticism of the masculinist bias of Christian theology. This bias has excluded women both from ordained ministry and from higher theological education throughout much of the church's history. Feminists therefore see Christian theology as having been done in exclusion of women's experience. Classical theology reflects a negative bias against women in its anthropological teachings...

Feminist theology seeks to analyse the effects of this exclusion of and negative anthropology about women in shaping the theological understandings of God, nature, sin, grace, christology, redemption and ecclesiology. Feminist criticism documents this male bias in theological doctrines and traces its effects in scripture, and in patristic, medieval and modern theologians...

The second agenda of feminist theology aims at the discovery of alternative historical traditions supportive of the full personhood of woman and her inclusion in leadership roles in church and society. There are two approaches to this quest for alternative tradition. Some feminists concerned with religion and spirituality have given up on the Judaeo-Christian tradition. They feel that this tradition is inherently patriarchal. Women should abandon Judaism or Christianity and seek alternative traditions outside them, by returning to ancient religions with female symbols for the divine and by drawing on their own experience...

Other feminists wish to affirm the possibility of feminist theology within the Judaeo-Christian tradition. They seek to uncover the more fundamental meaning of concepts of God, Christ, human personhood, sin and redemption that can criticise the deformation of these concepts as tools for male domination. The vindication of an alternative feminist reading of Christian origins is particularly important. Early Christianity is read as a counter-cultural movement subversive of the traditional hierarchical religious and social relationships. This radical vision was gradually submerged as institutional Christianity reintegrated itself back into patriarchical and slave-holding society and justified these household relationships, not only for the church but as a metaphor of Christian submission to God and to Christ. However, the radical vision of Christianity was not entirely extinguished, but continued to appear in both mystical and popular movements which affirmed the charismatic authority of women...

Feminists engaged in recovering alternative traditions for women in theology do not intend merely to supplement the present male tradition. They are construct-ing a new norm for interpretation of what is "true" and "false" in the tradition. Justifications of women's subordination in scripture and theology are no longer regarded as normative expressions of the gospel. Rather, they are judged as failures to apply the norms of equality in creation and redemption authentically, as perver-sion of the good news into an instrument of oppression. The full personhood of women is one of the touchstones for testing our faithfulness to the vision of redemption in Christ. By this norm much of mainstream tradition must be judged as deficient.

R.R. Ruether, in *A New Dictionary of Christian Theology*, edited by Alan Richardson and John Bowden, SCM Press Ltd., 1985, p.210.

FRIENDSHIP

*"Friendship"—"the state of being a friend; association of persons
as friends; a friendly intimacy, conformity, affinity,
correspondence, aptness to unite."*

The greatest experience I've had of friendship was our Oxford University Expedition to Nepal of 1963. Four of us got together and spent eighteen months in careful preparation. This meant we knew each other pretty well before we left England. We spent three months in the Himalayas, collecting blood for the Lister Institute in London who were doing a world-wide survey of blood groups. This was not an easy task. Persuading the Gurkhas to part with blood was one problem; getting it safely to the Lister Institute, within three days, was another. Yet we worked solidly as a team for two months, and much to everyone's surprise, completed our project.

We then set out on a trek in Western Nepal and spent three weeks on the slopes of Annapurna. Whilst two of the party attempted to get into Tibet, the other two made a film of village life which was later shown on TV.

The outstanding memory of the expedition was "friendship". In the whole of the time we were out there we had no serious argument. Problems were tackled corporately. Tasks were allotted to suit temperaments and our various strengths and weaknesses. There was a great deal of teasing and leg-pulling. Looking back, it was one of the happiest times of my life. I have a feeling that friendship lies in pursuing a common venture with like-minded people.

A faithful friend is a strong defence: and he that hath found such an one hath found a treasure.
Ecclesiasticus 6.14 (A.V.).

Whoso feareth the Lord shall direct his friendship aright: for as he is, so shall his neighbour be also.
Ecclesiasticus 6.17 (A.V.).

No longer do I call you servants, for the servant does not know what his master is doing; but I have called you friends, for all that I have heard from my Father I have made known to you.
John 15.15.

Welcome one another, therefore, as Christ has welcomed you, for the glory of God.
Romans 15.7.

A friend to all, is a friend to none.
Thomas Fuller, *Gnomologia*, Stearne Brock, 1733, p.5.

Be a friend to thy self, and others will be so too.
Thomas Fuller, *Gnomologia*, Stearne Brock, 1733, p.31.

It is not possible to be intimate with more than very few, because there are only very few in the world with whom we have practically everything in common.
Thomas Merton, *No Man Is an Island*, Burns & Oates Ltd., 1974, p.8.

To experience God's presence in earthly friendship and to be friendliness oneself—
that is the dialectic which rules the good man's life.

Ladislaus Boros, *Hidden God*, translated by Erika Young, Search Press Ltd., 1973, p.62.

How wonderful is thy friendliness toward me!
How deep! How unchanging.
Give me a grace to pass it on.

Alistair Maclean, in *God in our midst*, Martin Reith, Triangle/SPCK, 1989, p.26.

Fortunate people manage to gather two or three friends on their journey through
life. Others speak loosely of having hosts of friends, but what they mean is that they
have a lot of pleasant acquaintances.

Robert Standish, *The Big One Got Away*, Peter Davies Ltd., 1960, p.217.

There is a great reserve of incomprehensibility in all the few friends for whom I
really care. It is better that it should be so. What would a comprehensible friend be
worth? The impenetrable background gives the beauty to that which is in front of it.
The most unfathomable also of my friends are those who are most sincere and
luminous.

Mark Rutherford, *More Pages From a Journal*, Oxford University Press, 1910, p.252.

My friends have come to me unsought. The great God gave them to me. By oldest
right, by the divine affinity of virtue with itself, I find them, or rather, not I, but the
Deity in me and in them, both deride and cancel the thick walls of individual
character, relation, age, sex and circumstance, at which he usually connives, and
now makes many one.

Ralph Waldo Emerson, *Essay on Friendship*, Roycrofters, 1899, p.14.

We pine for a friend to whom we can unbosom our thoughts and emotions and we
are disappointed. We think only of ourselves in our discontent. Ought we not to
think a little of others and allow some small consideration to the possibility of doing
good? The friendship which proceeds from unselfishness will be firmer and more
intimate than that which is, after all, mere selfishness refined.

Mark Rutherford, *Last Pages From a Journal*, Oxford University Press, 1915, p.304.

The older I grow in years, the wonder and the joy increase when I see the power of
these words of Jesus—"I have called you friends"—to move the human heart. To the
rich and poor alike, to the learned and ignorant they bring with them a message of
peace and love. They are "spirit" and "life"; and the results that follow are
manifest... That one word "friend" breaks down each barrier of reserve, and we
have boldness in His presence... And so with thankfulness and joy our hearts go out
in love to meet His love.

Charles F. Andrews, *Christ in the Silence*, Hodder & Stoughton Ltd., 1933, p.220.

Christianity has at its centre the intense personal allegiance of Christ's followers to
him. While it includes a doctrine and implies a philosophy, it is in essence a Person.
Nowhere is this more vividly presented than in the discourse at the Last Supper in
the Gospel of St. John, where the intensity of the relationship between the disciples
and their Lord is seen in such imagery as "I am the vine, you are the branches; abide
in me and I in you", and "I have not called you servants, but friends".

Michael Ramsey, *Through the Year with Michael Ramsey*, edited by Margaret Duggan, Hodder & Stoughton Ltd., 1975, p.16.

The end of friendship is a commerce the most strict and homely that can be joined; more strict than any of which we have experience. It is for aid and comfort through all the relations and passages of life and death. It is fit for serene days, and graceful gifts, and country rambles, but also for rough road, and hard fare, shipwreck, poverty and persecution. It keeps company with the sallies of the wit and the trances of religion. We are to dignify to each other the daily needs and offices of man's life, and embellish it by courage, wisdom and unity.

Ralph Waldo Emerson, Essay on Friendship, Roycrofters, 1899, p.34.

Our friends are chosen for us by some hidden law of sympathy, and not by our conscious wills. All we know is that in our reactions to people we are attracted to some and are indifferent to others. And the ground of this mutual interest seems based on no discoverable principles of similarity of temperament or character. We have no time, when meeting a new person, to study him or her carefully; our reactions are swift and immediate. Our minds are made up instantly,—"friend, or non-friend." By some subtle intuitions, we know and have measured at their first words all the possibilities which their friendship has in store for us. We get the full quality of their personality at the first shock of meeting, and no future intimacy changes that quality.

Randolph Bourne, Youth and Life, Constable & Co. Ltd., 1913, p.140.

A blessed thing it is for any man or woman to have a friend, one human soul we can trust utterly, who knows the best and worst of us, and who loves us in spite of all our faults; who will speak the honest truth to us, while the world flatters us to our face, and laughs at us behind our back; who will give us counsel and reproof in the days of prosperity and self-conceit; but who, again, will comfort and encourage us in the day of difficulty and sorrow, when the world leaves us alone to fight our battle as we can.

It is only the great-hearted who can be true friends: the mean and cowardly can never know what true friendship means.

Charles Kingsley, Daily Thoughts, Macmillan Publishers Ltd., 1884, p.61.

What is friendship?

Friendship is an unpretentious relation, for "friend" is not a designation of office, nor an exalted title, nor a function one must perform from time to time, nor a role one is supposed to play in society. Friendship is a personal relation, "someone who likes you," someone you like . . .

Friendship also combines respect with affection . . . One does not have to submit to a friend. One neither looks up to nor down at a friend. One can look a friend in the face. In friendship one experiences oneself, just as one is, readily accepted and respected in one's own freedom. When one person likes another, then one respects the other in his or her individuality, and delights in his or her singularities as well.

Friendship is no passing feeling of affection. It combines affection with faithfulness. You can depend upon a friend. As a friend you become someone upon whom others can depend. A friend remains a friend even in misfortune, even in guilt. For between friends there rules no prejudice that defines one, and no ideal image after which one must strive. Nor is friendship an alliance for mutual advantage, as is the case with so-called business friends. Between friends there rules only the promise to walk with each other and to be there for each other, in other words, a faithfulness that has to do not with acting and possessing but with the individual person and with being.

Friendship is then a deep human relation that arises out of freedom, consists in mutual freedom, and preserves this freedom.

Jurgen Moltmann, *The Open Church*, SCM Press Ltd., 1978, p.51.

A true friend takes you for who you are rather than for who you pretend to be. There is great security in that kind of a friend. There can be a level of trust there that seems necessary to growth in human relationships. And friendship on this very basic level mirrors our relationship with God. Certainly Christ knows us, even better than we know ourselves. He sees the core without the accrued camouflage, without the layers of masks we have adopted to keep the real us from appearing. Christ sees us so intimately and continues to love us so deeply that we should learn a great deal about ourselves from this. Each of us feels inadequate on some level, to the task of being fully human and all that that implies. Christ knows our inadequacies, yet he loves us, even trusts us, to be ourselves. God trusts us so much that we were made free. We are created to develop along the path each of us chooses for our lives. No one else has given us that kind of liberty. The reason is, of course, that no one else loves us as fully as God does. As friends, how do we reciprocate? Am I essentially a friend who takes but one who seldom gives? I need to think about that question with some seriousness. God's love for us ought never to be one-sided. Clearly our love for Christ will never match his for us; nevertheless we must always be cultivating our love, nurturing it so it will grow toward fulfillment, even though never achieving it in this life. The various friendships that we have contain trust, love, respect, and time. We cannot have deep relationships without these elements. The same is true in the relationship that these worldly affiliations mirror—our personal interaction with Jesus Christ. The friendship that is always there, is always reliable, and one on which we can base our personal security. How fortunate we are.

Harry James Cargas, *Encountering Myself*, SPCK, 1978, p.92.

GREED

"Greed"—"inordinate or insatiate longing, especially for wealth; covetous desire."

I was involved in taking some relief supplies into "Biafra" during the Nigerian Civil War in 1968. This was an overland venture, going through territory which had recently been fought over. I was taking my shift as driver, and suddenly came across a vulture in the middle of the road, tearing away at the entrails of some poor unfortunate animal. This large voracious bird was so preoccupied in devouring its prey that it failed to notice our approach. At the last moment it spotted us, and in a panic, attempted a take-off. It was almost too late. It collided with the front of our vehicle; then with a great flapping of wings it bounced off the bonnet and smashed into the windscreen; and finally disappeared from view in complete disarray.

It reminded me strangely of a young English banker I once met in Switzerland. His avowed aim in life was to make as much money as he could, as quickly as possible, and he didn't really care how he did it. Already there was something of the attitude of the vulture imprinted in his features.

I sometimes wonder if our society is now based mainly on the acquisition of material wealth and that "greed" is euphemistically held up as "laudable enterprise".

Thou dost cause the grass to grow for the cattle, and plants for man to cultivate, that he may bring forth food from the earth, and wine to gladden the heart of man.
Psalm 104.14-15.

Hear, my son, and be wise, and direct your mind in the way. Be not among winebibbers, or among gluttonous eaters of meat; for the drunkard and the glutton will come to poverty, and drowsiness will clothe a man with rags.
Proverbs 23.19-20.

"Take heed, and beware of all covetousness; for a man's life does not consist in the abundance of his possessions." And he told them a parable, saying, "The land of a rich man brought forth plentifully; and he thought to himself, 'What shall I do, for I have nowhere to store my crops?' And he said, 'I will do this: I will pull down my barns, and build larger ones; and there I will store all my grain and my goods. And I will say to my soul, Soul, you have ample goods laid up for many years; take your ease, eat, drink, be merry.' But God said to him, 'Fool! This night your soul is required of you; and the things you have prepared, whose will they be?' So is he who lays up treasure for himself, and is not rich toward God."
Luke 12.15-21.

They have hearts trained in greed.
2 Peter 2.14.

What we desire is often more than we require.

A.C. Benson, *Extracts from the Letters of Dr. A.C. Benson to M.E.A.*, Jarrolds Publishing, 1927, p.42.

They are as sick that surfeit with too much as they that starve with nothing.

William Shakespeare, *The Merchant of Venice*, Act I. sc.ii. l.6.

Drink not the third glasse, which thou canst not tame,
When once it is within thee.

George Herbert, *The Poems of George Herbert*, Oxford University Press, 1979, *The Church Porch*, 5, *The Temple*, 1633, p.4.

Drunkenness turns a man out of himself, and leaves a beast in his room.

Thomas Fuller, *Gnomologia*, Stearne Brock, 1733, p.51.

The greedy man says the chief end of man is to glorify *gold*, and to enjoy it for ever.

Henry Ward Beecher, *Proverbs from Plymouth Pulpit*, Charles Burnet & Co., 1887, p.42.

Seek not proud riches, but such as thou mayest get justly, use soberly, distribute cheerfully, and leave contentedly.

Francis Bacon, *The Essays or Counsels, Civil and Moral*, Clarendon Press, 1985, p.109.

Drunkenness… is merely temporary suicide; the happiness that it brings is merely negative, a momentary cessation of unhappiness.

Bertrand Russell, *The Conquest of Happiness*, Unwin Paperbacks, 1984, p.19.

Drunkenness is never anything but a substitute for happiness. It amounts to buying the dream of a thing when you haven't money enough to buy the dreamed-of thing materially.

André Gide, *The Journals of André Gide* translated by Justin O'Brien, Martin Secker & Warburg Ltd., 1947, p.72.

Covetousness is close to but often distinguished from greed, which is an excessive desire for goods, especially wealth, and from avarice, which is an inordinate desire to acquire and hoard goods, usually money.

James F. Childress, in *A New Dictionary of Christian Ethics*, edited by James F. Childress and John Macquarrie, SCM Press Ltd., 1986, p.137.

All excess is ill; but drunkenness is the worst sort. It destroys health, dismounts the mind, and unmans man. It reveals secrets, is quarrelsome, lascivious, impudent, dangerous, and mad. In fine he that is drunk is not a man.

William Penn, *Fruits of Solitude*, A.W. Bennett, 1863, p.18.

If a man be discreet enough to take to hard drinking in his youth, before his general emptiness is ascertained, his friends invariably credit him with a host of shining qualities which, we are given to understand, lie balked and frustrated by his one unfortunate weakness.

Agnes Repplier, *Points of View*, Gay and Bird, 1893, p.26.

One night, under cover of darkness, and further concealed in a most cunning disguisement, a desperate burglar slid into his happy home, and robbed them all of everything. And darker yet to tell, the blacksmith himself did ignorantly conduct this burglar into his family's heart. It was the Bottle Conjuror! Upon the opening of that fatal cork, forth flew the fiend, and shrivelled up his home.

Herman Melville, *Moby Dick*, Penguin Books Ltd., 1978, p.595.

There are those who are *greedy* for this world's goods. Once again only Christianity can banish that spirit. If we judge things purely by material standards, there is no reason why we should not dedicate our lives to the task of getting. But Christianity introduces a spirit which looks outwards and not inwards. It makes love the highest value in life and service the greatest honour. When the love of God is in a man's heart, he will find his joy not in getting but giving.

William Barclay, *The Letters to the Corinthians*, The Saint Andrew Press, 1988, p.19.

> Say what we like, our civilisation has learnt a great lesson: It is sick of greed.
> It is sick of people out on the make.
> They are really low class, people out on the make.
> But what can you do, in a system which forces you to go out on the make
> Or practically starve?
> What can you do?
> Our fathers' and grandfathers' ideal
> Of success, money—
> Even while we admit the ghastly importance of money
> So base to us, and distasteful.
> And the destiny of mankind at last
> Not on what men think
> But on what they find distasteful, repulsive, or attractive.

D.H. Lawrence, *The Complete Poems of D.H. Lawrence*, edited by Vivian de Sola Pinto and Warren Roberts, William Heinemann Ltd., 1967, Volume II, *The Young Are Not Greedy*, p.831.

There is a close relation between lust and gluttony; no one knows this better than the doctors who have to deal with patients who are in despair about themselves. They have tried to satisfy all their greedy desires—of the intellect, the stomach, the emotions, and of sex—and the end of it all is the complete destruction of their happiness and peace of mind. All that is left is misery, dissatisfaction, loneliness, sickness and sexual frustration. For the glutton, as well as the lustful man, has lost all sense of the holiness of the body; he feels he can misuse it as much as he likes; That of course is where he is wrong: his body and all his appetites belong to God, who created him, and to all mankind, not to himself at all. And it is because he has lost his centre in God that he falls into these "sins of the flesh". He has ignored the truth that the body is "a temple of the Holy Ghost". In the words of St Paul: "Ye are not your own, for ye were bought with a price: glorify God therefore in your body." In other words, our whole personality belongs, by right, to God alone. To refuse Him our allegiance is to commit the sin of idolatry.

Olive Wyon, *On the Way*, SCM Press Ltd., 1958, p.52.

Gluttony at first sight looks like a survival from our animal ancestry. Certainly the urgent drive to search for food is one of the most powerful of animal instincts. But in fact excessive eating such as is common to man is rarely if ever found among animals, except those domesticated by men and so influenced by him. Men and women commonly overeat, at least in countries where there is an abundance of food, to fill the void caused by loneliness or boredom. This is even truer of excessive drinking. "The gin shop is the quickest way out of Manchester." Eating and drinking, despite excess, are clearly good and necessary. This is seen conspicuously when food and drink are shared in a meal between friends or in a family. It is not without reason that heaven has been likened to a feast.

Covetousness is an undue desire to possess. It gives to money or possessions, which are essentially only means to living, the value of ends, of objects to be clung to for their own sake. It can be powered by more than one motive. Avarice, like pride, can be an attempt to escape from the painful sense of insignificance and of dependence on the whim of others. The power which money gives and the wealth which surrounds a rich man can help a person to maintain the image of his superiority. But like lust, the urge to possess may have as its underlying motive the desire to escape from loneliness, from the fear of being unloved or even of being unlovable. Money, it is felt, can buy friendship, though in fact it is singularly unsuccessful in doing this. For the rich, though they can buy the company of their fellows, become painfully aware that their so-called friends love their money and the comfort it can obtain more than themselves. Wealth, especially when sought diligently and acquired with effort, tends to separate those who have it from those who have not. It makes the poor envious and the rich defensive. Covetousness has been called idolatry, for it has a unique power of blinding men to their dependence on God and their need to love and to be loved by their fellows. The splash of wealth can distract the rich from the needs of the poor and make them forget their humanity. Wealth also appears to be a source of perpetual anxiety. Our Western world has been called an acquisitive society because its economic system, for its efficient working, seems to require the constant stimulation, by means of advertising for example, of the desire to possess more and more. Nevertheless, despite all that can be said against either human avarice or the capitalist system, both possessions and money are means to the enhancement of human life. Seen as servants of human welfare they are to be valued. But recognised as powerful servants, ever liable to usurp the position of master, they need to be kept firmly in their subordinate place. We live at a time when science and technology have together enabled men to create immense wealth. It may be that the future of human life on this planet depends on the wisdom and determination really to subordinate the new-found wealth to the well-being of the race.

Christopher Bryant, SSJE, *The Heart in Pilgrimage*, Darton, Longman & Todd Ltd., 1980, p.40.

GRIEF

"Grief"— "deep or violent sorrow caused by loss or trouble; keen or bitter regret or remorse."

The deepest grief I have experienced so far came as a consequence of a broken relationship on which I had set much store. To me it was a "death" situation— the death of a valuable relationship.

I went through a very deep and painful bereavement. Nothing would console me. I would wake up at three in the morning and be unable to fall asleep again that night. A consequence of this was perpetual tiredness and a lack of energy. Food was distasteful to me, and I began to lose weight rapidly. I sank into some kind of depression and was thoroughly miserable. Before long my work suffered and I failed my exams. Other interests were abhorrent to me. What was even more distressing was the triggering off of a chain-reaction. Everything I touched somehow went wrong, and there seemed to be no end of trouble.

Eventually I came to the conclusion that I had to get on with the one thing needful, which was my work, as the future depended on that. Little by little and imperceptibly life picked up. In retrospect I came to see that what I had taken to be utter disaster was in reality the most valuable thing that I have yet experienced in life. Precious truths can be learnt in grief—but it takes time to realize them—and there is no easy way forward. Grief is costly.

Be gracious to me, O Lord, for I am in distress; my eye is wasted from grief, my soul and my body also.
Psalm 31.9.

Surely he has borne our griefs and carried our sorrows.
Isaiah 53.4.

I will not leave you desolate; I will come to you.
John 14.18.

He will wipe away every tear from their eyes, and death shall be no more, neither shall there be mourning nor crying nor pain any more.
Revelation 21.4.

Someone has called bereavement "loving in a new key".
J. Neville Ward, *Friday Afternoon*, Epworth Press, 1982, p.101.

Every man is a solitary in his griefs. One soon finds that out.
Norman Douglas, *An Almanac*, Chatto & Windus in association with Martin Secker & Warburg Ltd., 1945, p.11.

Passionate grief does not link us with the dead but cuts us off from them.
C.S. Lewis, *A Grief Observed*, Faber & Faber Ltd., 1961, p.44.

In the great complication or grief, only the saint can "see life steadily and see it whole".
J. Neville Ward, *Friday Afternoon*, Epworth Press, 1982, p.97.

One must go on living, in spite of anything tragic that may happen—and it's useless to break one's heart over troubles.
A.C. Benson, *Extracts from the Letters of Dr. A.C. Benson to M.E.A.*, Jarrold Publishing, 1927, p.19.

When we lose one we love, our bitterest tears are called forth by the memory of hours when we loved not enough.
Maurice Maeterlinck, *Wisdom and Destiny*, translated by Alfred Sutro, George Allen & Sons, 1898, p.113.

Grief is near-sighted, and holds its trouble close up; but love is long-sighted, and looks at them in all points of view.
Henry Ward Beecher, *Proverbs from Plymouth Pulpit*, Charles Burnet & Co., 1887, p.202.

But grief should be the instructor of the wise;
Sorrow is knowledge: they who know the most
Must mourn the deepest...
Lord Byron, *The Complete Poetical Works*, edited by Jerome J. McGann, Clarendon Press, 1986, Volume IV, *Manfred*, Act 1. sc.i. l.9, p.53.

I value sympathy in bereavement, because it seems—I won't say to *replace* the affection taken away, but to remind one that love is still there.

A.C. Benson, *Extracts from the Letters of Dr. A.C. Benson to M.E.A.*, Jarrold Publishing, 1927, p.18.

Grief is beautiful, as in winter ice-clad trees are beautiful when the sun shines upon them, but it is dangerous. Ice breaks many a branch, and so many persons are bowed down and crushed by their afflictions.

Henry Ward Beecher, *Proverbs from Plymouth Pulpit*, Charles Burnet & Co., 1887, p.209.

Do you imagine that it is in a fit of absent-mindedness that God has afflicted you? We have so much to learn, and grief must be our master. It is only through suffering that we can hope to come to self-knowledge.

Mary Craig, *Blessings*, Hodder & Stoughton Ltd., 1979, p.63.

The thought of death leaves me perfectly calm for I am fully convinced that our spirit is absolutely indestructible: it is something that works on from eternity to eternity, it is like the sun which only seems to sink judged by our earthly eyes and in reality never sinks at all but shines without ceasing.

Johann Wolfgang von Goethe, *The Practical Wisdom of Goethe*, chosen by Emil Ludwig, George Allen & Unwin Publishers Ltd , 1933, *To Eckermann*, 1824, p.75.

People often say, "My mother was such a good woman: why should she have suffered?" or "My boy was such a fine boy: why should he have died?" It is a very natural thing to say, but when we find ourselves saying it we should look at Jesus crowned with thorns, holiest of all, loveliest of all, and yet suffering more than all. His whole life, as He lived it amongst the people of His time, was a beauty and a glory, a flame of love passing by, and yet He was crucified.

Father Andrew, SDC, *A Gift of Light*, selected and edited by Harry C. Griffith, Mowbray, 1968, p.31.

Despair, when it comes from losing a person one loves, can go with a state of being unable to forget the loved one. If one could only despair completely, one thinks, one could forget. But the desire for the other keeps creating the hope of reunion, and the real situation keeps destroying that hope. So one finds oneself plunged into despair not once but over and over again. One hopes again every day and despairs again every day.

John S. Dunne, *The Reasons of the Heart*, SCM Press Ltd., 1978, p.97.

One further gain—the greater—was that my suffering did not, I think, withdraw me wholly into myself and fence me from the world: rather it gave me a sense of the brotherhood of grief. I was one with all the agonies that lie silent in the shadow of life; and though my suffering had no tangible cause, yet I was initiated into the fellowship of those who bear. I *understood*;—weak, faithless, and faulty as I was, I was no longer in the complacent isolation of the strong, the successful, the selfish, and even in my darkest hour I had strength to thank God for that.

A.C. Benson, *The House of Quiet*, John Murray Ltd., 1910, p.203.

I was not met as in intercourse with my fellow-men by the cold platitudes that fall so lightly from the lips of those whose hearts have never known one real pang, nor whose lives one crushing blow. I was not told that all things were ordered for the best, nor assured that the overwhelming disparities of life were but apparent, but I was met from the eyes and brows of Him who was indeed acquainted with grief, by a look of solemn recognition, such as may pass between friends who have endured between them some strange and secret sorrow, *and are through it united in a bond that cannot be broken.*

Dora Greenwell, *Colloquia Crucis*, Strahan & Co., Publishers, 1871, p.15.

They that love beyond the world, cannot be separated by it. Death cannot kill what never dies. Nor can spirits ever be divided, that love and live in the same divine principle, the root and record of their friendship. If absence be not death, neither is theirs. Death is but crossing the world, as friends do the seas; they live in one another still. For they must needs be present, that love and live in that which is omnipresent. In this divine glass they see face to face; and their converse is free, as well as pure.

This is the comfort of friends, that though they may be said to die, yet their friendship and society are, in the best sense ever present, because immortal.

William Penn, *Fruits of Solitude*, A.W. Bennett, 1863, p.80.

The most searing thing about death is that it creates a physical absence. But physical absence doesn't mean *absence of presence*. I understood that a long time ago, after the war, when before me in my office a husband and wife were tearing each other apart. They overflowed with the bitterness and despair of couples who have loved each other but have grown apart. Suddenly, the wife grasped her husband's arm and cried painfully: "Remember how close, how united we were two years ago when you were a prisoner in Poland." It is so true that genuine love can withstand distance. Jules Beaucarne (a French singer whose wife was murdered in the late 1970s) has some magnificent words: "Death is just a different kind of presence."

Michel Quoist, *With Open Heart*, translated by Colette Copeland, Gill and Macmillan Ltd., 1983, p.207.

I'm really in a most awful mental fix: no religion or philosophy has any validity over my trouble, nothing gives any value to life: it is a fatal folly to be as attached to anyone as I was to my wife: I still weep daily, uncontrollably, and scarcely dare to go out less I break down in public: the case seems to me to approach insanity, which I suppose includes emotional uncontrol as well as the intellectual. Music solaces me, but no reading and no thinking; they on the contrary put me "wronger". I find religion nothing: we know nothing: we can only guess, and our guess changes with our health and our environment: the one religion I have now is a longing to see my wife again, and like all other religions there's much more doubt than faith about it. I'm tortured too wondering would she want to see me: who can possibly tell what changes the habit of eternity may bring, supposing even, as on the whole I do, that we survive and know. Music, with one finger, and the calm beauty of fields and trees and the simplicity of children, these are the only things that keep me from the burst brain that at times seems to threaten—a sort of boiling in the brain pan with most singularly no sense of ill health, generally even no physical lassitude.

Stephen MacKenna, *Journal and Letters*, Constable & Co. Ltd., 1936, p.189.

The world is a cold, unfair place in which everything they held precious has been destroyed. But instead of giving up on this unfair world and life, instead of looking outward, to churches or to nature, for answers, they look inward to their own capacities for loving.

"Blow on the coal of the heart" for what little light and warmth we will be able to muster to sustain us . . .

Is there an answer to the question of why bad things happen to good people?

That depends on what we mean by "answer." If we mean "is there an explanation which will make sense of it all?"—why is there cancer in the world? Why did my father get cancer? Why did the plane crash? Why did my child die?—then there is probably no satisfying answer. We can offer learned explanations, but in the end, when we have covered all the squares on the game board and are feeling very proud of our cleverness, the pain and the anguish and the sense of unfairness will still be there.

But the word "answer" can mean "response" as well as "explanation", and in that sense, there may well be a satisfying answer to the tragedies in our lives. The response would be Job's response in MacLeish's version of the biblical story—to forgive the world for not being perfect, to forgive God for not making a better world, to reach out to the people around us, and to go on living it all.

In the final analysis, the question of why bad things happen to good people translates itself into some very different questions, no longer asking why something happened, but asking how we will respond, what we intend to do now it has happened.

Are you capable of forgiving and accepting in love a world which has disappointed you by not being perfect, a world in which there is so much unfairness and cruelty, disease and crime, earthquake and accident? Can you forgive its imperfections and love it because it is capable of containing great beauty and goodness, and because it is the only world we have?

Are you capable of forgiving and loving the people around you, even if they have hurt you and let you down by not being perfect? Can you forgive them and love them, because there aren't any perfect people around, and because the penalty for not being able to love imperfect people is condemning oneself to loneliness?

Are you capable of forgiving and loving God even when you have found out that He is not perfect, even when He has let you down and disappointed you by permitting bad luck and sickness and cruelty in His world, and permitting some of those things to happen to you? Can you learn to love and forgive Him despite His limitations, as Job does, and as you once learned to forgive and love your parents even though they were not as wise, as strong, or as perfect as you needed them to be?

And if you can do these things, will you be able to recognize that the ability to forgive and the ability to love are the weapons God has given us to enable us to live fully, bravely, and meaningfully in this less-than-perfect world?

Harold S. Kushner, *Why Bad Things Happen to Good People*, Pan Books Ltd., 1982, p.152.

GUILT

"Guilt"—"conduct involving guilt, shame and remorse."

During my time as Chaplain to University College, London, I had a remarkable experience one winter's evening in Gower Street. It was already dark, and fortunately, as it turned out, I wasn't wearing my dog-collar.

A young man, greatly distressed, was shouting and screaming so that people were crossing the road to avoid him. Instead of taking evasive action I went and sat quietly by him on a doorstep. He greeted my arrival with a string of verbal abuse ending up with a piercing scream. He ranted and raved for a couple of minutes and then spat at me before muttering quietly to himself. This was followed by another outburst and a further string of expletives.

What happened next took me completely by surprise. He grabbed me by the arm, and we walked up Gower Street together. Suddenly without warning he jumped into my arms and I had to cradle him, rather like a baby. He then started whispering something in my ear. He had no idea I was a priest, but what was coming out was a form of confession. In the space of three minutes or so he shed a great deal of guilt, shame and remorse, which had accumulated over the years. I listened carefully and muttered a few words of forgiveness. This was greeted with a great whooping noise and with that he ran off into the night.

Guilt can be a burden; freedom from guilt—a liberation to love.

Your guilt is taken away, and your sin forgiven.
Isaiah 6.7.

Create in me a clean heart, O God, and put a new and right spirit within me.
Psalm 51.10.

Let him who is without sin among you be the first to throw a stone at her.
John 8.7.

Since all have sinned and fall short of the glory of God.
Romans 3.23.

For every man who lives without freedom, the rest of us must face the guilt.
Lillian Hellman, *Watch on the Rhine*, The World Publishing Company, 1943, Act II, p.98.

Suspicion always haunts the guilty mind:
The thief doth fear each bush an officer.
William Shakespeare, *Henry VI Part III*, Act V. sc.vi. l.11.

There is a sort of man who pays no attention to his good actions, but is tormented by his bad ones.
W. Somerset Maugham, *The Summing Up*, Bernhard Tauchnitz, 1938, p.12.

A guilty mind can be *eased* by nothing but repentance; by which what was ill done, is revoked, and morally voided and undone.
Benjamin Whichcote, *Moral and Religious Aphorisms*, Elkin Mathews & Marrot, Ltd., 1930, Century VII, No.602.

Guilt is the source of sorrow; 'tis the fiend,
Th'avenging fiend that follows us behind,
With whips and stings. The blest know none of this:
But rest in everlasting peace of mind,
And find the height of all their heaven is goodness.
Nicholas Rowe, *The Fair Penitent*, Thomas Dolby, 1864, Act III, sc.i, p.27.

And, oh! that pang where more than Madness lies—
The Worm that will not sleep—and never dies—
Thought of the gloomy day and ghastly night,
That dreads the darkness, and yet loathes the light—

That winds around, and tears the quiv'ring heart—
Ah! wherefore not consume it—and depart!

Lord Byron, *The Complete Poetical Works*, edited by Jerome J. McGann, Clarendon Press, 1981, Volume III, *The Bride of Abydos*, Canto II. st.27, l.645, p.145.

When I contemplate the accumulation of guilt and remorse which, like a garbage-can, I carry through life, and which is fed not only by the lightest actions but by the most harmless pleasure, I feel Man to be of all living things the most biologically incompetent and ill-organized. Why has he acquired a seventy-years' life-span only to poison it incurably by the mere being of himself? Why has he thrown Conscience, like a dead rat, to putrefy in the well?

Cyril Connolly, *The Unquiet Grave*, Hamish Hamilton Ltd., 1945, p.4.

False guilt, cheap guilt. When I used to answer letters on a newspaper so many of the writers were sick with guilt—about their children, husbands, wives, parents, about existing at all. They had lost themselves somewhere and felt everlastingly at fault, caught in compulsive rituals to appease insatiable gods. There can be no true guilt for people at this stage of development; there *is* no real guilt without freedom and they were not free.

Monica Furlong, *Travelling In*, Hodder & Stoughton Ltd., 1971, p.82.

The mortification born of a shameful act does not usually last long. With most people it passes within forty-eight hours. And yet each mortification as it passes leaves a stain and a blemish on our feeling of well-being. Thus gradually an under-current of self-contempt begins coursing within us, and now and then it leaks out in bitterness and hatred towards others. It is in rare moments when we have a particular reason to be satisfied with ourselves that we realize the depression and dejection secreted in us by a guilty conscience.

Eric Hoffer, *The Passionate State of Mind*, Martin Secker & Warburg Ltd., 1956, p.92.

Were the people responsible for the crime of Calvary?

Not, I think, in the way which some scholars have supposed. Not with malice aforethought; not with a diabolically thought-out judgement given against Jesus.

They were guilty by inertia, guilty as we are guilty today—guilty of moral torpor, and of being so self-obsessed and comfort-loving that we will not stir ourselves and suffer for the truth.

On those counts the people were guilty then, and on those counts most of us are guilty now.

W.E. Sangster, *They Met at Calvary*, Secker & Warburg, 1956, Epworth Press, 1956, p.48.

Jung has written: "If only people could realize what an enrichment it is to find one's own guilt, what a sense of honour and spiritual dignity." This enrichment springs from the fact that to acknowledge guilt is to affirm solidarity with the human race in its estrangement from its true life. The Lord's Prayer similarly emphasizes the individual's solidarity with his fellows. "Forgive us our trespasses as we forgive those who trespass against us." There need be nothing cringing in the human cry of penitence. The individual frankly though ruefully acknowledges his share in the human crimes of violence and cruelty, of greed and hate, as well as his own personal missing the mark.

Christopher Bryant, SSJE, in *A Dictionary of Christian Spirituality*, edited by Gordon S. Wakefield, SCM Press Ltd., 1986, p.318.

Before God we experience guilt in the form of estrangement from the righteousness of God. We know ourselves to be unworthy of fellowship with God. Our problem is not primarily the fact that we have broken God's laws so it is useless to plead that our sins have been "small ones". Our primary guilt lies in the fact that we are prodigals in a far country. Our guilt can only be removed when the Father's forgiveness receives us home as a child. Jesus equated the guilt of a man who has lust in his heart with the guilt of a man who actually commits adultery (Matt. 5.28). To understand this, we must see that Jesus is speaking theologically. Ethically and legally, of course, there is a vast difference between the guilt in the two cases. Jesus' point is that both men are equally alienated from God.

William Hordern, in *A New Dictionary of Christian Theology*, edited by Alan Richardson and John Bowden, SCM Press Ltd., 1985, p.245.

Love bade me welcome: yet my soul drew back,
Guiltie of dust and sinne.
But quick-ey'd Love, observing me grow slack
From my first entrance in,
Drew nearer to me, sweetly questioning,
If I lack'd any thing.

A guest, I answer'd, worthy to be here:
Love said, You shall be he.
I the unkinde, ungratefull? Ah my deare,
I cannot look on thee.
Love took my hand, and smiling did reply,
Who made the eyes but I?

Truth Lord, but I have marr'd them: let my shame
Go where it doth deserve.
And know you not, sayes Love, who bore the blame?
My deare, then I will serve.
You must sit down, sayes Love, and taste my meat:
So I did sit and eat.

George Herbert, *The Poems of George Herbert*, Oxford University Press, 1979, *The Church, Love* III, p.180.

Nothing is more intensely real than the sense of guilt; it is as real as the eternal distinction between right and wrong in which it is rooted. And nothing is more intensely real than the sense of release from guilt which comes from the discovery and assurance of the remission of sins. The evil things which a man has done cannot be undone; but when they have been forgiven through Christ, the iron chain which so bound him to them as to make the guilt of them eternally his has been broken; before God and his own conscience he is no longer guilty of them. This is the Christian mystery of justification, which, according to Paul—and his words have been confirmed in the experience of millions of Christian men—is "the power of God unto salvation to every one that believeth." It changes darkness into light; despair into victorious hope; prostration into buoyancy and vigour. It is one of the supreme motives to Christian living, and it makes Christian living possible. The man who has received this great deliverance is no longer a convict, painfully observing all prison rules with the hope of shortening his sentence, but a child in the home of God.

There are experiences of another kind by which the faith of a Christian man is verified. Of these one of the most decisive and most wonderful is the consciousness that through Christ he has passed into the eternal and Divine order. He belongs to two worlds. He is just as certain that he is environed by things unseen and eternal as that he is environed by things seen and temporal. In the power of the life given to him in the new birth he has entered into the kingdom of God. He is conscious that that Diviner region is now the native land of his soul. It is there that he finds perfect rest and perfect freedom. It is a relief to escape to its eternal peace and glory from the agitations and vicissitudes, the sorrows and successes, of this transitory world. It is not always that he is vividly conscious of belonging to that eternal order; this supreme blessedness is reserved for the great hours of life; but he knows that it lies about him always, and that at any moment the great apocalypse may come. And even when it is hidden, its "powers" continue to act upon him, as the light and heat of the sun pass through the clouds by which the burning splendour is softened and concealed.

R.W. Dale, *The Living Christ and the Four Gospels*, Hodder & Stoughton Ltd., 1890, p.14.

HATE

"Hate"—"an emotion of extreme dislike or aversion; detestation, abhorrence, hatred."

One of the first students I met at University College, London, was a film addict. There was a memorable occasion when we both went to the National Film Theatre to see the film *Even Dwarfs Started Small*. The film director Werner Hertzog was present and available for questions afterwards.

I remembered a particular scene in the film which portrayed a brood of hens pecking at stray grains of wheat in a farm-yard—a peaceful scene. Then our attention was focussed on one particular hen. It was diseased and had a large bare patch on its hind quarters. Suddenly the other hens spotted this defect, and savagely moved in and pecked the poor unfortunate hen to death. It was a disturbing scene. It seemed as though the hens couldn't stand the sight of something that was the same as them in essence yet different. It stirred up feelings of savage hate, and a threat to their sense of identity so that they had to eliminate it.

I was intrigued and asked Werner Hertzog a question afterwards, about the nature of evil and hatred. Was he trying to get over to us that evil and hatred are in all of us and can easily break out and cause mayhem?—especially when faced with something which is essentially the same but different. I must have touched a raw nerve somewhere in the audience. Pandemonium broke out and everyone started shouting at each other and getting very angry. I think their reaction confirmed the point.

You shall not hate your brother in your heart, but you shall reason with your neighbour, lest you bear sin because of him.
Leviticus 19.17.

There are six things which the Lord hates, seven which are an abomination to him: haughty eyes, a lying tongue, and hands that shed innocent blood, a heart that devises wicked plans, feet that make haste to run to evil, a false witness who breathes out lies, and a man who sows discord among brothers.
Proverbs 6.16-19.

Love your enemies and pray for those who persecute you.
Matthew 5.44.

He who says he is in the light and hates his brother is in the darkness still. He who loves his brother abides in the light, and in it there is no cause for stumbling. But he who hates his brother is in the darkness and walks in the darkness, and does not know where he is going, because the darkness has blinded his eyes.
1 John 2.9-11.

An intellectual hatred is the worst.

W.B. Yeats, *Collected Poems of W.B. Yeats*, Macmillan Publishers Ltd., 1973, *A Prayer for my Daughter*, l.19, p.213.

And the intensest form of hatred is that rooted in fear.

George Eliot, *Daniel Deronda*, Virtue & Co., 1912, Volume III, p 195.

Now hatred is a feeling which leads to the extinction of values.

José Ortega Y Gasset, *Meditations on Quixote*, W.W. Norton & Company, 1985, p.32.

The price of hating other human beings is loving oneself less.

Elderidge Cleaver, *Soul on Ice*, McGraw-Hill Book Company, 1968, p.17.

Now hatred is by far the longest pleasure;
Men love in haste, but they detest at leisure.

Lord Byron, *The Complete Poetical Works*, edited by Jerome J. McGann, Clarendon Press, 1981, Volume V, *Don Juan*, Canto XIII, st.6, l.47, p.526.

When we hate a man, we hate in him something which resides in us ourselves. What is not in us does not move us.

Hermann Hesse, *Demian*, Henry Holt and Company, 1948, p.140.

Love thyself last; cherish those hearts that hate thee;
Corruption wins not more than honesty.

William Shakespeare, *Henry VIII*, Act III, sc. ii. l.444.

Hatred comes from the heart; *contempt* from the head; and neither feeling is quite within our control.

Arthur Schopenhauer, *Studies in Pessimism*, translated by T. Bailey Saunders, Swan Sonnenschein, 1981, p.61.

Man hitherto has been strongest in his capacity to hate. Christ sought to change the point of supreme power to love.

Henry Ward Beecher, *Proverbs from Plymouth Pulpit*, Charles Burnet & Co., 1887, p.14.

(The world) would not hate angels for being angelic; but it does hate men for being Christians. It grudges them their new character; it is tormented by their peace; it is infuriated by their joy.

William Temple, *Readings in St. John's Gospel* (First and Second Series), Macmillan Publishers Ltd., 1947, p.272.

Hatred rarely does any harm to its object. It is the hater who suffers. His soul is warped and his life is poisoned by dwelling on past injuries or projecting schemes of revenge. Rancour in the bosom is the foe of personal happiness.

Lord Beaverbrook, *The Divine Propagandist*, William Heinemann Ltd., 1962, p.25.

Forgiveness alone destroys enemies. Jesus knew that. That is why His Cross towers above all the selfish competition of our modern life, ugly and holy, crude and sublime, coarse and serene; it symbolises the single way by which hate can be overcome.

W.E. Sangster, *He is Able*, Hodder & Stoughton Ltd., 1936, p.101.

There is no passion of the human soul so persistent and universal as that of hatred. Race hatreds, religious hatreds, hatred of rivalry, of jealousy, of fear, of interest, abound. Every one has conscience enough to hate, few have religion enough to love.

Henry Ward Beecher, *Proverbs from Plymouth Pulpit*, Charles Burnet & Co., 1887, p.26.

It is proper to hate a corrupt person only for his defects, but in-so-far as he is endowed with a divine image, it is in order to love him. We must also realize that the precious dimension of his worth is a more authentic expression of his nature than the lower characteristics that developed in him through circumstances.

Abraham Isaac Kook, *The Moral Principles*, translated by Ben Zion Bokser, 1978, p.137.

The human heart as modern civilisation has made it is more prone to hatred than to friendship. And it is prone to hatred because it is dissatisfied, because it feels deeply, perhaps even unconsciously, that it has somehow missed the meaning of life, that perhaps others, but not we ourselves, have secured the good things which nature offers man's enjoyment.

Bertrand Russell, *The Conquest of Happiness*, Unwin Paperbacks, 1984, p.72.

> All hatred driven hence,
> The soul recovers radical innocence
> And learns at last that it is self-delighting,
> Self-appeasing, self-affrighting,
> And that its own sweet will is Heaven's will.

W. B. Yeats, *Collected Poems of W.B. Yeats*, Macmillan Publishers Ltd., 1973, *A Prayer for my Daughter*, st.9, p.213.

The pleasure of hating, like a poisonous mineral, eats into the heart of religion, and turns it to rankling spleen and bigotry; it makes patriotism an excuse for carrying fire, pestilence, and famine into other lands: it leaves to virtue nothing but the spirit of censoriousness, and a narrow, jealous, inquisitorial watchfulness over the actions and motives of others.

William Hazlitt, *The Complete Works of William Hazlitt*, J.M. Dent & Sons Ltd., 1931, Volume 12, *The Plain Speaker*, p.130.

There is no hate without fear. Hate is crystallized fear... where hate is, fear will be lurking. Thus we hate what threatens our person, our liberty, our privacy, our income, popularity, vanity and our dreams and plans for ourselves. If we can isolate this element in what we hate we may learn to cease from hating. Analyse in this way the hatred of ideas, or of the type of people in whom one has once loved and whose face is preserved in Spirits of Anger. Hate is the consequence of fear.

Cyril Connolly, *The Unquiet Grave*, Hamish Hamilton Ltd., 1945, p.77.

Hatred, as ill will, hostility, and enmity, is the direct opposite of love, and it may be directed against God, against the neighbour, or against oneself. Hence, it violates the love commandment (Matt. 22.37-40 and parallels), which includes two major parts, love of God and love of neighbour as oneself. According to Jesus, hatred is ruled out and love required of his disciples, even toward enemies (Matt. 5.43ff.), because of God's perfect righteousness which humans should emulate. The attitude of hatred is condemned not only because of the evil actions that result from it but also because of its own intrinsic nature.

James F. Childress, in *A New Dictionary of Christian Ethics*, edited by James F. Childress and John Macquarrie, SCM Press Ltd., 1986, p.261.

There is in every weak, lost and isolated member of the human race an agony of hatred born of his own helplessness, his own isolation. Hatred is the sign and the expression of loneliness, of unworthiness, of insufficiency. And in so far as each one of us is lonely, is unworthy, each one hates himself. Some of us are aware of this self-hatred, and because of it we reproach ourselves and punish ourselves needlessly. Punishment cannot cure the feeling that we are unworthy. There is nothing we can do about it as long as we feel that we are isolated, insufficient, helpless, alone.

Others, who are less conscious of their own self-hatred, realize it in a different form by projecting it on to others. There is a proud and self-confident hate, strong and cruel, which enjoys the pleasure of hating for it is directed outward to the unworthiness of another. But this strong and happy hate does not realize that, like all hate, it destroys and consumes the self that hates, and not the object that is hated. Hate in any form is self-destructive, and even when it triumphs physically it triumphs in its own spiritual ruin...

The beginning of the fight against hatred, the basic Christian answer to hatred, is not the commandment to love, but what must necessarily come before in order to make the commandment bearable and comprehensible. It is a prior commandment *to believe*. The root of Christian love is not the will to love, but *the faith that one is loved*. The faith that one is loved *by God*. That faith that one is loved by God although unworthy—or, rather irrespective of one's worth!

Thomas Merton, *New Seeds of Contemplation*, Burns & Oates Ltd., 1962, p.57.

HEART

"Heart"—"the seat of feeling, understanding, and thought. The seat of one's inmost thoughts and secret feelings; one's inmost being."

One of the characters I remember from Bradford days was an elderly woman called Mrs Scott. She lived on the ground floor of a high-rise block of flats near the centre of the city and kept an open house—particularly for the young.

She suffered from several disabilities. She had very little behind her in the way of formal education. She was blind, and had an artificial limb. She had lost her husband prematurely in life. She had more than ample grounds to feel sorry for herself. Yet self pity formed no part of her itinerary. Instead she was cheerful and optimistic, and had that rare gift of being "big-hearted" which seemed to originate from a deep-seated faith. She was kind, generous, and outgoing. She had acquired along the way a unique form of life wisdom. It was not surprising she was a great favourite with the local teenagers.

I think it was her blindness and other physical disabilities that had turned her inwards and enabled her to discover the life of the heart. Through this she had discovered how to help people with their feelings. Like most blind people she was a good listener, and sensitive and aware as to what was actually going on. I always left her flat feeling better for the visit. Her knowledge of the "heart" was infectious.

Walk in the ways of your heart.
Ecclesiastes 11.9.

Keep your heart with all vigilance; for from it flow the springs of life.
Proverbs 4.23.

Out of the abundance of the heart the mouth speaks.
Matthew 12.34.

But in your hearts reverence Christ as Lord.
1 Peter 3.15.

The same heart beats in every human breast!
Matthew Arnold, *The Poems of Matthew Arnold*, edited by Kenneth Allott, Longmans, Green & Co. Ltd., 1965, *The Buried Life*, l.23, p.272.

The human heart is vast enough to contain all the world.
Joseph Conrad, *Lord Jim*, J.M. Dent & Sons Ltd., 1926, p.323.

There's nobody but God can control the heart of man.
George Eliot, *Adam Bede*, Virtue & Co., 1908, Volume 1, p.63.

Unauthorized and abhorrent thoughts will sometimes invade the best human heart.
Herman Melville, *Israel Potter*, Jarrold Publishing, 1925, p.45.

Great beauty, great strength, and great riches are really and truly of no great use; a right heart exceeds all.
Benjamin Franklin, *Poor Richard's Almanack*, Taurus Press, 1962, p.5.

It is the heart that makes a man rich. He is rich or poor according to what he *is*, not according to what he *has*.
Henry Ward Beecher, *Proverbs from Plymouth Pulpit*, Charles Burnet & Co., 1887, p.66.

Among all possessions on earth a heart of one's own is the most priceless, and there are scarcely two among thousands possessed of it.
Johann Wolfgang von Goethe, *Wisdom and Experience*, selected by Ludwig Curtius, translated and edited by Hermann J. Weigand, Routledge & Kegan Paul, 1949, p.190.

The mystery of God has its seat in man's heart, and even if it starts making itself felt in his brain, he still finds the answer only in love.
    It is by loving you understand.
Carlo Carretto, *The Desert in the City*, translated by Barbara Wall, William Collins Sons & Co. Ltd., 1983, p.40.

They understand by "heart" not primarily the emotions and feelings but—as in scripture—the moral and spiritual centre of the human person, the seat of wisdom and intelligence, the place where the individual becomes most truly personal, and at the same time closest to God.

Kallistos Ware, in *A Dictionary of Christian Spirituality*, edited by Gordon S. Wakefield, SCM Press Ltd., 1986, p.315.

Discipline of the heart means the control of the emotions and the affections; this is often very difficult, and seems impossible. It is only with God's help that we can voluntarily detach our desires from that which we want most (however good and desirable it may be in itself) when we see clearly that this "way" or achievement or relationship is not for us.

Olive Wyon, *On the Way*, SCM Press Ltd., 1958, p.75.

But the word heart in the Jewish-Christian tradition refers to the source of all physical, emotional, intellectual, volitional, and moral energies.

From the heart arise unknowable impulses as well as conscious feelings, moods, and wishes. The heart, too, has its reasons and is the centre of perception and understanding. Finally the heart is the seat of the will: it makes plans and comes to good decisions. Thus the heart is the central and unifying organ of our personal life. Our heart determines our personality, and is therefore not only the place where God dwells but also the place to which Satan directs his fiercest attacks. It is this heart which is the place of prayer.

Henri J.M. Nouwen, *The Way of the Heart*, Darton, Longman & Todd Ltd., 1981, p.77.

A flower has opened in my heart...
What flower is this, what flower of spring,
What simple, secret thing?
It is the peace that shines apart,
The peace of daybreak skies that bring
Clear song and wild swift wing.

Heart's miracle of inward light,
What powers unknown have sown your seed
And your perfection freed?...
O flower within me wondrous white,
I know you only as my need
And my unsealed sight.

Siegfried Sassoon, *The Heart's Journey*, William Heinemann Ltd., 1927, No.28.

It is by the things that we *feel* that life is dominated and controlled.

That principle governs every department of human experience. The entire history of mankind goes to show that men are more easily reached and more powerfully affected by the things that they *feel* than by the things that they *see*. In one of the finest passages in *Coningsby* Lord Beaconsfield shows that, without an exception, all the great epoch-making movements that have convulsed mankind—the siege of Troy, the rise of the Saracens, the Crusades, the French Revolution, and so on,—have been inspired, not by the *reason*, but by the emotions. It was not that men's minds were illuminated by a new *light*; it was that their hearts suddenly glowed with a new *passion*... The priceless evangel of the New Testament is not a system of philosophy, appealing to the intellect, but a divine letter, making its appeal direct to the heart.

F.W. Boreham, *The Gospel of Uncle Tom's Cabin*, Epworth Press, 1956, p.28.

I confess that I do not see why the very existence of an invisible world may not in part depend on the personal response which any one of us may make to the religious appeal. God himself, in short, may draw vital strength and increase of very being from our fidelity. For my own part, I do not know what the sweat and blood and tragedy of this life mean, if they mean anything short of this. If this life be not a real fight, in which something is eternally gained for the universe by success, it is no better than a game of private theatricals from which one may withdraw at will. But it *feels* like a real fight,—as if there were something really wild in the universe which we, with all our idealities and faithfulness, are needed to redeem; and first of all to redeem our own hearts from atheisms and fears. For such a half-wild, half-saved universe our nature is adapted. The deepest thing in our nature is this... dumb region of the heart in which we dwell alone with our willingnesses and unwilling-nesses, our faiths and fears. As through the cracks and crannies of caverns those waters exude from the earth's bosom which then form the fountain-heads of springs, so in these crepuscular depths of personality the sources of all our outer deeds and decisions take their rise. Here is our deepest organ of communication with the nature of things; and compared with these concrete movements of our soul all abstract statements and scientific arguments—the veto, for example, which the strict positivist pronounces upon our faith—sound to us like the mere chatterings of the teeth.

William James, *The Will to Believe*, Longmans, Green & Co Ltd., 1879, p.61.

HUMANISM

"Humanism"—"any system of thought or action which is concerned with merely human interests, or with those of the human race in general."

During National Service I was sent from Singapore on a short language course to Sungei Patani in northern Malaya. I had only been learning Gurkhali for a week when a telegram arrived ordering me back to base without delay. My orderly was waiting for me with my equipment, and we transferred from one plane to another—bound for a month in Sarawak. Half our battalion was to patrol up to the Indonesian border as a show of force and a warning to President Sukarno.

Our main approach was by the River Rejang, going up in small power boats. At night we stayed in long-houses—villages built by the river, consisting of a single row of houses joined together—about a quarter of a mile long. We slept on the verandas, and were inevitably joined by the odd dog who nestled up to us during the night for warmth and comfort.

I was impressed with the Australian Police Commissioner who had oversight of the whole operation. He was a man of quiet integrity who carried out his responsibilities in a manner akin to devotion. He was concerned for the people of Sarawak—the Dyaks—and for the future of their country. His gentle sense of humour went down well with the Gurkhas, and he was very efficient in his organization and administration. He was a cultured man and had a great respect for the individual. A humanist by conviction, he was certainly doing his best to make this a better world to live in.

And I applied my mind to seek and to search out by wisdom all that is done under heaven.

Ecclesiastes 1.13.

I searched with my mind how to cheer up my body with wine—my mind still guiding me with wisdom—and how to lay hold on folly, till I might see what was good for the sons of men to do under heaven during the few days of their life.

Ecclesiastes 2.3.

I am speaking in human terms, because of your natural limitations. For just as you once yielded your members to impurity and to greater and greater iniquity, so now yield your members to righteousness for sanctification.

Romans 6.19.

From now on, therefore, we regard no one from a human point of view; even though we once regarded Christ from a human point of view, we regard him thus no longer. Therefore, if any one is in Christ, he is a new creation; the old has passed away, behold, the new has come.

2 Corinthians 5.16-17.

The humanist wants man to believe in man himself, in his abilities and potentialities.

Monica Furlong, *With Love to the Church*, Hodder & Stoughton Ltd., 1965, p.11.

But while ancient apologetics was confronted with a humanism that was pagan in substance, the distinctive factor in modern apologetics is its confrontation with a humanism that is Christian in substance.

Paul Tillich, *On the Boundary*, William Collins Sons & Co. Ltd., 1967, p.61.

"Humanism" is perhaps too "whole-hearted" for the use of philosophers, who are a bloodless breed; but, save for that objection, one might back it, for it expresses the essence of the new way of thought, which is, that it is impossible to strip the human element out from even our most abstract theorizing.

William James, *Collected Essays and Reviews*, Longmans, Green & Co. Ltd., 1920, p.450.

Humanism has come to mean a reverence for man and a concern for his dignity, morality, and happiness linked with a belief that these ends are best served by the advance of the scientific outlook and by the demise of religion, since religion thwarts the scientific outlook and distracts man from his effectiveness in this world by an irrelevant preoccupation with another.

Michael Ramsey, *Canterbury Pilgrim*, SPCK, 1974, p.45.

The difficulty comes from this, that Christianity (Christian orthodoxy) is exclusive and that belief in *its* truth excludes belief in any other truth. It does not absorb; it repulses.

And humanism, on the contrary, or whatever other name you give it, tends to understand and absorb all forms of life, to explain to itself if not assimilate all beliefs, even those that repulse it, even those that deny it, even the Christian belief.

André Gide, *The Journals of André Gide*, 1926, translated by Justin O'Brien, Martin Secker & Warburg Ltd., 1947, Volume II, p.380.

Humanism . . . commonly connotes wide human interests, a rich and genial appreciation of human nature and its manifold works, and the fascinating lights and shadows of character. It means to love people more than theories; to enjoy the rich movement and colour of the ever-moving drama of human life; to be sensitive to all true forms of value, to discriminate the real from the counterfeit; to practise historical imagination, in a word, to be truly educated.

F.R. Barry, *The Relevance of Christianity*, James Nisbet & Co. Ltd., 1932, p.115.

Humanism costs so much less, the more it is directed to all mankind and the less it is open to the approach of the individual man with his needs. It is easier to plead for peace in the Far East than for peace in one's own family or in one's own sphere of influence. The humane European can more easily identify with the Negroes in North America and in South Africa than with immigrant workers in his own country. The more distant our fellow men, the easier it is to profess our love in words.

Hans Küng, *On Being a Christian*, translated by Edward Quinn, William Collins Sons & Co. Ltd., 1977, p.256.

On to the Young Humanists... I enjoyed myself thoroughly in their company. My topic was Christian and Humanist approaches to penal reform. Both groups believe in what Christians call the duty to one's neighbour, Humanists without the support of a belief in a deity. On the ethical side Christians have sin, forgiveness and the infinite worth of an immortal soul. What about the Humanists? Answer, nothing very coherent. But at the end of the evening the right words came to me for my adieu: "If you can't believe in God, humanism is the next best thing." Everyone went away happy, assuring me that they and I were equally attached to the individual human person.

Lord Longford, *Diary of a Year*, George Weidenfeld & Nicolson Ltd., 1982, p.13.

We require a religion which is both scientific and humanistic. Religion, science, and humanism were sisters in ancient India; they were allies in Greece. They must combine to-day if we are to attract all those who are equally indifferent to organized religion and atheism, to supernaturalism and nihilism. We need a spiritual home, where we can live without surrendering the rights of reason or the needs of humanity. Reverence for truth is a moral value. It is dearer than Buddha or Jesus. Truth is opposed, not to reason or the Greek spirit, but to dogma and fossilized tradition. We cannot rest the case of religion any more on dogmatic supernaturalism.

Sir Sarvepalli Radhakrishnan, *Eastern Religions and Western Thought*, Oxford University Press, 1940, p.294.

The four ends of life point to the different sides of human nature, the instinctive and the emotional, the economic, the intellectual and the ethical, and the spiritual. There is implanted in man's fundamental being a spiritual capacity. He becomes completely human only when his sensibility to spirit is awakened. So long as man's life is limited to science and art, technical invention, and social programmes, he is incomplete and not truly human. If we are insolent and base, unfair and unkind to one another, unhappy in personal relationships, and lacking in mutual understanding, it is because we remain too much on the surface of life and have lost contact with the depths. When the fountains of spirit from which creative life of the individual and society is fed dry up, diseases of every description, intellectual, moral, and social, break out. The everlasting vagrancy of thought, the contemporary muddle of conflicting philosophies, the rival ideologies which cut through natural frontiers and geographical divisions, are a sign of spiritual homelessness. The unrest is in a sense sacred, for it is the confession of the failure of a self-sufficient humanism with no outlook beyond the world. We cannot find peace on earth through economic planning or political arrangement. Only the pure in heart by fostering the mystical accord of minds can establish justice and love. Man's true and essential greatness is individual. The scriptures could point out the road but each man must travel it for himself.

Sir Sarvepalli Radhakrishnan, *Eastern Religions and Western Thought*, Oxford University Press, 1940, p.354.

In the broadest sense, the term includes any philosophy or teaching which emphasizes the worth and dignity of human beings, seeks the welfare of the human race and rejoices in human achievements. It might seem that any human being would be committed to such attitudes, just in virtue of being human. But this is not so, and the human race has often been denigrated, sometimes by religious teachings which contrast human sinfulness with the divine goodness, and sometimes by secular world-views which see man as a mere accident or even misfortune in the cosmos...

But the more typical humanism eschews even the appearance of being a religion. It claims that its values such as love are purely human values and need no religious support. There are various forms of humanism. Scientific humanism seeks to found its values on science, while for existentialist humanism, the chief value is freedom, and God is seen as an obstacle to the exercise of such freedom. But not all humanists are anti-Christian, and perhaps increasingly humanists are stressing the affirmative elements in their position and recognizing that on matters like the quest for peace and opposition to tyranny they should co-operate with Christians and others.

John Macquarrie, in *A New Dictionary of Christian Theology*, edited by Alan Richardson and John Bowden, SCM Press Ltd., 1985, p.272.

There is a real Christian form of Humanism which sings its way through the New Testament, especially the Epistle to the Ephesians. It offers all that romanticism stands for—the ample vista of Man's potentialities, a far-flung reach and range of aspirations, a claim on life that has scarcely any limit to it—but all sustained, disciplined and fructified by a burning conviction about God and the vision of His transcendent love and holiness. This is the "humanism" of the Gospel...

We find it there in individual lives—vital interest in all that is interesting, gladness in all the good things of life, a reverence for and trust in human nature, hallowed and controlled at the core of selfhood by faith, hope, love and consecration enkindled by the vision of God in Christ. This is a faith which is built on foundations. Christianity, when it is true to its own genius, is able to believe in Man recklessly, despite all that saddens and discourages, because it has seen the vision of God, the eternal source of all worth and wonder—lifting us up to become sons of God.

That is the spring of all creative effort, sureness of touch and mastery in life. On the whole and in the long run those men and women have been most effective in changing and remodelling the present world, who have realized that goodness, in whatever form, is not in the end something that we produce, but something that claims us and is imparted to us by the eternal and unchanging Goodness. The vision of God is the spring of moral fruitfulness. The source of all creative conviction is the vision of One who is "Faithful and True", unchanged in underived perfection. The real lesson of the present age is not that faith in a living God is absolute, but rather that we have made too small a claim on the glory and majesty of the Lord. The irreligiousness of our contemporaries is in fact a standing rebuke to the poverty of the Church's thought of God.

F.R. Barry, *The Relevance of Christianity*, James Nisbet & Co. Ltd., 1932, p.130.

HUMILITY

"Humility"— "the faculty of being humble, or having a lowly opinion of oneself; meekness, lowliness, humbleness; the opposite of pride or haughtiness."

I was in my last year at Theological College. The Church of England at the time was at a low ebb, and we were making the mistake of being hyperactive, in an attempt to get things moving. We rushed here, there and everywhere, and got nowhere. Exhaustion set in. The future looked bleak and gloomy.

We had a short visit from a black South African priest. He spoke very little and there was no trace at all of him being in a rush. On the contrary he was very relaxed. A quiet warm confidence emanated from him. It was as if he had allowed his ego to be dissolved in order to make way for the love of God to work through him. I can remember looking at him and thinking "phew—he's got the grace of God in him— one need no longer doubt the reality of God—the evidence is there, right in front of me." At the sight of him I was able to relax and be reassured. It was a pleasure to be in his company.

I'm sure he had no idea of the power and influence that was radiating from him. In those few days we got an insight into true humility. Here was a simple human being, who had decided to let go, in order to make room for the love of God. Through him we were able to get a glimpse of the glory of God in action.

He leads the humble in what is right and teaches the humble his way.

Psalm 25.9.

For thus says the high and lofty One who inhabits eternity, whose name is Holy: "I dwell in the high and holy place, and also with him who is of a contrite and humble spirit."

Isaiah 57.15.

Unless you turn and become like children, you will never enter the kingdom of heaven. Whoever humbles himself like this child, he is the greatest in the kingdom of heaven.

Matthew 18.3-4.

Clothe yourselves, all of you, with humility toward one another, for "God opposes the proud, but gives grace to the humble." Humble yourselves therefore under the mighty hand of God, that in due time he may exalt you.

1 Peter 5.5-6.

An humble able man is a jewel worth a kingdom.

William Penn, *Fruits of Solitude*, A.W. Bennett, 1863, p.92.

Humility... is the ground-work of Christian virtues.

Charlotte Brontë, *Jane Eyre*, Clarendon Press, 1969, p.514.

All paths open up before me because I walk in humility.

Johann Wolfgang von Goethe, *Wisdom and Experience*, selected by Ludwig Curtius, translated and edited by Hermann J. Weigand, Routledge & Kegan Paul, 1949, p.189.

The Churches must learn humility as well as teach it.

George Bernard Shaw, *The Complete Bernard Shaw Prefaces*, Paul Hamlyn, 1965, *St Joan*, p.622.

The humble man, because he sees himself as nothing, can see other things as they are.

Iris Murdoch, *The Sovereignty of Good*, Routledge & Kegan Paul, 1970, p.103.

In itself, humility is nothing else but a true knowledge and awareness of oneself as one really is.

The Cloud of Unknowing, translated by Clifton Wolters, Penguin Books Ltd., 1971, p.70.

The surest sign that we have received a spiritual understanding of God's love for us is the appreciation of our own poverty in the light of his infinite mercy.

Thomas Merton, *Thoughts in Solitude*, Burns & Oates Ltd., 1958, p.32.

The humble are not those who are most troubled by their own defects and dwell upon them. True humility is begotten by the worship of superiority, and chiefly by the worship of God.

Mark Rutherford, *Last Pages From a Journal*, Oxford University Press, 1915, p.301.

Humility is a head-on quality—not a dragging, miserable, mean feeling. It is not mortified pride. It is one of the noblest and one of the most resplendent of all the experiences of the soul.

Henry Ward Beecher, *Proverbs from Plymouth Pulpit*, Charles Burnet & Co., 1887, p.175.

Now I find hidden somewhere away in my nature something that tells me that nothing in the whole world is meaningless, and suffering least of all. That something hidden away in my nature, like a treasure in a field, is Humility.

Oscar Wilde, *The Works of Oscar Wilde*, William Collins Sons & Co. Ltd., 1948, *De Profundis*, p.858.

I shall recommend humility to you, as highly proper to be made the constant subject of your devotions... earnestly desiring you to think no day safe, or likely to end well, in which you have not... called upon God to carry you through the day, in the exercise of a meek and lowly spirit.

William Law, *A Serious Call to a Devout and Holy Life*, J.M. Dent & Sons Ltd., 1898, p.245.

> Thrice happy they who sleep in humble life,
> Beneath the storm Ambition blows. 'Tis meet
> The great should have the fame of happiness,
> The consolation of a little envy,
> 'Tis all their pay for those superior cares,
> Those pangs of heart, their vassals ne'er can feel.

Edward Young, *The Complete Works of Edward Young*, William Tegg, 1854, Volume II, *The Brothers*, Act I. sc.i, p.255.

I believe the first test of a truly great man is his humility. I do not mean, by humility, doubt of his own power, or hesitation in speaking his opinions; but a right understanding of the relation between what *he* can do and say and the rest of the world's sayings and doings. All the great men not only know their business, but usually know that they know it; and are not only right in their main opinions, but usually know that they are right in them; only, they do not think much of themselves on that account.

John Ruskin, *Modern Painters*, George Allen & Sons, 1910, Volume III, p.276.

This virtue is so essential to the right state of our souls, that there is no pretending to a reasonable or pious life without it. We may as well think to see without eyes, or live without breath, as to live in the spirit of religion without the spirit of humility.

And although it is thus the soul and essence of all religious duties, yet is it, generally speaking, the least understood, the least regarded, the least intended, the least desired and sought after, of all other virtues, amongst all sorts of Christians.

William Law, *A Serious Call to a Devout and Holy Life,* J.M. Dent & Sons Ltd., 1898, p.245.

Humility is the recognition on your part and mine of our mind and spirit's need of God. Humility is the spirit of courage that looks squarely at the facts of being—at the wonder and perfection of our bodies, for example, but at the animal pull downwards that is in every body, of yours and mine as well, so that man or woman cries out, "I cannot handle this body of mine, O God, unless Thou show me how." Humility is the greatness of thought that dares to step down from the pedestal of half-knowledge and to say, "My Father, I walk in a world where beauty is and song and many a joy; where mystery halts my thought and sorrow keeps her court, I cannot walk safely unless Thou hold my hand and guide my feet."

Alistair Maclean, *The Happy Finder,* Allenson and Co. Ltd., 1949, p.13.

It is almost impossible to overestimate the value of true humility and its power in the spiritual life. For the beginning of humility and consummation of humility is the perfection of all joy. Humility contains in itself the answer to all the great problems of the life of the soul. It is the only key to faith, with which the spiritual life begins: for faith and humility are inseparable. In perfect humility all selfishness disappears and your soul no longer lives for itself: and it is lost and submerged in God and transformed into Him.

At this point of the spiritual life humility meets the highest exaltation of greatness. It is here that every one who humbles himself is exalted because, living no longer for himself or on the human level, the spirit is delivered of all the limitations and vicissitudes of creaturehood and of contingency, and swims in the attributes of God, whose power, magnificence, greatness and eternity have, through love, through humility, become our own.

Thomas Merton, *New Seeds of Contemplation,* Burns & Oates Ltd., 1962, p.140.

Humility is not self-abnegation; it is self-affirmation made possible by the calling and power of Christians to be the light of the world and the salt of the earth. This work cannot be done by the habitually self-centred even if they are concerned with fulfilling a wish to be humble. The humble man loses his self-centredness by his habitual attempts to proclaim the gospel with his whole being. In essence, humility is exposing oneself by a wholehearted attempt to express deep feelings and beliefs in a manner neither uncontrolled nor self-conscious. This is what the apostle means when he says " . . . we have the mind of Christ" (1 Cor. 2.16).

One of the most familiar Christian images of humility is found in Phil. 2: "Have this mind among yourselves, which you have in Christ Jesus, who, though he was in the form of God, did not count equality with God a thing to be grasped, but emptied himself, taking the form of a servant, being born in the likeness of men. And being found in human form he humbled himself and became obedient unto death, even death on a cross."

In the medieval attempt to describe the good life by use of the table of the seven virtues humility is omitted. The omission may presuppose either that the practice of the seven virtues makes for humility or that only the humble man could practise them.

In the second half of the twentieth century people tend to explain the good life in terms of human relationships and would think of humility in that context. The humble would be described as neither boastful nor domineering, not given to self-display, always prepared to do well what he can do well and, as occasion demands, to attempt what he cannot do well. If an official of an institution he will think more of the work pertaining to his office than of his own importance as an official.

No man can make himself humble by acts of will; continued attempts to do so produce a condition which is not humility. Others cannot make him humble though they may humiliate him, and yet humiliation is part of the raw material out of which humility is so mysteriously made. There is no single activity which could be called being humble; it is rather a quality which flavours what a man does. Humility is given to men obliquely; it is, as it were, a by-product of the Christian style of living. This style is made through the consistent attempt to love God, neighbour and self in thought, word and deed—aware that each individual is at the same time first, a creature limited in knowledge and power; secondly, a being made in the image of God, capable of a relationship with God; thirdly, a sinner in constant need of repentance.

R.E.C. Browne, in *A Dictionary of Christian Ethics*, edited by John Macquarrie, SCM Press Ltd., 1967, p.159.

HUMOUR

"Humour"—"the faculty of perceiving what is ludicrous or amusing, or of expressing it."

H umour is one of the most valuable gifts we possess. I recall a time of hospital visiting. I was asked to cover a ward, not normally on my rota. It was an orthopaedic ward, notorious for its long-stay patients.

At the far end of the ward were two "ton-up" lads in traction. Their attitude suggested they had been strung up for several weeks and were more than familiar with the routine of the ward. As I approached I noticed one of them wink at the other and knew they would be up to something. Sure enough, when I got to their bed-side, one of them ostentatiously whipped out a bottle of Newcastle brown, effortlessly flicked off the top, and poured out the contents into two glasses. They were going to show the Reverend how they could "drink" in the ward. Keeping a dead-pan face, and not allowing the froth to settle, I quickly took a glass and quietly said "Thank you very much" and promptly put the glass to my lips. They were absolutely horrified. I then gave them a wicked grin, leered at them, and passed on the glass to the mate. They roared with laughter, and from then I could do no wrong as far as they were concerned. Humour had broken down a barrier, and opened the way to friendship.

God has made laughter for me.
Genesis 21.6.

He will yet fill your mouth with laughter, and your lips with shouting.
Job 8.21.

He who sits in the heavens laughs; the Lord has them in derision.
Psalm 2.4.

For everything there is a season, and a time for every matter under heaven... a time to weep, and a time to laugh.

Ecclesiastes 3.1,4.

Big heads have little wit.

French Proverb.

Humour, thy laugh is divine.

Herman Melville, *Mardi*, The New American Library of Literature, Inc., 1964, p.510.

A laugh is the wisest, easiest answer to all that's queer; and come what will, one comfort's always left.

Herman Melville, *Moby Dick*, Penguin Books Ltd., 1978, p.268.

Blessed is he who has a sense of the humourous. He has that which is worth more than money.

Henry Ward Beecher, *Proverbs from Plymouth Pulpit*, Charles Burnet & Co., 1887, p.186.

One horse-laugh is worth ten thousand syllogisms. It is not only more effective; it is also vastly more intelligent.

H.L. Mencken, *Prejudices: Fourth Series*, Jonathan Cape Ltd., 1925, p.140.

Mirth resting on earnestness and sadness, as the rainbow on black tempest: only a right valiant heart is capable of that.

Thomas Carlyle, *Sartor Resartus, Heroes and Hero-Worship, and Past and Present*, Ward Lock, 1841, *On Heroes, Hero-Worship, and the Heroic in History*, p.28.

Among those whom I like or admire, I can find no common denominator, but among those whom I love, I can: all of them make me laugh.

W.H. Auden, *The Dyer's Hand and Other Essays*, Faber & Faber Ltd., 1975, p.372.

Wit makes its own welcome, and levels all distinctions. No dignity, no learning, no force of character, can make any stand against good wit.

Ralph Waldo Emerson, *The Works of Ralph Waldo Emerson*, edited by George Sampson, George Bell & Sons Ltd., 1906, Volume III, *Society and Social Aims, Addresses, The Comic*, p.266.

What monstrous absurdities and paradoxes have resisted whole batteries of serious arguments, and then crumbled swiftly into the dust before the ringing death-knell of a laugh!

Agnes Repplier, *Points of View*, Gay and Bird, 1893, p.28.

True Wit, I believe, may be defin'd a Justness of Thought, and a Facility of Expression or: (in the Midwives phrase) a perfect Conception with an easy Delivery.

Alexander Pope, *Correspondence of Alexander Pope*, edited by George Sherburn, Clarendon Press, 1956, Volume 1, *Letter to William Wycherley*, 26 December 1704, p.2.

A sense of humour keen enough to show a man his own absurdities, as well as those of other people, will keep him from the commission of all sins, or nearly all, save those that are worth committing.

Samuel Butler, in *The Note-Books of Samuel Butler*, A.C. Fifield, 1912, p.11.

I may perhaps be wrong, but it seems to me that a man's character may be recognized by his mere laugh. If you know a man whose laugh inspires you with sympathy, be assured he is an honest man.

Fyodor Dostoyevsky, *The House of the Dead*, translated by H. Sutherland Edwards, J.M. Dent & Sons Ltd., 1962, p.39.

The sense of humour is, in many respects, a more adequate resource for the incongruities of life, than the spirit of philosophy. If we are able to laugh at the curious quirks of fortune in which the system of order and meaning which each life constructs within and around itself is invaded, we do not at least make the mistake of prematurely reducing the irrational to a nice system.

Reinhold Niebuhr, *Discerning the Signs of the Times*, SCM Press Ltd., 1946, p.110.

The essence of humour is sensibility; warm, tender fellow-feeling with all forms of existence... True humour springs not more from the head than from the heart; it is not contempt, its essence is love; it issues not in laughter, but in still smiles, which lie far deeper. It is a sort of inverse sublimity; exalting, as it were, into our affections what is below us, while sublimity draws down into our affections what is above us.

Thomas Carlyle, *Critical and Miscellaneous Essays*, Chapman and Hall, 1899, Volume 1, *Jean Paul Friedrich Richter*, Edinburgh Review, June 1827, p.16.

Our Lord is with us in all our troubles and always gives us sufficient help to carry us through.

Smile and even laugh at yourself when you feel all this inner hubbub going on. It is the childish language of nature; plaintiff, fearful, unreasonable; we always have it with us. It is a splendid habit to laugh inwardly at yourself. It is the best way of regaining your good humour and of finding God without further anxiety.

Abbé de Tourville, *Letters of Direction*, translated by Lucy Menzies, Mowbray, 1982, p.92.

Laughter is a sane and healthful response to the innocent foibles of men; and even to some which are not innocent. All men betray moods and affectations, conceits and idiosyncrasies which could become the source of great annoyance to us if we took them too seriously. It is better to laugh at them. A sense of humour is indispensable to men of affairs who have the duty of organizing their fellow men in common endeavours. It reduces the frictions of life and makes the foibles of men tolerable.

Reinhold Niebuhr, *Discerning the Signs of the Times*, SCM Press Ltd., 1946, p.102.

Holiness is close to, but not quite the same as, a return to innocence and to the life of spontaneous impulse... For holiness is the life of spontaneity and self-abandon-ment *with humour*, which includes the wisdom of serpents as well as the gentleness of doves, because humour is nothing other than perfect self-awareness. It is the delighted recognition of one's own absurdity, and a loving cynicism with regard to one's pretentions. A person who has learned to be *fully* self-aware can safely return to living by impulse. Humour is the transformation of anxiety into laughter: the same trembling, but with a different meaning. Holy humour is the discovery of the ultimate joke on oneself.

Alan Watts, *Beyond Theology*, Hodder & Stoughton Ltd., 1966, p.97.

I am afraid that all this may sound rather frivolous and out of place in face of the great issues of life and death. But surely one reason why a kindly Providence gave us a sense of humour is that it may relieve tension when it threatens to overwhelm us. One morning I came upon a sentence in a most solemn letter of condolence. I read it, and read it again with unbelieving eyes. Then I exploded into gusts of laughter. I had not felt less like laughing in my life, but tears and laughter are often not far apart. Wild horses would not drag that wonderful sentence out of me, nor make me reveal its author. But it did me a power of good! I hope that, whatever else may fail, a sense of humour will remain to the end.

Leslie J. Tizard, *Facing Life and Death*, George Allen & Unwin Publishers Ltd., 1959, p.138.

A sense of humour leads you to take pleasure in the discrepancies of human nature; it leads you to mistrust great professions and look for the unworthy motive that they conceal; the disparity between appearance and reality diverts you and you are apt when you cannot find it to create it. You tend to close your eyes to truth, beauty and goodness because they give no scope to your sense of the ridiculous. The humorist has a quick eye for the humbug; he does not always recognize the saint. But if to see men one-sidedly is a heavy price to pay for a sense of humour there is a compensation that has a value too. You are not angry with people when you laugh at them. Humour teaches tolerance, and the humorist, with a smile and perhaps a sigh, is more likely to shrug his shoulders than to condemn. He does not moralize, he is content to understand; and it is true that to understand is to pity and forgive.

W. Somerset Maugham, *The Summing Up*, William Heinemann Ltd., 1938, p.68.

We need laughter, just as we need love. Were we entirely rational, without any hang-ups, neuroses or tensions, then we would need neither. Laughter is like the pearl which the oyster forms around the speck of irritation. The entirely healthy oyster produces no pearls, and the inhabitants of Utopia (like Jesus) do not laugh. Laughter exists in an imperfect world, and it makes us rejoice that it *is* imperfect. Sydney Smith, who was right about so many things, was right about this.

"Man could direct his ways by plain reason, and support his life by tasteless food; but God has given us wit, and flavour, and brightness, and laughter, and perfumes, to enliven the days of man's pilgrimage, and to 'charm his pained steps over the burning marle'."

Richard Boston, *An Anatomy of Laughter*, William Collins Sons & Co. Ltd., 1974, p.239.

But it does not seem to have occurred to most Christians that the means of grace might include trickery—that in his care of souls the Lord might use placebos, jokes, shocks, deceptions, and all kinds of indirect and surprising methods of outwitting men's wonderfully defended egocentricity...

But, alas, the Lord is supposed to be totally devoid of wit or humour. His official utterances, the holy scriptures, are understood as if they were strictly Solemn Pronouncements—not, perhaps, to be taken quite literally, but certainly as bereft of any lightness of touch, innuendo, irony, exaggeration, self-caricature, leg-pulling, drollery, or merriment. Yet what if this show of solemnity is actually a sort of dead-pan expression? If the Lord is said to veil his glory, lest it be too bright for mortal eyes, might he not also veil his mirth—perhaps as something much, much too funny for men to stand?

Alan Watts, *Beyond Theology*, Hodder & Stoughton Ltd., 1966, p.55.

I discovered in myself a sense of humour, that extraordinary and blessed weapon which makes it possible to take the sting out of reality just when it is preparing to strike. All along my road, humour offered me a constant protection; behind its armour, I felt invincible and secure; it has been a heartening companion, a source of strength, helping me to endure and to prevail, until it has become a living presence, almost a deity, a miracle that has never failed to work. To humour I owe my only genuine triumphs over adversity. No one has ever succeeded in wrenching that weapon from me, and I am the more willing to turn it against myself since, behind the disguise of the "I" and the "me" at which I thus strike out, it is really with the very essence of our human condition that I am at odds. Humour is an affirmation of dignity, a declaration of man's superiority to all that befalls him.

Romain Gary, Promise at Dawn, Michael Joseph Ltd., 1962, p.109.

The sense of humour is even more important provisionally in dealing with our own sins than in dealing with the sins of others. Humour is a proof of the capacity of the self to gain a vantage point from which it is able to look at itself. The sense of humour is thus a by-product of self-transcendence. People with a sense of humour do not take themselves too seriously. They are able to "stand off" from themselves, see themselves in perspective and recognize the ludicrous and absurd aspects of their pretensions. All of us ought to be ready to laugh at ourselves because all of us are a little funny in our foibles, conceits and pretensions. What is funny about us is precisely that we take ourselves too seriously.

We are rather insignificant little bundles of energy and vitality in a vast organization of life. But we pretend that we are the very centre of this organization. This pretension is ludicrous; and its absurdity increases with our lack of awareness of it. The less we are able to laugh at ourselves the more it becomes necessary and inevitable that others laugh at us.

Reinhold Niebuhr, Discerning the Signs of the Times, SCM Press Ltd., 1946, p.106.

JEALOUSY

*"Jealousy"—"the state of mind arising from the suspicion,
apprehension, or knowledge of rivalry."*

I remember one of our Reflection Groups. There was just one person in it, an undergraduate in his third year. Having carefully looked through the list of topics, he chose "Jealousy".

We spent the first half hour looking through the material in silence, each of us working out what we thought and felt about jealousy. When we got to the start of the second half hour—the discussion part—I asked him if there was any particular reason for choosing this topic? He looked bashful for a moment and replied, "Yes. I have a girlfriend in another university, and I'm jealous of her. You see, she's very attractive and I'm afraid of rivals. We've actually talked about it but I'm still jealous. She is also jealous of me, fearful of possible rivals from the women in College. So we're both jealous, and it's wrecking our relationship."

I asked him if he'd found anything helpful in the quotations and we went on to discuss ways and means of dealing with jealousy. He ended by asking if he could possible have a copy of the material, as he wanted to use them for a Reflection Group with his girlfriend. I don't know what the outcome was, but I hoped it helped to develop their relationship. In my own experience, I have found jealousy very difficult to cope with.

For jealousy makes a man furious, and he will not spare when he takes revenge. He will accept no compensation, nor be appeased though you multiply gifts.
Proverbs 6.34-35.

Jealousy is cruel as the grave. Its flashes are flashes of fire, a most vehement flame.
Song of Solomon 8.6.

Love is patient and kind; love is not jealous or boastful.
1 Corinthians 13.4.

But if you have bitter jealousy and selfish ambition in your hearts, do not boast and be false to the truth. This wisdom is not such as comes down from above, but is earthly, unspiritual, devilish. For where jealousy and selfish ambition exist, there will be disorder and every vile practice.
James 3.14-16.

It is not love that is blind, but jealousy.
Laurence Durrell, *Justine*, Faber & Faber Ltd., 1957, p.151.

The jealous are troublesome to others, but a torment to themselves.

William Penn, *Fruits of Solitude*, A.W. Bennett, 1863, Part II, No.190.

Anger and jealousy can no more bear to lose sight of their objects than love.

George Eliot, *The Mill on the Floss*, Virtue & Co., 1908, Volume 1, p.153.

O, beware, my lord, of jealousy;
It is the green-ey'd monster which doth mock
The meat it feeds on.

William Shakespeare, *Othello*, Act III. sc.iii. l.169.

There is a sort of jealousy which needs very little fire; it is hardly a passion, but a blight bred in the cloudy, damp despondency of uneasy egoism.

George Eliot, *Middlemarch*, J.M. Dent & Sons Ltd., 1959, Volume 1, p.186.

Of all the passions, jealousy is that which exacts the hardest service, and pays the bitterest wages. Its service is—to watch the *success* of our enemy; its wages—to be *sure* of it.

Charles Caleb Colton, *Lacon*, William Tegg, 1866, p.168.

All jealousy
Must still be strangled in its birth, or time
Will soon conspire to make it strong enough
To overcome the truth.

Sir William Davanant, *The Dramatic Works of Sir William Davanant*, Sotheran & Co., 1932, Volume the First, *The Cruel Brother*, p.170.

I don't know anything so entirely *flattening* and disconcerting as the consciousness of malevolence and personal jealousy. It can't be conciliated—indeed, it generally has something *insane* about it!

A.C. Benson, *Extracts from the Letters of Dr. A.C. Benson to M.E.A.*, Jarrold Publishing, 1927, p.10.

That it is Jealousy's peculiar nature
To swell small things to great; nay, out of nought
To conjure much; and then to lose its reason
Amid the hideous phantoms it has form'd.

Edward Young, *Young's Complete Poems*, William Tegg, 1854, Volume II, *The Revenge*, Act III, p.220.

But jealous souls will not be answer'd so;
They are not ever jealous for the cause,
But jealous for they are jealous. 'Tis a monster
Begot upon it self, born on it self.

William Shakespeare, *Othello*, Act III. sc.iv. l.159.

Love may exist without jealousy, although this is rare; but jealousy may exist without love, and this is common; for jealousy can feed on that which is bitter, no less than on that which is sweet, and is sustained by pride as often as by affection.

Charles Caleb Colton, *Lacon*, William Tegg, 1866, p.197.

Ten thousand fears
Invented wild, ten thousand frantic views
Of horrid rivals hanging on the charms
For which he melts in fondness, eat him up
With fervent anguish and consuming rage.

James Thomson, *Poetical Works*, edited by J. Logie Robertson, Oxford University Press, 1965, *Spring*, l.1092, p.44.

Foul Jealousy, thou turnest love divine
To joyless dread, and mak'st the loving heart
With hateful thoughts to languish and to pine;
And feed itself with self-consuming smart?
Of all the passions of the mind thou vilest art.

Edmund Spenser, *The Works of Edmund Spenser*, The Johns Hopkins Press, 1934, *The Faerie Queene*, Book Three, XI. i. l.5, p.154.

Oh, jealousy! thou bane of pleasing friendship,
How does thy rancour poison all our softness,
And turn our gentle nature into bitterness!
See, where she comes! once my heart's dearest blessing,
Now my chang'd eyes are blasted with her beauty,
Loath that known face, and sicken to behold her.

Nicholas Rowe, in *Dolby's British Theatre*, T. Dolby, Britannia Press, 1824, *Jane Shore*, Act III, sc.i. p.24.

Jealousy is a terrible thing. It resembles love, only it is precisely love's contrary. Instead of wishing for the welfare of the object loved, it desires the dependence of that object upon itself, and its own triumph. Love is the forgetfulness of self; jealousy is the most passionate form of egotism, the glorification of a despotic, exacting, and vain *ego*, which can neither forget nor subordinate itself. The contrast is perfect.

Henri Frédéric Amiel, *Amiel's Journal*, translated by Mrs. Humphry Ward, Macmillan Publishers Ltd., 1918, p.284.

Jealousy is the dragon in paradise; the hell of heaven; and the most bitter of the emotions because associated with the sweetest. There is a specific against jealousy, namely conscious love; but this remedy is harder to find than the disease is to endure. But there are palliatives of which the first therapeutic condition is the recognition of the disease and the second the wish to cure oneself. In these circumstances let the sufferer deliberately experiment. Much may be forgiven him or her during this process. He may, for instance, try to forward the new plans of his former beloved—but this is difficult without obvious hypocrisy. Or he may plunge into new society. Or he may engage himself in a new work that demands all his energy. Or he may cast a spell on his memory and regard his former beloved as dead; or as having become enchanted. Best, however, if he "let go" completely with no lingering hope of ever meeting her again.

Be comforted. Our life is but one day of our Life. If not today, tomorrow! Let go!

A.R. Orage, *On Love*, The Janus Press, 1957, p.19.

The second of the Ten Commandments (Ex.20.5) describes God as being a jealous God; that is, not tolerating people who find satisfaction in relationship with any being other than himself. Christian revelation has broken up this primitive conception of God as jealous and vengeful.

People do not decide to behave jealously, they drift into such behaviour with little or no conscious knowledge of what is happening until they find themselves imprisoned. The detection of jealousy is usually difficult because it is often born of the warmth of a generous love—thus parents in their protective love for their children will try to limit their companionships, thereby robbing them of their human birthright of independence and ability to develop freely. Jealousy in an engaged couple is a sign of danger, in marriage a sign of disaster because jealousy breeds suspicion, distrust and deception.

Churchmen, in the name of the Church, are often jealous of social institutions because of the amount of time given by church members to them and the place and power they hold in society. To alter St. Paul's words, the institutions that be are ordained of God, to be accepted, loved and criticized but never to be ignored, destroyed or regarded as permanent.

There is no simple cure for jealousy, no sure way of stopping it at its first sign. Its absence is a tribute to a loving disposition which feeds and is fed by a regard for the individuality of each person and a sense of responsibility for his, or her, full human development which requires a width of relationship far beyond a limited companionship. The masters of spirituality continually remind us, century by century, of the beauty of ordinate affection where people share a love of God, which is greater than their love for one another.

R.E.C. Browne, in *A Dictionary of Christian Ethics*, edited by John Macquarrie, SCM Press Ltd., 1967, p.115.

JOY

"Joy"—"pleasurable emotion due to well-being or satisfaction; the feeling or state of being highly pleased; exultation of spirit, gladness, delight."

N atural things such as the sea, mountains, dawns and sunsets, have always been a great source of joy to me. I have just been reminded of this after three weeks in the French Alps. In my youth I was a very keen sportsman, and playing rugby, hockey and cricket was another source of joy. As a member of a team engaged in a common endeavour I've experienced companionship and friendship—and this has led to a great deal of joy in human relationships. Music has also been another important source of joy—particularly singing in choirs.

C.S. Lewis, in his book *Surprised by Joy*, opened my eyes to another source of joy—namely something to be found in the depths of our being. This really came alive to me on reading the book *The Choice is Always Ours* by Dorothy Berkley Phillips. Through this book I came to see that "Joy" is one of the fruits of the Spirit, and a part of our inheritance, when life is lived in supernatural regard.

I now believe the main source of joy is to be found in the depths of ourselves. Here we can discover an enormous resource of life—"a pearl of great price"—that can be enjoyed at first hand. This can be experienced in a wide variety of ways, for instance, an awareness of a "Presence"—or as a feeling of oneness, harmony or wholeness. Sometimes there can be an ecstatic element in all this, and a feeling that you simply want to burst with joy.

For the joy of the Lord is your strength.

Nehemiah 8.10.

The gladness of the heart is the life of man, and the joyfulness of a man prolongeth his days.

Ecclesiasticus 30.22 (A.V.).

These things I have spoken to you, that my joy may be in you, and that your joy may be full.

John 15.11.

But now I am coming to thee; and these things I speak in the world, that they may have my joy fulfilled in themselves.

John 17.13.

Joy untouched by thankfulness is always suspect.

Theodor Haecker, *Journal in the Night*, translated by Alexander Dru, The Harvill Press Ltd., 1950, p.1.

Every joy, great or small, is akin and always a refreshment.

Johann Wolfgang von Goethe, *The Practical Wisdom of Goethe*, chosen by Emil Ludwig, Martin Secker & Warburg Ltd., 1933, *Travels in Italy*, p.26.

But the fulness of joy is in God's immediate presence.

Richard Baxter, *The Saints' Everlasting Rest*, Blackie and Son, 1817, p.16.

These little thoughts are the rustle of leaves: they have their whisper of joy in my mind.

Rabindranath Tagore, *Collected Poems & Plays of Rabindranath Tagore*, Macmillan & Co., Limited, 1936, *Stray Birds*, XV11, p.289.

The joy which a man finds in his work and which transforms the tears and sweat of it into happiness and delight—that joy is God.

H.A. Williams, C.R., *The True Wilderness*, William Collins Sons & Co. Ltd., 1983, p.111.

Joy is the sentiment that is born in a soul, conscious of the good it possesses. The good of our intelligence is truth; the more this truth is abundant and luminous, the deeper is our inward joy.

D. Columba Marmion, *Christ in His Mysteries*, Sands & Company, 1924, p.9.

Our faith is faith in what the synoptic gospels call "the Kingdom of God" and the Kingdom of God is simply God's power enthroned in our hearts. This is what makes us light of heart and it is what Christian joy is all about.

John Main, O.S.B., *Moment of Christ*, Darton, Longman & Todd Ltd., 1984, p.80.

The Christian joy and hope do not arise from an ignoring of the evil in the world, but from facing it at its worst. The light that shines for ever in the Church breaks out of the veriest pit of gloom.

William Temple, *Readings in St. John's Gospel* (First and Second Series), Macmillan Publishers Ltd., 1947, p.295.

"The fruit of the spirit is love—joy." So the opaque Christian is a slander on God. The thing which the church has been so much afraid of—joy, cheerfulness, hopefulness, gentleness, sweetness, overflowing manhood—this is one of the fruits of the Spirit. Love and joy are put first.

Henry Ward Beecher, *Proverbs from Plymouth Pulpit*, Charles Burnet & Co., 1887, p.170.

If a man has sought first and chiefly the soul's treasure—goodness, kindness, gentleness, devoutness, cheerfulness, hope, faith, and love—he will extract more joy from the poorest furniture and outfitting of life than otherwise he would get from the whole world.

Henry Ward Beecher, *Proverbs from Plymouth Pulpit*, Charles Burnet & Co., 1887, p.185.

"To be a joy-bearer and a joy-giver says everything," she wrote, "for in our life, if one is joyful, it means that one is faithfully living for God, and that *nothing else counts*; and if one gives joy to others one is doing God's work; with joy without and joy within, all is well... I can conceive no higher way."

Janet Erskine Stuart, in *Life and Letters of Janet Erskine Stuart*, Maud Monahan, Longmans, Green & Co. Ltd., 1922, p.88.

> Life, I repeat, is energy of love
> Divine or human; exercised in pain,
> In strife, in tribulation; and ordained
> If so approved and sanctified, to pass,
> Through shades and silent rest, to endless joy.

William Wordsworth, *The Excursion*, Book Fifth, l.1012.

For the final deep abiding sense of rest—in Thee;
For the touch of Thyself growing continually out of everything more actual, starlike, perfect;
And for all experience;
Joy, joy and thanks for ever.

Edward Carpenter, *Towards Democracy*, George Allen & Unwin Publishers Ltd., 1931, p.105.

At first the Lark, when she means to rejoice, to cheer herself and those that hear her; she then quits the earth, and sings as she ascends higher into the air, and having ended her heavenly employment, grows then mute, and sad, to think she must descend to the dull earth, which she could not touch, but for necessity.

Izaak Walton, *The Compleat Angler*, Macmillan & Co. Ltd., 1906, p.15.

Joy is the affect which comes when we use our powers. Joy, rather than happiness, is the goal of life, for joy is the emotion which accompanies our fulfilling our natures as human beings. It is based on the experience of one's identity as a being of worth and dignity, who is able to affirm his being, if need be, against all other beings and the whole organic world.

Rollo May, *Man's Search for Himself*, Souvenir Press Ltd., 1975, p.96.

But if a man here on earth is enlightened with the Holy Ghost from the fountain of Jesus Christ, so that the spirits of nature, which signify the Father, are kindled in him, then there ariseth such a joy in his heart, and it goeth forth into all his veins, so that the whole body trembleth, and the soulish animal spirit triumpheth, as if it were in the holy Trinity, which is understood only by those who have been its guests in that place.

Jacob Boehme, *The Aurora*, translated by John Sparrow, John M. Watkins, 1914, p.72.

A soul in commerce with her God, is heav'n;
Feels not the tumults and the shocks of life;
The whirls of passions, and the strokes of heart.
A Deity believ'd, is joy begun;
    A Deity ador'd is joy advanc'd;
    A Deity belov'd is joy matur'd.

Edward Young, *Night Thoughts*, William P. Nimmo, 1868, Night Eight, Virtue's Apology, l.710, p.216.

Christian joy is completely independent of health or circumstances. It appears in the saints when "strength and health and friends" are gone: when circumstances are not only unkind but savage; when every "comfort" is withdrawn. In all the miracles of sanctity, there is nothing more miraculous than the joy of the saint in pain and persecution.

W.E. Sangster, *The Pure in Heart*, Epworth Press, 1954, p.110.

I have learned that it was more honouring to God to see him in all things generally than to concentrate on any one thing in particular. If I were wise enough to act on this advice I should not be made glad by anything specially, nor on the other hand should I be much distressed by anything else, for "Everything will be all right." The fullness of joy is to see God in all things.

Julian of Norwich, *Revelations of Divine Love*, translated by Clifton Wolters, Penguin Books Ltd., 1976, p.114.

Joy, the Greek word is *chara*, and the characteristics of this word is that it most often describes that joy which has a basis in religion, and whose real foundation is God . . . It is not the joy that comes from earthly things or cheap triumphs; still less is it the joy that comes from triumphing over someone else in rivalry or competition. It is a joy whose basis is God.

William Barclay, *The Letters to the Galatians and Ephesians*, The Saint Andrew Press, 1958, p.55.

Joy, shipmate, joy!
(Pleas'd to my soul at death I cry,)
Our life is closed, our life begins,
The long, long anchorage we leave,
The ship is clear at last, she leaps!
She swiftly courses from the shore,
Joy, shipmate, joy.

Walt Whitman, *The Complete Poems*, edited by Francis Murphy, Penguin Books Ltd., 1982, *Joy, Shipmate, Joy!* p.510.

Mark, then, how joy springs out at once as the unfailing token of the Holy Spirit's presence, the first sign that He is having His Own way with a man's heart. The joy of the Lord, the joy that is strength, the joy that no man taketh from us, the joy wherewith we joy before God, the abundant joy of faith and hope and love and praise,—this it is that gathers like a radiant, fostering, cheerful air around the soul that yields itself to the grace of God, to do His holy, loving Will.

Francis Paget, *The Spirit of Discipline*, Longmans, Green & Co. Ltd., 1891, p.58.

Lord, "in your presence is the fullness of joy",
For "the gods whom earth holds sacred are all worthless".
The gods of status and power and success,
The images that attract our reverence and worship,
All are emptied of ultimate meaning.

On this I make my stand, though you know full well
the strength of their hold on me.
"Enlarge my boundaries."
Widen my horizons.
"Show me the path of life."
Let us dwell together so that your joy may be mine,
and my joy complete.

Rex Chapman, *A Glimpse of God*, SCM Press Ltd., 1973, p.102.

The only true joy on earth is to escape from the prison of our own false self, and enter by love into union with the Life who dwells and sings within the essence of every creature and in the core of our own souls. In His love we possess all things and enjoy fruition of them, finding Him in them all. And thus as we go about the world, everything we meet and everything we see and hear and touch, far from defiling, purifies us and plants in us something more of contemplation and of heaven.

Short of this perfection, created things do not bring us joy but pain. Until we love God perfectly, everything in the world will be able to hurt us. And the greatest misfortune is to be dead to the pain they inflict on us, and not realize what it is.

Thomas Merton, *New Seeds of Contemplation*, Burns & Oates Ltd., 1962, p.20.

Consider first, that although the kingdom of heaven abounds with all that can be imagined good and delightful, yet there is but one sovereign good, in the enjoyment of which consists the essential beatitude of heaven, and that is God himself, whom the blessed ever see as he truly is, face to face; and see him in the very centre of their own souls; and by the eternal contemplation of his infinite beauty and truth, together with all his divine attributes and attractions, they are quite ravished and set on fire with seraphic flames of eternal love. By means of this contemplation and love they are closely united by a most pure and amiable union with this sovereign and infinite good, and they eternally enjoy him. He surrounds and penetrates them on all sides with inexpressible delights; he fills their whole souls with himself, the overflowing source of all good; he gives himself to them to be their joy, their treasure, their never-ending bliss; he transforms them in manner to himself, as when brass or iron in the furnace is perfectly penetrated by fire it loseth in a manner its own nature, and becomes all flame and fire. O happy creatures! what can be wanting to complete your joys, who have within and without you the immense ocean of endless felicity?

Richard Challoner, *Meditations*, Society of SS. Peter & Paul, 1915, p.522.

KINDNESS

"Kindness"—"the quality or habit of being kind; kind feeling; affection, love."

I f someone was to ask me what has been the greatest influence in my life, I would have to say—"loving-kindness".

I have experienced it in my parents, in my sisters, in numerous friends, and in several exceptional teachers.

Kindness is one of the great qualities of the Gurkhas. As well as being fierce soldiers, they have many commendable qualities, such as loyalty, courage, truthfulness, bravery, cheerfulness, but the quality which I found most appealing in them was loving-kindness.

I have found loving-kindness in the Church, at many different levels and social settings. The Bishop who ordained me was kind-hearted and an inspiration. As I have gone along I have experienced kindness alike in clergy and lay-people, and in situations where you would least expect to find it.

Although University College, London, is a "godless" institution, as Chaplain to the College for several years, I experienced a great deal of kindness and understanding, at all levels, particularly amongst the students.

This has also been my experience in my current appointment as Chaplain/ Fellow of University College, Oxford.

For me the supreme quality coming out of the Gospels in the life of Christ is— loving-kindness.

Blessed be the Lord: for he hath shewed me his marvellous kindness.
Psalm 31.21 (A.V.).

He who pursues righteousness and kindness will find life and honour.
Proverbs 21.21.

But love your enemies, and do good, and lend, expecting nothing in return; and your reward will be great, and you will be sons of the Most High; for he is kind to the ungrateful and the selfish.
Luke 6.35.

Note then the kindness and the severity of God; severity towards those who have fallen, but God's kindness to you, provided you continue in his kindness.
Romans 11.22.

A kind word is like a Spring Day.
Russian Proverb.

Kindnesses, like grain, grow by sowing.

Proverb.

Kind hearts are more than coronets.

Alfred, Lord Tennyson, *The Complete Works of Alfred Lord Tennyson*, Macmillan Publishers Ltd., 1898, *Lady Clara Vere de Vere*, p.49.

Kindliness in judgment is nothing less than a sacred duty.

William Barclay, *The Gospel of Matthew*, The Saint Andrew Press, 1987, Volume 1, p.262.

The heart benevolent and kind
The most resembles GOD.

Robert Burns, *The Poems and Songs of Robert Burns*, edited by James Kinsley, Clarendon Press, 1968, Volume 1, *A Winter Night*, l.95, p.305.

Gentleness as the fruit of the Spirit is a strong man's treating all men with lenity, and kindness, and forbearance, and patience.

Henry Ward Beecher, *Proverbs from Plymouth Pulpit*, Charles Burnet & Co., 1887, p.154.

Kindness is the quality which lifts a man out of the ruck of ordinary men. Eloquence will be forgotten; mental cleverness may live on the printed page; but kindness lives on enthroned in the hearts of men.

William Barclay, *The Letters to Timothy, Titus & Philemon*, The Saint Andrew Press, 1987, p.216.

I have had that curiously *symbolical* and reassuring pleasure, of being entertained with overflowing and simple kindness by a family of totally unknown people—an adventure which always brings home to me the goodwill of the world.

A.C. Benson, *Extracts from the Letters of Dr. A.C. Benson to M.E.A.*, Jarrold Publishing, 1927, p.40.

True kindness presupposes the faculty of imagining as one's own the suffering and joy of others. Without imagination, there can be weakness, theoretical or practical philanthropy, but not true kindness.

André Gide, *Pretexts, Reflections on Literature and Morality*, selected by Justin O'Brien, Martin Secker & Warburg Ltd., 1960, p.313.

Not to speak of myself or my works. To be simple, true, always humble. To maintain calm and never betray distress. To be friendly and full of sympathy for men and ideas, to be sure to understand them. To be kind, with that true kindness which comes not from the lips but from the heart. To devote myself, spend myself, all without excitement or useless dispersion.

Elizabeth Leseur, *A Wife's Story—The Journal of Elizabeth Leseur*, Burns & Oates Ltd., 1919, p.107.

Let the weakest—let the humblest... remember, that in his daily course he can, if he will, shed around him almost a heaven. Kindly words, sympathizing attentions, watchfulness against wounding men's sensitiveness—these cost very little, but they are priceless in their value. Are they not... almost the staple of our daily happiness? From hour to hour, from moment to moment, we are supported, blest, by small kindnesses.

F.W. Robertson, *Sermons*, Kegan Paul, Trench, Trubner & Co. Ltd., 1897, Second Series, p.293.

And it is here that the saints serve us yet again. Kindness recovers all its apostolic quality in them. In the saint it is never sentimental: never divorced from reality: never undisciplined: never evasive. On the other hand, it is ever-present: never excluded by their concern for God's holiness: never driven away by any pride in their own virtue. The cheapening of the word in the world, and the neglect of this grace in the sanctuary, are both corrected in the saint. He reveals kindness *as a fruit of the Spirit.* He shows it grounded in the nature of God. It flows directly from his faith. It is supernatural love disclosing itself in costly affection towards his fellow-men. That is why it does not cease when it is snubbed, injured and lied about. That is why it has a robustness and pertinacity unknown to the sentimental kindness of the world...

Kindness has been described... as "a constant feeling in us about our *kind*"— a resolute recollection of our one-ness with our race as objects of the love and the mercy of God: the moving out of supernatural love to our fellow-travellers on life's hard and flinty road. Properly understood, it is a virtue of the strong. Only those equipped from heaven are able, while bearing their own burden, to thrust their shoulder under somebody else's. It calls in those able to give it—for strength of mind as well as strength of heart.

W.E. Sangster, *The Pure in Heart,* Epworth Press, 1954, p.136.

In the Gospel we often see one word: "come to me all", "he that cometh to me I will not cast out", "suffer little children to come to me". We must be always ready to receive, to forgive, to love and to make sure we understand what God means when he says, "I say to you, as long as you did it to one of these my least brethren, you did it to me". One thing will always secure heaven for us—the acts of charity and kindness with which we have filled our lives. We will never know just how much good a simple smile can do. We tell people how kind, forgiving and understanding God is but are we the living proof? Can they really see this kindness, this forgiveness, this understanding alive in us?

Be kind and merciful. Let no one ever come to you without leaving better and happier. Be the living expression of God's kindness—kindness in your face, kindness in your eyes, kindness in your smile, kindness in your warm greeting. In the slums we are the light of God's kindness to the poor. To children, to the poor, to all who suffer and are lonely, give always a happy smile. Give them not only your care but also your heart. Because of God's goodness and love every moment of our life can be the beginning of great things. Be open, ready to receive and you will find him everywhere. Every work of love brings a person face to face with God.

Mother Teresa of Calcutta, *In the Silence of the Heart,* compiled by Kathryn Spink, SPCK, 1983, p.42.

Kindness is the overflowing of self upon others. We put others in the place of self. We treat them as we would wish to be treated ourselves. We change places with them. For the time self is another, and others are self. Our self-love takes the shape of complacence in unselfishness. We cannot speak of the virtues without thinking of God. What would the overflow of self upon others be in Him the ever-blessed and Eternal? It was the act of creation. Creation was divine kindness. From it as from a fountain, flow the possibilities, the powers, the blessings of all created kindness. This is an honourable genealogy for kindness. Then, again, kindness is the coming to the rescue of others, when they need it and it is in our power to supply what they need; and this is the work of the Attributes of God towards His creatures...

Moreover kindness is also like divine grace; for it gives men something which neither self nor nature can give them. What it gives them is something of which they are in want, or something which only another person can give, such as consolation; and besides this, the manner in which this is given is a true gift itself, better far than the thing given: and what is all this but an allegory of grace? Kindness adds sweetness to everything. It is kindness which makes life's capabilities blossom, and paints them with their cheering hues, and endows them with their invigorating fragrance...

Last of all, the secret impulse out of which kindness acts is an instinct which is the noblest part of ourselves, the most undoubted remnant of the image of God, which was given us at the first. We must therefore never think of kindness as being a common growth of our nature, common in the sense of being of little value. It is the nobility of man. In all its modifications it reflects a heavenly type. It runs up into one, and it is human because it springs from the soul of man just at the point of where the divine image was graven deepest.

Such is kindness.

F.W. Faber, *Spiritual Conferences*, Thomas Richardson and Son, 1859, p.2.

In '41 Mama took me back to Moscow. There I saw our enemies for the first time. If my memory is right, nearly 20,000 German war prisoners were to be marched in a single column through the streets of Moscow.

The pavements swarmed with onlookers, cordoned off by soldiers and police.

The crowd were mostly women—Russian women with hands roughened by hard work, lips untouched by lipstick and thin hunched shoulders which had borne half the burden of the war. Every one of them must have had a father or a husband, a brother or a son killed by the Germans.

They gazed with hatred in the direction from which the column was to appear.

At last we saw it.

The generals marched at the head, massive chins stuck out, lips folded disdainfully, their whole demeanour meant to show superiority over their plebian victors.

"They smell of eau-de-cologne, the bastards," someone in the crowd said with hatred.

The women were clenching their fists. The soldiers and policemen had all they could do to hold them back.

All at once something happened to them.

They saw German soldiers, thin, unshaven, wearing dirty blood-stained bandages, hobbling on crutches or leaning on the shoulders of their comrades; the soldiers walked with their heads down.

The street became dead silent—the only sound was the shuffling of boots and the thumping of crutches.

Then I saw an elderly women in broken-down boots push herself forward and touch a policeman's shoulder, saying: "Let me through." There must have been something about her that made him step aside.

She went up to the column, took from inside her coat something wrapped in a coloured handkerchief and unfolded it. It was a crust of black bread. She pushed it awkwardly into the pocket of a soldier, so exhausted that he was tottering on his feet. And now suddenly from every side women were running towards the soldiers, pushing into their hands bread, cigarettes, whatever they had.

The soldiers were no longer enemies.

They were people.

Yevgeny Yevtushenko, *A Precocious Autobiography*, translated by Andrew R. MacAndrew, Collins Harvill, 1963, p.24.

LONELINESS

"Loneliness"—"dejected at the consciousness of being alone; having a feeling of solitariness, dreary."

L oneliness is something we all feel from time to time. I had an acute experience of it during National Service. Shortly after arriving in Singapore, following a 24-day sea journey on a troopship, I was ordered into the jungle in Malaya with my platoon. I couldn't speak a word of Gurkhali, and the Gurkhas with me knew very little English. I was a stranger in the jungle and initially found it confusing. A great wave of loneliness hit me. My orderly, sensing my predicament, tried to help by lending me his *kukri* (the Gurkha knife). By sign language he indicated snakes might come during the night, and that I ought to be prepared for them. That somehow made the sense of isolation even worse. I was reduced to abject misery.

Still, the brief visit to the jungle had its desired effect. Learning Gurkhali became the number one priority. Once verbal communication was under way, loneliness gradually disappeared.

Loneliness is a problem for most students, particularly those away from home for the first time. This material is designed to help readers overcome loneliness and equip them with ways and means of dealing with it creatively.

Even though I walk through the valley of the shadow of death, I fear no evil; for thou art with me: thy rod and thy staff, they comfort me.
Psalm 23.4.

Turn thou to me, and be gracious to me; for I am lonely and afflicted. Relieve the troubles of my heart, and bring me out of my distresses.
Psalm 25.16-17.

I will not leave you desolate; I will come to you.
John 14.18.

Yet I am not alone, for the Father is with me.
John 16.32.

The quiet and exalted thoughts
Of loneliness.
William Wordsworth, *Prelude*, Book Third, l.210.

Pray that your loneliness may spur you into finding something to live for, great enough to die for.
Dag Hammarskjöld, *Markings*, translated by W.H. Auden & Leif Sjoberg, with a foreword by W.H. Auden, Faber & Faber Ltd., 1964, p.85.

The deepest need of man... is the need to overcome his separateness, to leave the prison of his aloneness.

Erich Fromm, *The Art of Loving*, George Allen & Unwin Publishers Ltd., 1974, p.14.

When one does give one's heart over to the loneliness of God ... one does actually experience a transformation of loneliness into love.

John S. Dunne, *The Reasons of the Heart*, SCM Press Ltd., 1978, p.50.

Does not all creativity ask for a certain encounter with our loneliness, and does not the fear of this encounter severely limit our possible self-expression?

Henri J.M. Nouwen, *Reaching Out*, William Collins Sons & Co. Ltd., 1980, p.29.

Our language has wisely sensed the two sides of man's being alone. It has created the word "loneliness" to express the pain of being alone. And it has created the word "solitude" to express the glory of being alone.

Paul Tillich, *The Eternal Now*, SCM Press Ltd., 1963, p.11.

> What makes loneliness an anguish
> Is not that I have no one to share my burden,
> But this:
> I have only my own burden to bear.

Dag Hammarskjöld, *Markings*, translated by W.H. Auden & Leif Sjoberg, with a foreword by W.H. Auden, Faber & Faber Ltd., 1964, p.85.

It is true, "loneliness is not the sickness unto death", but when there is no passing over, no entering into the lives of others, then the longing in loneliness becomes something dark at work in our lives, something "evil and lonely", a nightmare of soul, a "heart of darkness".

John S. Dunne, *The Church of the Poor Devil*, SCM Press Ltd., 1983, p.18.

When loneliness is haunting me with its possibility of being a threshold instead of a dead end, a new creation instead of a grave, a meeting place instead of an abyss, then time loses its desperate clutch on me. Then I no longer have to live in a frenzy of activity, overwhelmed and afraid for the missed opportunity.

Henri J.M. Nouwen, *Reaching Out*, William Collins Sons & Co. Ltd., 1980, p.35.

I never know what people mean when they complain of loneliness.

To be alone is one of life's greatest delights, thinking one's own thoughts, doing one's own little jobs, seeing the world beyond and feeling oneself uninterrupted in the rooted connection with the centre of all things.

D.H. Lawrence, *The Complete Poems of D.H. Lawrence*, edited by Vivian de Sola Pinto and Warren Roberts, William Heinemann Ltd., 1967, Volume Two, *Loneliness*, p.610.

We are always being told that no man is an island, but are not most of us islands? Desert islands at that. Each man has his empty shore of sand, his jungle thicket, his struggle for survival. Left to himself he deals with whatever habitation there is as best he can. But the point is that if he has faith in the presence and providence of God he is not left to himself.

Hubert van Zeller, *Considerations*, Sheed & Ward Ltd., 1974, p.23.

People who complain of loneliness must have lost something,
lost some living connection with the cosmos, out of themselves,
lost their life-flow
like a plant whose roots are cut.
And they are crying like plants whose roots are cut.
But the presence of other people will not give them new-rooted connection
it will only make them forget.
The thing to do is in solitude slowly and painfully put forth new roots
into the unknown, and take roots by oneself.

D.H. Lawrence, *The Complete Poems of D.H. Lawrence*, edited by Vivian de Sola Pinto and Warren Roberts, William Heinemann Ltd., 1967, Volume Two, *The Uprooted*, p.610.

Social acceptance, "being liked", has so much power because it holds the feelings of loneliness at bay. A person is surrounded with comfortable warmth; he is merged in the group. He is reabsorbed—as though, in the extreme psychoanalytical symbol, he were to go back into the womb. He temporarily loses his loneliness; but it is at the price of giving up his existence as an identity in his own right. And he renounces the one thing which would get him constructively over the loneliness in the long run, namely the developing of his own inner resources, strength and sense of direction, and using this as a basis of meaningful relations with others.

The "stuffed men" are bound to become more lonely no matter how much they "lean together"; for hollow people do not have a base from which to learn to love.

Rollo May, *Man's Search For Himself*, Souvenir Press Ltd., 1975, p.33.

Loneliness is one of the most universal sources of human suffering today. Psychiatrists and clinical psychologists speak about it as the most frequently expressed complaint and the root not only of an increasing number of suicides but also of alcoholism, drug use, different psychosomatic symptoms—such as headaches and stomach and low-back pains—and of a large number of traffic accidents. Children, adolescents, adults, and old people are in growing degree exposed to the contagious disease of loneliness in a world in which a competitive individualism tries to reconcile itself with a culture that speaks about togetherness, unity, and community as the ideals to strive for...

The roots of loneliness are very deep and cannot be touched by optimistic advertisement, substitute love images, or social togetherness. They find their food in the suspicion that there is no one who cares and offers love without conditions, and no place where we can be vulnerable without being used.

Henri J.M. Nouwen, *Seeds of Hope*, edited by Robert Durback, Darton, Longman & Todd Ltd., 1989, p.12.

There is a deep loneliness... that is not taken away even when one is very intimate with another human being, and that loneliness is a longing for intimacy, for communion. It is... a longing for communion with God. Yet the longing itself does not know that it longs for God. It does not differentiate between communion with God and communion with other beings. It is an undifferentiated longing for intimacy. And thus it is dark; it is pervaded with unknowing. It will look to other human beings for an intimacy that can only be had with God. It will expect others to enter into the soul, to understand one in full... to enter where only God can enter, to understand as only God can understand, to love as only God can love.

When it fails to do so, the longing will be disappointed and will tend to turn against the self for causing the failure and the apparent rejection by others. What began by being an unknowing, a darkness, ends by becoming also an unloving, a coldness towards others and toward the self. In the unknowing, though, it appears that it is others who are unloving, for they appear to refuse the intimacy, the communion that is sought. At the same time, it appears that the self is incapable of love, incapable of entering into any deep communion with others, or perhaps so unlovely, so unloveable, that others will not enter into communion with it.

John S. Dunne, The Reasons of the Heart, SCM Press Ltd., 1978, p.58.

Lonely is not a synonym for *alone*. The word *lonely* connotes isolation and dejection, a missed absence of companions when it is applied to persons. The root of *alone*, however, is in two words: *all one*. This means the opposite of isolation and dejection. The emphasis is not on the *one* but on the *wholly* one. It means complete by oneself. How many of us can actually feel that way? It is not easy to be full in oneself, to respect oneself, and to self-develop to such a degree that a person looks forward to long periods of being alone. For some who enjoy this oneness, they realize that because of their relationship with Christ they are never lonely. They cultivate the chances to be alone so that they can actually savor the moments with God alone, the moments when their unity with the Creator can be both enjoyed and developed. This implies quite a special human being. Too often we are frantic for companionship—for the team or the club or the class or the party or the movie or the TV. Immersion in such activities will free us from having to face the basic issues of existence. Such trivial busyness will keep us from intimate contact with ourselves. The kingdom of heaven is within each of us, yet how seriously do we try to make contact with it? Not only is there no need to go "out there" in most instances, but rather it is spiritually harmful to look outside of ourselves while ignoring what is by nature within us. The woman or man who can be alone—can be *together* in the self—is the kind of person we can admire, can hold as a model. The quest for wholeness for individual unity is one of the great journeys a life can make, indeed should make. There is no easy route to being properly alone. But making the trip is learning to find what the meaning of life is.

Harry James Cargas, Encountering Myself, SPCK, 1978, p.108.

LOVE

"Love"—"warm affection, attachment, liking, or fondness. In its deepest expression, a self-sacrificial form of love as exemplified in the life of Christ."

There are many different forms of love, stretching from the sensuous passion of the romantic to the self-sacrificial life of the saint.

I've been greatly influenced by the life of Albert Schweitzer. He was one of the great men of the 20th century, with doctorates in Music, Philosophy, Theology, and Medicine. He was a superb organist and gave recitals in the concert-halls of Europe. The world lay at his feet, and yet in his mid-thirties, he set out as a missionary doctor for a remote part of Africa. At Lambarene, in equatorial West Africa (now the Gabon Republic), he built a hospital and spent the rest of his life working there under very difficult conditions. He believed actions spoke louder than words, and concentrated on the medical work and outreach of the hospital.

Whilst out there he discovered a single concept which he felt lay at the very heart of philosophy and theology. This was his "Reverence for Life". Through it he developed an attitude to all forms of life. It influenced the way he looked at people, creed, race and background. It determined his attitude towards animals, nature, and the material world. We might in turn find "Reverence for Life" helpful as a practical guide to loving. I suspect it is sorely needed in the world we are living in today.

You shall love your neighbour as yourself.
Leviticus 19.18.

You shall love the Lord your God with all your heart, and with all your soul, and with all your might.
Deuteronomy 6.5.

A new commandment I give to you, that you love one another; even as I have loved you.
John 13.34.

As the Father has loved me, so have I loved you; abide in my love. If you keep my commandments, you will abide in my love, just as I have kept my Father's commandments and abide in his love.
John 15.9-10.

The great tragedy of life is not that men perish, but that they cease to love.
W. Somerset Maugham, *The Summing Up*, William Heinemann Ltd., 1938, p.312.

The highest love of all finds its fulfilment not in what it keeps but in what it gives.
Father Andrew, SDC., *Seven Words from the Cross*, Mowbray, 1954, p.32.

For even as love crowns you so shall he crucify you. Even as he is for your growth so is he for your pruning.
Kahlil Gibran, *The Prophet*, William Heinemann Ltd., 1970, p.11.

There is no surprise more magical than the surprise of being loved; it is God's finger on man's shoulder.
Charles Morgan, *The Fountain*, Macmillan Publishers Limited, 1932, p.211.

We should take pains to be polite to those whom we love.
Politeness preserves love, is a kind of sheath to it.
Mark Rutherford, *More Pages From a Journal*, Oxford University Press, 1910, p.244.

Love it is—not conscious—that is God's regent in the human soul, because it can govern the soul as nothing else can.
Henry Ward Beecher, *Proverbs from Plymouth Pulpit*, Charles Burnet & Co., 1887, p.106.

Nothing is sweeter than love, nothing stronger, nothing higher, nothing broader; nothing is more lovely, nothing richer, nothing better in heaven or in earth.
Thomas à Kempis, *The Imitation of Christ*, translated by Betty I. Knott, William Collins Sons & Co. Ltd., 1963, p.117.

Love, all alike, no season knows, nor clime,
Nor hours, days, months, which are the rags of time.

John Donne, *The Elegies and The Songs and Sonnets*,
edited by Helen Gardner, Clarendon Press, 1965, *The Sun Rising*, l.9-10, p.72.

Love to God is the slowest development to mature in the soul. No man ever learned to love God with all his heart, and his neighbour as himself, in a day.

Henry Ward Beecher, *Proverbs from Plymouth Pulpit*, Charles Burnet & Co., 1887, p.180.

All noble qualities feed and exalt Love. They in turn are by Love fed and exalted. Love, even as a *passion*, derives singular strength from its alliance with them.

Mark Rutherford, *Last Pages From a Journal*, Oxford University Press, 1915, p.283.

"Come with me into the desert." There is something much greater than human action: prayer; and it has a power much stronger than the words of men: love.
And I went into the desert.

Carlo Carretto, *Letters from the Desert*, translated by Rose Mary Hancock,
Darton, Longman & Todd Ltd., 1972, p.xviii.

When you love you should not say, "God is in my heart," but rather, "I am in the heart of God."
And think not you can direct the course of love, for love, if it find you worthy, directs your course.

Kahlil Gibran, *The Prophet*, William Heinemann, 1970, p.12.

When a person loves, all that is in his power is invested with a sense of purpose, as available for the other, or becomes a cause or occasion of gratitude, as received by gift from the other.

W.H. Vanstone, *Love's Endeavour, Love's Expense*,
Darton, Longman & Todd Ltd., 1978, p.45.

We must learn to *love*... Christian love, *agape*, is that unconquerable benevolence, that undefeatable good-will, which will never seek anything but the highest good of others, no matter what they do to us, and no matter how they treat us.

William Barclay, *The Gospel of Matthew*,
The Saint Andrew Press, 1987, Volume 1, p.224.

God's richness is such that he can totally give himself to every man, can be there only for him. And likewise for a second man, and a third, for millions and thousands of millions. That is the mystery of his infinity and inexhaustible richness.

Ladislaus Boros, *Hidden God*, translated by Erika Young, Search Press Ltd., 1973, p.122.

Few are they who, after the first enraptured steps on the path of love, stick to it all the way to its heroic conclusion, allowing its power to humble, to discipline, to purify, to let in truth, to toughen with responsibility, and so enable the lover, in Charles Williams' words, "to become the perfection he has seen".

John V. Taylor, *The Go-Between God*, SCM Press Ltd., 1973, p.47.

In everyone there sleeps
A sense of life lived according to love.
To some it means the difference they could make
By loving others, but across most it sweeps

As all they might have done had they been loved.
That nothing cures.

Philip Larkin, *The Whitsun Weddings*, Faber & Faber Ltd., 1977, *Faith Healing*, p.15.

"Being loved" is something that happens to someone else. Loving is what happens to you. Without it and the desire that always goes with it to make gifts of love, life is maimed, mutilated, deprived, depraved. Without it, life is soured at the source. With it, anything can be borne. To live without being loved is sorrowful. Without loving there *is* no real life.

Jessamyn West, *To See the Dream*, Hodder & Stoughton Ltd., 1958, p.142.

Existence will remain meaningless for you if you yourself do not penetrate into it with active love and if you do not in this way discover its meaning for yourself. Everything is waiting to be hallowed by you; it is waiting for this meaning to be disclosed and to be realised by you... Meet the world with the fullness of your being and you shall meet God. If you wish to believe, love!

Martin Buber, in *Encounter with Martin Buber*, Aubrey Hodes, Allen Lane The Penguin Press, 1972, p.66.

Essentially man is not a slave either of himself or of the world; but he is a lover. His freedom and fulfilment is in love, which is another name for perfect comprehension. By this power of comprehension, this permeation of his being, he is united with the all-pervading Spirit, who is also the breath of his soul. Where a man tries to raise himself to eminence by pushing and jostling all others, to achieve a distinction by which he prides himself to be more than everybody else, there he is alienated from that Spirit.

Rabindranath Tagore, *Sadhana*, Macmillan Publishers Limited, 1930, p.15.

God is a Being, loving, gentle, and tender. He is love. And he who dwells in love dwells in God, and God in him. Therefore, if you would walk with Him, be gentle and tender and full of love in all your works and ways. Let the spirit of the love of Jesus tame and sweeten the rough, oppositious, crabbed tempers of your natural mind, melt down your hardness, and bend your obstinate self-will; and should any of the bitterness of the old nature rise up, let yourself sink down at once into the deep sea of the gentleness and love of God.

Gerhard Tersteegen, in *Sketches of the Quiet in the Land*, Frances Bevan, John F. Shaw and Co., 1891, p.400.

Really meeting the God who is love means stepping willingly into the refining fire to be slowly remade and changed into the kind of love that one has confronted. Some even turn away from human love to escape this demand upon them. They realize how powerful that experience can be, and they resist being opened up to forces outside themselves which might loosen their ego control of life and change them. Love is indeed a powerful experience; one can be caught by it and forced to change, which is painful for most human beings. And the touch of a loving God is no less powerful and dangerous than that of a human love affair.

Morton T. Kelsey, *The Other Side of Silence*, SPCK, 1977, p.17.

It is possible to be inspired by another person..., to be drawn to the new and unknown life one sees in the other, without really loving the other. In fact, it is not possible to love "with all your heart, and with all your soul, and with all your might" until you have found your own soul. Here is a paradox. As long as another person is my "soul" and "the life of my heart", as Beatrice was for Dante when he first met her and, perhaps even more intensely, when he had lost her, I do not yet have the heart and soul to love the other. It is only when I find my soul by willingly letting go of the other that I become capable of loving with all my heart and all my soul and all my might.

John S. Dunne, *The Reasons of the Heart*, SCM Press Ltd., 1978, p.117.

Love has a marvellous property of feeling in another. It can enjoy in another, as well as enjoy him. Love is an infinite treasure to its object, and its object is so to it. God is Love, and you are His object. You are created to be His Love: and He is yours. He is happy in you, when you are happy: as parents in their children. He is afflicted in all your afflictions. And whosoever toucheth you, toucheth the apple of His eye. Will not you be happy in all His enjoyments? He feeleth in you; will not you feel in Him? He hath obliged you to love Him. And if you love Him, you must of necessity be Heir of the World, for you are happy in Him. All His praises are your joys, all His enjoyments are your treasures, all His pleasures are your enjoyments. In God you are crowned, in God you are concerned. In Him you feel, in Him you love, and move, and have your being, in Him you are blessed. Whatsoever therefore serveth Him, serveth you and in Him you inherit all things.

Thomas Traherne, *Centuries*, The Faith Press Ltd., 1969, p.24.

Love cannot be confined to the realm of personal relationships and personal needs. It includes the artist's and scientist's respect and wonder at the grain and structure of the material world, the realization that the world of nature is infinitely knowable and may well be discovered to have other significances for its Creator than to be merely the stage upon which the drama of God and man takes place, and the refusal to entertain any idea of the fulfilment of life that does not include all mankind and the whole created universe. What we long for is the transformation of nature into a clear manifestation of the love of God till all is glory and grace, not an escape from it or an abandonment of it at some point at which we imagine it has served its purpose as an adjunct of human life.

J. Neville Ward, *Five for Sorrow, Ten for Joy*, Epworth Press, 1971, p.128.

LUST

"Lust"—"a strong desire especially, though not exclusively, for sexual pleasure."

I remember a conversation with a young poet. He had a striking appearance, a bright agile mind, and a great zest for living. He was extremely articulate and spoke enthusiastically of his original interest in Philosophy and English Literature. On going to university he had rapidly become bored with the academic study of these subjects, but his imagination had been fired by the romantic poets. Much to his delight he discovered he had a gift for writing poetry and was now concentrating on getting his poems published.

As one would expect he was extremely popular with the opposite sex, so the conversation moved on apace. Yes, there was a new girlfriend, who, of course, was fantastic. They had known each other for about four months. Suddenly he stopped talking. A thought had just struck him. "Do you know, I've just realized. I haven't written any poetry since I've met her. How very odd."

We talked about it. I recalled an observation, that when lust comes in at the door, creativity goes out of the window. This seemed to strike a chord. Sometimes I wonder if "Lust" is *the* besetting sin of the twentieth century, particularly in the West.

Can a man carry fire in his bosom and his clothes not be burned?
Proverbs 6.27.

The righteousness of the upright delivers them, but the treacherous are taken captive by their lust.
Proverbs 11.6.

But I say to you that every one who looks at a woman lustfully has already committed adultery with her in his heart.
Matthew 5.28.

Do not love the world or the things in the world. If any one loves the world, love for the Father is not in him. For all that is in the world, the lust of the flesh and the lust of the eyes and the pride of life, is not of the Father but is of the world. And the world passes away, and the lust of it; but he who does the will of God abides for ever.
1 John 2.15-17.

The new lust gives the lecher the new thrill.
John Masefield, *The Collected Poems of John Masefield*, William Heinemann Ltd., 1926, *The Widow in the Bye Street*, l.22, p.139.

Th'expense of spirit in a waste of shame
Is lust in action.
William Shakespeare, *Sonnets*, 129.

If it is love or pleasure, or flirting, fawning, and flattering, for another or for yourself—then it is *Lust*.
The Cloud of Unknowing, translated by Clifton Wolters, Penguin Books Ltd., 1978, p.76.

It subverts kingdoms, overthrows cities, towns, families, mars, corrupts, and makes a massacre of men; thunder and lightning, wars, fires, plagues, have not done that mischief to mankind, as this burning lust, this brutish passion.

Robert Burton, *The Anatomy of Melancholy*, J.M. Dent & Sons Ltd., 1949, Volume Three, p.49.

The natural sex drive if repressed from fear of its seductive strength may take on the character of lust, but if accepted it can become a source of vigour and delight in the marriage relationship and the building of a home. It can also infuse warmth into all human relationships.

Christopher Bryant, SSJE, *Jung and the Christian Way*, Darton, Longman & Todd Ltd., 1983, p.79.

> For glances beget ogles, ogles sighs,
> Sighs wishes, wishes words, and words a letter...
> And then, God knows what mischief may arise,
> When love links two young people in one fetter,
> Vile assignations, and adulterous beds,
> Elopements, broken vows, and hearts, and heads.

Lord Byron, *The Complete Poetical Works*, edited by Jerome J. McGann, Clarendon Press, 1986, Volume IV, *Beppo*, st.16, p.134.

> Love comforteth like sunshine after rain,
> But Lust's effect is tempest after sun;
> Love's gentle spring doth always fresh remain:
> Lust's winter comes ere summer half be done.
> Love surfeits not: Lust like a glutton dies.
> Love is all truth: Lust full of forged lies.

William Shakespeare, *Venus and Adonis*, l.799.

To look with lust is much more than simply to look: it is to expend one of the finer substances of which complete sex-energy is composed: something passes in the act of vision which is irrecoverable; and for the want of it the subsequent sex-life is incomplete. It is the same with the other senses, though less easily realized. In short, it is possible to become completely impotent by means of the senses alone—yes, by the eyes alone—while remaining continent in the ordinary meaning of the word.

A.R. Orage, *On Love*, The Janus Press, 1957, p.15.

It is the difference betwixt lust and love, that this is fixed, that volatile. Love grows, lust wastes, by enjoyment: and the reason is, that one springs from an union of souls, and the other springs from an union of sense. They have diverse originals, and so are of different families: that inward and deep, this superficial; this transient, and that permanent.

They that marry for money, cannot have the true satisfaction of marriage; the requisite means being wanting.

William Penn, *Fruits of Solitude*, A.W. Bennett, 1863, p.19.

"Lust" is defined as a strong desire especially, though not exclusively for sexual pleasure. Many expressions of lust, such as fornication and adultery, are condemned in the scriptures (see Rom. 1:24-28, which denounces the "shameful lusts" of the pagans, and Gal. 5.19-20, which condemns "works of the flesh"), and lust itself has been viewed as one of the seven deadly, or capital, sins because it leads to so many other vices and sins. It is opposed to the specific virtue of chastity and the general virtue of temperance.

James F. Childress, in *A New Dictionary of Christian Ethics*, edited by James F. Childress and John Macquarrie, SCM Press Ltd., 1986, p.360.

Lust . . . is an excessive love of the pleasures of the flesh—for themselves and nothing else. It is not love, but the perversion of love. Real love is for a person, respected and reverenced as a unique human being, made "in the image of God". Lust is due to a wrong attitude towards sex. Those who indulge in it have no idea of the meaning of sex as an element of God's glorious purpose for human life. They treat it as something unworthy of respect, and when they do this they do not respect the other person involved. A married man, for instance, will tell his doctor, in confidence, that he is being unfaithful to his wife with a clear conscience, because, after all, "this is merely a little sensual adventure! it has nothing to do with my love for my wife, which is on a higher plane altogether"! Thus, "lust is the isolation of sex from pure love", that is, the severance of two elements which should never be divided.

Olive Wyon, *On the Way*, SCM Press Ltd., 1958, p.52.

The lust to get (pleonexia). The Greek word is built up of two words which mean *to have more.* The Greeks themselves defined *pleonexia* as the *accursed love of having.* It is an aggressive vice. It has been described as the spirit which will pursue its own interests with complete disregard for the rights of others, and even for the considerations of common humanity. The keynote of it is *rapacity.* Theodoret, the Christian writer, describes it as the spirit that aims at more, the spirit which grasps at things which it has no right to take. It may operate in every sphere of life. If it operates in the material sphere, it means grasping at money and goods, regardless of honour and honesty. If it operates in the ethical sphere, it means the ambition which tramples on others to gain something which is not properly meant for it. If it operates in the moral sphere, it means the unbridled lust which takes its pleasure where it has no right to take.

Pleonexia is the desire which knows no law.

William Barclay, *The Letter to the Romans*, The Saint Andrew Press, 1969, p.27.

Lust is the idolatry of sexual pleasure and in a broader sense of all pleasure that accompanies loving. Pleasure has been called the bloom which grows on the actions which nature intends. In its place it is matter for rejoicing. Sexual pleasure belongs primarily within the context of marriage and is nature's way of strengthening the relationship of husband and wife, important for the bringing up of a family. Owing to the disorder of original sin we all suffer a certain loneliness because we do not sufficiently enjoy the loving relationships that we cannot help wanting. Lust is the grasping at sexual pleasure to compensate oneself for this loneliness. It could also be called possessive loving... Possessive love is of the nature of lust. Lust treats persons whether in reality or in fantasy as means not as ends in themselves, as objects to gratify desires not as persons existing in their own right. But it needs no arguing that sex and sexuality form an essential part of humanity and must be seen as basically good. It is also clear that the immensely strong sexual drive inherited from our ancestors is difficult to control. Perhaps it is true to say that the work of humanising sex, of bringing it under the sway of loving relationships, relationships in which the good of the loved one outweighs the lover's pleasure, is one of the greatest tasks which mankind must carry out if it is to achieve its destiny, now fully humanised and at one with his Maker. Perhaps historically we have tended to alternate between periods when too much licence has been given to the exuberance of instinct and periods when society has imposed excessive restraint upon it.

Christopher Bryant, SSJE, *The Heart in Pilgrimage*, Darton, Longman & Todd Ltd., 1980, p.39.

MARRIAGE

"Marriage"—"the relation between married persons—intimate union."

As an undergraduate I used to play golf for the university. I remember a conversation with an opponent towards the end of a round. He was a middle-aged man, and happily married. There was one thing, though, which blighted his marriage. Before he met his wife, he had been intimately involved with another woman, and somehow had never been able to tell his wife about this. He was fearful of the consequences. After many years he was still deeply in love with his wife but bitterly regretted his early indiscretion. I wondered why he was telling me all this. Was he trying to teach me something?

I've learnt some helpful things from couples I've married. I met a husband a few months into married life. "How's it going?" I asked. His face fell. "Ooh," he said, "it's hard work," but then his face brightened up, and he added, "but it's worth it." As far as I can see they have had a very successful marriage. A wife (originally one of our first women undergraduates in College), after several years of married life, admitted that there had been ups and downs, but the crucial thing for them was sticking to their marriage vows through thick and thin. A husband confided to me that he and his wife had tremendous rows. I was shocked. I had always regarded them as my ideal couple. Seeing my distressed face he winked and said it was marvellous when they made it up afterwards. Forgiveness, for them, and humour, were crucial ingredients in their happy married life. One final point. Every marriage is unique and has to be worked out anew.

It is not good that the man should be alone; I will make a helper fit for him.
Genesis 2.18.

He who finds a wife finds a good thing, and obtains favour from the Lord.
Proverbs 18.22.

Have you not read that he who made them from the beginning made them male and female, and said, "For this reason a man shall leave his father and mother and be joined to his wife, and the two shall become one flesh"? So they are no longer two but one flesh. What therefore God has joined together, let not man put asunder.
Matthew 19.4-6.

Let marriage be held in honour among all, and let the marriage bed be undefiled.
Hebrews 13.4.

Don't get married unless you really have to.
Anon.

Never marry but for love; but see that thou lovest what is lovely.

William Penn, *Fruits of Solitude*, A.W. Bennett, 1863, Part 1, No.79, p.19.

But the highest form of affection is based on full sincerity on both sides.

Thomas Hardy, *Jude the Obscure*, Macmillan Publishers Ltd., 1924, p.325.

It is an essential condition for the proper choice of partners that both should be on the same plane of existence.

Count Hermann Keyserling, *The Book of Marriage*, Harcourt, Brace & Company, 1926, p.286.

Long, long ago Plutarch laid it down, that "marriage cannot be happy unless husband and wife are of the same religion."

William Barclay, *The Letters to the Corinthians*, The Saint Andrew Press, 1984, p.71.

It is a great mistake to criticize or even notice the small failings of one you love. Pay no attention to them: let love drown them far out of sight.

Mark Rutherford, *Last Pages From a Journal*, Oxford University Press, 1915, p.317.

For this is one of the miracles of love; it gives—to both, but perhaps especially to the woman—a power of seeing through its own enchantments and yet not being disenchanted.

C.S. Lewis, *A Grief Observed*, Faber & Faber Ltd., 1961, p.56.

The most precious gift that marriage gave me was this constant impact of something very close and intimate yet all the time unmistakably other, resistant—in a word, real.

C.S. Lewis, *A Grief Observed*, Faber & Faber Ltd., 1961, p.18.

For the rest let him attend to his work, be glad in it, love his wife, be glad in her, bring up his children with joyfulness, love his fellow men, rejoice in life.

Søren Kierkegaard, *Training in Christianity*, translated by Walter Lowrie, Princeton University Press, 1942, p.71.

If love be not thy chiefest motive, thou will soon grow weary of a married state, and stray from thy promise, to search out thy pleasures in forbidden places.

William Penn, *Fruits of Solitude*, A.W. Bennett, 1863, p.19.

As man is essentially a dynamic, aspiring, evolutionary being; marriage can bring fulfilment only inasmuch as it intensifies life. Wherever it causes diminution it fails in its purpose.

Count Hermann Keyserling, *The Book of Marriage*, Harcourt, Brace & Company, 1926, p.290.

The fulfilment of marriage is that joy in which each lover's true being is flowering because its growth is being welcomed and unconsciously encouraged by the other in the infinite series of daily decisions which is their life together.

J. Neville Ward, *Five for Sorrow, Ten for Joy*, Epworth Press, 1971, p.17.

The joy of going through life hand in hand with the comrade of one's choice, sharing one another's burdens, stimulating one another's courage, doubling one another's sagacity, buckling on one another's armour, wearing one another's laurels and easing one another's pain.

W.C. Willoughby, *Race Problems in the New Africa*, Clarendon Press, 1923, p.104.

The love that has lasted for years, which has resisted all weakness and defect; has been constant in all moods and circumstances better and worse; has exacted nothing; has been content with silence; always soft and easy as the circumambient air, a love with no reserve; what is there in any relationship to person or thing worth a straw compared with it!

Mark Rutherford, *More Pages From a Journal*, Oxford University Press, 1910, p.246.

Parenthood does not begin with the birth of the child, nor with the germination of the seed. It has its beginnings even before the child's conception, and is part and parcel of the marriage and the love from the expression of which the baby owes his being. If this is so, our abilities as good mothers and fathers—and our failures too—cannot be viewed in isolation, apart from the sum total—the interaction and fusing of personalities—which makes up the marriage.

Sheila Kitzinger, *The Experience of Childbirth*, Penguin Books Ltd., 1978, p.309.

The essence of a good marriage is respect for each other's personality combined with that deep intimacy, physical, mental, and spiritual, which makes a serious love between man and woman the most fructifying of all human experiences. Such love, like everything that is great and precious, demands its own morality, and frequently entails a sacrifice of the less to the greater, but such sacrifice must be voluntary, for where it is not, it will destroy the very basis of the love for the sake of which it is made.

Bertrand Russell, *Marriage and Morals*, George Allen & Unwin Publishers Ltd., 1976, p.203.

Some conflict is a natural and healthy aspect of intimacy. Its absence in a supposedly ideal marriage could be a sign of positive good but it could on the other hand be due to a deep fear that the marriage will not stand the expression of differences or to the fact that husband and wife are driven by perfectionist interpretations of Christian love. In either case it is not an authentic love that presents that serene exterior to the world. Where there is deep love, in spirit and in truth, husbands and wives are free to be themselves to one another and can share their negative as well as their positive feelings. In this sense a certain amount of conflict can be, instead of the sign of waning love it may seem, one of the many forms of deep mutual involvement and unity.

J. Neville Ward, *Friday Afternoon*, Epworth Press, 1982, p.71.

I have seen the failure of too many marriages, and warmed my hands before a few glowing successes, and in every case have thought and examined and wondered, and never found any logic, for marriage is as mysterious as life or fire. I know only that there is no objective existence to it. It cannot be studied from the outside and conclusions drawn, for it lives only inside itself, and what is presented to the observer or the listener bears only the relationship of a distorted shadow to the reality inside. There is no right and no wrong; there is no truth and no falsehood, neither wronged husband nor betrayed wife. There is only marriage, which is a mystical union, and when the partners to it cease to know that they are one flesh, when the mystical sense goes, there is no marriage. There is instead a practical problem, with a hundred factors pressing on the mind and the emotions. What to do? To pretend, to fight? To stay, to go? To deaden the senses or quicken them? To think of the children, who must be loved, or think of the mystery, which must be refound, without which there is no love? To die, to live?

John Masters, *The Road Past Mandalay*, Michael Joseph Ltd., 1962, p.103.

Two fears alternate in marriage, of loneliness and of bondage. The dread of loneliness being keener than the fear of bondage, we get married. For one person who fears being thus tied there are four who dread being set free. Yet the love of liberty is a noble passion and one to which most married people secretly aspire—in moments when they are not neurotically dependent—but by then it is too late; the ox does not become a bull, nor the hen a falcon.

The fear of loneliness can be overcome, for it springs from weakness; human beings are intended to be free, and to be free is to be lonely, but the fear of bondage is the apprehension of a real danger, and so I find it all the more pathetic to watch young men and beautiful girls taking refuge in marriage from an imaginary danger, a sad loss to their friends and a sore trial to each other. First love is the one most worth having, yet the best marriage is often the second, for we should marry only when the desire for freedom be spent; not till then does a man know whether he is the kind who can settle down. The most tragic breakings up are of those couples who have married young and who have enjoyed seven years of happiness, after which the banked fires of passion and independence explode—and without knowing why, for they still love each other, they set about accomplishing their common destruction.

Cyril Connolly, The Unquiet Grave, Hamish Hamilton Ltd., 1973, p.11.

What is the "end" of marriage? What is the meaning of sex in the light of the Christian revelation?

The basic answer in the Bible is the verse in Genesis: "And God created man in His own image, in the image of God created He him; male and female created He them" (Gen. 1.27). This truth is underlined and confirmed by our Lord when He said:

"From the beginning of the creation, male and female made He them" (Mark 10.6). This means that the term "man" includes both sexes; they are complementary. This does not mean, of course, that every man needs some particular woman for completion, or the other way round, but simply that men and women together make up mankind, that they complement each other, and that both equally are needed to live out their vocation to the glory of God. Here the words of St Paul are very much to the point: "Know ye not that your body is a temple of the Holy Ghost which is in you, which ye have from God? and ye are not your own; for ye were bought with a price: glorify God therefore in your body." Thus it is the purpose of God to use us for His designs in and through the body, in and through sex; to deny or ignore this causes all kinds of difficulties, and often affects the body itself. But what we do not always realize is this; that God does this in two ways: through marriage, and through celibacy.

For most people marriage is the normal and the right way of fulfilling the will of God for their lives. As has been well said: "When two people marry, the incompleteness of male and female severally is done away, and they become one new being 'made in the image of God'" ... They are made in the image of God, and privileged to take part in His creative work of making new people. The completeness of a Christian marriage is effected by the irrevocable offering of themselves in mutual loyalty, as a pair, to God for Him to make of them what He will.

But if marriage is a vocation, so is celibacy, even "involuntary celibacy", imposed on a woman (more rarely upon a man) by circumstances. For both in marriage and in celibacy God calls for an absolute obedience; in the one instance this obedience is rendered through the total loyalty of the Christian couple, of each partner to God, through the other. In the second case, God's call comes through the whole body of the Church. In principle the unmarried man or woman is "detached" from the exclusive claims of the family, in order that he or she may be free for God's use in and through the Church, in whatever sphere their vocation may lie. Indeed, there are many forms of service which can only be given by men and women who have no other absolute human ties.

Olive Wyon, *On the Way*, SCM Press Ltd., 1958, p.70.

MERCY

"Mercy"— "loving kindness and forgiveness."

I t was Evensong at Christ the King, the University Church in London. I was sitting in the congregation. A sidesman beckoned me. There was a problem in the Lady Chapel. Could I come and help?

I found a distraught young man. It emerged he had been living with his girlfriend; their relationship had broken down; she was now in hospital nearby; he had been to visit her, to find her being visited by another man—the opposition! He was so upset he'd slashed her face with a razor and was now on the run. He believed the Church to be a place of refuge, but should he give himself up to the police?

I was in my dog-collar, and had scruples about handing him over to the police. We talked over what to do and rang the hospital. The duty doctor suggested we came round to see him. On the way the young man told me more about himself. He and his girlfriend were registered drug addicts. They were treated by a professor at the hospital, a "character" with a bushy beard, who wore jeans and a great leather belt.

We reached the hospital and met the duty doctor. He told us the police had already been round, but respecting the wishes of the girlfriend, were not going to press charges. The Professor had been summoned and was expected soon. After a few minutes the door opened and there he was, as described.

He was quickly brought up to date on the events. I left when he started to work on their relationship. I observed that mercy had been shown at every stage in trying to resolve this problem.

Nevertheless in thy great mercies thou didst not make an end of them or forsake them; for thou art a gracious and merciful God.

Nehemiah 9.31.

But thou, O Lord, art a God merciful and gracious, slow to anger and abounding in steadfast love and faithfulness.

Psalm 86.15.

Blessed are the merciful, for they shall obtain mercy.

Matthew 5.7.

May mercy, peace, and love be multiplied to you.

Jude 2.

A God all mercy, is a God unjust.

Edward Young, *Young's Complete Poems*, William Tegg, 1854, Volume 1, *Night Thoughts*, Night IV, l.233, p.52.

We hand folks over to God's mercy, and show none ourselves.
George Eliot, *Adam Bede*, Virtue & Co., 1908, Volume II, p.214.

And every misery that I miss is a new mercy; and therefore let us be thankful.
Izaak Walton, *The Compleat Angler*, The Nonesuch Press Ltd., 1929, p.189.

How would you be
If He, which is the top of judgment, should
But judge you as you are? O, think on that,
And mercy then will breathe within your lips,
Like man new made.
William Shakespeare, *Measure for Measure*, Act II. sc.ii. l.75.

O mercy, heav'nly born! sweet attribute!
Thou great, thou best prerogative of pow'r!
Justice may guard the throne, but, join'd with thee,
On rocks of adamant it stands secure,
And braves the storm beneath.
William Somervile, *The Chase*, George Redway, 1896, Third Book, p.64.

In the New Testament God's mercy, expressed especially as forgiveness, serves as both a motive and a standard for human actions: "Be merciful, even as your Father is merciful" (Luke 6.36) and "Blessed are the merciful, for they shall obtain mercy" (Matt. 5.7). Augustine (*City of God* 9.5) defines "mercy" as "heartfelt sympathy for another's distress, impelling us to succour him if we can..."
James F. Childress, in *A New Dictionary of Christian Ethics*, edited by James F. Childress and John Macquarrie, SCM Press Ltd., 1986, p.381.

If it be the earnest Desire and Longing of your Heart to be merciful as he is merciful; to be full of his unwearied Patience, to dwell in his unalterable Meekness; if you long to be like him in universal, impartial Love; if you desire to communicate every Good, to every Creature that you are able; if you love and practise everything that is good, righteous and lovely, for its own sake, because it is good, righteous, and lovely; and resist no Evil, but with Goodness; then you have the utmost Certainty, that the Spirit of God lives, dwells, and governs in you.
William Law, *The Spirit of Prayer and the Spirit of Love*, edited by Sidney Spencer, James Clarke & Co. Ltd., 1969, p.156.

And to be true, and speake my soule, when I survey the occurrences of my life, and call into account the finger of God, I can perceive nothing but an abysse and masse of (his) mercies, either in generall to mankind, or in particular to my selfe. And whether out of the prejudice of my affection, or an inverting and partiall conceit of his mercies, I know not, but those which others term crosses, afflictions, judgments, misfortunes, to me, who enquire farther into them than their visible effects, they both appeare, and in event have ever proved, the secret and dissembled favours of his affection.
Sir Thomas Browne, *The Works of Sir Thomas Browne*, edited by Geoffrey Keynes, Faber & Faber Ltd., 1964, Volume 1, *Religio Medici*, Part 1, sec.53, p.63.

The quality of mercy is not strain'd;
It droppeth as the gentle rain from heaven
Upon the place beneath. It is twice blessed:

It blesseth him that gives and him that takes.
'Tis mightiest in the mightiest; it becomes
The throned monarch better than his crown;
His sceptre shows the force of temporal power,
The attribute to awe and majesty,
Wherein doth sit the dread and fear of kings;
But mercy is above his scept'red sway,
It is enthroned in the hearts of kings,
It is an attribute to God himself;
And earthly power doth then show likest God's
When mercy seasons justice.

William Shakespeare, *The Merchant of Venice*, Act IV. sc.i. l.179.

From the Old Testament onwards, there are two related but distinct aspects of mercy, the divine and the human, the theological and the moral. It is a word which traditionally describes both an attitude (even *the* attitude) of God to man and a disposition which should characterize human dealings. On the former side, it is bound up with considerations like God's justice; on the latter, it is a basic moral duty. But the two aspects, though distinct, are related and intertwined. Thus, mercy (or "steadfast love" or "loving kindness" as it is commonly rendered in recent versions of the Old Testament) which should mark human relationships marks, in the first place, God's relationship with human beings. And in so far as human creatures exercise justice on God's behalf, they are confronted with the question of the bounds of mercy. In the Bible, the two aspects are bound together in the deeper setting of the covenant. As this links not only God and his people but his people among themselves, so the character of the covenant is stamped on them all by virtue of their status within it. In other words, the moral aspect flows from the theological, the human from the divine.

J.L. Houlden, in *A New Dictionary of Christian Theology*, edited by Alan Richardson and John Bowden, SCM Press Ltd., 1985, p.356.

Those who have known what it is to be freed from great mental distress and brought out again into light and joy by God lose all desire to pass judgment and bear grudges. They feel the same if God has sent them someone to whom they can open their minds. They knew that helpless people are apt to resent the offer of help, don't want assistance. Nevertheless, they came to realize that the helping hand to freedom was fraternally given in God's name. All they want now is to help share their neighbour's troubles, to serve, help, forgive unconditionally and endlessly. It is experiences of this kind that encourage spiritual growth in those who are enabled to open out new horizons of forgiveness and hope for others, to understand their mental distress and help them bear it. Spiritual men of this kind, sealed with the Spirit, have existed in Christianity from the beginning. They are an integral part of the Church. In a certain sense, each of us is a man of the spirit, for each of us sooner or later is called to alleviate the mental suffering of his brethren by the spiritual works of mercy, and thereby find relief for his own mind and spirit.

Ladislaus Boros, *We Are Future*, Search Press Ltd., 1971, p.136.

"How great is the loving-kindness of the Lord our God, and His compassion unto such as turn unto Him in holiness!"
Why do we delay to cast ourselves into the depths of this abyss? The more we lose ourselves therein, in faith and love, the safer we are. Let us give ourselves up to

God, without reserve or apprehension of danger. He will love us, and make us to love Him; and that love increasing daily, shall produce in us all the other virtues. He alone shall fill our heart, which the world has agitated and intoxicated, but could never fill. He will take nothing from us but what makes us unhappy. He will only make us despise the world, which perhaps we do already. He will alter little in our actions, and only correct the motive of them by making them all be referred to Himself. Then the most ordinary and seemingly indifferent actions shall become exercises of virtue, sources of consolation. We shall cheerfully behold death approach as the beginning of life immortal; and, as S. Paul speaks, "we shall not be unclothed, but clothed upon that mortality might be swallowed up of life." (2 Cor 5.4). And we shall then discover the depth of God's mercy which He has exercised toward us.

Consider, in the presence of God, the effects of that infinite mercy which you have already experienced, the lights which Christ has given you, the good thoughts He has inspired you with, the sins He has pardoned, the dangers from which He has preserved you, and the extraordinary assistance He has afforded you. Endeavour to excite your love towards Him by these precious marks of His goodness; add to these the remembrance of the crosses He has dispensed for your sanctification, for those also are the riches of His mercy, which you ought to consider as signal testimonies of His love. Let a sense of past favours inspire you with a trust in Him for the future. Learn from these that He has loved you too much not to love you still. Distrust not Him, but only yourself. Remember that, as His Apostle speaks, "He is the Father of mercies, and the God of all comfort." (2 Cor 1.3). He sometimes separates these two, His *comforts* are withdrawn, but His *mercies* still continue. He takes away what is sweet and sensible in grace, because you want to be humbled and punished for having sought consolation elsewhere. Such chastisement is still a new depth of His mercy.

François de la M. Fénelon, Spiritual Thoughts for Busy People, SPCK, 1894, p.64.

MORALS

"Morals"—"concerned with the distinction between right and wrong."

I 've tried to work out why I behave the way I do. Looking back, I'm aware of several strands which have influenced me in my patterns of behaviour. First of all, there is home, and the upbringing of one's parents. Secondly, there is the local community, taking into account the mass media. Thirdly, there is school, and for me, National Service and university. I shall always remember my room in Balliol being invaded by an ardent socialist, who challenged every single thing I believed in. At least he made me realize my beliefs were second-hand and not my own, acquired along the way almost without question. It was then that I reached an important stage of life—thinking out my own values— and conscious of coming into being as a person in my own right.

The most important influence for me has been an evolving Christian faith. As a foundation there is the Bible and the person of Jesus Christ. Then there are the findings of theology, broadly construed, and the tradition of the Church down the ages. For me especially an important influence has been the recorded experience of the saints over the last two thousand years, still being collected, and the object of reflection. And lastly there is conscience, in constant need of education for fresh truth. And dare one end this section without mentioning the influence of "grace" and the "Holy Spirit"?

And you shall do what is right and good in the sight of the Lord, that it may go well with you.

Deuteronomy 6.18.

I will instruct you in the good and the right way.

1 Samuel 12.23.

And as you wish that men would do to you, do so to them.

Luke 6.31.

Aim at righteousness, godliness, faith, love, steadfastness, gentleness.

1 Timothy 6.11.

Morality is often grace working out into a noble life-form.

Henry Ward Beecher, *Proverbs from Plymouth Pulpit*, Charles Burnet & Co., 1887, p.96.

Half at least of all morality is negative and consists in keeping out of mischief.

Aldous Huxley, *The Doors of Perception*, Harper & Row, Publishers, 1970, p.43.

A right moralist is a great and good man; but, for that reason, he is rarely to be found.

William Penn, *Fruits of Solitude*, A.W. Bennett, 1863, p.67.

Morality without spirituality has no roots. It becomes a thing of custom, transient, and optional.

Henry Ward Beecher, *Proverbs from Plymouth Pulpit*, Charles Burnet & Co., 1887, p.97.

Without civic morality communities perish; without personal morality their survival has no value.

Bertrand Russell, *Authority and the Individual*, George Allen & Unwin Publishers Ltd., 1949, p.111.

The moral man is he that loves God above all, and his neighbour as himself: which fulfils both tables at once.

William Penn, *Fruits of Solitude*, A.W. Bennett, 1863, p.68.

The whole spectrum about morality is an effort to find a way of living which men who live it will instinctively feel is good.

Walter Lippmann, *A Preface to Politics*, Ann Arbor Publications, 1962, p.152.

So far, about morals, I know only that what is moral is what you feel good after and what is immoral is what you feel bad after . . .

Ernest Hemingway, *Death in the Afternoon*, Jonathan Cape Ltd., 1968, p.11.

The ultimate foundation for morality is that immorality doesn't work, it doesn't pay off. It doesn't lighten the burden of living. It increases it.

Norman Vincent Peale, *Man, Morals and Maturity*, World's Work Ltd., 1970, p.77.

The Christian moral standard is, after all, not a code which has to be defended against the attacks of a forward generation: it is an insight to be achieved.

F.R. Barry, *The Relevance of Christianity*, James Nisbet & Co. Ltd., 1932, p.8.

The real immorality, as far as I can see it
Lies in forcing yourself or somebody else
Against all your deeper instincts and your intuition.

D.H. Lawrence, *The Complete Poems of D.H. Lawrence*, edited by Vivian de Sola Pinto and Warren Roberts, William Heinemann Ltd., 1967, Volume II, *Immorality*, p.836.

We can offer this summary of moral obligation: Your being is personal; live as a person in fellow-membership with all others who, being personal, are your fellow-members in the community of persons. Strive to grow in fullness of personality, in width and depth of fellowship; and seek to draw the energy for this from that to which you and all things owe their origin, the Personal Love which is Creator and Sustainer of the world.

William Temple, *Nature, Man and God,* Macmillan Publishers Ltd., 1934, p.196.

It is true that man is a moral animal, but it is not true that there is but one morality; there are a thousand, the morality of each race is different, the morality of each individual differs. The origin of each sect is the desire to affirm certain moral ideas which particularly appeal to it; every charge of faith is determined by the moral temperament of the individual; we prefer this religion to that religion because our moral ideas are more implicit in these affirmations than in those.

George Moore, *Evelyn Innes,* Bernhard Tauchnitz, 1898, Volume II, p.106.

In the more distant past, even if parental affection was lacking, working-class children grew up in a community which had strong views of right and wrong; this morality perhaps owed more to the solidarity of a group who shared rough times than to the formal Christian ethics in which better-class children were instructed. Today, however, both the popular and churchgoing types of morality have slipped into disuse. Popular morality is now a wasteland, littered with the debris of broken convictions. Concepts such as honour, or even honesty, have an old-fashioned sound; but nothing has taken their place. The confusion is perhaps greatest over sexual morality; here the former theological canons of behaviour are seldom taken seriously. In their place a new concept is emerging, of sexual relationships as a source of pleasure, but also as a mutual encountering of personalities in which each explores the other and at the same time discovers new depths in himself or herself.

G.M Carstairs, *This Island Now,* Hogarth Press, 1963, p.54.

If we are to be genuinely in earnest with a high ethical rule of living, it would seem to be indispensable that we should be convinced that there is something really at stake in moral effort, and that the something which may be won or lost is no less than the supreme good which makes life worth living. What we endanger by sloth must be something more than a quantity of interesting and agreeable incident; it must be the life of the soul itself. Eternal life itself must be something which conceivably may be missed, and, for that reason, the eternity to be achieved by right living must be something not inherent in humanity from the start, but something to be *won,* and therefore something communicated and derivative. Hence humanity and divinity cannot simply be equated by a theology which is to be true to the demands of ethics. The divinity accessible to man must not be *deity,* but *deiformity,* transfiguration into a character which is not ours by right of birth, but is won by an effort, and won as something communicated from another source, where it is truly underived and original.

A.E. Taylor, *The Faith of a Moralist,* Macmillan Publishers Ltd., 1930, Volume 1, p.124.

There is a universal moral law, as distinct from a moral code, which consists of certain statements of fact about the nature of man; and by behaving in conformity with which, man enjoys his true freedom. This is what the Christian Church calls "the natural law". The more closely the moral code agrees with the natural law, the more it makes for freedom in human behaviour; the more widely it departs from the natural law, the more it tends to enslave mankind and to produce the catastrophes called "judgments of God".

The universal moral *law* (or natural law of humanity) is discoverable, like any other law of nature, by experience. It cannot be promulgated, it can only be ascertained, because it is a question not of opinion but of fact. When it has been ascertained, a moral *code* can be drawn up to direct human behaviour and prevent men, as far as possible, from doing violence to their own nature. No code is necessary to control the behaviour of matter, since matter is apparently not tempted to contradict its own nature, but obeys the law of its own being in perfect freedom. Man, however, does continually suffer this temptation and frequently yields to it. This contradiction within his own nature is peculiar to man, and is called by the Church "sinfulness"; other psychologists have other names for it.

Dorothy Sayers, *The Mind of the Maker*, Methuen & Co. Ltd., 1941, p.7.

Morality has always been connected with religion and with mysticism. The disappearance of the middle term leaves morality in a situation which is certainly more difficult but essentially the same. The background to morals is properly some sort of mysticism, if by this is meant a non-dogmatic essentially unformulated faith in the reality of the Good, occasionally connected with experience. The virtuous peasant knows, and I believe he will go on knowing, in spite of the removal or modification of the theological apparatus, although what he knows he might be at a loss to say. This view is of course not amenable even to a persuasive philosophical proof and can easily be challenged on all sorts of empirical grounds. However, I do not think that the virtuous peasant will be without resources...

I think the "machinery of salvation" (if it exists) is essentially the same for all. There is no complicated secret doctrine. We are all capable of criticizing, modifying and extending the area of strict obligation which we have inherited. Good is non-representable and indefinable. We are all mortal and equally at the mercy of necessity and chance.

These are the true aspects in which all men are brothers.

Iris Murdoch, *The Sovereignty of Good*, Routledge & Kegan Paul, 1970, p.74.

Hence Jesus Christ takes as man a place alike in the realms of ethics and of faith. He gives to us the moral standard of life, the ethical ideal; He discloses the culminating power of the religious consciousness, for He is, in the deep harmony of his relationship with God, the mystic ideal also.

While men were labouring to establish relationship with the unseen; while some, failing and despairing, broke into angry revolt against life, and others, deceiving themselves, reached a false repose by shutting out of sight the facts of ugly moral problems; Jesus Christ, keenly alive to evil and warm to defend the weak and the oppressed, keeping the ethical standard high and the ethical perception clear, lived a life of simple and unruffled heart repose. He realizes, and we see that He realizes, the double ideal, the ideal of righteousness and of inward peace. He realizes the perfect harmony, the peace which is no counterfeit; He lives a human life, but we feel that He lives all the time in the serene atmosphere of Heaven. In Him we get a glimpse of what the soul is whose birth and being are from the eternal love.

He seems something more than a soul filled with the divine; He seems to be one whose manhood is taken into God, and we no longer wonder that His utterances are sweet and satisfying; we listen to Him, and His teaching comes to us fresh on the breath of the sea and musical as the sound of falling rain.

William Boyd Carpenter, *The Witness to the Influence of Christ*, Constable & Co., Ltd., 1905, p.59.

NEIGHBOUR

"Neighbour"—"dweller in the same street or district, or as one having claims on others' friendliness."

This is a limited definition of "neighbour". On the lines of the Parable of the Good Samaritan I would extend it to include "anyone close by in need".

I was in a tube in South-East London. Four of us, from University College, London, were returning from a hockey match against our old rivals—King's. It was evening and I was wearing a dog-collar. There was a fracas on the platform. Suddenly we found ourselves in the middle of violence. A man leaped into our compartment, followed by a gang of youths, beating him up. The doors closed and the tube set off.

I put my things down and rushed over to them. "What's going on?" I shouted angrily.

One of the gang tried to mollify me. "He's given us some lip, Vicar, and we're teaching him a lesson."

"Well, pack it in," I cried out, greatly distressed.

Things then moved rather quickly. I didn't see this but behind me, another member of the gang seized my hockey stick, and was about to hit me. At this point the three members of our hockey team came to my rescue. Angry verbal exchanges took place. These continued until we reached the next station and the tube came to a halt. The doors opened. In the confusion the man managed to slip out unobserved. The doors shut and he was safe. The gang got caught inside with us and the tube set off. With a howl of frustration they glared angrily at us, then opened the inner door and disappeared along the tube. We were relieved to have come out of it unscathed, but learned that loving one's neighbour can sometimes be a costly business.

You shall not covet your neighbour's house; you shall not covet your neighbour's wife, or his manservant, or his maidservant, or his ox, or his ass, or anything that is your neighbour's.

Exodus 20.17.

You shall love your neighbour as yourself.

Leviticus 19.18.

As you did it to one of the least of these my brethren, you did it to me.

Matthew 25.40.

Let each of us please his neighbour for his good, to edify him.

Romans 15.2.

They who are all things to their neighbours cease to be anything to themselves.

Norman Douglas, *An Almanac*, Chatto & Windus in association with Martin Secker & Warburg Ltd., 1945, p.10.

Each man can learn something from his neighbour; at least he can learn this—to have patience with his neighbour, to live and let live.

Charles Kingsley, *Daily Thoughts*, Macmillan Publishers Ltd., 1884, p.59.

But it is His long-term policy, I fear, to restore to them a new kind of self-love—a charity and gratitude for all selves, including their own; when they have really learned to love their neighbours as themselves, they will be allowed to love themselves as their neighbours.

C.S. Lewis, *The Screwtape Letters*, Chivers Press, 1983, p.58.

Jesus, however, is not interested in universal, theoretical or poetical love... It is a love, not of man in general, of someone remote, with whom we are not personally involved, but quite concretely love of one's immediate neighbour... *anyone who wants me here and now.*

Hans Küng, *On Being a Christian*, translated by Edward Quinn, William Collins Sons & Co. Ltd., 1977, p.256.

We must... not mix ourselves up uninvited in other people's business. On the other hand we must not forget the danger lurking in the reserve which our practical daily life forces upon us. We cannot possibly let ourselves get frozen into regarding everyone we do not know as an absolute stranger.

Albert Schweitzer, *Memories of Childhood and Youth*, translated by C.T. Campion, George Allen & Unwin Publishers Ltd., 1924, p.95.

The ultimate measure of a man is not where he stands in moments of comfort and convenience, but where he stands at times of challenge and controversy. The true neighbour will risk his position, his prestige, and even his life for the welfare of others. In dangerous valleys and hazardous pathways, he will lift some bruised and beaten brother to a higher and more noble life.

Martin Luther King, *The Words of Martin Luther King*, selected by Coretta Scott King, William Collins Sons & Co. Ltd., 1986, p.24.

Strive to love your neighbours actively and indefatigably. And the nearer you come to achieving this love, the more convinced you will become of the existence of God and the immortality of your soul. If you reach the point of complete selflessness in your love of your neighbours, you will most certainly regain your faith and no doubt can possibly enter your soul. This has been proved. This is certain.

Fyodor Dostoyevsky, *The Brothers Karamazov*, translated by David Magarshack, Penguin Books Ltd., 1963, Volume 1, p.61.

The remarkable thing is that we really love our neighbour as ourselves: we do unto others as we do unto ourselves. We hate others when we hate ourselves. We are tolerant towards others when we tolerate ourselves. We forgive others when we forgive ourselves. We are prone to sacrifice others when we are ready to sacrifice ourselves.

It is not love of self but hatred of self which is at the root of all the troubles that afflict the world.

Eric Hoffer, *The Passionate State of Mind*, Martin Secker & Warburg Ltd., 1956, p.54.

The love of our neighbour in all its fullness simply means being able to say to him: "What are you going through?" It is a recognition that the sufferer exists, not only as a unit in a collection, or a specimen from the social category labelled "unfortunate", but as a man, exactly like us, who was one day stamped with a special mark by affliction. For this reason it is enough, but it is indispensable, to know how to look at him in a certain way.

This way of looking is first of all attentive. The soul empties itself of all its own contents in order to receive into itself the being it is looking at, just as he is, in all his truth.

Only he who is capable of attention can do this.

Simone Weil, *Waiting on God*, translated by Emma Craufurd, William Collins Sons & Co. Ltd., 1974, p.75.

"Love your neighbour as yourself." What does it mean if not putting him first, if he is less fortunate than yourself, as Abbé Pierre puts it.

It's at once simple and frightening.

Given this definition, who can confidently say that he truly loves his brothers, the way Christ intended? So many lives are built on illusion! A few kind gestures, a commitment or two, and you have a good conscience. We give a little of our lives and we're so proud of ourselves. We place ourselves in the ranks of "authentic Christians", but all we've given is a crumb or two.

As for me, what can I say for myself, I who have made a career of total giving?

Michel Quoist, *With Open Heart*, translated by Colette Copeland, Gill and Macmillan Ltd., 1983, p.155.

Because of its use by Jesus when, highlighting Lev. 19.18, he stated the two great commandments (Mark 12.28-34 and parallels), the term "neighbour" has become customary in discussion of Christian duty to other people. Its characteristic appearance in the singular ("thy neighbour," not "others") focuses attention on the specific case. Love is to be for *this* person in his or her individuality rather than for the human race in general. The Lucan version of the command, with the appended parable of the good Samaritan (Luke 10.25-37), made this even more striking: the neighbour is the one who acts for good precisely where there is no normal obligation. With the original reference to the fellow Jew, the definition of the neighbour was a subject of intense controversy in the time of Jesus. His teaching opens the gate as wide as possible.

From this beginning, the word has become the common Christian term for speaking, in ethical contexts, of the status of other people in relation to oneself, and so of the claims that they exercise.

J.L. Houlden, in *A New Dictionary of Christian Ethics*, edited by James F. Childress and John Macquarrie, SCM Press Ltd., 1986, p.418.

It is assumed that man loves himself. And it is just this obvious attitude of man toward himself which should be the measure—in practice, beyond measure—of love of neighbour. I know only too well what I owe myself and I am no less aware of what others owe me. In everything that we think, say and feel, do and suffer, we tend quite naturally to protect, shield, advance ourselves, to cherish ourselves. And now we are expected to give exactly the same care and attention to our neighbour. With this all reserves are broken down. For us, who are egoists by nature, it means a radical conversion: to accept the other person's standpoint; to give the other exactly what we think is due to ourselves: to treat our fellow man as we wish to be treated by him. As Jesus himself shows, this certainly does not mean any feebleness or softness, any renunciation of self-confidence, any annihilation of self in devout meditation or strenuous asceticism in the Buddhist or supposedly Christian sense. But it certainly does mean the orientation of ourselves towards others: an alertness, an openness, a receptivity for our fellow man, a readiness to help without reserve. It means living not for ourselves, but for others: in this—from the standpoint of the person who loves—is rooted the indissoluble unity of undivided love of God and the unlimited love of neighbour.

Hans Küng, *On Being a Christian*, translated by Edward Quinn, William Collins Sons & Co. Ltd., 1977, p.257.

PACIFISM

"Pacifism"—"the doctrine that the abolition of war is both desirable and possible."

I'm really horrified now by the efficiency of weapons systems. It seems as though the modern serviceman doesn't stand much of a chance in the warfare of today.

As a youth I accepted call-up without question. We were still very much in the aftermath of the Second World War. Basic training at Topsham Barracks, Exeter, was a mixed experience, but chiefly remembered for the deep belly laughs it produced. I greatly enjoyed my time at Mons Officer Cadet School, Aldershot, and learnt a great deal as well as having some good laughs there too. The fourteen months with the 2nd Gurkhas in Singapore were some of the most memorable months of my life. When the time approached to be demobbed, the C.O. took me to the "Club" for a game of tennis, and afterwards, asked me if I'd consider signing on. I thought it over. I'd really enjoyed my time with the Gurkhas. They were a delightful people to work with, keen, loyal, and efficient. The outdoor life suited my temperament. As a regular soldier the pay would be good—and the prospects promising. Yet in the last analysis I came to see that they were there to kill. I was unable to justify this as a life-time aim. I needed a more creative purpose in life, so had to say "no".

With the passage of time I now believe that the abolition of war is desirable, but not possible in our day and age. What we need is a spiritual revolution leading to a change of consciousness throughout the world before a full pacifist position is tenable. In the meantime we must work towards it.

He makes wars cease to the end of the earth; he breaks the bow, and shatters the spear, he burns the chariots with fire!

Psalm 46.9.

And they shall beat their swords into plowshares, and their spears into pruning hooks; nation shall not lift up sword against nation, neither shall they learn war any more.

Isaiah 2.4.

You have heard that it was said, "An eye for an eye and a tooth for a tooth." But I say to you. Do not resist one who is evil. But if any one strikes you on the right cheek, turn to him the other also.

Matthew 5.38-39.

All who take the sword will perish by the sword.

Matthew 26.52.

If you have a nation of men who have risen to that height of moral cultivation that they will not declare war or carry arms, for they have not so much madness left in their brains, you have a nation of lovers, of benefactors, of true, great, and able men.

Ralph Waldo Emerson, *Society and Solitude, Miscellanies*, "War," J.M. Dent & Sons Ltd., 1912, p.287.

I remain pacifist but I quite see that at present the Christian world is not "there" and attempts to preach it at the moment can only rouse resistance and reduce charity. Like you I think the final synthesis must reconcile the lion and the lamb—but meanwhile the crescendo of horror and evil and wholesale destruction of beauty is hard to accept...

Evelyn Underhill, *The Letters of Evelyn Underhill*, Longmans, Green & Co. Ltd., 1947, p.310.

The nonviolent approach does not immediately change the heart of the oppressor. It first does something to the hearts and souls of those committed to it. It gives them new self-respect; it calls up resources of strength and courage that they did not know they had. Finally it reaches the opponent and so stirs his conscience that reconciliation becomes a reality...Admittedly, nonviolence in the truest sense is not a strategy that one uses simply because it is expedient at the moment; nonviolence is ultimately a way of life that men live by because of the sheer morality of its claim. But even granting this, the willingness to use nonviolence as a technique is a step forward. For he who goes this far is more likely to adopt nonviolence later as a way of life.

Martin Luther King, *The Words of Martin Luther King*, selected by Coretta Scott King, William Collins Sons & Co. Ltd., 1986, p.79.

The principle of nonviolent resistance seeks to reconcile the truths of two opposites—acquiescence and violence—while avoiding the extremes and immoralities of both. The nonviolent resister agrees with the person who acquiesces that one should not be physically aggressive toward his opponent; but he balances the equation by agreeing with the person of violence that evil must be resisted. He avoids the nonresistance of the former and the violent resistance of the latter. With nonviolent resistance, no individual or group need submit to any wrong, nor need anyone resort to violence in order to right a wrong.

Martin Luther King, *The Words of Martin Luther King*, selected by Coretta Scott King, William Collins Sons & Co. Ltd., 1986, p.79.

Pacifism, which means "making peace", encompasses many different activities because "peace" itself can be narrow or broad, because "making" involves various positive and negative actions, and because it can be applied to personal, group, or national policies. Peter Brock holds that contemporary pacifism combines "advocacy of personal nonparticipation in war of any kind or in violent revolution with an endeavour to find nonviolent means of resolving conflict". A minimal, negative definition covers a wide range of historical positions: opposition to war and/or to direct participation in war through military service. Both violent resistance and revolution raise somewhat different problems about the Christian's relation to the state and have often been rejected even by Christians who have accepted war and participation in war. They have frequently drawn a sharp distinction between using violence *for* the state and using violence *against* it.

Despite the emphasis on "peace" in several senses in the New Testament, there is considerable debate about whether the New Testament is a pacifist document, in part because of ambiguities in Jesus' attitude toward violent resistence. Although Jesus' response to the centurion (Luke 7.9) suggested that it was not necessary to reject military service in order to enter the Kingdom of God, many non-pacifists concede that the dominant tendency of Jesus' life and message is pacifist. However, it is clear that Paul and others justified the government's use of the sword, both internally and externally (see Rom. 13.1-7; I Peter 2.14). Until A.D. 170-180, there is no direct evidence that Christians participated in military service or that they abstained from such service. For various reasons, including their position in society and their relations to the Roman Empire, it is probable that few Christians were soldiers. In the 2nd century, Celsus criticized Christians for not participating in military service, but there is evidence from A.D. 170-180 that some Christians were in the army. Their numbers increased in subsequent decades, and it appears that soldiers who converted to Christianity were not expected to leave the army. Dramatic changes occurred in the early 4th century with the conversion of Constantine, and by A.D. 416 only Christians could serve in the army. Nevertheless, Roland Bainton's comment is apt: "The age of persecution down to the time (of) Constantine was the *age of pacifism* to the degree that during this period no Christian author to our knowledge approved of Christian participation in battle."

James F. Childress, in *A New Theology of Christian Ethics*, edited by James F. Childress and John Macquarrie, SCM Press Ltd., 1986, p.446.

Pacifism means *peace-making*. The pacifist is literally a peace-maker. He is not a passive or negative person who proposes to lie back and do nothing in the face of injustice, unrighteousness and rampant evil. He stands for "the fiery positive". Pacifism is not a theory; it is a way of life. It is something you *are and do*.

I am a good deal disillusioned over the value of propaganda as a method of achieving moral and spiritual ends. It is no doubt immensely successful as a means of advertising commodities or of accomplishing utilitarian purposes. If you say a thing often enough, and if you say it emphatically enough, vast numbers of people will believe it. Practically any theory about life or about society will accumulate a following if vivid writers write it up, and if "peppy" speakers proclaim it as a panacea for the ills of the world.

But theories like good resolutions are very thin and abstract until they are put into operation and tried in practice...

St. Paul knew enough about the forces of evil to know that they could be conquered only by greater *forces*, and so he set forth his famous method—"overcome evil with good". There is no other way to overcome it. Something else, something better, must be put in its place. Something strong and positive must put it down, conquer it and make it cease to be. The evil that concerns us, the evil that really matters, is always embodied; it is incarnate in a person, or in a social institution, and consequently our new way of life, our pacifism, to meet it and overcome it, must be incarnate, too, and must have the dynamic of personal lives in it and behind it.

We shall not get very far with phrases like "passive resistance" or "non-resistance," or "the use of force is immoral". One can neither train a life nor build a world on those or any other slogans. In the last analysis children are trained and worlds are built by persons who are living concrete and positive lives, whose theories have taken on flesh and blood and have behind them the attractive power of a strong personality. There would be little use having our Government and all the other governments of the world adopt abstract resolutions to the effect that military force shall be outlawed and shall never be resorted to again, if at the same time all the selfish and unjust methods of life and business and social relations were left to work just as they are now working. War is a fruit which grows and ripens like other fruit. No magic phrase, no written scrap of paper, will stop the ripening of it if the tree which bears it is planted and watered and kept in the sunshine and warm air. The axe must first be laid to the root of the tree. The old way of life must be abolished and a new way of life must be produced and made to flourish. We shall never succeed in stopping war until we have a human society permeated with persons who practice a way of life which removes and abolishes the grounds and occasions of war, and which at the same time matures and ripens a spirit of mutual understanding and personal co-operation...

If we are to be effective peace-makers we must be vastly more than propagandists. We must demonstrate the power of the kind of life which conquers evil and produces the fruits of peace and good will. Under the old system, armies invaded countries and conquered them with force. Our method, too, must be one of *invasion.* God invaded Africa through David Livingstone and He has invaded Labrador through Sir Wilfred Grenfell. Both these men are types of the overcoming way of life. They conquer men as surely as Alexander or Napoleon did, only their force is different. It is good will and kindness, it is love and gentleness, it is health and strength, it is light and healing. It invades and conquers, overcomes, transforms, rebuilds and inaugurates the new day. Let us join the ranks of the "invaders"

Rufus M. Jones, The New Quest, Macmillan Publishers Ltd., 1928, p.97.

PASSION

"Passion"— "strong emotion; outburst of anger; sexual love; strong enthusiasm."

P assion can be used for good or ill. A memory comes back of the voyage to Singapore on the troopship, the Empire Fowey. It was about 10.00pm. We were probably somewhere in the Indian Ocean. I was in my cabin, quietly reading a novel, when a colleague from the 6th Gurkhas knocked on the door. He was concerned about the safety of a seventeen-year-old girl, the daughter of an older officer. One of our colleagues had drunk too much, and was thought to be making off with her. I allowed myself to be manipulated and we went off to see what we could do. His fears proved to be entirely correct. I tried to do a rescue operation, and promptly got belted. It taught me to be more cautious when sexual passion is aroused.

But passion can be an extremely valuable part of our nature. We had an undergraduate who used his abundant energy creatively. He spent his teenage years in getting well read. This greatly enriched his student years. At College he studied Mods and Greats (Classics), a demanding four year course, and came out with a good degree. He was a keen rugger player and before coming up to university, had already toured New Zealand, playing in distinguished company. An international blocked his attempts to play against Cambridge for two consecutive years. However he persevered and managed to get a Blue in his final year. You couldn't hope to meet a nicer person. He was someone who had learnt to use his passion creatively, and in a wholesome way.

A tranquil mind gives life to the flesh, but passion makes the bones rot.

Proverbs 14.30.

And those who belong to Christ Jesus have crucified the flesh with its passions and desires.

Galatians 5.24.

So shun youthful passions and aim at righteousness, faith, love, and peace.

2 Timothy 2.22.

These are grumblers, malcontents, following their own passions, loud-mouthed boasters, flattering people to gain advantage.

Jude 16.

If Passion drives, let Reason hold the Reins.

Benjamin Franklin, *Poor Richard's Alamanack*, Taurus Press, 1962, p.8.

Conquer your passions and you conquer the whole world.

Hindu Proverb.

Passion, though a bad regulator, is a powerful spring.

Ralph Waldo Emerson, *The Conduct of Life*, J.M. Dent & Sons Ltd., 1911, p.276.

Our passions are wild beasts. God grant us power to muzzle them.

Sir Walter Scott, *The Journal of Sir Walter Scott*, Oxford University Press, 1951, p.162.

Do not give too much way to thy passions, if thou dost expect happiness.

Henry Fielding, *Joseph Andrews*, J.M. Dent & Sons Ltd., 1973, p.249.

Religion is a restraint on man's passions and appetites, and so promotes his prosperity.

Henry Ward Beecher, *Proverbs from Plymouth Pulpit*, Charles Burnet & Co., 1887, p.124.

To control our passions we must govern our habits, and keep watch over ourselves in the small details of everyday life.

Sir John Lubbock, *The Pleasures of Life*, Macmillan Publishers Ltd., 1891, p.44.

Our passions are regular phoenixes. As the old one is consumed, straightway the new rises out of the ashes.

Johann Wolfgang von Goethe, *Wisdom and Experience*, selected by Ludwig Curtius, translated and edited by Hermann J. Weigand, Routledge & Kegan Paul, 1949, p.188.

Give me that man
That is not passion's slave.

William Shakespeare, *Hamlet*, Act III. sc.ii. l.69.

And passion makes us Cowards grow,
What made us brave before.

John Dryden, *The Poems and Fables of John Dryden*, edited by James Kinsley, Oxford University Press, 1970, *An Evening's Love*, Song 1, l.15, p.125.

The passion to get ahead is sometimes born of a fear lest we get left behind.

Eric Hoffer, *The Passionate State of Mind*, Martin Secker & Warburg Ltd., 1956, p.115.

The way to avoid evil is not by maiming our passions, but by compelling them to yield their vigour to our moral nature.

Henry Ward Beecher, *Proverbs from Plymouth Pulpit*, Charles Burnet & Co., 1887, p.6.

The natural man has only two primal passions, to get and to beget,—to get the means of sustenance (and today a little more) and to beget his kind.

William Osler, *Science and Immortality*, Constable & Co. Ltd., 1919, p.20.

> Take heed least Passion sway
> Thy Judgement to do aught, which else free Will
> Would not admit.

John Milton, *The Poetical Works of Milton*, edited by H.C. Beeching, Oxford University Press, 1950, *Paradise Lost*, Bk.VIII, l.635, p.349.

The passions are never doing their proper work unless they are like locomotives behind a train; the functions of the passions in a Christian is to go behind conscience and love, and make them powerful and fruitful.

Henry Ward Beecher, *Proverbs from Plymouth Pulpit*, Charles Burnet & Co., 1887, p.165.

The fugitive, brief, though intense satisfactions that come to the nerves through the appetite and passions are not the foundations of joy in this world: they come in a moment's flush, and are disastrous in their flight.

Henry Ward Beecher, *Proverbs from Plymouth Pulpit*, Charles Burnet & Co., 1887, p.186.

Passion is a sort of fever in the mind, which ever leaves us weaker than it found us ... It, more than any thing, deprives us the use of our judgment; for it raises a dust very hard to see through ... It may not unfitly be termed the mob of the man, that commits a riot upon his reason.

William Penn, *Fruits of Solitude*, A.W. Bennett, 1863, p.41.

Every man is a tamer of wild beasts, and these wild beasts are his passions. To draw their teeth and claws, to muzzle and tame them, to turn them into servants and domestic animals, fuming, perhaps, but submissive—in this consists personal education.

Henri Frédéric Amiel, *Amiel's Journal*, translated by Mrs. Humphry Ward, Macmillan Publishers Ltd., 1918, p.83.

Whenever a man talks loudly against religion,—always suspect that it is not his reason, but his passions which have got the better of his CREED. A bad life and a good belief are disagreeable and troublesome neighbours, and where they separate, depend upon it, 'tis for no other cause but quietness' sake.

Laurence Sterne, *The Life and Opinions of Tristram Shandy*, edited by Melvyn New and Joan New, The University Presses of Florida, 1978, Volume 1, p.164.

There is in most passions a shrinking away from ourselves. The passionate pursuer has all the earmarks of a fugitive.

Passions usually have their roots in that which is blemished, crippled, incomplete and insecure within us. The passionate attitude is less a response to stimuli from without than an emanation of an inner dissatisfaction.

Eric Hoffer, *The Passionate State of Mind*, Martin Secker & Warburg Ltd., 1956, p.1.

Passion enslaves us: the love which God gives sets us free. Passion blinds us to the defects of the loved one: this love sees the defects in other mortals, but loves just the same. Passion is hungry, demanding, exclusive: this love is generous, releasing, eager to be shared. Passion can turn to sudden anger and destroy the object of its fierce desire: this love is never ungovernable and always creative. It is by love that man comes to freedom, and there is no other way.

W.E. Sangster, *The Pure in Heart*, Epworth Press, 1954, p.243.

I am capable of all the passions, for I bear them all within me. Like a tamer of wild beasts, I keep them caged and lassoed, but sometimes hear them growling... I will have none of those passions of straw which dazzle, burn up, and wither; I invoke, I await, and I hope for the love which is great, pure, and earnest, which lives and works in all the fibres and through all the powers of the soul. And even if I go lonely to the end, I would rather my hope and my dream died with me, than that my soul should content itself with any meaner union.

Henri Frédéric Amiel, *Amiel's Journal*, translated by Mrs. Humphry Ward, Macmillan Publishers Ltd., 1918, p.30.

It is strange how the moment we have reason to be dissatisfied with ourselves we are set upon by a pack of clamourous desires. Is desire somehow an expression of the centrifugal force that tears and pulls us away from an undesirable self? A gain of self-esteem usually reduces the pull of the appetites, while a crisis in self-esteem is likely to cause a weakening or a complete breakdown of self-discipline.

Asceticism is sometimes a deliberate effort to reverse a reaction in the chemistry of our soul: by suppressing desire we try to rebuild and bolster self-esteem.

Eric Hoffer, *The Passionate State of Mind*, Secker & Warburg, 1956, p.3.

The sources of individual power and personal influence... are not in the first instance in the head but in the heart. "Out of the heart are the issues of life." The power of the person is the *passion* of the person. It is the *passion* for truth which marks the important philosopher or teacher. It is the *passion* for righteousness which makes the great moral leader. It is the *passion* for justice which distinguishes the leader among jurists. And in industry it is not the passion for profits but for *people* which distinguishes the leader from the mere executive. Nor is it without significance in this connection that passion means in its original sense, capacity to suffer and endure.

Ordway Tead, *The Art of Leadership*, McGraw-Hill Book Company, 1935, p.103.

Both the spiritual and bodily powers of a man increase, and are perfected and strengthened by exercise. By exercising yourself in good works or in conquering your vices and temptation, you will in time learn to do good works easily and with delight: and with the help of God's grace you will easily learn to conquer your vices. If you cease praying, or pray seldom, prayer will be oppressive to you. If you do not fight against your sinful habits, or only do so seldom and feebly, you will find it very difficult to fight, and you will often be conquered by them; if you do not learn how to conquer them, they will give you no rest, and your life will be poisoned by them.

Father John of Kronstadt, *Spiritual Counsels of Father John of Kronstadt*, W. Jardine Grisbrooke, James Clarke & Co. Ltd., 1966, p.133.

Men torture and kill other men in order to satisfy their animal instincts, and to gratify the urges of matter in them.

The spark of light, which ought to illumine their road towards their Maker, burns dim, and the voice of their conscience, which is the voice of their Maker speaking through them, cannot always be heard. When it is heard, it helps them to master their instincts and to behave as individuations all born from the same source; whenever they hear it is too late, it shows them the extent of their betrayal of the brotherhood or oneness to which they belong, and the loss which their inhuman behaviour imposes upon the one which created them. But all these failings, all the hatred which men have for other men, together with their blindness to truth, their selfishness, and their pride, which leads some of them to believe that they alone know the truth, and that therefore they can dispose of their fellow-beings' lives, as if they were worthless insects, cannot be ascribed to any imaginary original fall. These failings are part of their finitude, and therefore part of the human condition. Yet man, like the rest of creation, is not static, he is part of the continuous creativity which informs the Universe. In fact, although very young on this earth, he has already accomplished immense strides, which consist in having become aware of the direction in which he is going, and of the possibilities of his brief, yet precious, life.

J. Chiari, *Religion and Modern Society*, Herbert Jenkins, 1964, p.165.

PATIENCE

"Patience"—"calm endurance of pain or any provocation; perseverance."

I was visiting a block of high rise flats in Bradford. One of the doors was slightly ajar, so I knocked and was invited in. I met Doreen for the first time—a woman in her late thirties. She was a paraplegic, with hardly any legs, and a hunchback. She had great difficulties with one of her arms, which hung loosely from her shoulder. Numerous operations had failed to remove the roots of a troublesome abcess. The arm looked to be held to the shoulder by skin. Life had not been easy for Doreen. She had been like this from birth. She was kept going by the patience of Job.

We became friends, and I used to see her on a regular basis. Each visit was a challenge. She was well endowed with Yorkshire directness and very much a no-nonsense person. There were no easy answers for her. Any false utterance was quickly demolished by caustic invective. God was no help to her in her suffering. Frank Sinatra was. So was her cat Chloe—a vicious creature when hungry—but a constant source of comfort and affection for Doreen when fed.

I learnt a lot about patience from Doreen when visiting her in her flat, in hospital, and later on in a Cheshire Home. Not surprisingly, "patience" is one of the fruits of the Spirit. It is often found in unusual places—and people.

Be still before the Lord, and wait patiently for him.
Psalm 37.7.

But they who wait for the Lord shall renew their strength, they shall mount up with wings like eagles, they shall run and not be weary, they shall walk and not faint.
Isaiah 40.31.

We have peace with God through our Lord Jesus Christ. Through him we have obtained access to this grace in which we stand, and we rejoice in our hope of sharing the glory of God. More than that, we rejoice in our sufferings, knowing that suffering produces endurance, and endurance produces character, and character produces hope, and hope does not disappoint us, because God's love has been poured into our hearts through the Holy Spirit which has been given to us.

Romans 5.1-5.

But let patience have her perfect work, that ye be perfect and entire, wanting in nothing.

James 1.4 (A.V.).

Patience and application will carry us through.

Thomas Fuller, *Gnomologia*, Stearne Brock, 1733, p.164.

Though God take the sun out of the heaven, yet we must have patience.

George Herbert, *The Works of George Herbert*, edited by F.E. Hutchinson, Clarendon Press, 1945, *Outlandish Proverbs*, No.980, p.353.

This impatience or strenuousness is the white man's characteristic, and his curse.

Norman Douglas, *An Almanac*, Chatto & Windus in association with Martin Secker & Warburg Ltd., 1945, p.26.

I know how unbearable is suspense of mind, to have to face a situation which one cannot alter or even affect, and have to wait.

A.C. Benson, *Extracts from the Letters of Dr. A.C. Benson to M.E.A.*, Jarrold Publishing, 1927, p.7.

I can see that patience is essential in this life, for there is much that goes against the grain. Whatever I do to ensure my peace, I find that fighting and suffering are inevitable.

Thomas à Kempis, *The Imitation of Christ*, translated by Betty I. Knott, William Collins Sons & Co. Ltd., 1979, p.129.

People are always talking of perseverance, and courage, and fortitude; but patience is the first and worthiest part of fortitude—and the rarest too.

John Ruskin, *Ethics of the Dust*, George Allen & Sons, 1907, p.61.

I do oppose
My patience to his fury, and am armed
To suffer with a quietness of spirit
The very tyranny and rage of his.

William Shakespeare, *The Merchant of Venice*, Act IV. sc.i. l.9.

To be silent, to suffer, to pray, when there is no room for outward action, is an acceptable offering to God. A disappointment, a contradiction, an injury received and endured for God's sake, are of as such value as a long prayer.

François de la M. Fénelon, *Spiritual Thoughts for Busy People*, SPCK, 1894, p.80.

Patience and diligence, like faith, remove mountains. Never give out while there is hope; but hope not beyond reason: for that shews more desire than judgment. It is a profitable wisdom, to know when we have done enough; much time and pains are spared, in not flattering ourselves against probabilities.

William Penn, *Fruits of Solitude*, A.W. Bennett, 1863, p.36.

We must wait for God, long, meekly, in the wind and wet, in the thunder and the lightning, in the cold and the dark. Wait, and He will come. He never comes to those who do not wait. He does not go their road. When He comes, go with Him, but go slowly, fall a little behind; when He quickens His pace, be sure of it, before you quicken yours. But when He slackens, slacken at once. And do not be slow only, but silent, very silent, for He is God.

F.W. Faber, *Growth in Holiness*, Thomas Richardson and Son, 1855, p.148.

The exercise of patience involves a continual practice of the presence of God; for we may be come upon at any moment for an almost heroic display of good temper. And it is a short road to unselfishness; for nothing is left to self. All that seems to belong most intimately to self, to be self's private property, such as time, home, and rest, are invaded by these continual trials of patience. The family is full of such opportunities, and the sanctity of marriage abounds with them.

F.W. Faber, *Growth in Holiness*, Thomas Richardson and Son, 1855, p.137.

Let this be plainly said again, however elementary it must seem to those who deeply think on the things of God. He does not work our way. His might finds fitting expression, not in the power to wound, but in the power to woo. His power is not coercion, but constraint. Never does He violate the personality that He has made. With infinite patience, He seeks to win the wayward and the wicked by all the dear inducements of love, and our hard task is this: *to have patience with the patience of God.*

W.E. Sangster, *These Things Abide*, Hodder & Stoughton Ltd., 1939, p.70.

Patience is the most difficult thing of all and the only thing that is worth learning. All nature, all growth, all peace, everything that flowers and is beautiful in the world depends on patience, requires time, silence, trust, and faith in long-term processes which far exceed any single lifetime, which are accessible to the insight of no one person, and which in their totality can be experienced only by peoples and epochs, not by individuals.

Hermann Hesse, in *Reflections*, Volker Michels, translated by Ralph Manheim, Jonathan Cape Ltd., 1977, p.58.

Most men and women catch a gleam of God's glory at some point of their earthly pilgrimage. But the cares of this world, and our fatal preoccupation with ourselves, keep our eyes cast downwards. We neither watch, nor long, nor expect to see it again. The saint watches, longs, and expects. He watches unto prayer, longs with a growing intensity, has patience in the dark, and faith to believe that his eyes will behold it. The vision of God begets humility in his soul as naturally as our eyes blink when we step into strong sunshine....

Not only is humility a necessary consequence of seeing God. The saint learns that the more humility he has, the more of God he will have also.

W.E. Sangster, *The Pure in Heart*, Epworth Press, 1954, p.164.

"In your patience, possess ye your soul." (S. Luke 21.19). The soul loses itself by impatience; whereas, when it submits without repining, it possesses itself in peace, and it also possesses God. To be impatient is to will what one has not; or not to will what one has. An impatient soul is a slave to passion, having cast off the restraints of reason and faith.

What weakness! what error in this! As long as we *will* the evil we endure, it is not evil; why then should we make it a real evil, by refusing to bear it willingly? The inward peace resides, not in the senses, or inferior appetites, but in the will. It may be preserved amidst the bitterest sorrows, as long as the will continues in a firm resignation. Peace here below consists not in an exemption from suffering, but in a voluntary acceptance of it.

François de la M. Fénelon, *Spiritual Thoughts for Busy People*, SPCK, 1894, p.24.

Not only are the saints brave:

They are patient. The fruit of the Spirit is longsuffering. It is the courage which *endures.* They go on when everything seems knocked out of them and the cause itself quite lost. In their early days, many of the saints were in a hurry but, when they learned that God is not in a hurry, they found patience. The things they longed for were coming as fast as God could bring them, and they learned patience with the patience of God. Perhaps nothing helped them more than the recollection of God's long patience with their own unsanctified souls.

Someone has said that the secret of patience is "doing something else in the meantime". The "something else" the saints do is to dwell on the use God can make even now of the trials which beset them. "Let me receive them with patient meekness," they seem to say "and perhaps by this means, God will polish His jewel."

W.E. Sangster, *The Pure in Heart*, Epworth Press, 1954, p.129.

A waiting person is a patient person. The word *patience* means the willingness to stay where we are and live the situation out to the fullest in the belief that something hidden there will manifest itself to us. Impatient people are always expecting the real thing to happen somewhere else and therefore want to go elsewhere. The moment is empty. But patient people dare to stay where they are. Patient living means to live actively in the present and wait there. Waiting, then, is not passive. It involves nurturing the moment, as a mother nurtures the child that is growing in her. Zechariah, Elizabeth, and Mary were present to the moment. That is why they could hear the angel. They were alert, attentive to the voice that spoke to them and said, "Don't be afraid. Something is happening to you. Pay attention."

Henri J.M. Nouwen, *Seeds of Hope*, edited by Robert Durback, Darton, Longman & Todd Ltd., 1989, p.103.

To be patient with self is an almost incalculable blessing, and the shortest road to improvement, as well as the quickest means by which an interior spirit can be formed within us, short of that immediate touch of God which makes some souls interior all at once. It breeds considerateness and softness of manner towards others. It disinclines us to censoriousness, because of the abiding sense of our own imperfections. It quickens our perception of utterest dependence on God and grace, and produces at the same time evenness of temper and equality of spirits, because it is at once an effort, and yet a quiet sustained effort. It is a constant source of acts of the most genuine humility. In a word, by it we act upon self from without, as if we were not self, but self's master, or self's guardian angel. And when this is done in the exterior life as well as the interior, what remains in order to perfection?

F.W. Faber, *Growth in Holiness*, Thomas Richardson and Son, 1855, p.140.

PEACE

"Peace"—"freedom from, cessation of, war, freedom from civil disorder, quiet tranquillity, mental calm, bring person, oneself, back into friendly relations."

I can clearly remember the Japanese surrender, heralding the end of the Second World War. For the first time for several years we experienced peace. There was an immediate lessening of tension everywhere and a great communal sense of relief. At last we could relax and start enjoying life again.

At a more personal level, and twenty years later, I recall a visit to the Bradford Royal Infirmary. There I met a man in one of the wards. He was dying of cancer and knew it. I was struck by his appearance. He had a calm, serene disposition and quiet demeanour. He had come to terms with the fact that he was shortly to die, and I was impressed by his faith and peace of mind—so rarely to be found.

He was troubled by a row in the ward between a patient and a nurse. This had somehow tarnished the atmosphere, so he set about trying to sort it out. He first of all became friendly with the patient, and got to know him well. Then he befriended the nurse and later reconciled the two. He was delighted with the outcome, especially as the peaceful atmosphere of the ward was restored. I was impressed by his action and wondered why a man, shortly to die, should concern himself with what might seem to be a trivial thing. But peace is supremely important and many of us can be instruments of peace, wherever we are—in the home, at school, at work, even in hospital. Peace, as with patience, is one of the fruits of the Spirit, and is its own reward.

The Lord is my shepherd, I shall not want; he makes me lie down in green pastures. He leads me beside still waters; he restores my soul. He leads me in paths of righteousness for his name's sake.

Psalm 23.1-3.

Thou dost keep him in perfect peace, whose mind is stayed on thee, because he trusts in thee.

Isaiah 26.3.

Blessed are the peacemakers, for they shall be called sons of God.

Matthew 5.9.

Peace I leave with you; my peace I give to you; not as the world gives do I give to you. Let not your hearts be troubled, neither let them be afraid.

John 14.27.

Peace,
The central feeling of all happiness.

William Wordsworth, *The Excursion*, Book Third, l.382.

Peace comes not by establishing a calm outward setting so much as by inwardly surrendering to whatever the setting.

Hubert van Zeller, *Leave Your Life Alone*, Sheed and Ward Ltd., 1973, p.103.

Peace hath her victories
No less renowned than war.

John Milton, *The Poetical Works of John Milton*, the Clarendon Press, edited by Helen Darbishire, 1955,Volume II, *Sonnet XVI*, l.10, p.154.

Live in peace yourself and then you can bring peace to others—a peaceable man does more good than a learned one.

Thomas à Kempis, *The Imitation of Christ*, translated by Betty I. Knott, William Collins Sons & Co. Ltd., 1979, p.87.

I am a child of peace and am resolved to keep the peace for ever and ever, with the whole world, inasmuch as I have concluded it at last with my own self.

Johann Wolfgang von Goethe, *Wisdom and Experience*, selected by Ludwig Curtius, translated and edited by Hermann J. Weigand, Routledge & Kegan Paul, 1949, p.295.

This is certain, that there is no peace but in the will of God. God's will is our peace and there is no other peace. God's peace is perfect freedom and there is no other freedom.

Father Andrew SDC, *The Life and Letters of Fr. Andrew SDC*, Mowbray, 1948, p.121.

Calm soul of things! make it mine
To feel amid the city's jar,
That there abides a peace of thine,
Man did not make, and cannot mar!

Matthew Arnold, *In Kensington Gardens*, l.37.

When people are praying for peace, the cause of peace is being strengthened by their very act of prayer, for they are themselves becoming immersed in the spirit of peace, and committed to the cause of peace.

John Macquarrie, *The Concept of Peace*, SCM Press Ltd., 1973, p.81.

Peace does not mean the end of all our striving,
Joy does not mean the drying of our tears;
Peace is the power that comes to souls arriving
Up to the light where God Himself appears.

G.A. Studdert Kennedy, *The Unutterable Beauty*, Hodder & Stoughton Ltd., 1964, *The Suffering God*, p.13.

There will be true peace, where none will suffer attack from within himself nor from any foe outside.
        The reward of virtue will be God himself, who gave the virtue, together with the promise of himself, the best and greatest of all possible promises.

St. Augustine of Hippo, *The City of God*, edited by David Knowles, Penguin Books Ltd., 1972, p.1088.

No man has touched the essential characteristic of Christianity, and no man has entered into the interior spirit of Christianity, who has not reached to a certain extent that peace which Christ said He gave to His disciples, and which at times they declared to be past all understanding.

Henry Ward Beecher, *Proverbs from Plymouth Pulpit*, Charles Burnet & Co., 1887, p.169.

There is an experience of being in pure consciousness which gives lasting peace to the soul. It is an experience of the Ground or Depth of being in the Centre of the soul, an awareness of the mystery of being beyond sense and thought, which gives a sense of fulfilment, of finality, of absolute truth.

Bede Griffiths, O.S.B., *Return to the Centre*, William Collins Sons & Co. Ltd., 1976, p.136.

The past is prophetic in that it asserts loudly that wars are poor chisels for carving out peaceful tomorrows. One day we must come to see that peace is not merely a distant goal that we seek, but a means by which we arrive at that goal. We must pursue peaceful ends through peaceful means. How much longer must we play at deadly war games before we heed the plaintive pleas of the unnumbered dead and maimed of past wars?

Martin Luther King, *The Words of Martin Luther King*, selected by Coretta Scott King, William Collins Sons & Co. Ltd., 1986, p.83.

Peace is only to be found in reconciliation with destiny, when destiny seems, in the religious sense of the word, *good*; that is to say, when man feels himself directly in the presence of God. Then, and then only, does the will acquiesce. Nay, more, it only completely acquiesces when it adores. The soul only submits to the hardness of fate by virtue of its discovery of a sublime compensation—the lovingkindness of the Almighty.

Henri Frederic Amiel, *Amiel's Journal*, translated by Mrs. Humphry Ward, Macmillan Publishers Ltd., 1918, p.222.

In the Bible the word *peace, shalom*, never simply means the absence of trouble. Peace means everything which makes for our highest good. The peace which the world offers us is the peace of escape, the peace which comes from the avoidance of trouble, the peace which comes from refusing to face things. The peace which Jesus offers us is the peace of conquest. It is the peace which no experience in life can ever take from us. It is the peace which no sorrow, no danger, no suffering can make less. It is the peace which is independent of outward circumstances.

William Barclay, *The Gospel of John*, The Saint Andrew Press, 1974, Volume Two, p.199.

There are periods which can be called "the peace of the Church", but all history shows how brief and transitory they are. Each such period is followed by new, unforeseen and different conflicts and problems; the Church is challenged to fresh discoveries of truth, and to new kinds of victory. Have we any right to suppose that it will be different for the individual who is a member of the Church? Can he claim a permanent and undisturbed peace, such as is not granted to the Church as a whole? Must he not expect that the pattern of his life too will be in conflict until the very end? He has indeed been translated into the kingdom of God's dear Son (Col. 1.13). He may hope, like his Master, to have the peace of God in his heart. But for all that, he still lives in the old world-order, with which the new is at death grips; and this must furnish the basic pattern of Christian living in the world.

Stephen Neill, *Christian Holiness*, Lutterworth Press, 1960, p.41.

All that matters is to be at one with the living God
to be a creature in the house of the God of Life.
Like a cat asleep on a chair
at peace, in peace
and at one with the master of the house, with the mistress,
at home, at home in the house of the living,
sleeping on the hearth, and yawning before the fire.
Sleeping on the hearth of the living world
yawning at home before the fire of life

feeling the presence of the living God
like a great reassurance
a deep calm in the heart
a presence
as of the master sitting at the board
in his own and greater being,
in the house of life.

D.H. Lawrence, *The Complete Poems of D.H. Lawrence*, edited by Vivian de Sola Pinto and Warren Roberts, William Heinemann Ltd., Volume Two, *Pax*, p.700.

The fact is that true peace cannot come save from God. It has only one name: the peace of Christ. It has one aspect, that impressed on it by Christ who, as if to anticipate the counterfeits of man, emphasized: "Peace I leave with you, my peace I give to you."

The appearance of true peace is threefold:

Peace of heart: Peace is before all else an interior thing, belonging to the spirit, and its fundamental condition is a loving and filial dependence on the will of God. "Thou has made us for thyself, O Lord, and our heart is restless till it rest in thee."

Social peace: This is solidly based on mutual and reciprocal respect for the personal dignity of man. The Son of God was made man, and his redeeming act concerns not only mankind as a whole, but also the individual man... Such is the teaching of the Church, which, for the solution of these social questions, has always fixed her gaze on the human person and has taught that things and institutions— goods, the economy, the state—are primarily for man, not man for them...

International peace: The basis of international peace is, above all, truth. For in international relations, too, the Christian saying is valid: "The truth shall make you free."

It is necessary, then, to overcome certain erroneous ideas: the myths of force, of nationalism, or of other things that have poisoned fraternal life among peoples. And it is necessary that peaceful "living-together" be based on moral principles and be in accord with the teaching of right reason and of Christian doctrine.

Pope John XXIII, *Readings from Pope John*, edited by Vincent A. Yzermans, Mowbray, 1968, p.55.

"Peace I leave with you: my peace I give unto you, not as the world giveth."—John 14.27.

All men seek for peace, but they do not seek it where it is to be found. The peace that the world can give is as different from that which God bestows, as God is different from men; or rather, the world promises peace, but never gives it.

It presents some passing pleasures to us, but these cost more than they are worth. It is only the religion of Jesus that can give us peace. This sets us at peace with ourselves; it subdues our passions, and regulates our desires; it consoles us with the hope of everlasting good; it gives us the joy of the holy Spirit; it enables us to be happy; it gives us peace of mind in the midst of outward trials; and as the source from whence it springs is inexhaustible, and as the recesses of the soul which it inhabits are inaccessible to the malignity of man, it is to the righteous a treasure that can never fail.

True peace is the possession of the favour of God. This is found only in submission, faith, and obedience to his laws; it is the result of a pure and holy love for him. Resign every forbidden joy; restrain every wish that is not referred to his will; banish all eager desires, all anxiety. Desire only the will of God, seek him alone, and you will find peace; you shall enjoy it in spite of the world. What is it that troubles you? poverty, neglect, want of success, external or internal troubles? Look upon everything as in the hands of God, and as real blessings that he bestows upon his children, of which you receive your portion. Then, the world may turn its face from you, but nothing will deprive you of peace.

François de la M. Fénelon, *Selections from the Writings of Fénelon*, Mrs Follen, Edward T. Whitfield, 1850, p.237.

PENITENCE

"Penitence"—"concerned with making a full and sincere confession of sins, declaring sorrow for them, and promising to amend his or her life, and so make restitution to those whom he or she had wronged."

I was troubled by something I had done, and decided to go to an elderly and experienced priest to make a confession—not my normal practice at all. Somewhat dreading the ordeal, I found myself in the presence of a monk with bright penetrating eyes. We talked for a while, enough to put me at ease, and establish some kind of rapport. I became aware of being in the presence of a real man of God, kindly disposed and understanding, but also direct and down to earth. He inspired confidence.

I made my confession. He listened with a calm semi-detached air. When I finished speaking, there were a few moments of silence—a pause for thought. He then gave me some simple words of advice, as a penance, and pronounced absolution.

I left the monastery feeling as though I was off to a fresh start. An enormous burden had been lifted from my shoulders. I experienced a sense of delight at the prospect of new life ahead. It was as if my soul had undergone a radical spring-clean. Penitence thus experienced was not all sorrow—the prevailing element was joy and a new quality of life.

If you return to the Almighty and humble yourself, if you remove unrighteousness far from your tents . . . then you will delight yourself in the Almighty, and lift up your face to God.

Job 22.23,26.

I acknowledged my sin to thee, and I did not hide my iniquity; I said, "I will confess my transgressions to the Lord"; then thou didst forgive the guilt of my sin.

Psalm 32.5.

And they were baptized by him in the river Jordan, confessing their sins.

Matthew 3.6.

Draw near to God and he will draw near to you. Cleanse your hands . . . and purify your hearts, you men of double mind.

James 4.8.

One mustn't be truly penitent because one anticipates God's forgiveness, but because one already possesses it.

John Osborne, *Luther*, Faber & Faber Ltd., 1961, Act II, sc.ii, p.56.

When we have heartily repented of wrong we should let all the waves of forgetfulness roll over it, and go forward unburdened to meet the future.

Henry Ward Beecher, *Proverbs from Plymouth Pulpit*, Charles Burnet & Co., 1887, p.163.

Bad I am, but yet thy child.
Father, be thou reconciled.
Spare thou me, since I see
With thy might that thou art mild.

Gerard Manley Hopkins, *The Poems of Gerard Manley Hopkins*, edited by W.H. Gardner and N.H. Mackenzie, Oxford University Press, 1970, No.155, p.194.

Hasn't *my* penitence been spurious at times? Have I been sorry, not because I have offended God, but because I have lost my inner peace, or found my spirit clouded, or missed the sweets of communion with Heaven? Am I cast down, not because I have offended against His holy laws, but because I have suffered some personal deprivations? This is not true repentance.

W.E. Sangster, *Westminster Sermons*, Epworth Press, 1960, Volume One, *At Morning Worship*, p.21.

The word (Penance) derives from the Latin *paenitentia*, meaning penitence or repentance. In Christian history it has variously designated an inner turning to God or a public returning to the church, any of a series of ecclesiastical disciplines, designed to facilitate such inward or outward reconversion, and the various works that had to be performed as part of such disciplines.

J. Martos, in *A New Dictionary of Christian Theology*, edited by Alan Richardson and John Bowden, SCM Press Ltd., 1985, p.435.

It is a brave thing to be penitent, to get down on our knees and ask for the courage to face our souls and the fact of our own failure. Every saint is a penitent; only the bravery of their penitence went very far, and they had the courage of faith. The virtues of humility and courage shine in their halos. When they fell, they got up again and owned their fault; they fell again, and again they rose, until the day came when they fell and rose and fell no more, because the courage of their faith had won the victory.

Father Andrew SDC, *Meditations for Every Day*, Mowbray, 1941, p.88.

Penitence can never spring from the realization of one's sins . . . On the contrary, it is the result of adoration. It flows naturally out of the security that comes into one's life as one is led to a positive view of the goodness of life and the glory and love of God. It flowers and fruits only in fertile stretches of happiness. If any one had the luck really to see life as a welcoming love he would begin to feel nervous and ashamed about what his current attempt at being human amounted to.

J. Neville Ward, *The Use of Praying*, Epworth Press, 1967, p.41.

People have such wrong ideas of penitence. They think that you are only to be penitent if you are a great sinner, but you can only be perfectly penitent if you are a great saint. It is the musician who knows when the instrument is out of tune; it is the artist who knows the agony of a great piece of work being spoilt; and it was the soul of Jesus that knew supremely the agonizing darkness that has lost the sense of God.

The perfect penitence of the Son of Mary accepted and offered to the Divine Majesty the supreme darkness that a soul must know that has willed to reject God.

Father Andrew SDC, *The Seven Words from the Cross*, Mowbray, 1954, p.44.

The prayer of *penitence* is the response of the soul to the revelation of the divine holiness. True penitence is the reaction of love to the revelation of greater love, the reaction of humility to the manifestation of beauty, so that... the purest penitence will be the penitence of the pure. There may be a morbid condition of wounded self-love. It may come to the prayer of penitence, but is certainly, while it is tainted by self-centredness and egotism, not yet the prayer of penitence. The prayer of penitence will go on all our lives, if we are seeking God in purity, for it is the fruit of the growth of our apprehension of the divine sanctity and the expression of our loving return to the divine holiness after any and every departure therefrom.

Father Andrew SDC, *In the Silence*, Mowbray, 1947, p.83.

Natural religion, if you understand it rightly, is a most excellent thing, it is a right sentiment of heart, it is so much goodness in the heart, it is its sensibility both of its separation from and its relation to God; and therefore it shows itself in nothing but in a penitential sentiment of the weight of its sins, and in an humble recourse by faith to the mercy of God. Call but this the religion of nature and then the more you esteem it, the better; for you cannot wish well to it without bringing it to the Gospel state of perfection.

For the religion of the Gospel is this religion of penitence and faith in the mercy of God, brought forth into its full perfection. For the Gospel calls you to nothing but to know and understand and practise a full and real penitence, and to know by faith such heights and depths of the divine mercy towards you, as the religion of nature had only some little uncertain glimmerings of.

William Law, *Selected Mystical Writings of William Law*, edited by Stephen Hobhouse, Rockliff, 1948, p.3.

In terms of time, penitence may be divided into two parts: sudden penitence and gradual penitence.

Sudden penitence comes about as a result of a certain spiritual flash that enters the soul. At once the person senses all the evil and the ugliness of sin and he is converted into a new being; already he experiences inside himself a complete transformation for the better. This form of penitence dawns on a person through the grace of some inner spiritual force, whose traces point to the depths of the mysterious.

There is also a gradual form of penitence. No sudden flash of illumination dawns upon the person to make him change from the depth of evil to the good, but he feels that he must mend his way of life, his will, his pattern of thought. By heeding this impulse he gradually acquires the ways of equity, he corrects his morals, he improves his actions, and he conditions himself increasingly to becoming a good person until he reaches a high level of purity and perfection.

Abraham Isaac Kook, *The Lights of Penitence*, SPCK, 1978, p.45.

Surely it grows evident in this age, which is so critical of everything but itself, that the world is to be brought round, made clean, right and peaceful, just and true, only by a great act of penitence at the feet of God on the part of us all. We must all make a great act of social responsibility. We must bear the sin of the world upon our own hearts, as our own sins. We are all the time washing our hands, saying this is not our affair, not our sin, not our fault.

Stop blaming Russians, Germans, Egyptians, Easterns, Westerns, rich or poor, capitalists or labourers, and see ourselves as a great family with a stain upon us all because on some, who are capable of crucifying Jesus—see the wounds of God, the broken heart of our would-be Saviour; see them until the vision blinds our eyes to our complaints, suspicions, memories, and every grievance.

Juliana of Norwich saw the wound in the side of her Lord, like a fair delectable place large enough to gather all humanity therein. To gather to that wound, to see it, to know how greatly He loves and suffers in our sin—in that gathering is healing for man and God.

A.E. Whitham, *The Catholic Spirit*, Hodder & Stoughton Ltd., 1940, p.101.

Don't be afraid of anything. Do not ever be afraid. And don't worry. So long as you remain sincerely penitent, God will forgive you everything. There's no sin, and there can be no sin in the whole world which God will not forgive to those who are truly repentant. Why, man cannot commit so great a sin as to exhaust the infinite love of God. Or can there be a sin that would exceed the love of God? Only you must never forget to think continually of repentance, but dismiss your fear altogether. Believe that God loves you in a way you cannot even conceive of. He loves you in spite of your sin and in your sin. And there's more joy in heaven over one sinner that repents than over ten righteous men. This was said a long time ago. So go and do not be afraid. Do not be upset by people and do not be angry if you're wronged... if you are sorry for what you did, then you must love. And if you love, you are of God... Everything can be atoned for, everything can be saved by love. If I, a sinner like you, have been moved by your story and am sorry for you, how much more will God be. Love is such a priceless treasure that you can redeem everything in the world by it, and expiate not only your own but other people's sins. Go and do not be afraid.

Fyodor Dostoyevsky, *The Brothers Karamazov*, translated by David Magarshack, Penguin Books Ltd., 1963, Volume 1, p.56.

PLEASURE

"Pleasure"—"enjoyment, delight; sensuous enjoyment as chief object of life."

F irst recollections of pleasure come from childhood. These mainly centred on our garden. This consisted of a spacious lawn, numerous flower-beds and a wide variety of trees. My twin sister and I spent many happy hours playing in this garden. We got a great deal of enjoyment and delight simply in being close to nature.

Second recollections of pleasure come from sport. In my teens I got a great deal of enjoyment from rugby, hockey and cricket. I loved the games themselves, the outdoor life, the people I met, and the friendships which evolved.

Third recollections of pleasure come from travel. National Service took me out to the Far East and triggered off an urge to see the world. Asia was quickly followed by Africa, and later I went to Russia and America. Recently I've found the Alps a great source of pleasure, in winter and summer.

Fourth recollections of pleasure come from my present stage of life. I'm getting a great deal of enjoyment from my work. As a College Chaplain this has partly to do with an interest in people, and partly to do with being reflective and meditative. The real pleasure comes however, when something creative has taken place. This is a great source of enjoyment and delight.

In thy right hand are pleasures for evermore.
Psalm 16.11.

I kept my heart from no pleasure, for my heart found pleasure in all my toil.
Ecclesiastes 2.10.

Rejoice in the Lord always; again I will say, Rejoice.
Philippians 4.4.

But understand this, that in the last days there will come times of stress. For men will be lovers of self... lovers of pleasure.
2 Timothy 3.1,4.

It is *god-like*, to take pleasure in the good of others.
Benjamin Whichcote, *Moral and Religious Aphorisms*, Elkin Mathews & Marrot, Ltd., 1930, Century VI, No.549.

Pleasure, wrong or rightly understood,
Our greatest evil, or our greatest good.
Alexander Pope, *The Poems of Alexander Pope*, Methuen & Co. Ltd., 1954, Volume III-1, *An Essay on Man*, Epistle 11, l.91, p.65.

Life is full of untapped sources of pleasure. Education should train us to discover and exploit them.
Norman Douglas, *An Almanac*, Chatto & Windus in association with Martin Secker & Warburg Ltd., 1945, p.17.

Consecrating the life to Christ is not giving up all the pleasures and beauties of life.
Henry Ward Beecher, *Proverbs from Plymouth Pulpit*, Charles Burnet & Co., 1887, p.176.

Pleasure is the only thing one should live for. Nothing ages like happiness.
Oscar Wilde, *The Artist as Critic*, edited by Richard Ellmann, Random House, Inc., 1969, p.433.

All physical pleasures are momentary, however intense they may be, and there is very little memory of them.
Henry Ward Beecher, *Proverbs from Plymouth Pulpit*, Charles Burnet & Co., 1887, p.185.

Enjoying things which are pleasant; that is not the evil; it is the reducing of our moral self to slavery by them that is.
Thomas Carlyle, *On Heroes, Hero-Worship and the Heroic in History*, Ward Lock, 1841, p.54.

We are always searching for something extraordinary which shall give life its pleasure and value. The extraordinary must be contributed by our own minds and feelings.
Mark Rutherford, *More Pages From a Journal*, Oxford University Press, 1910, p.221.

The purest pleasures lie within the circle of useful occupation. Mere pleasure— sought outside of usefulness—is fraught with poison.
Henry Ward Beecher, *Proverbs from Plymouth Pulpit*, Charles Burnet & Co., 1887, p.37.

Reality, union with reality, is the true state of the soul when confident and healthy... Unreality is what keeps us from ourselves and most pleasure is unreal.
Cyril Connolly, *The Unquiet Grave*, Hamish Hamilton Ltd., 1973, p.88.

Pleasure is the only thing to live for?—I think that the realization of oneself is the prime aim of life and to realize oneself through pleasure is finer than to do so through pain.

Oscar Wilde, *The Artist as Critic*, edited by Richard Ellmann, Random House, Inc., 1969, p.437.

Every quest for pleasure is fundamentally a striving for the infinite. Every pleasure attracts us because we hope, by savouring it, to get a foretaste of something that will exceed it in intensity and joy.

Fulton J. Sheen, *Lift Up Your Heart*, Burns & Oates Ltd., 1962, p.42.

The world was not made for man: but man, like all the world, was made for God. Not for man's pleasure merely, not for man's use, but for God's pleasure all things are, and for God's pleasure they were, created.

Charles Kingsley, *Daily Thoughts*, Macmillan Publishers Ltd., 1884, p.261.

Enjoy pleasures, but let them be your own, and then you will taste them: but adopt none; trust to nature for genuine ones. The pleasures that you would feel you must earn; the man who gives himself up to all, feels none sensibly.

Lord Chesterfield, *Letters of Lord Chesterfield to His Son*, J.M. Dent & Sons Ltd., 1929, May 8, 1750, p.174.

Life takes on meaning when we remove it as far as possible from the naïve striving for selfish pleasure, and put it in the service of something. If we take this service seriously, the "meaning" comes of itself.

Hermann Hesse, in *Reflections*, Volker Michels, translated by Ralph Manheim, Jonathan Cape Ltd., 1977, p.49.

Pleasure is the rock which most young people split upon; they launch out with crowded sails in quest of it, but without a compass to direct their course, or reason sufficient to steer the vessel; for want of which, pain and shame, instead of Pleasure, are the returns of their voyage.

Lord Chesterfield, *Letters of Lord Chesterfield to His Son*, J.M. Dent & Sons Ltd., 1929, March 27, 1747, p.23.

Do not suppress pleasures, but let them flop. Pleasure is like the fringe of your dress, the afterness of an act. Ignore them, let them flop, never work directly for them.

God always gives joy, even in spiritual things there is a concomitant pleasure. There is a great joy in renunciation.

Baron Friedrich von Hügel, *Letters to a Niece*, J.M. Dent & Sons Ltd., 1929, p.xxiii.

All purely physical pleasures have a way of wearing out. At each successive enjoyment of them the thrill becomes less thrilling. It requires more of them to produce the same effect. They are like a drug which loses its initial potency and which becomes increasingly less effective. A man is a foolish man who finds his pleasures in things which are bound to offer diminishing returns...

There are certain pleasures which inevitably lose their attraction as a man grows older. It may be that he is physically less able to enjoy them; it may be that as his mind matures they cease in any sense to satisfy him. In life a man should never give his heart to the joys the years can take away; he should find his delight in the things whose thrill time is powerless to erode.

William Barclay, *The Gospel of Matthew*, The Saint Andrew Press, 1987, Volume 1, p.240.

Freedom... for Augustine, cannot be reduced to a sense of choice: it is a freedom to act fully. Such freedom must involve the transcendence of a sense of choice. For a sense of choice is a symptom of the disintegration of the will: the final union of knowledge and feeling would involve a man in the object of his choice in such a way that any other alternative would be inconceivable.

Throughout his sermons against the Pelagians, Augustine repeats this as his fundamental assertion on the relation of grace and freedom: that the healthy man is one in whom knowledge and feeling have become united; and that only such a man is capable of allowing himself to be "drawn" to act by the sheer irresistible pleasure of the object of his love. The notorious tag of Vergil... "Let each man's pleasure draw him," occurs, surprisingly, in a sermon by the old man on the Gospel of S. John: "And have the senses of the body those delights, while the soul is left devoid of pleasure? If the soul does not have pleasures of its own, why is it written: *The soul of men shall hope under the shadow of Thy wings; they shall be made drunk with the fullness of Thy house; and of the torrents of Thy pleasures Thou wilt give them to drink; for in Thee is the Fountain of Life, and in Thy Light shall we see the light?* Give me a man in love: he knows what I mean. Give me one who yearns; give me one who is hungry; give me one far away in this desert, who is thirsty and sighs for the spring of the Eternal country. Give me that sort of man: he knows what I mean. But if I speak to a cold man, he just does not know what I am talking about..." (Tract. in Joh. 26,4.)

Peter Brown, *Augustine of Hippo*, Faber & Faber Ltd., 1975, p.374.

Then a hermit... came forth and said, Speak to us of Pleasure.

And he answered, saying:
Pleasure is a freedom-song,
But it is not freedom.
It is the blossoming of your desires,
But it is not the fruit.
It is a depth calling unto a height,
But it is not the deep nor the high.
It is the caged taking wing,
But it is not space encompassed.
Ay, in very truth, pleasure is a freedom-song.
And I fain would have you sing it with fullness of heart; yet I would not have you lose your hearts in the singing.

Some of your youth seek pleasure as if it were all, and they are judged and rebuked.
I would not judge nor rebuke them. I would have them seek.
For they shall find pleasure, but not her alone;
Seven are her sisters, and the least of them is more beautiful than pleasure.
Have you not heard of the man who was digging in the earth for roots and found a treasure?

And some of your elders remember pleasures with regret like wrongs committed in drunkenness.
But regret is the beclouding of the mind and not its chastisement.
They should remember their pleasures with gratitude, as they would the harvest of a summer.
Yet if it comforts them to regret, let them be comforted.

And there are among you those who are neither young to seek nor old to remember;
And in their fear of seeking and remembering they shun all pleasures, lest they neglect the spirit or offend against it.
But even in their foregoing is their pleasure.
And thus they too find a treasure though they dig for roots with quivering hands.
But tell me, who is he that can offend the spirit?
Shall the nightingale offend the stillness of the night, or the firefly the stars?
And shall your flame or your smoke burden the wind?
Think you the spirit is a still pool which you can trouble with a staff?

Oftentimes in denying yourself pleasure you do but store the desire in the recesses of your being.
Who knows but that which seems omitted today, waits for to-morrow?
Even your body knows its heritage and its rightful need and will not be deceived.
And your body is the harp of your soul,
And it is yours to bring forth sweet music from it or confused sounds.

And now you ask in your heart, "How shall we distinguish that which is good in pleasure from that which is not good?"
Go to your fields and your gardens, and you shall learn that it is the pleasure of the bee to gather honey of the flower.
But it is also the pleasure of the flower to yield its honey to the bee.
For to the bee a flower is a fountain of life,
And to the flower a bee is a messenger of love,
And to both, bee and flower, the giving and the receiving of pleasure is a need and an ecstasy.

... be in your pleasures like the flowers and the bees.

Kahlil Gibran, The Prophet, William Heinemann Ltd., 1970, p.83.

PRAISE

"Praise"— "glorify, extol the attributes of God."

I find the direct praise of God difficult. Glorifying and extolling the attributes of God—as Creator through His Creation—come far more easily. For me it is in the heart of nature that praise comes spontaneously. I love mountains and have been fortunate in spending time in the Himalayas on an expedition to Nepal. One mountain in particular was awe-inspiring—Macchapuchare in Western Nepal. No wonder the Gurkhas thought the gods resided up on the summit.

At Christmas, I frequently go to Switzerland to look after a Church in the village of Mürren, four thousand feet up in the mountains. Here, whilst skiing, I am faced with the beauty of the Eiger and the Jungfrau. In such surroundings it is easy to adopt an attitude of praise. In summer I usually go to a chalet in the French Alps on a reading/walking party with undergraduates, and walk on the slopes of Mont Blanc. Here again, praise comes naturally, surrounded by mountain snows and glaciers.

The sea not only exercises its charm over me, but additionally leads me into an attitude of praise, as do dawns and sunsets. I've had many memorable holidays in Scotland and the Lake District, and three unforgettable visits to Africa, giving rise to praise. Music, especially singing, has also been a great source of praise, and I'm particularly fond of singing and listening to anthems as a way of praising God. With all these "aids" the direct praise of God is made possible and through them we are able "to glorify God and enjoy Him for ever".

Because thy steadfast love is better than life, my lips will praise thee. So I will bless thee as long as I live; I will lift up my hands and call on thy name.

Psalm 63.3-4.

O praise God in his holiness: praise him in the firmament of his power.
Praise him in his noble acts: praise him according to his excellent greatness.
Praise him in the sound of the trumpet: praise him upon the lute and harp.
Praise him in the cymbals and dances: praise him upon the strings and pipe.
Praise him upon the well-tuned cymbals: praise him upon the loud cymbals.
Let every thing that hath breath: praise the Lord.

Psalm 150, Book of Common Prayer.

Through him then let us continually offer up a sacrifice of praise to God, that is, the fruit of lips that acknowledge his name.

Hebrews 13.15.

Great and wonderful are thy deeds, O Lord God the Almighty! Just and true are thy ways, O King of the ages!

Revelation 15.3.

Seven whole days, not one in seven,
I will praise thee.

George Herbert, The Poems of George Herbert, Oxford University Press, 1961, Praise, l.17, p.137.

Praise Him, therefore, whether in His gifts or in His scourges. The praise of the scourges is the medicine for the wound.

St. Augustine of Hippo, An Augustine Synthesis, arranged by Erich Przywara SJ, Sheed & Ward Ltd., 1936, p.398.

Ascription of praise to God is the utterance of the joy and gladness which the divine excellence tends to excite in us, and may be called a caress of words.

Henry Ward Beecher, Proverbs from Plymouth Pulpit, Charles Burnet & Co., 1887, p.222.

Prayer is praise of God; our whole life is that constant prayer, and I wish to know no other; it can be inspired by love, by distress, or by humility. I should like it to spring only from love.

André Gide, The Journals of André Gide, 1894, translated by Justin O'Brien, Martin Secker & Warburg Ltd., 1947, p.40.

In the deserts of the heart,
Let the healing fountain start,
In the prison of his days
Teach the free man how to praise.

W.H. Auden, Collected Shorter Poems, 1927-1957, Faber & Faber Ltd., 1977, In Memory of W.B. Yeats, III, p.143.

GOD, sing the meadow-streams with gladsome voice,
And pine groves with their soft, and soul-like sound,
And silent snow-mass, loos'ning, thunders GOD! . . .
Ye signs and wonders of the element,
Utters forth, GOD! and fills the hills with praise!

Samuel Taylor Coleridge, *The Complete Poetical Works of Samuel Taylor Coleridge*, edited by Ernest Hartley Coleridge, Clarendon Press, 1975, *Chamouny: The Hour Before Sunrise, A Hymn*, l.58, p.1075.

O God, for ever praise be to thee
For the blessings thou bestow'st on me—
For my food, my work, my health, my speech,
For all the good gifts bestowed on each.
O God, for ever praise to thee.

Traditional Gaelic, in *God in our midst*, Martin Reith, Triangle/SPCK, 1989, p.43.

Let all the world in ev'ry corner sing,
My God and King.
The heav'ns are not too high,
His praise may thither flie:
The earth is not too low,
His praises there may grow.
Let all the world in ev'ry corner sing,
My God and King.

George Herbert, *The Poems of George Herbert*, Oxford University Press, 1961, *The Temple Antiphon*, p.45.

He opened the book beside the window. At that hour even the veiled panes seemed to grow translucent as crystal. So, while the true light remained to him, he continued to read, in such desperate and disorderly haste that he introduced here and there words and phrases, whole images of his own. His secret self was singing at last in great bursts:
"Praise ye Him, sun and moon: praise Him all ye stars of light.
Praise Him, ye heavens of heavens, and ye waters that be above the heavens;
And wires of aerials, and grey, slippery slates, praise, praise the Lord."

Patrick White, *Riders in the Chariot*, Eyre & Spottiswoode Publishers Ltd., 1961, p.397.

Pray night and day, very quietly, like a little weary child, to the good and loving God, for everything you want, in body as well as soul—the least thing as well as the greatest. Nothing is too much to ask God for—nothing too great for Him to grant: glory be to Thee, O Lord! And try to thank Him for everything.
. . . I sometimes feel that eternity will be too short to praise God in, if it was only for making us live at all! And then not making us idiots or cripples, or even only ugly and stupid! What blessings we have! Let us work in return for them—not under the enslaving sense of paying off an infinite debt, but with the delight of gratitude, glorying that we are God's debtors.

Charles Kingsley, *Daily Thoughts*, Macmillan Publishers Ltd., 1884, p.89.

To give praise to God is the natural expression of all creation. "All Thy works praise Thee, O Lord." "The heavens declare the glory of God, and the firmament showeth His handy work." "Thou art worthy, O Lord, to receive glory and honour, and power; for Thou hast created all things, and for Thy pleasure they are and were created." To give praise and glory to the Creator is the reasonable aim and end of all created intelligence. "O, praise the Lord, ye angels of His; . . . ye servants of His that do His pleasure." "Let all the angels of God worship Him." As Christian men and women, at all times and in all places our bounden duty and service is to offer to Him the sacrifice of praise and thanksgiving for our *Creation, Redemption, Salvation,* and for the *hope of glory*...

I will praise Him for my family, my father and my mother, my brothers and sisters, my home, for my husband, for my wife, for the kindness of servants, and the love of children.

Edward King, Sermons and Addresses, Longmans, Green & Co. Ltd., 1911, p.31 & p.38.

A Praise of Glory

"In Christ it was our lot to be called, singled out beforehand to suit His purpose; (for it is He who is at work everywhere carrying out the designs of His will); we were to manifest His glory." (Ephesians 1.11-12).

It is St Paul who speaks thus, St Paul, taught by God Himself. How can we realize this great dream of God's heart, this changeless design for our souls? How, in a word, can we respond to our vocation and become a perfect praise of the glory of the Blessed Trinity?

In heaven every soul is established in pure love and no longer lives its own life, but the life of God. Then, says St Paul, "I shall recognize God as He has recognized me". (1 Cor. 13.12). In other words, "a praise of glory" is a soul who abides in God, who loves Him with a pure and unselfish love, without self-seeking in the pleasure of that love, who loves Him above all His gifts, who would love Him as much even if it had received nothing from Him, and who desires good for God, except by doing His will, since that will orders all things to His greater glory? Such a soul, then, must give itself up completely and blindly to God's will, so that it can will only what He wills.

"A praise of glory" is a silent soul which rests like a lyre under the mysterious trials of the Holy Spirit, that He may bring forth divine harmonies. Knowing that suffering is a string which produces the most beautiful sound of all, this soul loves to see it on its own instrument, that it may move God's heart with great delight.

"A praise of glory" is a soul who gazes on God, in faith and simplicity. It reflects all that He is, and is like a fathomless abyss into which He can flow and outpour Himself. It is a crystal through which He can shine and contemplate all his perfections and splendour. A soul who thus allows the divine Being to satisfy within it His need to communicate all that He is and all that He has, is a true praise of glory of all His gifts.

Finally "a praise of glory" is a being forever giving thanks. Every action, every movement, every thought and aspiration, while rooting the soul more deeply in love, is like an echo of the eternal Sanctus.

Sister Elizabeth of the Trinity, Spiritual Writings, Geoffrey Chapman, 1962, p.152.

PROVIDENCE

"Providence"—"beneficent care of God or nature."

A t the age of nine I became aware of a painful lump in my neck. The doctor was called and a gland was found to be infected with TB. An operation was required to remove it. I was not unduly frightened. Somehow I thought all would be well. The anaesthetic turned out to be unpleasant, and the large incision painful for a few days.

However all was well and I soon recovered.

This feeling that all would be well, no matter what happens, has never left me, and I take this to be what we sometimes mean by faith in Providence.

Another setback occurred at the age of eleven—failure to pass the Eleven Plus. Instead of going on to the local Grammar School as expected, I went away to School—and thrived.

Two more operations in rapid succession. These were not so serious but had to be faced and gone through. Again I felt all would be well, and that Providence would see me through. This emerging pattern of failure, setback and disappointment in life has never left me. Neither has Providence. I have come to see that disasters, accepted and worked through, can be put to good use, and that something of real value can come out of them. Perhaps this is one of the ways in which we experience something of the love of God and of his beneficent care of us.

The Lord will provide.

Genesis 22.14.

Thou visitest the earth and waterest it, thou greatly enrichest it; the river of God is full of water; thou providest their grain, for so thou hast prepared it.

Psalm 65.9.

And God is able to provide you with every blessing in abundance, so that you may always have enough of everything and may provide in abundance for every good work.

2 Corinthians 9.8.

Since God had foreseen something better for us, that apart from us they should not be made perfect.

Hebrews 11.40.

And dare trust in His providence; and be quiet; and go a Angling.

Izaak Walton, *The Compleat Angler*, The Nonesuch Press, 1929, p.180.

God's providence is His capacity to use natural laws and make them serve men.

Henry Ward Beecher, *Proverbs from Plymouth Pulpit*, Charles Burnet & Co., 1887, p.126.

Behind a frowning providence,
He hides a smiling face.

William Cowper, *The Poetical Works of William Cowper*, Oxford University Press, 1950, *Olney Hymns*, XXXVI, *Light Shining Out of Darkness*, l.15-16, p.455.

Who finds not Providence all good and wise,
Alike in what it gives, and what denies?

Alexander Pope, *The Poems of Alexander Pope*, Methuen & Co. Ltd., 1954, Volume III-1, *An Essay on Man*, Epistle 1, l.205, p.40.

Happy the man who sees a God employ'd
In all the good and ill that chequer life!

William Cowper, *Poetical Works*, edited by H.S. Milford, Oxford University Press, 1967, *The Task*, Book II, l.161, p.149.

There is a Providence—a broad, beneficent system, which has such a relation to you that you cannot afford to be uneasy.

Henry Ward Beecher, *Proverbs from Plymouth Pulpit*, Charles Burnet & Co., 1887, p.173.

The doctrine of providence deals with the history of created being as such, in the sense that in every respect and in its whole span this proceeds under the fatherly care of God the Creator.

Karl Barth, *Church Dogmatics*, T. & T. Clark, 1961, Volume III, Part Three, p.3.

God did not create the world and set it going, as a man might wind up a clockwork toy and leave it to run down. God is all through His world, guiding, directing, sustaining, upholding, loving. In everything and through everything the providence of God is active and operative and powerful.

William Barclay, *The Letters to the Galatians and Ephesians*, The Saint Andrew Press, 1958, p.168.

> All Nature is but Art, unknown to thee;
> All Chance, Direction, which thou canst not see;
> All Discord, Harmony, not understood;
> All partial Evil, universal Good:
> And, spite of Pride, in erring Reason's spite,
> One truth is clear, "Whatever is, is RIGHT."

Alexander Pope, *The Poems of Alexander Pope*, Methuen & Co. Ltd., 1954, Volume III-1, *An Essay on Man*, Epistle 1, 1.289, p.50.

Providence means that there is a creating and saving possibility implied in every situation, which cannot be destroyed by any event. Providence means that the daemonic and destructive forces within ourselves and our world can never have an unbreakable grasp upon us, and that the bond which connects us with the fulfilling love can never be disrupted.

Paul Tillich, *The Shaking of the Foundations*, SCM Press Ltd., 1949, p.106.

Cheered by the presence of God, I will do at each moment, without anxiety, according to the strength which he shall give me, the work that his providence assigns me. I will leave the rest without concern; it is not my affair...

I ought to consider the duty to which I am called each day, as the work that God has given me to do, and to apply myself to it in a manner worthy of his glory, that is to say, with exactness and in peace. I must neglect nothing; I must be violent in nothing.

François de la M. Fénelon, *Selections from the Writings of Fénelon*, Mrs Follen, Edward T. Whitfield, 1850, p.233.

Trust in the providence of God is not a heaven-sent formula for the indolent, not a way of bypassing responsibility with regard to social and material concerns. However much you commit yourself to God's care you still have to calculate, decide, work. Where fatalism and Christian trust part company is in the willingness to cooperate. You cannot simply say "it will take care of itself" and sit back. You do not have to worry about the outcome any more than does the fatalist but you do have to make the effort; you have to take on the affairs that come your way, knowing that they come from God and must be steered back again to him. Looked at in one way the outcome is in your hands, looked at in another the outcome is wholly in God's.

Hubert van Zeller, *Leave Your Life Alone*, Sheed and Ward Ltd., 1973, p.21.

A visit to a museum or art gallery, the reading of a classical author, or going to the theatre where a play from the past is being performed—these activities give one a sense of relatedness to the past, some awareness of *a* communion of saints, if not the specifically Christian understanding of that phrase. Similarly, walking in the countryside or cultivating our back garden can maintain our awareness of the natural world and our participation in that creatureliness that is full of the throb of life and the threat of death. These activities can provoke some sense of the continuity of life and of the glory of God in creation and providence, and accordingly become sources of thankfulness and joy at the way life is arranged.

J. Neville Ward, *The Use of Praying*, Epworth Press, 1967, p.36.

Providence consists above all in a *change of heart*, and not so much, or at least not in the first place, in the intervening of God in a marvellous way in our life, removing all threats, warding off attacks. Providence means essentially that there remains a last way out, all can be turned to grace; and every need can be given a new significance through the mercy of God. Perhaps everything goes in the old way. The threat grows no less. A man has still to endure his fears, and has still to make his way through a hostile world. Nevertheless, everything has changed. In and through all that can now be seen the goodness of God in our life. A man can say, I suffer, but fundamentally it doesn't matter.

Ladislaus Boros, *In Time of Temptation*, Burns and Oates Ltd., 1968, p.28.

The primary source for a Christian doctrine of providence is the rule of God as this is portrayed in the Bible. It is possible to detect several elements in this overall rule, though the original writers would not always have recognized the distinctions that were later to be made. There is God's creative activity, especially as recounted in Genesis; there is the sustaining activity of God when he upholds the world or man (e.g. Isa. 41.10); there is the activity that came to be called "general providence", that is the work of God in and through natural things, as when the rain falls on the just and the unjust (Matt. 5.45); there is what some would later call "special providence", when God speaks to a prophet, or works through some other specific action; finally, there is what some would later call "miracle", when the specific action is one that must defy any purely natural explanation. In a broad sense all of these activities fall under providence, but in a narrower sense only the two that came to be called general and special providence.

M.J. Langford, in A Dictionary of Christian Spirituality, edited by Gordon S. Wakefield, SCM Press Ltd., 1986, p.320.

It is a commonplace of religious experience that when a Christian looks back over his own individual life—his secular career as well as his spiritual development—it becomes apparent to him that there has been a mysterious pattern running through it all, and that, not by his own initiative, and not always by his own volition, his life has been brought into conformity with that pattern by the hand of God. No hypothesis but that of an overruling Providence is sufficient to account for what has happened. Character is shaped by destiny as truly as destiny is shaped by character: and as the Christian reviews in retrospect the events by which his progress has been determined and controlled, the opportunities that have been granted to him, and all the other blessings of this life, he cannot fail to recognise, not with complacency or spiritual pride, but rather with humility and penitence and thankfulness and trust, the hand of God patiently moulding him in accordance with His eternal purpose for that one individual soul. A man can see this most clearly in his own life, for obvious reasons: but it is often strikingly apparent to him in the lives of others, as if all the resources of the omniscience and loving providence of God had been concentrated upon this single object, of fashioning that one soul precisely for the specific end for which it was created, and of making that particular individual all that God intended him to be.

The evidence for this doctrine of particular Providence in human lives is far too strong to be neglected or ignored.

Charles Smyth, *Cyril Forster Garbett*, Hodder & Stoughton Ltd., 1959, p.515.

PURITY

"Purity"—"pureness, cleanness, freedom from physical or moral pollution."

I used to play the oboe. In London, my teacher had only recently qualified, so she was much younger than me. We both used to sing in the University Church Choir, and knew each other socially as well as professionally.

One day she surprised us by announcing she was going to be a nun, and would shortly be entering an enclosed order. The Choir completed a tour in Germany in a long vacation and she then disappeared into a convent in Oxford. That was the last we saw of her in London.

I later returned to Oxford as Chaplain/Fellow of University College, and decided to visit her in the convent. Being a priest I was allowed to see her for a few minutes. When she came into the room I was immediately struck by her appearance. She seemed to be ten years younger, and looked extremely fit. She spent much time in meditation and was greatly enjoying her new life.

I visited her again twelve months later. She again looked a picture of health, and was pleased with her new assignment—a year in the convent garden. She would really enjoy the fresh air and gardening. I went again after a reasonable lapse of time, and found her again in good spirits. I asked her if she ever came into the city? "Oh no," she said, "it's not very nice there is it?" Here was someone who valued purity so much, she was not interested in visiting a city, which thousands of tourists consider to be beautiful. I could see exactly what she meant. She was better off in the confines of the convent, living out her vows.

Therefore the Lord has recompensed me according to my righteousness, according to the cleanness of my hands in his sight... with the pure thou dost show thyself pure.

Psalm 18.24,26.

Who shall ascend the hill of the Lord? And who shall stand in his holy place? He who has clean hands and a pure heart, who does not lift up his soul to what is false, and does not swear deceitfully. He will receive blessing from the Lord, and vindication from the God of his salvation.

Psalm 24.3-5.

Blessed are the pure in heart, for they shall see God.
Matthew 5.8.

Beloved, we are God's children now; it does not yet appear what we shall be, but we know that when he appears we shall be like him, for we shall see him as he is. And everyone who thus hopes in him purifies himself as he is pure.

1 John 3.2-3.

It is from a pure heart that the harvest of a good life comes.

Thomas à Kempis, *The Imitation of Christ*, translated by Betty I. Knott, William Collins Sons & Co. Ltd., 1979, p.161.

Refin'd himself to Soul, to curb the Sense;
And made almost a Sin of Abstinence.

John Dryden, *The Poems and Fables of John Dryden*, edited by James Kinsley, Oxford University Press, 1970, *The Character of a good Parson*, p.811.

One of the striking peculiarities of Christ's teaching, and the teaching of those who were inspired by Him, was the unconditional acquisition of moral purity. The very first step in a religious life was one of personal purification.

Henry Ward Beecher, *Proverbs from Plymouth Pulpit*, Charles Burnet & Co., 1887, p.92.

One of the characteristics of the world in which we live is the lowering of standards. Standards of honesty, standards of diligence in work, standards of conscientiousness, moral standards, all tend to be lowered. The Christian must be the person who holds aloft the standard of absolute purity in speech, in conduct, and even in thought.

William Barclay, *The Gospel of Matthew*, The Saint Andrew Press, 1987, Volume 1, p.119.

God is purity itself, true and clear as the unclouded light. And in fellowship with Him all that is in your heart must be pure and clear and true. Let the single eye of your heart look straight to God, with no other object besides; no mixture of self-seeking, and of side aims and purposes; no known or unknown hypocrisy or pretence or show. And should any false or mixed motive rise up involuntarily, bring it honestly and restfully into His presence, and lay it before His face, where it will vanish away; and let the clear sunlight of His countenance shine down upon all your thoughts and purposes, spread out in simplicity before Him.

Gerhard Tersteegen, in *Sketches of the Quiet in the Land*, Frances Bevan, John F. Shaw and Co., 1891, p.399.

By *purity* I understand a due abstractedness from the body, and mastery over the inferior appetites, or such a temper and disposition of mind as makes a man despise and abstain from all the pleasures and delights of sense or fancy which are sinful in themselves, or tend to extinguish or lessen our relish of more divine and excellent pleasures; which doth also infer a resoluteness to undergo all those hardships he may meet with in the performance of his duty; so that not only chastity and temperance, but also Christian courage and magnanimity, may come under this head.

Henry Scougal, *The Life of God in the Soul of Man*, C.J.G. & F. Rivington, 1829, p.16.

I was a little stranger, which at my entrance into the world was saluted and surrounded with innumerable joys. My knowledge was Divine... My very ignorance was advantageous. I seemed as one brought into the Estate of Innocence. All things were spotless and pure and glorious: yea, and infinitely mine, and joyful and precious. I knew not that there were any sins, or complaints or laws. I dreamed not of poverties, contentions or vices. All tears and quarrels were hidden from mine eyes. Everything was at rest, free and immortal. I knew nothing of sickness or death or rents or exaction, either for tribute or bread. In the absence of these I was entertained like an Angel with the works of God in their splendour and glory, I saw all in the peace of Eden; Heaven and Earth did sing my Creator's praises, and could not make more melody to Adam, than to me. All Time was Eternity, and a perpetual Sabbath. Is it not strange that an infant should be heir of the whole World, and see those mysteries which the books of the learned never unfold?

Thomas Traherne, Centuries, The Faith Press Ltd., 1969, p.109.

"Blessed are the pure in heart: for they shall see God."

If we are to take part in the kingdom, there must be singleness of purpose. Purity of heart is, of course, continally taken in its narrower meaning of absence of sensual defilement and pollution. That is an important part of purity; and may I say a word about the pursuit of purity in this narrower sense? A great many people are distressed by impure temptations, and they very frequently fail to make progress with them for one reason, namely, that while they are anxious to get rid of sin in this one respect, they are not trying after goodness as a whole. Uncleanness of life and heart they dislike. It weighs upon their conscience and destroys their self-respect. But they have no similar horror of pride, or irreverence, or uncharity. People very often say that it is impossible to lead a "pure" life. The Christian minister is not pledged to deny this, if a man will not try to be religious all round, to be Christ-like altogether. For the way to get over uncleanness is, in innumerable cases, not to fight against that only, but to contend for positive holiness all round, for Christ-likeness, for purity of heart in the sense in which Christ used the expression, in the sense in which in the 51st Psalm a clean heart is coupled with a "right spirit"—that is, a will set straight towards God, or simplicity of purpose. There is an old Latin proverb— "Unless the vessel is clean, whatever you pour into it turns sour." It is so with the human will. Unless the human will is directed straight for God, whatever you put into the life of religious and moral effort has a root of bitterness and sourness in it which spoils the whole life. Our Lord means "Blessed are the single-minded", for they, though as yet they may be far from seeing God, though as yet they may not believe a single article of the Christian Creed, yet at last shall attain the perfect vision; yes, as surely as God is true, they shall be satisfied in their very capacity for truth and beauty and goodness; they shall behold God.

Charles Gore, The Sermon on the Mount, John Murray Ltd., 1896, p.40.

What... does Christ mean by the pure in heart? He means more than sexually or even morally pure. He means rather what we call single-minded. He is always telling us that we profit by things only when we cease to seek our own profit in them. The single-minded are those who are, as we say, interested in people or things for their own sake, and not with an eye to any profit that can be got out of them...

A man can do nothing supremely well unless in his work he expresses some interest in things themselves. He cannot make a pair of boots supremely well unless he is interested in the making of boots, not merely in the earning of wages. He cannot teach children well at all unless he is interested in the children; and, the higher the activity, the more surely is single-mindedness a condition of excellence in it. That we all know by experience; but Christ goes further. He says that those who are single-minded, that is to say single-minded altogether and not only in some one interest, are blessed, that is to say happy, because they shall see God. We are so used to His words, and to the assumption that they have no precise meaning, that they do not seem daring to us. But they would seem daring to us if we understood precisely what they mean, and if we believed that Christ meant what He said in them. He did not, of course, mean that the single-minded would see God as we see a cow in a field, actually with their eyes. As St. John says, "No man hath seen God at any time." But He did mean that they would see a reality we do not see, in such a way that it would become more real to them than the world of sense is to us; and further, that they would know this reality to be supremely good. And He meant more even than that, namely, that they would know this reality to be God, to be living and personal, more living, more personal, than human beings are. Most of us can hardly believe that He meant that, actually meant it as more than a pious opinion. But Christ, as we can see from the Gospels, was not given to uttering pious opinions. We speak of the Sermon on the Mount: but His sayings are not at all like what we hear in most sermons. Many of them must have seemed to the divines of His day to be in exceedingly bad taste; indeed they said that He had a devil. So whether we believe Him or not, we may take it that, when He said anything, He did mean it, not as a pious opinion, but in some very precise sense, even though we ourselves find it difficult to grasp that sense. When He said that the pure in heart would see God, He meant that they would be aware of God with the most extreme certainty that the human mind is capable of...

Why we listen to Christ, why we are enthralled by His words, even when we do not understand them, is because He does convince us that He Himself saw this reality, and was part of it. But it is not enough to be enthralled; we need also to understand. His truth, if it is truth, is not merely His, but the truth; and we can apply it illimitely, far beyond the applications of it that He gave us...

If I am to experience music as it is, I must forget about myself and all my demands and expectations, and allow myself to fall in love with it, if I can; I must allow that relation, which is the music, to happen in me.

Now, according to Christ, the universe, in its nature, is not cabbages which we grow for our own kitchens; it is like music. Its reality consists in a relation which is not a relation of use to us at all; and we must get ourselves and our own wants and demands and expectations out of the way, if we are to be aware of that reality. But, further, to be aware of that reality of the music of the universe is the highest, the highest happiness. Then we ourselves become part of the music; we are by hearing the music constrained to make ourselves part of it; for it is a real music, irresistible in its beauty, and we cannot but dance to it when we hear it.

A. Clutton-Brock, *What is the Kingdom of Heaven*, Methuen & Co. Ltd., 1919, p.35.

RELATIONSHIPS

*"Relationships"—"what one person or thing has to do with another,
way in which one stands or is related to another."*

I want to take a radical line with relationships. In this area of life I think we've lost sight of the fact that man and woman are made in the image and likeness of God, and therefore have something of the divine in them. The New Testament confirms this in stating that our bodies are the temples of the Holy Spirit. As we grow up our first task should be to develop this inner relatedness with the divine. In theory we do this in infant baptism, with its emphasis on "spiritual rebirth", but do we acknowledge it in practice, and act accordingly? I suspect this is practically unheard of in homes, schools and the media.

The early years should be spent in developing this spiritual side of our nature, along with the physical and the intellectual. There is nothing new in this—merely the education of the whole person. But once we become grounded and rooted in the divine we have a firm foundation and a secure framework in which to work out our future relationships. This is based on respect for the individual.

This is not usually how our relationships are worked out at the present time. Men and women are generally regarded as being "sophisticated animals" and we treat each other as such. We therefore tend to use (and abuse) each other. Is this another facet of a consumer society?

Three things are too wonderful for me; four I do not understand: the way of an eagle in the sky, the way of a serpent on a rock, the way of a ship on the high seas, and the way of a man with a maiden.

Proverbs 30.18-19.

Set me as a seal upon your heart, as a seal upon your arm; for love is strong as death... Many waters cannot quench love, neither can floods drown it. If a man offered for love all the wealth of his house, it would be utterly scorned.

Song of Solomon 8.6-7.

Love is patient and kind; love is not jealous or boastful; it is not arrogant or rude. Love does not insist on its own way; it is not irritable or resentful; it does not rejoice at wrong, but rejoices in the right. Love bears all things, believes all things, hopes all things, endures all things. Love never ends.

1 Corinthians 13.4-8.

And above all these put on love, which binds everything together in perfect harmony.

Colossians 3.14.

The emotionally crippled person is always the produce of a love gone wrong.

Michel Quoist, *With Open Heart*, translated by Colette Copeland, Gill and Macmillan Ltd., 1983, p.36.

An intimate relationship between people not only asks for mutual openness, but also for mutual respectful protection of each other's uniqueness.

Henri J.M. Nouwen, *Reaching Out*, William Collins Sons & Co. Ltd., 1980, p.32.

Good judgment in our dealings with others consists not in seeing through deceptions and evil intentions but in being able to waken the decency dormant in every person.

Eric Hoffer, *The Passionate State of Mind*, Martin Secker & Warburg Ltd., 1956, p.70.

A man needs something which is more than friendship and yet is not love as it is generally understood. This something nevertheless a woman only can give.

Mark Rutherford, *Last Pages From a Journal*, Oxford University Press, 1915, p.261.

What does real love do for us? It teaches the discernment and adoration of human worth, despite its obscuration by the petty trifles of common life.

Mark Rutherford, *Last Pages From a Journal*, Oxford University Press, 1915, p.298.

No matter how intimate you may be with your beloved there is or ought to be in her a mystery, a something unpenetrated and impenetrable. It is as necessary as that which is known.

Mark Rutherford, *Last Pages From a Journal*, Oxford University Press, 1915, p.317.

I like direct and simple relations with people, and dread complex, subtle, intricate relations—and above all *claims*. One gives, and does the best one can, but the moment that *claims* come in, the atmosphere is uneasy.

A.C. Benson, *Extracts from the Letters of Dr. A.C. Benson to M.E.A.*, Jarrold Publishing, 1927, p.12.

When a love-affair is broken off, the heaviest blow is to the vanity of the one who is left. It is therefore reasonable to assume that, when a love-affair is beginning, the greatest source of satisfaction is also to the vanity. The first signs of a mutual attraction will induce even the inconsolable to live in the present.

Cyril Connolly, *The Unquiet Grave*, Hamish Hamilton Ltd., 1973, p.12.

We discover, perhaps to our astonishment, that our greatest moments come when we find that we are not unique, when we come upon another self that is very like our own. The discovery of a continent is mere idle folly compared with this discovery of a sympathetic other-self, a friend or a lover.

J.B. Priestley, *All About Ourselves and Other Essays*, William Heinemann Ltd., 1956, p.232.

What an awesome thing it is to feel oneself on the verge of the possibility of really knowing another person. Can it ever happen? I'm not sure. I don't know that any two people can really strip themselves that naked in front of each other. We're so filled with fears of rejection and pretences that we scarcely know whether we're being fraudulent or real ourselves.

Beverly Axelrod, in *Soul on Ice*, by Eldridge Cleaver, McGraw-Hill Book Company, 1968, p.146.

In the sphere of human relationships there are no rules to be found for knowing the appropriate behaviour in a particular situation. No ethical code could have made it obvious that the breaking of the alabaster box of precious ointment was fitting to a strange occasion. The roots of human behaviour are mysterious and partly seen, not so much in making and carrying out decisions as in the spontaneous response made to sudden demands or unexpected opportunities.

R.E.C. Browne, *The Ministry of the Word*, SCM Press Ltd., 1958, p.111.

True relationship with others involves humility of attitude, refusal to treat others as things or slaves, refusal to pass judgement upon them, acceptance of their limitations and culpability, readiness to welcome and to listen to what they have to say, respect for their uniqueness, progressive understanding of their mystery, trust in what they can become, stimulation of their spiritual progress, appreciation of both the value and insufficiency of ethical norms and moral virtues.

Emile Rideau, in *Journey for a Soul*, William Collins Sons & Co. Ltd., 1976, p.26.

Human beings seek nearness to one another. When they are in one another's direct physical presence and seek to love one another in these circumstances, they seek to exist not only in a physiological contact of flesh on flesh, but to render such contact, when it is to be meaningful, the expression of a really total, personal, fully mutual and reciprocal exchange of love between them. Here we have a mystery that we cannot hope to solve at this point in our discussion—if indeed it can be solved at all.

Karl Rahner, *The Love of Jesus and the Love of Neighbour*, translated by Robert Barr, St. Paul Publications, 1983, p.20.

If we think about it, we find our life *consists* in this achieving of a pure relationship between ourselves and the living universe about us. This is how I "save my soul" by accomplishing a pure relationship between me and another person, me and other people, me and a nation, me and a race of men, me and the animals, me and the trees or flowers, me and the earth, me and the skies and sun and stars, me and the moon: an infinity of pure relations, big and little, like the stars of the sky: that makes our eternity, for each one of us, me and the timber I am sawing, the lines of force I follow; me and the dough I knead for bread, me and the very motion with which I write, me and the bit of gold I have got. This, if we knew it, is our life and our eternity: the subtle, perfected relation between me and my whole circumambient universe.

D.H. Lawrence, *The Phoenix*, edited with an introduction by Edward D. McDonald, William Heinemann Ltd., 1936, p.528.

How special then can a relationship be without falling into error?
Not so special that any other friend is neglected or considered a nuisance.
Not so special that one can really only enjoy the times when one is alone with that person.
Not so special that jealousy creeps in.
Not so special that one is constantly re-living memories of the past, or eagerly anticipating meetings of the future, never able to enjoy to the full what J.P. de Caussade has called "the sacrament of the present moment".
Not so special that the prospect of separation at some future date is like a sword of Damocles hanging over the relationship.
Not so special that it affects normal relationships with the opposite sex.
Not so special that the two lives become inseparably intertwined.

Margaret Evening, *Who Walk Alone*, Hodder & Stoughton Ltd., 1974, p.46.

The handsome and self-absorbed young man
looked at the lovely and self-absorbed girl
and thrilled.
    The lovely and self-absorbed girl
looked back at the handsome and self-absorbed young man
and thrilled.
    And in that thrill he felt:
Her self-absorption is even as strong as mine.
I must see if I can't break through it
and absorb her in me.
    And in that thrill she felt:
His self-absorption is even stronger than mine!
What fun, stronger than mine!
I must see if I can't absorb this Samson of self-absorption.
    So they simply adored one another
and in the end
they were both nervous wrecks, because
In self-absorption and self-interest they were equally matched.

D.H. Lawrence, *The Complete Poems of D.H. Lawrence*, edited by Vivian de Sola Pinto and Warren Roberts, William Heinemann Ltd., 1967, Volume Two, *True Love at Last*, p.605.

I have come to be very much of a cynic in these matters; I mean that it is impossible to believe in the permanence of man's or woman's love. Or, at any rate, it is impossible to believe in the permanence of any early passion. As I see it, at least, with regard to man, a love affair, a love for any definite woman, is something in the nature of a widening of the experience. With each new woman that a man is attracted to there appears to come a broadening of the outlook, or, if you like, an acquiring of new territory. A turn of the eyebrow, a tone of the voice, a queer characteristic gesture—all these things, and it is these things that cause to arise the passion of love—all these things are like so many objects on the horizon of the landscape that tempt a man to walk beyond the horizon, to explore. He wants to get, as it were, behind those eyebrows with the peculiar turn, as if he desired to see the world with the eyes that they overshadow. He wants to hear that voice applying itself to every possible proposition, to every possible topic; he wants to see those characteristic gestures against every possible background. Of the question of the sex-instinct I know very little and I do not think that it counts for very much in a really great passion. It can be aroused by such nothings—by an untied shoe-lace, by a glance of the eye in passing—that I think it might be left out of the calculation. I don't mean to say that any great passion can exist without a desire for consummation. That seems to me to be a commonplace and to be therefore a matter needing no comment at all. It is a thing, with all its accidents, that must be taken for granted, as, in a novel, or a biography, you take it for granted that the characters have their meals with some regularity. But the real fierceness of desire, the real heat of a passion long continued and withering up the soul of a man is the craving for identity with the woman he loves. He desires to see with the same eyes, to touch with the same sense of touch, to hear with the same ears, to lose his identity, to be enveloped, to be supported. For, whatever may be said of the relation of the sexes, there is no man who loves a woman that does not desire to come to her for the renewal of his courage, for the cutting asunder of his difficulties. And that will be the mainspring of his desire for her. We are all so afraid, we are all so alone, we all so need from the outside the assurance of our own worthiness to exist.

So, for a time, if such a passion come to fruition, the man will get what he wants. He will get the moral support, the encouragement, the relief from the sense of loneliness, the assurance of his own worth. But these things pass away; inevitably they pass away as the shadows pass across sun-dials. It is sad, but it is so. The pages of the book will become familiar; the beautiful corner of the road will have been turned too many times. Well, this is the saddest story.

And yet I do believe that for every man there comes at last a woman—or, no, that is the wrong way of formulating it. For every man there comes at last a time of life when the woman who then sets her seal upon his imagination has set her seal for good. He will travel over no more horizons; he will never again set the knapsack over his shoulders; he will retire from those scenes. He will have gone out of the business.

Ford Madox Hueffer, *The Good Soldier*, John Lane, Bodley Head, 1915, p.134.

REVERENCE

"Reverence"— "regarding something as sacred or exalted—
showing respect or regarding something or someone with awe."

Once a year every Gurkha soldier in the Regiment had to swear allegiance to the Crown. This was done by saluting the Queen's Truncheon—the equivalent of Colours in a British Regiment. The Truncheon had been presented to the Regiment by Queen Victoria, and for security reasons was housed in the Quarter-Guard.

I was ordered to march my platoon to the Quarter-Guard and carry out this annual duty. With about fifty yards to go I was surprised by the men suddenly breaking ranks. This took me unawares. Was a mutiny about to take place? I watched carefully, trying to look unperturbed. They each hurriedly picked a flower by the roadside, and resumed ranks. At the Quarter-Guard they came to a smart halt, turned about, and stood at ease. They then approached the Truncheon one at a time. With a look of awe and wonder in their eyes they placed the flowers on the Truncheon, took a pace backwards, and came up with a pukka salute. It was a most moving experience. It taught me something of the nature of reverence. There was something almost sacred in the manner they swore their allegiance to the Crown. I do wish there was more reverence in our everyday life. We would be the richer for it, whether it be for nature, work, or people.

Those who honour me I will honour, and those who despise me shall be lightly esteemed.
1 Samuel 2.30.

Be silent, all flesh, before the Lord; for he has roused himself from his holy dwelling.
Zechariah 2.13.

Therefore let us be grateful for receiving a kingdom that cannot be shaken, and thus let us offer to God acceptable worship, with reverence and awe; for our God is a consuming fire.
Hebrews 12.28-29.

Be subject to one another out of reverence for Christ.
Ephesians 5.21.

Reverence thyself.
W.H. Brown, *The Power of Sympathy*, Columbia University Press, 1937, Volume II, p.16.

The most common trait of all primitive peoples is a reverence for the lifegiving earth...
Stewart L. Udall, *The Quiet Crisis*, Holt, Rinehart & Winston, 1963, p.4.

Does not every true man feel that he is himself made higher by doing reverence to what is really above him?
Thomas Carlyle, *On Heroes, Hero-Worship and the Heroic in History*, Ward Lock, Limited, p.12.

The ethic of Reverence for Life is the ethic of Jesus brought to philosophical expression, extended into cosmical form, and conceived of as intellectually necessary.
Albert Schweitzer, in *Albert Schweitzer: Christian Revolutionary*, George Seaver, James Clarke & Co. Ltd., 1944, p.92.

Reverence God in *thyself*: for God is *more* in the *mind* of man, than in any part of this world besides; for we (and we *only* here) are made after the image of God.
Benjamin Whichcote, *Moral and Religious Aphorisms*, Elkin Mathews & Marrot, Ltd., 1930, Century VIII, No. 798.

All real joy and power of progress in humanity depend on finding something to reverence, and all the baseness and misery of humanity begin in a habit of disdain.
John Ruskin, *The Crown of Wild Olive*, George Allen & Sons, 1910, p.177.

I felt deep within me that the highest point a man can attain is not Knowledge, or Virtue, or Goodness, or Victory, but something even greater, more heroic and more despairing: Sacred Awe!
Nikos Kazantzakis, *Zorba the Greek*, translated by Carl Wildman, Faber & Faber Ltd., 1961, p.273.

Of course, God is the "wholly other"; but he is also the wholly same: the wholly present. Of course he is the *mysterium tremendum* that appears and overwhelms; but he is also the mystery of the self-obvious that is closer to me than my own!
Martin Buber, *I and Thou*, translated by Walter Kaufmann, T. & T. Clark, 1970, p.127.

The nature of the numinous can only be suggested by means of the special way in which it is reflected in the mind in terms of feeling... We are dealing with something for which there is only one appropriate expression, *mysterium tremendum*.
Rudolph Otto, *The Idea of the Holy*, translated by John W. Harvey, Oxford University Press, 1975, p.12.

Why should not my body, which is the symbol and organ of my spirit, make a bodily gesture symbolic of spiritual reverence before those material objects which have been consecrated to be the symbols and vehicles of Christ's spiritual self-giving?
William Temple, *Thoughts on Some Problems of the Day*, Macmillan Publishers Ltd., 1931, p.164.

Dear Lord and Father of mankind,
Forgive our foolish ways!
Reclothe us in our rightful mind,

In purer lives Thy service find,
In deeper reverence, praise.

John Greenleaf Whittier, *The Brewing of Soma*, 1872, Hymn.

For centuries my civilization contemplated God in the person of man. Man was created in the image of God. God was revered in Man. Men were brothers in God. It was this reflection of God that conferred an invaluable dignity upon every man. The duties of each towards himself and towards his kind were evident from the fact of the relation between God and man. My civilization was the inheritor of Christian values.

Antoine de Saint-Exupéry, *Flight to Arras*, translated by Lewis Galantiere, William Heinemann Ltd., 1942, p.146.

Respect for the personality of others, a strong sense of the dignity and intrinsic worth of each person, realization that all men are similar and on an equal footing in more ways than they are different—all this is essentially a religious and a democratic outlook in the best and deepest sense. It introduces a qualitative basis into human dealings and enhances the values of good human relations by taking account of the true community of interests among men.

Ordway Tead, *The Art of Leadership*, The McGraw-Hill Book Company, 1935, p.284.

Late on the third day, at the very moment when, at sunset, we were making our way through a herd of hippopotamuses, there flashed upon my mind, unforeseen and unsought, the phrase, "Reverence for Life". The iron door had yielded: the path in the thicket had become visible. Now I had found my way to the idea in which affirmation of the world and ethics are contained side by side! Now I knew that the ethical acceptance of the world and of life, together with the ideals of civilization contained in this concept, has a foundation in thought.

Albert Schweitzer, *Out of My Life and Thought*, translated by C.T. Campion, Henry Holt and Company, 1949, p.156.

Christian belief in the sanctity of human life is derived from the doctrine of God as Creator. Humankind was made in God's image with power to reason and the capacity to choose. Each individual is infinitely precious to God and made for an eternal destiny. Thus the Christian attitude to human life can only be one of reverence—enjoined by the whole of the Decalogue (not only the sixth commandment) and confirmed by the incarnation—which is to be extended to every individual from the moment of conception to extreme old age and death. Our right to life, grounded in our divine origin, is the basis of all other human rights, natural and legal, and the foundation of civilized society.

Thomas Wood, in *A New Dictionary of Christian Ethics*, edited by James F. Childress and John Macquarrie, SCM Press Ltd., 1986, p.353.

When we look at the Ten Commandments, which are the essence and the foundation of all law, we can see that their whole meaning can be summed up in one word—*respect*, or even better, *reverence*. Reverence for God and for the name of God, reverence for God's day, respect for parents, respect for life, respect for property, respect for personality, respect for the truth and for another person's good name, respect for oneself so that wrong desires may never master us—these are the fundamental principles behind the Ten Commandments, principles of reverence for God, and respect for our fellow men and for ourselves. Without them there can be no such thing as law. On them all law is based.

William Barclay, *The Gospel of Matthew*, The Saint Andrew Press, 1987, Volume 1, p.130.

Be reverent before the dawning day. Do not think of what will be in a year, or in ten years. Think of to-day. Leave your theories. All theories, you see, even those of virtue, are bad, foolish, mischievous. Do not abuse life. Live in to-day. Be reverent towards each day. Love it, respect it, do not sully it, do not hinder it from coming to flower. Love it even when it is grey and sad like to-day. Do not be anxious. See. It is winter now. Everything is asleep. The good earth will awake again. You have only to be good and patient like the earth. Be reverent. Wait. If you are good, all will go well. If you are not, if you are weak, if you do not succeed, well, you must be happy in that. No doubt it is the best you can do. So, then, why will? Why be angry because of what you cannot do? We all have to do what we can . . .

Romain Rolland, *John Christopher*, translated by Gilbert Cannan, William Heinemann Ltd., 1911, Volume II, *Storm and Stress*, p.149.

There is now no reverence for anything; and the reason is, that men possess conceptions only, and all their knowledge is conceptional only. Now, as to conceive is a work of the mere understanding, and as all that can be conceived may be comprehended, it is impossible that a man should reverence that, to which he must always feel something in himself superior. If it were possible to conceive God in a strict sense, that is, as we conceive a horse or a tree, even God himself could not excite any reverence, though he might excite fear or terror, or perhaps love, as a tiger or a beautiful woman. But reverence, which is the synthesis of love and fear, is only due from man, and, indeed, only excitable in man, towards ideal truths, which are always mysteries to the understanding, for the same reason that the motion of my finger behind my back is a mystery to you now—your eyes not being made for seeing through my body. It is the reason only which has a sense by which ideas can be recognized, and from the fontal light of ideas only can a man draw intellectual power.

Samuel Taylor Coleridge, *The Table Talk and Omniana of Samuel Taylor Coleridge*, Oxford University Press, 1917, p.156.

RIGHTEOUSNESS

"Righteousness"—"just, uprightness, virtuous, law-abiding,—of person, life, and action."

As an undergraduate I remember going to the University Mission in 1963. It was led by Trevor Huddleston—then Bishop of Masasi, in Tanganyika.

The main addresses were given in the Examination Schools. They were well attended. Many of us arrived in good time hoping to get a seat near the front. We were chatting excitedly amongst ourselves, waiting for the Bishop to arrive. I was curious to see him, having been deeply moved by his book, *Naught for Your Comfort*—about apartheid in Sophiatown, South Africa.

There was a sudden silence. We all turned round and looked at the entrance. Yes, the Bishop had indeed arrived. All eyes were fixed on him. In complete silence he walked slowly up the hall, not hurrying. I studied his demeanour carefully. First impressions are important.

Here was someone I immediately took to be righteous. "Righteousness" was somehow written into his features. This observation was later confirmed by what he said and by the kind of life he lived. Four hours a day in prayer and worship were impressive. That this devotional life was balanced by thought and action completely won me over. I concluded he was a man in a "right" relationship with God, and in a "right" relationship with people, hence for me a living example of "righteousness."

For the Lord is righteous, he loves righteous deeds; the upright shall behold his face.
Psalm 11.7.

Then justice will dwell in the wilderness, and righteousness abide in the fruitful field. And the effect of righteousness will be peace, and the result of righteousness, quietness and trust for ever. My people will abide in a peaceful habitation, in secure dwellings, and in quiet resting places.
Isaiah 32.16-18.

Blessed are those who hunger and thirst for righteousness, for they shall be satisfied.
Matthew 5.6.

The kingdom of God is not food and drink but righteousness and peace and joy in the Holy Spirit.
Romans 14.17.

The law of righteousness, is the law of God's nature, and the law of His actions.
Benjamin Whichcote, *Moral and Religious Aphorisms*, Elkin Mathews & Marrot, Ltd., 1930, Century V, No.401.

Aim at *righteousness*, which means giving both to men and to God their due.
William Barclay, *The Letters to Timothy, Titus & Philemon*, The Saint Andrew Press, 1987, p.180.

Better, though difficult, the right way to go,
Than wrong, though easy, where the end is woe.
John Bunyan, *The Pilgrim's Progress*, J.M. Dent & Sons Ltd., 1964, p.43.

But there remains the question: *what* righteousness really is. The method and secret and sweet reasonableness of Jesus.
Matthew Arnold, *The Complete Prose Works of Matthew Arnold*, The University of Michigan Press, 1968, Volume 6, *Dissent and Dogma, Literature and Dogma*, p.399.

The most general meaning is uprightness, rectitude, or justice, and the word may be applied to God or to humans.
James F. Childress, in *A New Dictionary of Christian Ethics*, edited by James F. Childress and John Macquarrie, SCM Press Ltd., 1986, p.556.

The revelation of Jesus Christ in the New Testament is like the revelation of the God of Israel in the Old, in being the eternal *not ourselves* which makes for righteousness.
Matthew Arnold, *The Complete Prose Works of Matthew Arnold*, The University of Michigan Press, 1968, Volume 6, *Dissent and Dogma, Literature and Dogma*, p.311.

Righteousness, or rather *the* righteousness, that character which God has marked out for us, the character of Christ—blessed are they which do hunger and thirst after it.
Charles Gore, *The Sermon on the Mount*, John Murray Ltd., 1897, p.35.

There are two good things about righteousness. It is right and it is perfect, like all the works of our Lord God. It has need neither of mercy nor of grace, for they too are righteous. Nothing is lacking.
Julian of Norwich, *Revelations of Divine Love*, Penguin Books Ltd., 1976, p.81.

It is the work and business of religion, and of our lives, to reconcile the *temper* of our spirits to the rule of righteousness; and to incorporate the principles of our religion, into the *complexion* of our minds.

Benjamin Whichcote, *Moral and Religious Aphorisms*, Elkin Mathews & Marrot, Ltd., 1930, Century I, No.25.

Jesus Christ came to reveal what righteousness really is... Nothing will do, except righteousness; and no other conception of righteousness will do, except Jesus Christ's conception of it—his *method*, his *secret*, and his *temper*.

Matthew Arnold, *The Complete Prose Works of Matthew Arnold*, The University of Michigan Press, 1968, Volume 6, *Dissent and Dogma, Literature and Dogma*, p.400.

Among the Greeks and Romans righteousness (Greek *dikaiosune*, Latin *iustitia*) had meanings which included both the strict justice with which states ought to be governed and laws administered, and more generally the correct behaviour of people within the various relationships of family, neighbourhood, society and state. In the second sense it was often synonymous with virtue itself.

J.A. Ziesler, in *A New Dictionary of Christian Theology*, edited by Alan Richardson and John Bowden, SCM Press Ltd., 1985, p.507.

Like as the earth engendereth not rain, nor is able by her own strength, labour and travail to procure the same, but receiveth it of the mere gift of God from above: so this heavenly righteousness is given us of God without our works or deservings. As much therefore as the earth of itself is able to do in getting and procuring to itself seasonable showers of rain to make it fruitful, even so much are we men able to do by our strength and words in winning this heavenly and eternal righteousness; and therefore we shall never be able to attain unto it, unless God himself by mere imputation and by his unspeakable gift do bestow it upon us.

Martin Luther, *A Commentary on St Paul's Epistle to the Galatians*, edited by Philip S. Watson, James Clarke & Co. Ltd., 1953, Preface, p.23.

The first great illumination to be found in the Old Testament is the interpretation of holiness as first and foremost righteousness. What exalts God most completely in our mind is not that He is so great or that He is so powerful, but that He is so good.

Again, this righteousness is first understood in terms of justice, and this manifestation in terms of justice is never superseded. Let us remember always that our Lord's most searching precepts concerning life and love are given in fulfilment or completion of the law and the prophets, and not in contradiction or supersession of them. "I came not to destroy the law or the prophets, but to fulfil (or complete) them."

William Temple, *Basic Convictions*, Hamish Hamilton Ltd., 1937, p.18.

There is one thing which came forcibly to me in my early studies of the Bible. It seized me immediately when I read one passage. The text was this: "Seek ye first the Kingdom of God and His righteousness, and all other things will be added unto you." I tell you that if you will understand, appreciate, and act up to the spirit of this passage, then you will not even need to know what place Jesus, or any other teacher, occupies in your heart or my heart. If you will do this moral scavenger's work, so as to clean and purify your hearts and get them ready you will find that all these mighty teachers will take their places without any invitation from us. That, to my mind, is the basis of a sound education. The culture of the mind must be subservient to the culture of the heart. May God help you to become pure!

Mohandas K. Gandhi, in *Mahatma Gandhi's Ideas*, C.F. Andrews, George Allen & Unwin Publishers Ltd., 1929, p.94.

Righteousness is a word that has been much misunderstood, because it means so much, and is hard to define. In common with words like Christianity, Socialism, Liberty, it is so difficult to define; it requires too much trouble, so that it has been left out and despised like words that need much pondering over. It goes to the root of our nature, strikes below the reason, is deeper than hunger and thirst, stronger than fear of death. Those are blessed who love righteousness most. Only those souls can grow to fulness, who will drive on to completion of development, to the final completion of human nature for which we are made. Righteousness is an intense desire for harmony springing out of a great sensibility to discord. So righteousness and peace have kissed each other.

G.A. Studdert Kennedy, *The New Creation in Christ,* Hodder & Stoughton Ltd., 1932, p.47.

When Paul uses the word *righteousness*, he means *a right relationship with God.* The man who is righteous is the man who is in a right relationship with God, and whose life shows it. Paul begins with a survey of the Gentile world. We have only to look at the decadence and corruption of that Gentile world to know that it had not solved the problem of righteousness. He looks at the Jewish world. The Jews had sought to solve the problem of righteousness by meticulous obedience to the law. Paul had tried that way himself, and it had issued in frustration and defeat, because no man on earth can ever fully obey the law, and, therefore, every man must have the continual consciousness of being in debt to God and under God's condemnation. So Paul finds the way to righteousness in the way of utter trust, and utter yieldedness. The only way to a right relationship with God is to take God at His word, and to cast oneself, just as one is, on the mercy and the love of God. It is the way of faith. It is to know that the important thing is, not what we can do for God, but what God has done for us. For Paul the centre of the Christian faith was that we can never earn or deserve the favour of God, nor do we need to. The whole matter is a matter of grace, and all that we can do is to accept in wondering love and gratitude and trust what God has done for us.

William Barclay, *The Letter to the Romans,* The Saint Andrew Press, 1969, p.xxv.

SACRAMENTS

"Sacraments"—"religious ceremony or act regarded as an outward and visible sign of an inward and spiritual grace."

I shall never forget a "Communion Service" in the hot summer of 1976. Twenty students from University College, London, went on a "pilgrimage" for a week. We set out from St. Ives in Cornwall, intending to walk to Truro Cathedral. Our route was the coastal path—until we had to cut inland to reach Truro. We planned to walk during the day, and rest up overnight on church hall floors. This had all been carefully planned beforehand.

About half way through the week we decided to have our informal Communion Service at lunch-time. Before we set out we noticed on the map a small remote bay, and our aim was to reach that by midday. Instead of our normal lunch, we would just have some fresh bread and wine—lunch and Communion in one.

The weather was superb. We found the beach and much to our delight it was sandy and almost deserted. Huge waves were crashing in. We changed into swimming costumes, and started our "Service". We simplified the set form. Lessons were read and a short address was given. The bread was broken and distributed. The wine was poured out and shared. There was something special about that service. We had an acute awareness, by the sea, of that inward and spiritual grace.

Unless you eat the flesh of the Son of man and drink his blood, you have no life in you; he who eats my flesh and drinks my blood has eternal life, and I will raise him up at the last day. For my flesh is food indeed, and my blood is drink indeed. He who eats my flesh and drinks my blood abides in me, and I in him.

John 6.53-56.

And Peter said to them, "Repent, and be baptized every one of you in the name of Jesus Christ for the forgiveness of your sins; and you shall receive the gift of the Holy Spirit."

Acts 2.38.

For I received from the Lord what I also delivered to you, that the Lord Jesus on the night when he was betrayed took bread, and when he had given thanks, he broke it, and said, "This is my body which is for you. Do this in remembrance of me." In the same way also the cup, after supper, saying, "This cup is the new covenant in my blood. Do this, as often as you drink it, in remembrance of me."

1 Corinthians 11.23-25.

And let him who is thirsty come, let him who desires take the water of life without price.

Revelation 22.17.

The Spiritual Presence cannot be received without a sacramental element, however hidden the latter might be.

Paul Tillich, *Systematic Theology*, James Nisbet & Co. Ltd., 1963, Volume III, 1964, p.130.

A symbol is a significant image, which helps the worshipping soul to apprehend spiritual reality. A sacrament is a significant deed, a particular use of temporal things, which gives to them the value of eternal things and thus incorporates and conveys spiritual reality.

Evelyn Underhill, in *The Wisdom of Evelyn Underhill*, edited by John Stobbart, Mowbray, 1951, p.25.

The sacrament of baptism applies itself, and has reference to the faith of conviction, and is, therefore, only to be performed once—it is the light of man. The sacrament of the eucharist is a symbol of all our religion—it is the life of man. It is commensurate with our will, and we must, therefore, want it continually.

Samuel Taylor Coleridge, *Table Talk and Omniana of Samuel Taylor Coleridge*, Oxford University Press, 1917, p.98.

At bottom, worship is a spiritual activity; but we are not pure spirits, and therefore we cannot expect to do it in purely spiritual ways. That is the lesson of the Incarnation. Thus liturgies, music, symbols, sacraments, devotional articles and acts have their rightful part to play in the worshipping life; it is both shallow and arrogant to reject them *en masse* and assume that there is something particularly religious in leaving out the senses when we turn to God.

Evelyn Underhill, in *The Wisdom of Evelyn Underhill*, edited by John Stobbart, Mowbray, 1951, p.25.

Human beings are very dependent on their feelings so far as the practice of their religion is concerned. Sacraments are particularly suited to the human condition because they deliver people from the enslavement to feelings. Sacraments are given by God, and provided that they are received in faith, we are promised the grace of God, whatever we may or may not feel. While sacraments need to be subjectively received in faith, their objectivity meets our need for assurance.

Hugh Montefiore, *Confirmation Notebook*, Fifth Edition, SPCK, 1985, p.33.

The whole sacramental theory is based on two great principles: one is that the movement of the soul towards God meets with a corresponding movement of God towards the soul; the other is that every material thing has been created that spirit may possess it and that spirit may be expressed thereby. When God's children come to Him, He comes to them. If they make a move towards Him spiritually, He comes to them spiritually; if they make a move towards Him sacramentally, He comes to them sacramentally.

Father Andrew SDC, *The Symbolism of the Sanctuary*, A.R. Mowbray & Co. Ltd., 1927, p.19.

Because sacraments are symbolic actions, God can communicate to us through them without our having to articulate precisely what is being done. And so sacraments are particularly helpful to those who find it hard to verbalize their faith. At the same time, words do illuminate the action of a sacrament, and also the reverse. Hence the conjunction of word and sacrament. The word is addressed to the discursive mind, and the sacrament speaks to those deeper levels of consciousness where imagination and subconscious mind are moved by sign and symbol.

Hugh Montefiore, *Confirmation Notebook*, Fifth Edition, SPCK, 1985, p.34.

The great point about the Sacraments is that they are the acts of God. The grace of God has never been dependent upon men but upon the gracious gift of God Himself. In the times when the Popes were at their worst, in the times when the priesthood has been most corrupt, there have been some of the richest manifestations of holiness, and that has been because the grace of God has never been in any way invalidated or affected by the unworthiness of the ministers who have imparted it to God's children. The security of the sacramental system of the Church is dependent upon the character and the good faith of God Himself. For the Church is the Body of Christ, a group of people brought into being through the action of God the Holy Spirit, and as the acts of Christ in His incarnate life were authentic acts of God, so the acts of the Body of Christ, the Catholic Church, are authentic acts of Christ in the matter of imparting the grace of God.

Father Andrew SDC, *The Way of Victory*, Mowbray, 1938, p.14.

If we are sensitive to the voice of nature, we might be able to hear sounds from a world where all of humanity and all of nature both find their shape. We will never fully understand the meaning of the sacramental signs of bread and wine when they do not make us realize that the whole of nature is a sacrament pointing to a reality far beyond itself. The presence of Christ in the Eucharist becomes a "special problem" only when we have lost our sense of his presence in all that is, grows, lives, and dies. What happens during a Sunday celebration can only be a real celebration when it reminds us in the fullest sense of what continually happens every day in the world which surrounds us. Bread is more than bread, wine is more than wine: it is God with us—not as an isolated event once a week but as the concentration of a mystery about which all of nature speaks day and night.

Therefore, wasting food is not a sin just because there are still so many hungry people in this world. It is a sin because it is an offence against the sacramental reality of all we eat and drink. But if we become more and more aware of the voices of all that surrounds us and grow in respect and reverence for nature, then we also will be able to truly care for a humanity embedded in nature like a sapphire in a golden ring.

Henri J.M. Nouwen, *Seeds of Hope*, edited by Robert Durback, Darton, Longman & Todd Ltd., 1989, p.100.

The greatest mystery of the Christian faith is that God came to us in the body, suffered with us in the body, rose in the body, and gave us his body as food. No religion takes the body as seriously as the Christian religion. The body is not seen as the enemy or as a prison of the Spirit, but celebrated as the Spirit's temple. Through Jesus' birth, life, death, and resurrection, the human body has become part of the life of God. By eating the body of Christ, our own fragile bodies are becoming intimately connected with the risen Christ and thus prepared to be lifted up with him into the divine life. Jesus says, "I am the living bread which has come down from heaven. Anyone who eats this bread will live forever; and the bread that I shall give is my flesh, for the life of the world." (John 6.51).

It is in union with the body of Christ that I come to know the full significance of my own body. My body is much more than a mortal instrument of pleasure and pain. It is a home where God wants to manifest the fullness of the divine glory. This truth is the most profound basis for the moral life. The abuse of the body—whether it be psychological (e.g., instilling fear), physical (e.g., torture), economic (e.g., exploitation), or sexual (e.g., hedonistic pleasure-seeking)—is a distortion of true human destiny: to live in the body eternally with God. The loving care given to our bodies and the bodies of others is therefore a truly spiritual act, since it leads the body closer towards its glorious existence.

Henri J.M. Nouwen, *Seeds of Hope*, edited by Robert Durback, Darton, Longman & Todd Ltd., 1989, p.118.

The sacraments belong to the order of signs. They manifest something more than themselves, something hidden. Indeed, a sacrament is at once something visible and something hidden. The Latin word *sacramentum* is the normal translation of the Greek *mysterion,* or mystery. In each sacramental "mystery" we have an outward sign, an action, the application or use of some material element… But also, in each sacrament, the outward sign is accompanied by an inward, spiritual reality, which it signifies. This inward reality is an effect produced by God in our soul, through the instrumentality of the sacramental action. And so the sacraments are very special signs, differing from other signs not only in their divine institution, but above all in the fact that they signify a spiritual reality, and at the very same time produce the reality which they signify.

At the same time, we must remember that the sacraments have a multiple signification. They point not only to a present spiritual effect in our own souls, but at the same time they link that effect with its cause, the mystery of Christ's Passion, and with its final end: the life of glory in heaven. Therefore in every sacrament we have not only a sign of the grace made present in the soul, but a sign of the Passion of Christ, which is the source and cause of that grace, and of the resurrection of all saints in Christ, which is the term and fulfilment of all grace. Every sacrament therefore unites in itself the past, the present and the future. It makes "present", in some way, the whole "mystery of Christ" by virtue of its own, proper sacramental signification.

Thomas Merton, *The New Man,* Burns & Oates Ltd., 1962, p.142.

SACRIFICE

"Sacrifice"— "giving up of thing for the sake of another that is higher or more urgent."

I once had the privilege of seeing Mother Teresa of Calcutta at close quarters. She came to England to receive the Templeton Prize, and I was privileged to be one of the guests at the prize-giving ceremony.

First impressions are often important. What immediately struck me was her quiet demeanour and an air of radiance about her personality. I remember thinking she could so easily have got some qualifications, married, had a family, and settled down. Yet she sacrificed all this, joined an order of nuns, and dedicated herself to a life of costly service.

For many years she has been working in the streets of Calcutta, ministering to the sick, the dying and the destitute. This must surely be one of the most difficult tasks in the world. On her own admission she can only do it through a life dedicated to prayer and worship, and then taking to the streets to care for people in need.

I remember being in the streets of Calcutta some thirty years ago, and was reduced to despair at the immensity of the problems facing that city. However, over the years, little by little, she and her order of nuns have transformed the lives of thousands of people in that city. She has been an inspiration throughout the world, and by her life and work we have learnt anew the meaning of Sacrifice.

But I will buy it of you for a price; I will not offer burnt offerings to the Lord my God which cost me nothing.

2 Samuel 24.24.

For thou hast no delight in sacrifice; were I to give him a burnt offering, thou wouldst not be pleased. The sacrifice acceptable to God is a broken spirit; a broken and contrite heart, O God, thou wilt not despise.

Psalm 51.16-17.

And to love him with all the heart, and with all the understanding, and with all the strength, and to love one's neighbour as oneself, is much more than all whole burnt offerings and sacrifices. And when Jesus saw that he answered wisely, he said to him, "You are not far from the kingdom of God."

Mark 12.33-34.

I appeal to you therefore, brethren, by the mercies of God, to present your bodies as a living sacrifice, holy and acceptable to God, which is your spiritual worship.

Romans 12.1.

Sacrifice is the heart of all religious worship.

Emil Brunner, *Revelation and Reason*, translated by Olive Wyon, SCM Press Ltd., 1947, p.41.

Life has become richer by the love that has been lost.

Rabindranath Tagore, *Collected Poems & Plays of Rabindranath Tagore*, Macmillan Publishers Ltd., 1935, *Stray Birds*, CCXXIII, p.316.

Nothing so much enhances a good as to make sacrifices for it.

George Santayana, *The Sense of Beauty*, A. & C. Black, 1896, p.111.

Good actions are the best sacrifice we can offer to God.

Thomas Fuller, *Gnomologia*, Stearne Brock, 1733, p.65.

We cannot be sure that we have something worth living for unless we are ready to die for it.

Eric Hoffer, *The True Believer*, The New American Library of World Literature, Inc., 1965, p.24.

Ever since his conversion, he (Paul) had offered everything to God—his money, his scholarship, his time, the vigour of his body, the acuteness of his mind, the devotion of his heart.

William Barclay, *The Letters to Timothy, Titus & Philemon*, The Saint Andrew Press, 1987, p.209.

Life is a great vocation, and Christ's disciples will put into it all they can of sacrifice, love, and labour. The Christian character is the flower of which sacrifice is the seed.

Father Andrew SDC, *A Gift of Light*, selected and edited by Harry C. Griffith, Mowbray, 1968, p.32.

Without self-sacrifice there can be no blessedness either in earth or in heaven. He that loveth his life will lose it. He that hateth his life in this paltry, selfish, luxurious world shall keep it to life eternal.

Charles Kingsley, *Daily Thoughts*, Macmillan Publishers Ltd., 1884, p.95.

Self-sacrificial love cannot be planted in someone's heart simply by bringing in a new economic order. Christianity is both about justice and about Christ changing people from inside out.

David Sheppard, *Bias to the Poor*, Hodder & Stoughton Ltd., 1983, p.155.

My brothers... the love of God is a hard love. It demands total self-surrender, disdain of our human personality. And yet it alone can reconcile us to suffering and the deaths of children, it alone can justify them, since we cannot understand them, and we can only make God's will ours.

Albert Camus, *The Plague,* translated by Stuart Gilbert, Hamish Hamilton Ltd., 1948, p.212.

In the name of all her members the Church comes up to the altar with awe and thanksgiving, and there, on the very frontiers of the unseen world, she gives herself that she may receive the Food of Eternal Life. So the inner life of each one of those members must have in it the colour of sacrifice, the energy of a redeeming love, if it is to form part of the living Soul of the Church.

Evelyn Underhill, in *The Wisdom of Evelyn Underhill,* edited by John Stobbart, Mowbray, 1951, p.29.

Every time we perform an act of kindness to any human being, ay, even to a dumb animal; every time we conquer our worldliness, love of pleasure, ease, praise, ambition, money, for the sake of doing what our conscience tells us to be our duty,—we are indeed worshipping God the Father in spirit and in truth, and offering Him a sacrifice which He will surely accept for the sake of His beloved Son, by whose Spirit all good deeds and thoughts are inspired.

Charles Kingsley, *Daily Thoughts,* Macmillan Publishers Ltd., 1884, p.181.

The Christian may have to sacrifice his personal ambitions, the ease and the comfort that he might have enjoyed, the career that he might have achieved; he may have to lay aside his dreams, to realize that shining things of which he has caught a glimpse are not for him. He will certainly have to sacrifice his will, for no Christian can ever again do what he likes; he must do what Christ likes. In Christianity there is always some cross, for it is the religion of the Cross.

William Barclay, *The Gospel of Matthew,* The Saint Andrew Press, 1987, Volume 1, p.396.

Most of us die *of* something; of disease, accident, old age. But occasionally there appears in our midst a man who resolves to die *for* something... This dying *for* something, instead of waiting to die *of* something, as most of us do, this deliberate dying for something deemed worthy of it, is the strongest form of self-affirmation I know of. The power and vitality of it are tremendous and the stamp that it leaves on the world is indelible. The Christian religion is an example of it.

L.P. Jacks, *The Inner Sentinel,* Hodder & Stoughton Ltd., 1930, p.130.

It is not easy to justify at the bar of reality the prayers for peace and for reunion which are now offered in countless churches, and by numerous individuals who are not in fact prepared to do one difficult thing, or to make a single sacrifice either of possessions or of prejudices, in the interests of peace and of reunion. Peace is very costly, and reunion will be very costly. Both will need great renunciation; a great acceptance of the Cross. To tell people to pray for either is unreal, unless we also tell them such prayer carries its own sacrificial obligation.

Evelyn Underhill, in *The Wisdom of Evelyn Underhill,* edited by John Stobbart, Mowbray, 1951, p.29.

What a strange mystery is that of mutual self-sacrifice! to exist for one moment for another! the perfection of human bliss! And does not love teach us two things? First, that self-sacrifice, the living for others, is the law of our perfect being, and next, that by and in self-sacrifice alone can we attain to the perfect apprehension of ourselves, our own personality, our own duty, our own bliss. So that the mysteries are utterly wrong when they fancy that self-sacrifice can be attained by self-annihilation. Self-sacrifice, instead of destroying the sense of personality, perfects it.

Charles Kingsley, *Daily Thoughts*, Macmillan Publishers Ltd.., 1884, p.55.

The greatest mystery of life is that satisfaction is felt not by those who take and make demands but by those who give and make sacrifices. In them alone the energy of life does not fail, and this is precisely what is meant by creativeness. Therefore the positive mystery of life is to be found in love, in sacrificial, giving, creative love. As has been said already, all creativeness is love and all love is creative.

If you want to receive, give, if you want to obtain satisfaction, do not seek it, never think of it and forget the very word; if you want to acquire strength, manifest it, give it to others.

Nicolas Berdyaev, *The Destiny of Man*, translated by Natalie Duddington, Geoffrey Bles: The Centenary Press, 1937, p.180.

And what is sacrifice? To sacrifice is literally to "make a thing sacred"; it is to take something out of common use and to make it over to God. It is a symbolic act by which we recognise that everything in this world derives from another order of being and seeks to enter into communion with that other world. But the outward thing which is sacrificed can never be more than a sign of an inward offering; what we desire is to offer ourselves. The essential sacrifice has to take place in the centre of our own being, in the darkness of the interior where alone we can encounter the God who is hidden in the depths of the soul. We have to pass beyond all the images of the senses, beyond all the concepts of the mind, beyond ourselves, if we are really to find God.

Bede Griffiths OSB, *The Golden String*, The Harvill Press Ltd., 1954, p.163.

SAINTS

"Saints"— "the holy people of God."

I grew up with a rather jaundiced view of saints. I spotted a few of them in stained-glass windows in Churches. They looked cold and severe in demeanour, and thin and emaciated in body. I thought golden plates round their heads made them look stupid.

The turning-point came in meeting a real live saint. I was surprised to be confronted with a warm and loving person. He was outgoing and fully alive. His disposition was kindly and sympathetic. His bright shining eyes were evidence of an inner energy and enthusiasm. I was relieved to find no sign of a golden plate round his head; rather something of "light" emanating from the depths of his personality. Ah, that's it. I should have known. That is how the artists tried to communicate this to us—something of the divine in the lives of the saints, best depicted as "light". I wonder how the saints got to be like that? Something of God in them coming alive, nurtured by prayer and worship, and finding an outlet in service?

I began to look around and soon discovered a whole bevy of saints. I call them my "heroes". Indirectly they have been an enormous help to me. In times of despair, when it feels as though all hope is gone, I've just thought about my "heroes" and immediately felt much better. Whatever else was happening in the world, they were quietly getting on with things—their lives giving ample evidence of the existence of God.

The recorded experience of the saints down the ages has also provided me with an invaluable source of inspiration. I love to reflect on their findings.

As for the saints in the land, they are the noble, in whom is all my delight.
Psalm 16.3.

The Lord loves those who hate evil; he preserves the lives of his saints; he delivers them from the hand of the wicked. Light dawns for the righteous, and joy for the upright in heart. Rejoice in the Lord, O you righteous, and give thanks to his holy name!
Psalm 97.10-12.

Called to be saints together with all those who in every place call on the name of our Lord Jesus Christ, both their Lord and ours.
1 Corinthians 1.2.

The grace of the Lord Jesus be with all the saints.
Revelation 22.21.

The heroes, the saints and sages—they are those who face the world alone.
Norman Douglas, *An Almanac*, Chatto & Windus in association with Martin Secker & Warburg Ltd., 1945, p.13.

The holiness of the saints is the restored image of God in them.
Benedicta Ward, in *A New Dictionary of Christian Theology*, edited by Alan Richardson and John Bowden, SCM Press Ltd., 1985, p.518.

To pray is to open oneself to the possibility of sainthood, to the possibility of becoming set on fire by the Spirit.
Kenneth Leech, *True Prayer*, Sheldon Press, 1980, p.36.

The saint is essentially someone who communicates and radiates the character of God, his love, his joy, his peace.
Kenneth Leech, *True Prayer*, Sheldon Press, 1980, p.36.

The loving acceptance of the saints is never mistaken by sinners as condoning their sins. Rather it lifts them to new aspirations.
Anon.

Through such souls alone
God stooping shows sufficient of His light
For us i' the dark to rise by. And I rise.
Robert Browning, *The Complete Poetical Works of Robert Browning*, Ohio University Press, 1988, Volume VIII, *The Ring and the Book*, VII, l.1826.

We may allow that the saints are specialists; but they are specialists in a career to which all Christians are called. The difference between them and us is a difference in degree, not in kind.
Evelyn Underhill, in *The Wisdom of Evelyn Underhill*, edited by John Stobbart, Mowbray, 1951, p.30.

A saint is a human creature devoured and transformed by love: a love that has dissolved and burnt out those instinctive passions—acquisitive and combative, proud and greedy—which commonly rule the lives of men.
Evelyn Underhill, in *The Wisdom of Evelyn Underhill*, edited by John Stobbart, Mowbray, 1951, p.30.

The saint is God's greatest work. All the world's "great" men seem small beside the saint. The great statesman, the great writer, the great soldier may be far above us, but he remains altogether of our world. The great saint fills us with awe and seems at times almost a visitor from another sphere.

W.E. Sangster, *The Pure in Heart*, Epworth Press, 1954, p.96.

The eyes of the saint make all beauty holy and the hands of the saint consecrate everything they touch to the glory of God, and the saint is never offended by anything and judges no man's sin because he does not know sin. He knows the mercy of God. He knows that his own mission on earth is to bring that mercy to all men.

Thomas Merton, *Seeds of Contemplation*, Anthony Clarke Books, 1972, p.20.

The saint . . . is sanctified not only by fasting when he should fast but also by eating when he should eat. He is not only sanctified by his prayers in the darkness of the night, but by the sleep that he takes in obedience to God, who made us what we are. Not only his solitude contributes to his union with God, but also his supernatural love for his friends and his relatives and those with whom he lives and works.

Thomas Merton, *No Man is an Island*, Burns & Oates Ltd., 1974, p.86.

A saint is a perfect man. He is a temple of the Holy Ghost. He reproduces, in his own individual way, something of the balance and perfection and order that we find in the human character of Jesus. The soul of Jesus, hypostatically united to the Word of God, enjoyed at the same time and without conflict the clear vision of God and the most common and simple and intimate of our human emotions—affection, pity and sorrow, happiness, pleasure or grief; indignation and wonder; weariness, anxiety and fear; consolation and peace.

Thomas Merton, *Thoughts in Solitude*, Burns & Oates Ltd., 1958, p.23.

The theocentric saint is impressive, not only for what he is, but also for what he does and says. His actions and all his dealings with the world are marked by disinterestedness and serenity, invariable truthfulness and a total absence of fear. These qualities are the fruits of the doctrine he preaches, and their manifestation in his life enormously reinforces that doctrine and gives him a certain strange kind of uncoercive but none the less compelling authority over his fellow men. The essence of this authority is that it is primarily spiritual and moral, and is associated with none of the ordinary social sanctions of power, position or wealth.

Aldous Huxley, *Collected Essays*, Chatto & Windus, 1960, p.281.

It is a wonderful experience to discover a new saint. For God is greatly magnified and marvellous in each one of His saints: differently in each individual one. There are no two saints alike: but all of them are like God, like Him in a different and special way. In fact, if Adam had never fallen, the whole human race would have been a series of magnificently different and splendid images of God, each one of all the millions of men showing forth His glories and perfections in an astonishing new way, and each one shining with his own particular sanctity, a sanctity destined for him from all eternity as the most complete and unimaginable supernatural perfection of his human personality.

Thomas Merton, *Elected Silence*, Hollis & Carter, 1949, p.304.

What is a *saint?* Saintliness is a known phenomenon. We call a man saintly not just because he is very good, nor yet because he is good and also religious. A saint is marked by a certain "otherworldliness", by a serenity and happiness as of one who is "yonder"—and yet there is no escapism, for he is very sensitive to the pains of his fellows and shares and bears with them acutely. And he is marked also by an unselfconscious awareness of God which is the secret of an unusual humility: virtues and achievements cannot inflate him, for he ascribes them to their source, and a hidden sense of unworthiness (sometimes very painful) makes him yet more receptive of God's gifts. He is not surprised to find that there is "a drop of poison in the chalice of the fullest secular happiness, a poison infused by the heavenly lover of all souls to prevent us from finding abiding happiness outside Himself."

Michael Ramsey, *Canterbury Pilgrim*, SPCK, 1974, p.50.

The true marvel of a saint is his life of continual faith through everything. If he had not that, the rest of his gifts would not make him holy. His holiness based on the loving faith which causes him to enjoy God in everything needs no exterior wonders; if such have their use it is for the sake of others who may need this testimony. As for the soul of faith contented in its obscurity, it does not rest on these brilliant manifestations; it lets them appear externally for the benefit of its neighbour, keeping for itself the most ordinary elements it can find, the order of God and his good pleasure which exercise its faith in obscurity rather than in manifestation. Faith asks for no proofs, and those who need them have less faith than those who do not. Those who live by faith do indeed receive proof, not as such but in the course of the divine order.

Jean-Pierre de Caussade, *Self-Abandonment to Divine Providence*, translated by Algar Thorold, William Collins Sons & Co. Ltd., 1972, p.88.

It is not being *virtuous* that makes a saint: the Pharisees were very virtuous, and they and their virtues needed conversion. It is not *doing good* that makes a saint; he often does do good, but so do many people whom we would never call saints. It is not the practice of *religion* which makes a saint. I expect you and I are pretty religious, but our religion, like every part of us, needs converting. No, the saint is one who has a strange nearness to God and makes God real and near to other people.

A saint embodies the parable of the corn of wheat that falls into the earth and dies. His virtues do not make him proud, for he is reaching out towards a perfection far beyond them and is humbled by the quest. His sins and failings, which may be many and bitter, do not cast him down, for the divine forgiveness humbles him and humbles him again. He shares and bears the griefs of his fellows, and he feels the world's pains with a heightened sensitivity; but with that sensitivity he has an inner serenity of an unearthly kind which brings peace and healing to other people.

This strange blending of humility, sorrow, and joy is the mark of a saint, and through him God is real and near.

Michael Ramsey, *Through the Year with Michael Ramsey*, edited by Margaret Duggan, Hodder & Stoughton Ltd., 1975, p.38.

We need heroes. They show us the wonders of life, the possibilities in life. They fill us with a sense of pride and gratitude in our humanity. Life and love are communal. It is through community that we mature. So it is proper that we seek a community, a neighbourhood, of people who inspire us to better living. Churches have realized that and have given us saints. However, these need to be supplemented with our personal set of human champions... whose experiences are more particularly like our own... Heroes are necessary for our sense of humanity, of growth, of community in which we are spiritually nourished. If we fail to see the heroic in otherwise ordinary mortals, we may be in such a state of despair that it is dangerous to our own development. Are we so discouraged by political chicanery, by military lying, by ecclesiastical blundering, by friends letting us down that we finally believe that everybody has a price? Or can we find those human beacons that will guide us through the ordinariness of existence? One further note on this may also be put in the form of a rhetorical question: Do we have the confidence to lead our lives so that we may be beacons for others?

Harry James Cargas, Encountering Myself, SPCK, 1978, p.110.

SANCTIFICATION

"Sanctification"— "holiness of life, saintliness, being made
productive or conducive to holiness."

One of my "heroes" is Archbishop Anthony Bloom. I met him once in London and asked him for a way of growing in the devotional life. He recounted his first experiences of being in the monastery, training for the priesthood. He was allocated a spiritual director, and went to see him at the appointed hour. The "sage" gave him a verse from Scripture and asked him to meditate on it for a week. He was to return again at the same hour, to discuss the findings.

Anthony Bloom meditated on that one verse for a week, and went back to see the spiritual director as arranged. The sage listened carefully for an hour, and concluded: "Well, you've scratched the surface of this verse. Go into it a little deeper next week, and we'll meet again at our appointed hour."

All told, seven weeks were spent in meditating on that one verse. Eventually the sage said: "You seem to have got something out of this now. I think the time has come for a different verse." The process started all over again.

Anthony Bloom attributed his progress in holiness to this demanding training. Perhaps the contents of this anthology may help to stimulate the practice of meditation.

Consecrate yourselves therefore, and be holy; for I am the Lord your God. Keep my statutes, and do them; I am the Lord who sanctify you.

Leviticus 20.7-8.

Sanctify yourselves; for tomorrow the Lord will do wonders among you.

Joshua 3.5.

Sanctify them in the truth; thy word is truth.

John 17.17.

He is the source of your life in Christ Jesus, whom God made our wisdom, our righteousness and sanctification and redemption.

1 Corinthians 1.30.

Do we not need to rehabilitate sanctity in the modern world and to place it humbly before our contemporaries?

Charles S. Duthie, God in His World, Independent Press Ltd., 1955, p.193.

Christians are called to be saints (Rom. 1.7; etc.). The being, character and action of God determine holiness. Creatures become holy when they reflect or participate in God.

Geoffrey Wainwright, in *A New Dictionary of Christian Theology*, edited by Alan Richardson and John Bowden, SCM Press Ltd., 1985, p.521.

Prayer is the secret of a holy life. Reduced to its minimum, the way of sanctity centres in two words: *attend* and *obey*. The saints of all communions come by grace to their serene and unself-conscious distinction by the same means: they attend to God and they obey His word.

W.E. Sangster, *Power in Preaching*, Epworth Press, 1958, p.109.

The cardinal features of sanctity are alike whenever we meet it, and the major elements of method are alike as well. Similarity to Jesus binds all the saints together. Purity and prayer, faith and love... these are the salient characteristics in all the methods by which they ascended the heights.

W.E. Sangster, *The Pure in Heart*, Epworth Press, 1954, p.196.

People often talk about "the secret of the saints" but, in so far as the phrase has any meaning at all, it must be an open secret...

Reduced to a minimum, and put in the plainest words, it comes to this. They ATTEND and OBEY. These two principles underlie all Christian sanctity. Examine holiness wherever it is found in Christendom, and seek what is elemental in the methods employed, and it will bring you to attention and obedience.

But observe! It is *absorbing* attention and *utter* obedience. By this docility on the part of the saints, the Holy Spirit enters and the work is done.

W.E. Sangster, *The Pure in Heart*, Epworth Press, 1954, p.197.

Sanctity in God is therefore the love which He bears in His own supreme goodness, a love which is supremely wise and of the most absolute rectitude.

In its full perfection sanctity exists in God alone, for He alone has a perfect love of his infinite goodness. The three divine Persons possess this essential tribute but each in His own personal "relation".

It will always be beyond our powers of understanding to have an exact idea of divine sanctity in itself. On the other hand, when we contemplate it in Jesus, divine sanctity reveals itself to us and commends our admiration. Man recognizes it as something which is accessible, close to him.

D. Columba Marmion, *Christ—the Ideal of the Priest*, Sands & Company, 1952, p.41.

Sanctification, not redemption, is the chief work of Jesus Christ—"God with us" rather than "God for us". For this reason, to know only the benefits of Christ is not to know Christ. To know Christ only as Redeemer is not to know Christ. To love Christ only with gratitude because of what He has done or will do for us is not to know Christ. Rather, to know Christ is to enjoy the presence of His person, to take delight in His nearness, to love Him as a friend "being with" whom is its own sufficient reason. Only after we first know Jesus as "God with us" can we truly know Him as "God for us". Only after we know Him as friend can we know Him as Redeemer.

The western concentration upon sin and redemption has pushed this correct understanding of the incarnation into the background.

Herbert W. Richardson, *Theology for a New World*, SCM Press Ltd., 1968, p.130.

The sanctification of the soul is a supernatural work. What is the true concept of the supernatural? It is the realization in time of the eternal designs of the Father. God, in His goodness, has destined man to find His final beatitude in the vision of the divinity face to face, a vision which is natural to God alone. Revelation, the Incarnation, the Redemption, the Church, faith, the sacraments, grace, and sanctity, all belong to the munificence of this plan of which Christ and our adoption in Him form the centre. This communication is absolutely gratuitous; it exceeds the needs and the requirements of all created nature, whether angelic or human: that is why it is *supernatural.* We have a glorious ensemble, a world of graces to which is connected the whole activity of the man destined to celestial beatitude.

D. Columba Marmion, *Christ—the Ideal of the Priest,* Sands & Company, 1952, p.33.

There was a simple peasant, a good father of a family, an unlettered husbandman, whose fervent piety was the joy of his pastor's heart. Whether going to his work or returning from it, never did that good man pass the church-door without entering it to adore his Lord. He would leave his tools, his spade, hoe, and pickaxe, at the door, and remain for hours together sitting or kneeling before the tabernacle. M. Vianncy, who watched him with great delight, could never perceive the slightest movement of the lips. Being surprised at this circumstance, he said to him one day, "My good father, what do you say to our Lord in these long visits you pay Him every day and many times a day?" "I say nothing to Him," was the reply; "I look at Him, and He looks at me." "A beautiful and sublime answer," says M. Monnin. "He said nothing, he opened no book, he could not read; but he had eyes,—eyes of the body and eyes of the soul,—and he opened them, those of the soul especially, and fixed them on our Lord. 'I look at Him.' He fastened upon Him his whole mind, his whole heart; all his senses, and all his faculties. There was an interchange of ineffable thought in those glances which came and went between the heart of the servant and the heart of the Master. This is the secret, the great secret, of attaining sanctity."

Alfred Monnin, *Life of the Blessed Curé D'Ars,* Burns & Oates Ltd., 1907, p.47.

It was the glory of Christ again to sanctify, i.e., declare the sacredness of, all things natural. All natural relationships—all natural enjoyments.

All natural relationships. What He sanctified by His presence was a marriage. Now remember what had gone before this. The life of John the Baptist was the highest form of religious life known in Israel. It was the life ascetic. It was a life of solitariness and penitential austerity. He drank no wine: he ate no pleasant food: he married no wife: he entered into no human relationship. It was the law of that stern and in its way sublime life, to cut out every human feeling as a weakness, and to mortify every natural instinct, in order to cultivate an intenser spirituality. A life in its own order grand, but indisputably unnatural.

Now the first public act of our Redeemer's life is to go with His disciples to a marriage. He consecrates marriage, and the sympathies which lead to marriage. He declares the sacredness of feelings which had been reckoned carnal, and low, and human. He stamped His image on human joys, human connections, human relationships. He pronounces that they are more than human—as it were sacramental: the means whereby God's presence comes to us; the types and shadows whereby higher and deeper relationships become possible to us. For it is through our human affections that the soul first learns to feel that its destiny is Divine: it is through a mortal yearning, unsatisfied, that the spirit ascends, seeking a higher object: It is through the gush of our human tenderness that the Immortal and the Infinite in us reveals itself.

Never does a man know the force that is in him till some mighty affection or grief has humanized the soul. It is by an earthly relationship that God has typified to us and helped us to conceive the only true Espousal—the marriage of the soul to her Eternal Lord.

It was the glory of Christianity to pronounce all these human feelings sacred: therefore it is that the church asserts their sacredness in a religious ceremony; for example, that of marriage. Do not mistake. It is not the ceremony that makes a thing religious: a ceremony can only *declare* a thing religious. The church cannot make sacred that which is not sacred: she is but here on earth as the moon, the witness of the light in heaven; by her ceremonies and by her institutions to bear witness to eternal truths... She cannot make the bond of marriage sacred and indissoluble: she can only witness to the sacredness of that which the union of two spirits has already made: and such are her own words. Her minister is commanded by her to say— "Forasmuch as these two persons have *consented together*," there is the sacred Fact of Nature, "I pronounce that they be man and wife"—here is the authoritative witness to the fact.

Again, it was His glory to declare the sacredness of all natural enjoyments. It was not a marriage only, but a marriage-*feast* to which Christ conducted His disciples. Now we cannot get over this plain fact by saying that it was a religious ceremony: that would be mere sophistry. It was an indulgence in the festivity of life; as plainly as words can describe here was a banquet of human enjoyment. The very language of the master of the feast about men who had well drunk, tells us that there had been, not excess of course, but happiness there and merry-making.

Neither can we explain away the lesson by saying that it is no example to us, for Christ was there to do good, and that what was safe for him might be unsafe for us. For if His life is no pattern for us here in this case of accepting an invitation, in what can we be sure it *is* a pattern? Besides, He took His disciples there, and His mother was there: they were not shielded as he was, by immaculate purity. He was there as a guest at first, as Messiah only afterwards: thereby He declared the sacredness of natural enjoyments.

Here again then, Christ manifested His peculiar glory. The Temptation of the Wilderness was past: the baptism of John, and the life of abstinence to which it introduced were over; and now the Bridegroom comes before the world in the true glory of Messiah—not in the life of asceticism, but in the life of Godliness—not separating from life, but consecrating it; carrying a Divine spirit into every simplest act—accepting an invitation to a feast—giving to water the virtue of a nobler beverage. For Christianity does not destroy what is natural, but ennobles it. To turn water into wine, and what is common into what is holy, is indeed the glory of Christianity.

F.W. Robertson, *Sermons*, Kegan Paul, Trench, Trubner & Co. Ltd., 1897, Second Series, p.246.

SEEING

"Seeing"— "having or exercising the power of discerning objects with the eyes— discern mentally, ascertain by search or inquiry or reflection, consider."

A reflection group was under way. The topic chosen was "Maturity". We had been reflecting silently for about ten minutes when one of our women under-graduate members suddenly exclaimed: "Gosh, that's it! Of course, I see it now!"

The penny had dropped. She had seen something profound that moved her deeply, and her eyes were opened. For her, this was the gateway to faith. Following on from this experience, she became deeply committed in her faith.

"Seeing" in this way is rare in reflection groups. Things usually work much more slowly. I remember a Canadian post-graduate coming to see me, having been in a group for about a year. "You know, Bill," he said, "I have to go away after our reflection group for a period of up to about three hours. I need this time just to digest everything I've seen in the reflection group. I thought this was something peculiar to me, but I've been asking the others about it, and they all have to do it in their own particular way."

Two of them used to go to a coffee house across the road. I had heard of others who used to resume and chat well into the night. I suppose "discern mentally" is an important part of "seeing"—especially in a university environment—but "seeing" can happen anywhere, for those with the desire to see.

Open my eyes, that I may behold wondrous things out of thy law.
Psalm 119.18.

How great are his signs, how mighty his wonders! His kingdom is an everlasting kingdom, and his dominion is from generation to generation.
Daniel 4.3.

"Go your way; your faith has made you well." And immediately he received his sight and followed him.
Mark 10.52.

When he was at table with them, he took the bread and blessed, and broke it, and gave it to them. And their eyes were opened and they recognized him.
Luke 24.30-31.

We can see through others only when we see through ourselves.
Eric Hoffer, *The Passionate State of Mind*, Martin Secker & Warburg Ltd., 1956, p.78.

What you are you do not see, what you see is your shadow.
Rabindranath Tagore, *Collected Poems & Plays of Rabindranath Tagore*, Macmillan Publishers Ltd., Limited, 1936, *Stray Birds*, XVIII, p.289.

The seership of a poet's heart, the insight that is given to faith.
Edward Bellamy, *Looking Backward*, Alvin Redman Ltd., 1948, p.111.

How another sees you depends on how you see him. Respect him, and he will respect you.
Michel Quoist, *With Open Heart*, translated by Colette Copeland, Gill and Macmillan Ltd., 1983, p.168.

He will see most without who has the best eyes within; and he who only sees with his bodily organs sees but the surface.

Henry Ward Beecher, *Proverbs from Plymouth Pulpit*, Charles Burnet & Co., 1887, p.27.

The only way to get our values right is to see, not the beginning, but the end of the way, to see things, not in the light of time, but in the light of eternity.

William Barclay, *The Gospel of Matthew*, The Saint Andrew Press, 1987, Volume 1, p.280.

Hundreds of people can talk for one who can think, but thousands can think for one who can see. To see clearly is poetry, prophecy, and religion,—all in one.

John Ruskin, *Modern Painters*, George Allen & Sons, 1910, Volume III, p.278, Part IV, ch. 16, sec.28.

Some things that are continually before our eyes we never see at all. Men only see what they attend to; if our attention is only fixed on small things we shall only see small details. The more we see and attend, the more the wonder ought to grow.

G.A. Studdert Kennedy, *The New Man in Christ*, Hodder & Stoughton Ltd., 1916, p.53.

The greatest need of our time is to clean out the enormous mass of mental and emotional rubbish that clutters our minds and makes of all political and social life a mass illness.

Without this housecleaning we cannot begin to *see*. Unless we *see* we cannot think. The purification must begin with the mass media. How?

Thomas Merton, *The Conjectures of a Guilty Bystander*, Burns & Oates Ltd., 1968, p.64.

Try to look at the reality in which you live—your work, your commitments, your relationships, your meetings, your walks, the shopping, the newspapers, the children—as a single whole from which you cannot disengage yourself, a whole which you have to think about. I shall say more: a whole by means of which God speaks to you and through which He guides you. So it is not by fleeing that you will find God more easily, but it is by changing your heart that you will see things differently.

Carlo Carretto, *The Desert in the City*, translated by Barbara Wall, William Collins Sons & Co. Ltd., 1983, p.21.

Early morning before sunrise: the valley was filled with mist; red clouds in the sky. For a minute or two the mist took the colour, but fainter, of the clouds. What patience is required in order to see! The sun had not risen, the grass in the field was obviously green, but not without intent fixture of the eyes upon it was the dark, twilight shade of green recognised which was its peculiar meaning and beauty. To most of us, perhaps not to artists, it is more difficult to look than to think.

Mark Rutherford, *More Pages From a Journal*, Oxford University Press, 1910, p.243.

Jesus said, "I am the light." One of the oldest hymns used by Christians—St Paul quotes it—was "Sleeper awake: rise from the dead: Christ shall give you light".

Jesus enables you to see. By your allegiance to him you begin to see God by faith. You begin to see yourself with your illusions about yourself shaken, and your pride shattered. You begin to see other people as they really are, through eyes like those of Jesus, and not through the eyes of your distorted prejudices.

You also see the world and its needs with new awareness, and know that to serve others in their suffering is to serve Jesus himself.

Michael Ramsey, *Through the Year with Michael Ramsey*, edited by Margaret Duggan, Hodder & Stoughton Ltd., 1975, p.204.

And there came upon me this thought, which doubtless has occurred to many another besides myself—why the scene should so influence me and yet make no impression on the men about me. Here were men with far keener eyesight than my own, and around me were animals with eyesight keener still. Their eyes looked on the same scene as mine did, and could distinguish each detail with even greater accuracy. Yet while I lay entranced by its beauty, the keen-eyed shikaris, the animals, and the soaring eagles above me, might have been stone blind for all the impression of beauty it left upon them. Clearly it is not the eye, but the soul that sees beauty. As the soul can respond so will beauty be seen. But then comes the still further reflection—what may there not be staring *me* straight in the face which I am as blind to as the Kashmir stags are to the beauties amidst which they spend their entire lives? The whole panorama may be vibrating with beauties man has not yet the soul to see. Some already living, no doubt see beauties that we ordinary men have not the souls to appreciate. It is only a century ago that mountains were looked upon as hideous, yet now they are one of our chiefest enjoyments. And in the long centuries to come may we not develop a soul for beauties unthought of now? Undoubtedly we must. And often in reverie on the mountains I have tried to conceive what further loveliness they may yet possess for men.

Sir Francis Younghusband, Kashmir, A. & C. Black Ltd., 1924, p.13.

All creatures are living in the hand of God; the senses perceive only the action of the creature, but faith sees the action of God in everything—faith believes that Jesus Christ is alive in everything and operates throughout the whole course of the centuries; faith believes that the briefest moment and the tiniest atom contain a portion of Christ's hidden life and his mysterious action. The action of creatures is a veil concealing the profound mysteries of the divine action. Jesus Christ after his resurrection took his disciples by surprise in his apparitions, he presented himself to them under appearances which disguised him; and as soon as he had revealed himself, he disappeared. This very same Jesus, always living and active, still takes by surprise souls whose faith is not sufficiently pure and penetrating.

There is no moment at which God does not present himself under the guise of some suffering, some consolation or some duty. All that occurs within us, around us and by our means covers and hides his divine action. His action is there, most really and certainly present, but in an invisible manner, the result of which is that we are always being taken by surprise and that we only recognize his operation after it has passed. Could we pierce the veil and were we vigilant and attentive, God would reveal himself continuously to us and we should rejoice in his action in everything that happens to us. At every occurrence we should say: *Dominus est.* It is the Lord; and in all circumstances we should find a gift from God: we should consider creatures as very feeble instruments in the hands of an almighty worker, and we should recognize without difficulty that nothing is lacking to us and that God's constant care leads him to give us each instant what is suited to us.

Jean-Pierre de Caussade, Self-Abandonment to Divine Providence, translated by Algar Thorold, William Collins Sons & Co. Ltd., 1972, p.50.

Christ in us knows both the loneliness of the outsider and the crabbed lives of the insider. He experiences in us the full diversity of the human condition. The meeting of Christ in us with the Christ in others will mean that we shall be willing to expose ourselves in openness to others without fear, seeing each person we meet as having a significance because both of us are accepted and loved by God.

"I can only acknowledge the unconditional significance of another person in him (without which true love is impossible) by affirming him in God, and therefore by belief in God himself, and in myself, as possessing in God the centre and root of my existence." (Vladimir Soloviev, *The Meaning of Love*, p.59)

To have a prayerful approach to people is to have eyes to see, a mind intent upon seeing, a heart hopeful of seeing the image of God in each person I meet, to see them in themselves and in God.

It is only when this significance has been given by us in our approach to people, when we have freed ourselves of the need to assess blame and responsibilities, that we can take them on to the next step on the road to redemption, namely, to be aware of their true selves and that which is blocking the potentialities which lie within them. It is this kind of freedom which the Christ in us brings in our personal approach: the Christ who revealed to the Samaritan woman the truths she was concealing from herself, who enabled the blind not only to see physically but to see spiritually, who enabled the prostitute to realize the real love which lay within her. As I said in my previous book:

"He is constantly opening the eyes of people to a reality greater than is at present known to them, so that they may surrender what they imagine or hope or fear they are to what in fullness they really are: so that they may not be guilty about themselves or hide themselves, but be themselves and love themselves." (*No New Morality*, p.26)

This will mean that in our encounters with people we shall do a great deal of listening in order that we may learn how people do see themselves. By sensitivity to what is heard, and by insight into the right kind of questions to be put, we may be able both to build up the fearful and insecure and rightly disturb and undermine the complacent—those who are "too much at ease in Zion".

Douglas Rhymes, *Prayer in the Secular City*, Lutterworth Press, 1967, p.68.

SELF

"Self"—"person's or thing's own individuality or essence, person or thing as object of introspection or reflexive action."

If I had been asked who I was when an undergraduate, I would probably have replied, "I'm Bill Sykes," and would have added—"and I'm a lawyer". That would mean something like this: "My name is Bill Sykes, but that doesn't really tell you much about me. If you really want to know what I'm like, then I'm reading Law. I spend most of my time reading Law, and that's essentially the sort of person I am, and where my sense of identity comes from"—and under my breath would probably have added—"and I'm dead boring!".

A real change of perspective came about when I began to be committed faith-wise. The focus of attention then moved away from Law, to something (or someone) more personal—Jesus Christ. He became the yardstick of my identity. That was when I began to get a new awareness of self and started to discover who I really was. It was like a breath of fresh air—a feeling of real freedom. Many years later when the full implications of the Genesis story of the Creation of mankind struck me, of man and woman made in the image and likeness of God, of the divine inbreathing, of finding something of the divine in the depths of my being, then I began to get a deeper and broader awareness of "self". Self-discovery became an exciting adventure. Life suddenly became full of endless possibilities, inwardly and outwardly.

Reflection, carefully balanced by outward action, has been for me an invaluable means of growing and progressing on the road of self-discovery and of enjoying one's unique essence.

I commune with my heart in the night; I meditate and search my spirit.
Psalm 77.6.

Let us test and examine our ways, and return to the Lord!
Lamentations 3.40.

But we have this treasure in earthen vessels, to show that the transcendent power belongs to God and not to us.
2 Corinthians 4.7.

Examine yourselves, to see whether you are holding to your faith. Test yourselves. Do you not realize that Jesus Christ is in you? unless indeed you fail to meet the test!
2 Corinthians 13.5.

Very often a change of self is needed more than a change of scene.
A.C. Benson, *Extracts from the Letters of Dr. A.C. Benson to M.E.A.*, Jarrold Publishing, 1927, p.64.

He, that has no government of himself, has no Enjoyment of himself.
Benjamin Whichcote, *Moral and Religious Aphorisms*, Elkin Mathews & Marrot, Ltd., 1930, p.30.

My business is not to remake myself,
But make the absolute best of what God made.
Robert Browning, *The Poetical Works of Robert Browning*, Smith, Elder, & Co., 1897, Volume 1, *Bishop Blougram's Apology*, p.533.

Self-knowledge comes to us only in the dark times, when we are stripped of illusion and naked to truth.
Mary Craig, *Blessings*, Hodder & Stoughton Ltd., 1979, p.104.

Resolve to be thyself; and know that he,
Who finds himself, loses his misery!
Matthew Arnold, *The Poems of Matthew Arnold*, edited by Kenneth Allott, Longmans, Green & Co. Ltd., 1965, p.144, "Self-Dependence," l.31.

Man is made "in God's image". God is a "subsequent relation". Within this relationship, man is made; through it, he becomes what he is. Out of it, he falls apart.
Michel Quoist, *With Open Heart*, translated by Colette Copeland, Gill and Macmillan Ltd., 1983, p.41.

The living self has one purpose only: to come into its own fullness of being, as a tree comes into full blossom, or a bird into spring beauty, or a tiger into lustre.
D.H. Lawrence, *The Phoenix*, edited by Edward D. McDonald, William Heinemann Ltd., 1936, p.714.

Remember that there is but one man in the world, with whom you are to have perpetual contention, and be always striving to exceed him, and that is yourself.
William Law, *A Serious Call to a Devout and Holy Life*, J.M. Dent & Sons Ltd., 1898, p.288.

Learning to know oneself is not just an affair of private introspection. It is also an affair of seeing how others behave and of recognizing and identifying feelings of theirs with feelings of one's own. Each is indispensable to the other.

John S. Brubacher, *Modern Philosophies of Education*, McGraw-Hill Book Company, 1969, p.9.

For it is precisely when all the bogus protective structures have collapsed, when the soul is "pulverised" or nihilated, when it cries out, as the soul of Jesus did, in its helplessness and pain—it is precisely then that God is discovered in the darkness and love shapes itself in the void.

David Anderson, *Simone Weil*, SCM Press Ltd., 1971, p.61.

Love of self is the basic sin, from which all others flow. The moment a man makes his own will the centre of life, divine and human relationships are destroyed, obedience to God and charity to men both become impossible. The essence of Christianity is not the enthronement but the obliteration of self.

William Barclay, *The Letters to Timothy, Titus & Philemon*, The Saint Andrew Press, 1987, p.184.

The more man goes out from himself or goes beyond himself, the more the spiritual dimension of his life is deepened, the more he becomes truly man, the more also he grows in likeness to God, who is Spirit. On the other hand, the more he turns inward and encloses himself in self-interest, the less human does he become. This is the strange paradox of spiritual being—that precisely by going out and spending itself, it realizes itself.

John Macquarrie, *Paths in Spirituality*, SCM Press Ltd., 1972, p.45.

We hide from God, we hide from one another and cover ourselves with all kinds of ethical, intellectual and spiritual garments, because we are ashamed to be found naked; we hide from ourselves, putting lofty screens around our thoughts. Now the first thing the Bible does for us is to uncover all our hiding places and wrappings; we have to stand before God as we are, we have to see ourselves in that crude light.

Suzanne de Dietrich, in *Journey for a Soul*, George Appleton, William Collins Sons & Co. Ltd., 1976, p.106.

Implicit in the command to love one's neighbour as one's self is the duty to love one's self, safeguarded by an equal love of neighbour. Each soul is valued and loved by God, and its individuality or divine image respected. Some people overvalue themselves in pride and self-confidence, though both of these self-regarding characteristics may spring from a hidden doubt. Others undervalue themselves and shrink from openness or helpful initiative to other people. The secret of mature balance will be to accept ourselves as we are and not try to imitate others, and then to rely on God's grace to build us up to the best of which we are capable.

George Appleton, *Journey for a Soul*, William Collins Sons & Co. Ltd., 1976, p.105.

Every human being is unique. It follows that every human being has some unique gift to give to his family: to his parents and brothers and sisters in the ordinary narrow sense, first of all, and thence to his country and to the world. The small world of the human home is built up of the gifts of each member of it; the larger world without is built up in the same way of the various gifts, economic, political, cultural, religious, of its individual citizens. If we are Christians we dismiss once and for all the idea that our business in the world is to serve ourselves and nobody else, to become holy ourselves and pay no attention to anyone else... Live your life in the unity of the home first of all: train yourself to think in terms of what will make the home a better and a happier place; and then in your building up of the home think of the needs and well-being of your immediate neighbours, and thence of your country and of the whole world; and so you will necessarily live a life of love, and fulfil that much at least—and it is a great deal—of the law of God.

Gerald Vann, The Divine Pity, William Collins Sons & Co. Ltd., 1956, p.56.

Just as we say that we must look at ourselves both as members of the entire world body and in individuals, so, too, I must seek universal truth as well as my own personal truth. These are not contradictory or exclusive truths, they are in harmony. Yet the part of the great truth which is my very own truth is unique to me. My task then is to search for that truth which is mine—which is me, really—find it, and then seize it, make it so conscious a part of my existence that it informs everything that I do. Another way of saying this is simply to realize that I am unique, and then to develop this uniqueness in the service of the common good. I must caution myself that this has nothing to do with eccentricity, showing off, cultivating a difference for the sake of being different. Rather I must try to find out in what way I am different from all others who live, have ever lived, and who will live, and offer this difference to God in the important effort to try to complete the reality of humanity. As youngsters we tried so hard to conform to what others did and were; we wished to be accepted as part of the crowd. We wanted, or seemed to want, the values, the ideas, the outer appearances (hair, clothing) similar to others. Advertisers and governments would love us to keep such an immature attitude: We would be much more manipulatable in this way. Hopefully, we are past that. But the growth of our spirit requires that we do other than just go along with the crowd, just live an unthoughtful life, just muddle on in time on a material, sensual, animal level only. The great adventure of my life is to find out who I am. This means finding my uniqueness, my truth, glorifying in it and living it as heroically as I can. It may mean, actually, to live unheroically on a heroic level.

Harry James Cargas, Encountering Myself, SPCK, 1978, p.14.

SELFISHNESS

"Selfishness"—"deficient in consideration for others, alive chiefly
to personal profit or pleasure, actuated by self-interest, that pursuit
of pleasure of one kind or another is the ultimate aim of every
action."

T here is a vital point we often miss in reading the Genesis story of the Creation of Man/Woman. We pass it by unnoticed. Yet it is essential for us to grasp if we want to have a correct understanding of human nature.

It comes out in the sentence: "That which was fashioned and shaped in the image and likeness of God *was taken from the dust of the earth.*" Interpreted, this means that although we have an enormous potential of divine life in the depths of our being, we are at one and the same time earthy and creaturely, and rightly so. This earthy and creaturely side is a valuable source of power and energy. What is required is an inner integration of these two sides of our nature, leading to a full-blooded person, as worked out in the life of Jesus Christ. This is wholeness—salvation.

What has happened in modern life is something like this. We have forgotten what is means to be made in the image and likeness of God. We no longer centre ourselves on God, we centre ourselves on ourselves, in the main on our earthy and creaturely side, and end up being selfish. We become actuated by self-interest. The cost is, we dampen down the enormous potential of divine life in the depths of ourselves, and we greatly restrict our relationships with others.

And do you seek great things for yourself? Seek them not.

Jeremiah 45.5.

A covetous man's eye is not satisfied with his portion; and the iniquity of the wicked dries up his soul.

Ecclesiasticus 14.9 (A.V.).

They all look after their own interests.

Philippians 2.21.

If any one has the world's goods and sees his brother in need, yet closes his heart against him, how does God's love abide in him?

1 John 3.17.

One suffers most who is most selfish.

Taoist saying.

Perhaps one should not think so much of oneself, though it is an interesting subject.

Norman Douglas, *An Almanac*, Chatto & Windus in association with Martin Secker & Warburg Ltd., 1945, p.60.

Egoism: measuring others by our likes and dislikes—not by their needs but by our preferences.

A.R. Orage, *On Love*, The Janus Press, 1957, p.60.

Selfish prosperity makes a man a vortex rather than a fountain; instead of throwing out, he learns only to draw in.

Henry Ward Beecher, *Proverbs from Plymouth Pulpit*, Charles Burnet & Co., 1887, p.49.

He who hates not in himself his self-love, and that instinct which leads him to make himself God, is indeed blinded.

Blaise Pascal, *Pensées*, translated by W.F. Trotter, Random House, Inc., 1941, p.161.

We are rearing up a brood of crafty egoists, a generation whose earliest recollections are those of getting something for nothing from the State.

Norman Douglas, *An Almanac*, Chatto & Windus in association with Martin Secker & Warburg Ltd., 1945, p.40.

Selfish man, who does not want to be selfish—that aspiration for something better, is of God. Worldly man, conscious of spiritual things—that consciousness is of God.

Henry Ward Beecher, *Proverbs from Plymouth Pulpit*, Charles Burnet & Co., 1887, p.154.

Every man must decide whether he will walk in the light of creative altruism or the darkness of destructive selfishness. This is the judgment. Life's most persistent and urgent question is, What are you doing for others?

Martin Luther King, *The Words of Martin Luther King*, selected by Coretta Scott King, William Collins Sons & Co. Ltd., 1986, p.17.

I may say that the growth has all been toward the elimination of selfishness. I do not mean simply the grosser, more sensual forms, but those subtler and generally unrecognized kinds, such as express themselves in sorrow, grief, regret, envy, etc.

William James, *The Varieties of Religious Experience*, William Collins Sons & Co. Ltd., 1974, p.136.

> All selfish souls, what'er they feign,
> Have still a selfish lot;
> They boast of Liberty in vain,
> Of Love, and feel it not.
> He whose bosom glows with Thee,
> He, and he alone, is free.

William Cowper, *The Poetical Works of William Cowper*, Oxford University Press, 1950, *Gratitude And Love To God*, l.19, p.490.

In your excessive self-love you are like a molecule closed in upon itself and incapable of entering easily into any new combination. God looks to you to be more open and more pliant. If you are to enter into him you need to be freer and more eager. Have done, then, with your egoism and your fear of suffering.

Pierre Teilhard de Chardin, *Let Me Explain*, William Collins Sons & Co. Ltd., 1970, p.137.

It seems to me that nothing is so important from the point of view of Christianising society as to recognise that competition is not a thing limited to business. It is a thing that pervades the whole of our life. It is simply organised selfishness, and, as things stand, from the moment we become conscious, almost throughout our lives, the whole influence of our environment is competitive, and suggests that our business is to do the utmost for ourselves in the struggle against other people.

William Temple, *The Kingdom of God*, Macmillan Publishers Ltd., 1912, p.96.

> How vainly seek
> The selfish for that happiness denied
> To aught but virtue! Blind and hardened they,
> Who hope for peace amid the storms of care,
> Who covet power they know not how to use,
> And sigh for pleasure they refuse to give—
> Madly they frustrate still their own designs;
> And, where they hope that quiet to enjoy
> Which virtue pictures, bitterness of soul,
> Pining regrets, and vain repentances,
> Disease, disgust, and lassitude, pervade
> Their valueless and miserable lives.

Percy Bysshe Shelley, *The Complete Works of Percy Bysshe Shelley*, edited by Thomas Hutchinson, Oxford University Press, 1934, *Queen Mab*, V, l.237, p.783.

In the possession of material goods, there is no such thing as satiety. One seems never able to accumulate enough to be a safeguard against the unpredictable future, and so the requirements of full security remain in principle unlimited. Thus, men who otherwise appeared quite normal and respectable were goaded by their insistent fears about the future into claiming all they could for themselves and their own. And concurrently, the needs of the neighbour receded into the dim background. Men in such a situation seemed hardly free to do the generous thing, but only free enough to act in their own self-interest.

As Brecht puts it in the *Threepenny Opera*:

> For even saintly folk will act like sinners
> Unless they have their customary dinners.

Langdon Gilkey, *Shantung Compound*, Anthony Blond, 1967, p.111.

All sufferings,
All injustices, bitternesses, humiliations, griefs, hates, despairs,
All sufferings are an unappeased hunger,
A hunger for love.
So men have built slowly, selfishness by selfishness, a disfigured world that crushes them;
So the men on earth spend their time feeding their self-love,
While around them others with outstretched arms die of hunger.
They have squandered love...
Help me to love, Lord, not to waste my powers of love, to love myself less and less in order to love others more and more,
That around me, no one should suffer or die because I have stolen the love they needed to live.

Michel Quoist, *Prayers of Life*, translated by Anne Marie de Commaile and Agnes Mitchell Forsyth, Gill and Macmillan Ltd., 1963, p.81.

SERENITY

"Serenity"— "calm, placid, tranquil, unperturbed."

One of the wards I used to visit had a special atmosphere—a certain calmness and serenity. The source was not difficult to find. It stemmed from the quality of the surgeons. These two men were highly skilled and experienced. Their professional expertise inspired confidence. Equally important was their bedside manner. They were kindly, compassionate men, and patients instinctively knew they were in the presence of someone who cared. They had a certain empathy. They would come on to the ward before an operation, and explain to the patients exactly what they were going to do. This would be extended to the immediate family. The follow-up was similarly thorough, full of the personal touch—gentle and sympathetic. They were quality men in themselves. The Ward Sister was of a similar disposition—calm and serene. She was wonderful in her co-operation. "Don't spend long with Mr—. He's very ill at the moment. Do spend time with Mrs—. She's recovering from her operation but getting bored. She'll enjoy a chat with you. Try and have a word with Nurse—. She's down at the moment." Her attitude to the patients and nurses matched that of the surgeons. A pleasant atmosphere prevailed. She too was a quality person, and the net result throughout the ward—was serenity.

He made the storm be still, and the waves of the sea were hushed. Then they were glad because they had quiet, and he brought them to their desired haven.

Psalm 107.29-30.

I have calmed and quieted my soul, like a child quieted at its mother's breast; like a child that is quieted is my soul.
Psalm 131.2.

We call those happy who were steadfast.
James 5.11.

Be patient, therefore, brethren, until the coming of the Lord. Behold, the farmer waits for the precious fruits of the earth, being patient over it until it receives the early and late rains. You also be patient. Establish your hearts.
James 5.7-8.

No one can achieve Serenity until the glare of passion is past the meridian.
Cyril Connolly, The Unquiet Grave, Hamish Hamilton Ltd., 1945, p.13.

In Jesus there is the quiet, strong serenity of one who seeks to conquer by love, and not by strife of words.
William Barclay, The Gospel of Matthew, The Saint Andrew Press, 1975, Volume 2, p.37.

We have yet to learn that strength is shown at least as well as by serenity and poise as in strenuous action.
Odell Shepard, The Joys of Forgetting, George Allen & Unwin Publishers Ltd., 1928, p.22.

Nothing but stillness can remain when hearts are full
Of their own sweetness, bodies of their loveliness.
W.B. Yeats, Collected Poems of W.B. Yeats, Macmillan Publishers Ltd., 1973, Meditations in Time of Civil War, VII, p.232.

An old age, serene and bright
And lovely as a Lapland night.
William Wordsworth, in The Secret of Radiant Life, W.E. Sangster, Hodder & Stoughton Ltd., 1957, p.14.

There is certainly something in angling... that tends to produce a gentleness of spirit, and a pure serenity of mind.
Washington Irving, The Sketch-Book, George Newnes Ltd., 1902, Volume II, p.226.

If you want inner peace find it in solitude, not speed, and if you would find yourself, look to the land from which you came and to which you go.
Stewart L. Udall, The Quiet Crisis, Holt, Rinehart & Winston, 1963, p.190.

True contemplative grace gently tranquillizes the personality, giving a wonderful serenity and a calm self-dominion.
William Johnston, The Mysticism of The Cloud of Unknowing, Anthony Clarke Books, 1978, p.265.

Only a soul full of despair can ever attain serenity and, to be in despair, you must have loved a good deal and still love the world.
Henry Miller, The Books in My Life, Village Press, 1974, p.59.

I am serene because I know thou lovest me.
    Because thou lovest me, naught can move me from my peace. Because thou lovest me, I am as one to whom all good has come.
Alistair Maclean, in God in our midst, Triangle/SPCK, 1989, p.27.

The serenity relevant for our time is a serenity that does not bypass the turmoil and torment of the atomic age but sends its roots down through the agonies to the life and power of God.

C.S. Duthie, *God in His World*, Independent Press Ltd., 1955, p.15.

God, give us grace to accept with serenity the things that cannot be changed, courage to change the things which should be changed, and the wisdom to distinguish the one from the other.

Reinhold Niebuhr, *The Serenity Prayer*, 1943, written for a service in the Congregational church of Heath, Massachusetts.

We can make our lives so like still water that beings gather about us that they might see, it may be, their own images, and so live for a moment with a clearer, perhaps even with a fiercer life, because of our quiet.

W.B. Yeats, in *The Joys of Forgetting*, Odell Shepard, George Allen & Unwin Publishers Ltd., 1928, p.143.

Whatever helps a person to use his resources productively and reduces his need to live up to a false image of strength and perfection is likely to add to his serenity and freedom from fear.

Arthur T. Jersild, in *Educational Psychology*, edited by Charles E. Skinner, Staples Press Ltd., 1952, p.93.

> Would you taste the tranquil scene?
> Be sure your bosom be serene;
> Devoid of hate, devoid of strife
> Devoid of all that poisons life;
> And much it 'vails you, in their place,
> To graft the love of human race.
>
> William Shenstone, *Inscription on a tablet.*

His chiefest study was to be free from all the things that are in the world, lest the serenity of his mind might even for a moment be troubled by the taint of any dust. He made himself insensible to the din of all outward things; and, gathering up with all his might from every side the outward senses, and keeping the natural impulses in check, occupied himself with God alone...

For his safest haven was prayer: not prayer for one moment, not vacant or presumptuous prayer, but long-continued, full of devotion, calm and humble.

Thomas of Celano, *The Life of St Francis*, translated by A.G. Ferrers Howell, Methuen & Co. Ltd., 1908, p.69.

The whole atmosphere has a luminous serenity, a limpid clearness. The islands are like swans swimming in a golden stream. Peace, splendour, boundless space!... And I meanwhile look quietly on while the soft hours glide away. I long to catch the wild bird, happiness, and tame it. Above all, I long to share it with others. These delicious mornings impress me indescribably. They intoxicate me, they carry me away. I feel beguiled out of myself, dissolved in sunbeams, breezes, perfumes, and sudden impulses of joy.

Henri Frédéric Amiel, *Amiel's Journal*, translated by Mrs. Humphry Ward, Macmillan Publishers Ltd., 1918, p.220.

Sometimes we meet a person who has a quiet serenity of spirit of which we become quickly conscious; who seems to be unhurried and unworried; uncomplaining about the past, content with the present, unafraid of the future; one who seems to live in another tempo of life, with a stillness that is not a technique but comes from a centre of stillness within himself; one who is relaxed and restful, unself-assertive; whose "isness" says more than his words, and will validate his words when he speaks of what he has discovered.

George Appleton, *Journey for a Soul*, William Collins Sons & Co. Ltd., 1976, p.99.

It was one of those moments of total serenity which the spiritual part of me, always aspiring to the heights of philosophical detachment, so often compelled me to seek in the days of my meditative youth; one of those moments when all the materialistic and cynical views of life collapse like pathetic fabrications before the sovereign evidence of life's beauty, meaning and wisdom, and when every man experiences the triumphant feeling of an artist of genius who has just entirely expressed himself.

Romain Gary, *Promise at Dawn*, Michael Joseph Ltd., 1962, p.26.

The dominant characteristic of our Lord's mind was harmony: harmony in itself, with God, and with his environment. It was the harmony of a mind unbrokenly God-centred and utterly free from self-preoccupation.

He was never muddled, never worried, never hurried, never on the edge of a breakdown, because his mind was anchored in God.

He was at ease with everyone he met, and gave each his full attention. He was never perturbed by interruptions.

He was in command of every situation—the hungry crowd, the frightened disciples, in the storm, the police and soldiers who came to arrest him, in his interrogation before the Roman governor.

Maisie Spens, in *Journey for a Soul*, George Appleton, William Collins Sons & Co. Ltd., 1976, p.158.

Go placidly amid the noise and haste and remember what peace there may be in silence. As far as possible without surrender be on good terms with all persons. Speak your truth quietly and clearly; and listen to others, even the dull and ignorant; they too have their story.

Avoid loud and aggressive persons, they are vexations to the spirit. If you compare yourself with others, you may become vain and bitter; for always there will be greater and lesser persons than yourself. Enjoy your achievements as well as your plans.

Keep interested in your own career, however humble; it is a real possession in the changing fortunes of time. Exercise caution in your business affairs; for the world is full of trickery. But let this not blind you to what virtue there is; many persons strive for high ideals; and everywhere life is full of heroism.

Be yourself. Especially, do not feign affection. Neither be cynical about love; for in the face of all aridity and disenchantment it is perennial as the grass.

Take kindly the counsel of the years, gracefully surrendering the things of youth. Nurture strength of spirit to shield you in sudden misfortune. But do not distress yourself with imaginings. Many fears are born of fatigue and loneliness. Beyond a wholesome discipline, be gentle with yourself.

You are a child of the universe, no less than the trees and the stars; you have a right to be here. And whether or not it is clear to you, no doubt the universe is unfolding as it should.

Therefore be at peace with God, whatever you conceive Him to be, and whatever your labours and aspirations, in the noisy confusion of life keep peace with your soul.

With all its shams, drudgery and broken dreams, it is still a beautiful world. Be careful. Strive to be happy.

Desiderata, Max Erhmann.

SEX

"Sex"—"act of intercourse, for procreation or pleasure."

A teacher came to see me. She was concerned about her girls and pre marital sex. Did I have any advice to offer?

I remembered an analogy given somewhere by Peter Ustinov. He likened sex and love to the gear box and the driving of a car. On the whole, he reckoned, it didn't pay to crash your gears and go straight through to top gear. "Ah," said the teacher thoughtfully, "I'll have to think through the implications of that one. It's just possible I might be able to get something over to them on those lines. Direct prohibitions seem to be counter-productive."

After she had gone I also thought about the implications of the analogy. Sex, we believe, is an extremely valuable gift, a sacred act, and best enjoyed in the context and security of a whole and lasting relationship. As in the definition the act of intercourse is twofold. Firstly for the procreation of children. This means bringing into existence children "made in the image and likeness of God". Seen from this angle, we can well understand why sex is regarded as a sacred act.

Secondly there is pleasure. What is involved here is an expression and sharing of love which involves body, mind and spirit—a union of two personalities, a joyful celebration. This is something not to be rushed. We are complex beings and know that a lasting friendship usually takes a long time to grow and develop. Not crashing one's gears means giving the relationship time to develop through several stages, before engaging in the ultimate act of sharing love and affection in depth. Such is the vision of love surrounding sex.

Be fruitful and multiply.
Genesis 1.28.

For I am sick with love. O that his left hand were under my head, and that his right hand embraced me!
Song of Solomon 2.5-6.

Do you not know that your body is a temple of the Holy Spirit within you, which you have from God?
1 Corinthians 6.19.

For this is the will of God, your sanctification; that you abstain from unchastity.
1 Thessalonians 4.3.

The sexual embrace, worthily understood, can only be compared with music and with prayer.
Havelock Ellis, *On Life and Sex*, William Heinemann Ltd., 1948, p.53.

The call to sexual morality is grounded in the understanding that the human body is "a shrine of the indwelling Holy Spirit".
Elizabeth R. Moberly, in *A Dictionary of Pastoral Care*, edited by Alastair V. Campbell, SPCK, 1987, p.29.

Like the bee its sting, the promiscuous leave behind them in each encounter something of themselves by which they are made to suffer.
Cyril Connolly, *The Unquiet Grave*, Hamish Hamilton Ltd., 1945, p.43.

The sex act is never the mere activity of a few organs but includes the whole personality... The Christian view of man requires one to find a significance in coitus, and its meaning is that it both builds up and consolidates the union between a man and his wife that they may be "one flesh".

J.G. Davies, *Every Day God*, SCM Press Ltd., 1973, p.171.

The modern treatment of sex, and of the human body. The most "real" has come to mean the sordid, the carnal, the plebeian; this is not accidental, since the natural world owes any qualities of the sacramental, the noble, or the sublime which it may possess precisely to its relation to higher causes.

Kathleen Raine, *Defending Ancient Springs*, Oxford University Press, 1967, p.112.

The physical aspect of love does not in itself carry any significance. It can be a communion or a separation: a wonderful communion, if it is mutual; a tragic separation, if it is just a way of taking from each other to fulfil personal desires. In the first case, it is a meeting of two people. In the second, it is a collision of two objects.

Michel Quoist, *With Open Heart*, translated by Colette Copeland, Gill and Macmillan Ltd., 1983, p.188.

If a man is alienated from his body, physical acts appear to him to be distasteful and he is incapable of any adequate understanding of sex. Obviously, if a man regards himself as a body only, his physical acts cannot be other than on the same level as those of the animals. Neither of the two is integrated. It is only when sex is recognised as both physical (secular) and spiritual (sacred) that it can be invested with a human meaning.

J.G. Davies, *Every Day God*, SCM Press Ltd., 1973, p.160.

The sexual act is not a mere pleasure of the body, a purely carnal act, but is a means by which love is expressed and life perpetuated. It becomes evil, if it harms others or if it interferes with a person's spiritual development, but neither of these conditions is inherent in the act itself. The act by which we live, by which love is expressed and the race continued is not an act of shame or sin. But when the masters of spiritual life insist on celibacy, they demand that we should preserve singleness of mind from destruction by bodily desire.

Sir Sarvapalli Radhakrishnan, *Mahatma Gandhi*, George Allen & Unwin Publishers Ltd., 1949, p.18.

There are the *fornicators*, those guilty of lax morality. Christianity alone can guarantee purity. The root cause of sexual immorality is a wrong view of man. In the end it views men as beasts.

It declares that the passions and instincts which they share with the beasts must be shamelessly gratified and regards the other person merely as an instrument through which that gratification may be obtained. Now Christianity regards man as a child of God, and, just because of that, as a creature who lives in the world but who always looks beyond it, a person who will not dictate his life by purely physical needs and desires, one who has a body but also a spirit. If men regarded themselves and others as sons and daughters of God, moral laxity would automatically be banished from life.

William Barclay, *The Letters to the Corinthians*, The Saint Andrew Press, 1988, p.47.

To drive home the close parallel between the sexual act and the mystical union with God may seem blasphemous today. Yet the blasphemy is not in the comparison, but in the degrading of the one act of which man is capable that makes him like God both in the intensity of his union with his partner and in the fact that by this union he is a co-creator with God. All the higher religions recognize the sexual act as something holy: hence their condemnation of adultery and fornication under all circumstances. These acts are not forbidden because they are demonstrably injurious on rational grounds; they are forbidden because they are a desecration of a holy thing, they are a misuse of what is most godlike in man.

R.C. Zaehner, *Mysticism Sacred and Profane*, Oxford University Press, 1967, p.152.

The virtue of chastity is not the complete renunciation of all sex, but simply the right use of sex. This means, according to most of the great religious traditions of the world, the restriction of all sex to married life, and, within the married state, to certain ordinate norms.

Nowhere is self-denial more important than in the area of sex, because this is the most difficult of all natural appetites to control and one whose undisciplined gratification completely blinds the human spirit to all interior light.

Sex is by no means to be regarded as evil. It is a natural good, willed by God, and entering into the mystery of God's love and God's mercy towards men. But though sex may not be evil in itself, inordinate attachment to sexual pleasure, especially outside of marriage, is one of man's most frequent and pitiable weaknesses. Indeed, it is so common that most people today simply believe that sex cannot be fully controlled—that it is not really possible for a normal human being to abstain from it completely. Hence they assume that one should simply resign himself to the inevitable and cease worrying about it.

Thomas Merton, *New Seeds of Contemplation*, Burns & Oates Ltd., 1962, p.67.

The *sexual* relation between man and woman consummates in the act of coition. Now what is the act of coition? We know its functional purpose of procreation. But, after all our experience and all our poetry and novels we know that the procreative purpose of sex is, to the individual man or woman, just a side-show. To the individual, the act of coition is a great psychic experience, a vital experience of tremendous importance. On this vital individual experience the life and very being of the individual largely depends.

But what is the experience? Untellable. Only, we know something. We know that in the act of coition the *blood* of the individual man, acutely surcharged with intense vital electricity—we we know no word, so say "electricity", by analogy—rises to a culmination, in a tremendous magnetic urge towards the magnetic blood of the female. The whole of the living blood in the two individuals forms a field of intense, polarized magnetic attraction. So, the two poles must be brought into contact. In the act of coition, the two seas of blood in the two individuals, rocking and surging towards contact, as near as possible, clash into a oneness. A great flash of interchange occurs, like an electric spark when two currents meet or like lightning out of the densely surcharged clouds. There is a lightning flash which passes through the blood of both individuals, there is a thunder of sensation which rolls in diminishing crashes down the nerves of each—and then the tension passes.

The two individuals are separate again. But are they as they were before? Is the air the same after a thunderstorm as before? No. The air is as it were new, fresh, tingling with newness.

D.H. Lawrence, *Fantasia of the Unconscious*, Thomas Seltzer, 1922, p.147.

Since, moreover, marriage is designed by Providence as a life—a state of being and becoming, and not merely as an act or series of acts—the worst possible way of embarking upon that life is by the premature exercise of what is meant to be its final consummation. The appropriate act of marriage is appropriate only *in* marriage: only in marriage is it the expression of the habit of love. For the climax to come in advance of what it is intended to perfect and culminate is an inversion which cannot but promote similar inversions all along the line. The initial exercise of the act is, putting aside for a moment its significance in the spiritual order, of such profound importance in the psychological make-up of both parties that, should it take place outside the state of matrimony (or, inside matrimony, under conditions running counter to its true nature), there is every likelihood of the sex-conscience being permanently warped. To start off wrong on such a vital issue is to prejudice the chances of thinking right—let alone acting right—in the future. The relationship leaves the sacramental level before it has a chance of knowing what advantages Christian marriage claims to provide. By sin the right to that happiness which the sacrament offers is waived: momentary pleasure is chosen in the place of settled peace. Men & women may not afterwards claim what they have done their selfish best earlier on to stifle. By deliberately following their lusts they have renounced what nature and grace intended for them, and it is no good their complaining about it when the ardour has cooled and when they are looking round for a happiness which is more lasting. For the woman the mental and physical upheaval occasioned by the first use of the act may be more fundamental than for the man, but for each of them it is both significant and so sacred that to perform it lightly, indifferently, cynically or brutally is to do something which is more than merely wasteful or meaningless: it is to do something which is monstrous. It is as monstrous for him as for her. It is a travesty. It is happiness committing suicide.

Hubert van Zeller, *We Work While the Light Lasts*, Sheed & Ward Ltd., 1950, p.35.

Sex becomes a problem when it is wrenched out of its context. And its true context is not duty, or the rearing of children, or family life, important as these are; the true context of sex is joy.

The Creator has shared with His children the gift of creation; man seeks to exercise that gift out of frustration, or to compensate for a feeling of inferiority, or as a means to some end, whereas of the Creator it was said that he saw everything that He had made and pronounced it good, and that at creation "the morning stars sang together and all the sons of God shouted for joy".

What do we find at the basis of unhappy or strained sexual relationships? That one or other of the partners is having recourse to physical intimacy out of a feeling of frustration, or in order to forget, or to flee from a feeling of inadequacy or disappointment. Instead of being a celebration, the act becomes a means of escape or of forgetfulness; it proceeds not from health but from disease, not out of strength but out of weakness, not from joy and health but from exasperation or self-pity. And the result is that one of the partners feels that he or she is being used as a thing, a drug, a medicine or as a hot-water bottle, is being prostituted as a person.

As a young and happily married man said to me last night, "I love my wife, and at moments when we have achieved real fellowship in mind and spirit, when we have a good day together, I turn to her in complete happiness to fulfil and consummate that deep, rich joy we have had in each other. But I am unhappy and somewhat repelled when Elizabeth, having had a frustrated day, feeling disappointed with herself, or being self-distrustful about her career, turns to the physical act in order to forget it all, in order to compensate for the happiness she feels she has missed on another level."

This is not an isolated case. And what is really happening is that people are using the flesh in order to solve the problems of the spirit. They obtain a momentary relief from the tension of self. But the relief is only a semblance of the true atonement. What is experienced is not spiritual identity with the loved one, but a momentary escape from separateness in the darkness of the unconscious. And so, far from being permanently enriched and cleansed by this experience, the self returns to the daylight world fundamentally unchanged, if not indeed corrupted.

Somebody once said that two people have no chance of being successfully married to each other if they are not already married to themselves. Of course we are incomplete as we are, and marriage wonderfully fulfils and integrates our lives. But it is the total experience of being married that does this, not one isolated act. People expect from physical union what can only come from growth and discipline at other levels. And so sex becomes an attempt to redeem the self instead of a sharing of the redeemed self.

W.B.J. Martin, *Five Minutes to Twelve*, William Collins Sons & Co. Ltd., 1957, p.104.

SILENCE

"Silence"—"abstinence from speech or noise, absence of sound, stillness."

At Mons Officer Cadet School, in Aldershot, we each had to do a night of guard duty. My turn duly came up, and I was instructed to guard the Adjutant's horse.

It was summer time, and the weather was settled. The sky was clear, so having said "how-do" to the horse, I went out and gazed at the stars. I quickly found Orion's belt and the Plough, and before long spotted a falling star. It was a beautiful night, and the stars were shining brightly.

I suddenly became aware of silence. Everyone had long since gone to bed. This was the first time I had actually been on my own for three months. I began to think. The Course at Mons was excellent but intense. We were kept on the go the whole time. Still, it was enjoyable, and all being well, only another month to go. I wondered where I'd be in two months' time—the Far East, Africa, or Germany? I hoped it would be the Far East. That could be exciting. I wondered what it would be like—commissioned? What was I going to do in life? Did I really want to become a lawyer? What about marriage and a family? I just didn't know. So many unanswered questions. I moved on to reflect about the deeper things in life, about God, about the nature of evil, and about our purpose in life, if any. I was so deeply engaged in this inward speculation I failed to notice the arrival of the dawn. However I made it to the Guardhouse just in time.

What I had learnt that night was something of the value of silence, and the importance of ultimate questions.

For God alone my soul waits in silence,
for my hope is from him.
Psalm 62.5.

But the Lord is in his holy temple;
let all the earth keep silence before him.

Habakkuk 2.20.

Let it be the hidden person of the heart with the imperishable jewel of a gentle and quiet spirit, which in God's sight is very precious.

I Peter 3.4.

There was silence in heaven...

Revelation 8.1.

God's silence ripens man's thoughts into speech.

Rabindranath Tagore, *Collected Poems & Plays of Rabindranath Tagore*, Macmillan Publishers Ltd., 1936, *Stray Birds*, CCCIV, p.326.

There is a complete protection available to you—silence.

A.R. Orage, *On Love*, The Janus Press, 1983, p.62.

Man goes into the noisy crowd to drown his own clamour of silence.

Rabindranath Tagore, *Collected Poems & Plays of Rabindranath Tagore*, Macmillan Publishers Ltd., 1936, *Stray Birds*, CX, p.300.

Silence isolates us from the crowds that love to pool their misery; an unhappy civilization is always gregarious.

Fulton J. Sheen, *Lift Up Your Heart*, Burns & Oates Ltd., 1962, p.30.

The best and most wonderful thing that can happen to you in this life, is that you should be silent and let God work and speak.

Dag Hammarskjöld, *Markings*, translated by W.H. Auden & Leif Sjoberg, with a foreword by W.H. Auden, Faber & Faber Ltd., 1964, p.134.

We are silent at the beginning of the day because God should have the first word, and we are silent before going to sleep because the last word also belongs to God.

Dietrich Bonhoeffer, *Life Together*, SCM Press Ltd., 1955, p.69.

I listened to the silence of the night and I felt as if I had all of a sudden penetrated the very heart of the universe. An immense happiness, such as I had never known, swept over me with a flow of fulfilment.

Carlo Levi, *Christ Stopped at Eboli*, translated by Frances Frenaye, Cassell, 1948, p.223.

In true silence strength is renewed, and the mind is weaned from all things, but as they may be enjoyed in the Divine will; and a lowliness in outward living, opposite to worldly honour, becomes truly acceptable to us.

John Woolman, *The Journal of John Woolman*, Edward Marsh, 1857, p.307.

To preserve the silence within—amid all the noise. To remain open and quiet, a moist humus in the fertile darkness where the rain falls and the grain ripens—no matter how many tramp across the parade-ground in whirling dust under an arid sky.

Dag Hammarskjöld, *Markings*, translated by W.H. Auden & Lief Sjoberg, with a foreword by W.H. Auden, Faber & Faber Ltd., 1964, p.85.

Silence is not much preached today, so it is for prayer to preach it. "Silence," says

Heraclitus, "is a listening to the truth of things." If we do not listen we do not come to truth. If we do not pray we do not even get as far as listening. The four things go together: silence, listening, prayer, truth.

Hubert van Zeller, *Leave Your Life Alone*, Sheed & Ward Ltd., 1973, p.70.

It is not easy in the busy-ness of our lives to still ourselves. Silence makes us uneasy; it is too immeasurably big to be comfortable. It beats on us; we want to shift and talk, to use our minds on problems they can tackle. But if we run from silence to noise we are running from the deeper to the shallower; from the silence of God to the noise of the world.

Michael Hollings, *I Will Be There*, Mowbray, 1975, p.13.

Then we discover what the spiritual life really is... It is the silence of our whole being in compunction and adoration before God, in the habitual realization that he is everything and we are nothing, that he is the centre to which all things tend, and to whom all our actions must be directed. That our life and strength proceed from him, that both in life and in death we depend entirely on him.

Thomas Merton, *Thoughts in Solitude*, Burns & Oates Ltd., 1958, p.45.

The word "desert"—for the man who lets himself be taken up by the Spirit who animates God's word—expresses the search for God in silence, it is a "suspension bridge" thrown by the soul in love with God over the dark abyss of its own spirit, over the strange deep crevasses of temptation, over the unfathomable precipices of its own fears which form an obstacle to the progress towards God.

Carlo Carretto, *The Desert in the City*, translated by Barbara Wall, William Collins Sons & Co. Ltd., 1983, p.18.

> How silently, how silently,
> The wondrous gift is given!
> So God imparts to human hearts
> The blessings of his heaven.
> No ear may hear his coming;
> But in this world of sin,
> Where meek souls will receive him, still
> The dear Christ enters in.

Phillips Brooks, *Carol: O Little Town of Bethlehem*, verse 3.

But in order to listen well, silence is needful; it is needful that we should often, like Jesus at the Transfiguration, go apart into a solitary place. Certainly Jesus is to be found everywhere, even in the turmoil of great cities, but He is only heard well in a peaceful soul surrounded by an atmosphere of silence. He is only well understood in a soul that prays. It is then above all that He reveals Himself to the soul, drawing her to Him and transfiguring her in Him.

D. Columba Marmion, *Christ in His Mysteries*, Sands & Company, 1924, p.244.

We must learn to use silence—not as emptiness, but as communication. We are embarrassed by it, we fidget and twist and squirm in our too-tight mental underwear, because we have never learned its properties and possibilities. We have always lived with a fear of gaps. We carry an odd-bucket of assorted hems and haws, ah-wells and you-sees, to stuff up any draughty chinks to find in conversations or speeches. But we need to be reminded that silences are the cracks in the dome of eternity, whence wisdom can seep through. We need, in the church, to come to the place where we can be silent...

J. Killinger, *Leave it to the Spirit*, SCM Press Ltd., 1971, p.134.

Be silent about great things; let them grow inside you. Never discuss them: discussion is so limiting and distracting. It makes things grow smaller. You think you swallow things when they ought to swallow you. Before all greatness, be silent—in art, in music, in religion: silence...

Christianity is a thing of the heart, and it's that that matters. No other knowledge counts but that that feeds and strengthens the mind and soul.

Christianity is an immense warning; a tremendous heroism. Christ teaches a great austerity. He teaches renunciation: the life of the Cross.

Baron Friedrich von Hügel, *Letters to a Niece*, J.M. Dent & Sons Ltd., 1929, p.ix.

God is the friend of silence...

We need to find God and he cannot be found in noise and restlessness. See how nature, the trees, the flowers, the grass grow in perfect silence—see the stars, the moon and the sun, how they move in silence...

Silence gives us a new outlook on everything. We need silence to be able to touch souls. The essential thing is not what we say but what God says to us and through us. Jesus is always waiting for us in silence. In that silence he will listen to us, there he will speak to our soul, and there we will hear his voice. Interior silence is very difficult but we must make the effort. In silence we will find new energy and true unity. The energy of God will be ours to do all things well. The unity of our thought with his thoughts, the unity of our prayers with his prayers, the unity of our actions with his actions, of our life with his life. All our words will be useless, unless they come from within—works which do not give the light of Christ increase the darkness.

Mother Teresa of Calcutta, in *In the Silence of the Heart*, compiled by Kathyrn Spink, SPCK, 1983, p.19.

Of recent years especially many travellers and explorers have discovered for themselves the values of silence and solitude. Forced to be much alone in wild regions, they have lost their fear of the desert, and have become "learners in its severe school"...

But many people feel the opposite. They dislike, fear, and hate silence. They have no desire to listen for "mysterious" voices from some strange region. Many of them say point-blank: "Silence is most unhealthy!" This fear of silence is a landmark in that country of the mind where God is not named. Even within the Christian Church silence is often disliked, and even feared. People say that "it makes them nervous"...

Yet, if we are to live fully and richly, a certain amount of silence is necessary for us all. Speaking of the value of Retreats and Quiet Days, Canon Peter Green says: "Silence has a wonderfully healing power. There is no surer proof of poverty of soul than a dislike of silence and an inability to be quiet, nor any better cure for such poverty than a few days of self-imposed abstinence from talking." Silence is indeed the essence of a good Retreat. The relief and refreshment of a few days, spent in worship and prayer in fellowship with others, with time for thought, has to be experienced to be believed. It is with an effort that we come out of Retreat, so precious is the experience of this quietness and concentration on the things of God.

Silence is precious: but we have to pay the price it demands. Silence does not reveal its treasures until we are willing to wait in darkness and emptiness. For a time it may seem very strange and difficult. But when we have passed through the preliminary stages of a new discipline we find that there is nothing negative about such silence; nor is it irksome. It is indeed a "positive creative condition, requisite for the due education of some of the deepest faculties we possess": those needed for clear thinking, power of concentration, and spiritual apprehension.

Olive Wyon, *On the Way*, SCM Press Ltd., 1958, p.102.

SORROW

"Sorrow"—"grief, sadness, caused by loss of good or occurrence of evil."

I n the summer vacation we usually take two reading parties, each with a dozen undergraduates, to the French Alps. For many years the College has had an interest in a chalet on the slopes of Mont Blanc. In our summer visits we get down to some academic reading, and walk in the mountains, close to glaciers.

Three years ago we had a serious accident. Two of our party had gone out on a long steep hill walk. They had found it relatively easy and decided to return by a different route. In the course of this, one of them fell, and suffered severe head injuries. He was taken to hospital by helicopter, and transferred to a Geneva clinic. Here he was put on a life support machine in intensive care.

We were deeply shocked. At first, we were hoping against hope he would regain consciousness and recover. As the days went by our hopes faded. There was little or no response to the life support machine—and on the eighth day, he died.

We were devasted. We drifted back to College in a shocked state. We felt awful, and just sat together, comforting each other, working through our grief and sorrow, trying to come to terms with what had happened. With heavy hearts we went to the funeral, and later to a Memorial Service, and eventually back to work again.

Occasions of sorrow hit all of us from time to time. There are no easy answers. We each have to work through our sorrow. The quotations are designed to elicit a positive and creative response.

I will turn their mourning into joy, I will comfort them, and give them gladness for sorrow.

Jeremiah 31.13.

Is it nothing to you, all you who pass by? Look and see if there is any sorrow like to my sorrow.

Lamentations 1.12.

Truly, truly, I say to you, you will weep and lament, but the world will rejoice; you will be sorrowful, but your sorrow will turn into joy. When a woman is in travail she has sorrow, because her hour is come; but when she is delivered of the child, she no longer remembers the anguish, for joy that a child is born into the world. So you have sorrow now, but I will see you again and your hearts will rejoice, and no one will take your joy from you.

John 16.20-22.

Blessed be the God and Father of our Lord Jesus Christ, the Father of mercies and God of all comfort, who comforts us in all our affliction, so that we may be able to comfort those who are in any affliction, with the comfort with which we ourselves are comforted by God.

2 Corinthians 1.3-4.

Two in distress makes sorrow less.

Proverb.

'Tis held that sorrow makes us wise.

Alfred, Lord Tennyson, *The Complete Works of Alfred Lord Tennyson*, Macmillan Publishers Ltd., 1898, *In Memoriam A.H.H.*, cxiii, p.279.

One must not torment oneself with fruitless sorrow.

A.C. Benson, *Extracts from the Letters of Dr. A.C. Benson to M.E.A.*, Jarrold Publishing, 1927, p.48.

A radiant heart lets forth its hope upon its sorrow, and all the blackness flies.

Henry Ward Beecher, *Proverbs from Plymouth Pulpit*, Charles Burnet & Co., 1887, p.211.

For gnarling sorrow hath less power to bite
The man that mocks at it and sets it light.

William Shakespeare, *King Richard II*, Act I. sc.iii. l.292.

The great thing with unhappy times is to take them bit by bit, hour by hour, like an illness. It is seldom the *present*, the exact present, that is unbearable.

C.S. Lewis, *Letters to an American Lady*, edited by Clyde S. Kilby, Hodder & Stoughton Ltd., 1969, p.55.

Let us rather be thankful that our sorrow lives in us as an indestructible force, only changing its form as forces do, and passing from pain to sympathy.

George Eliot, *Adam Bede*, Virtue & Co., 1908, Volume II, p.302.

Sorrow brings us closer to God than joys, usually; but sorrows to be of use must be borne, as Christ's were, victoriously, carrying with them sacred prophecies to the heart of Hope.

Henry Ward Beecher, *Proverbs from Plymouth Pulpit*, Charles Burnet & Co., 1887, p.207.

Now, one of the greatest dangers which can befall any man ... is that he should lapse into a state of self-pity; that he should look so long, and so intently at his troubles that he becomes a martyr to this most debilitating of mental disorders, and whine his way through life constantly seeking an audience which will listen to the long tale of his woe. It would be hard to exaggerate the dangers of self-pity.

W.E. Sangster, *He is Able*, Hodder & Stoughton Ltd., 1936, p.79.

It is sorrow which makes our experience; it is sorrow which teaches us to feel rightly for ourselves and others. We must feel deeply before we can think rightly. It is not in the tempest and storm of passions we reflect, but afterwards, when the waters have gone over our soul; and, like the precious gems and the rich merchandise which the wild wave casts on shore out of the wreck it has made, such are the thoughts left by retiring passions.

Anon.

Sorrow can do two things for us. It can show us, as nothing else can, the essential kindness of our fellow-men; and it can show us as nothing else can the comfort and the compassion of God. Many and many a man in the hour of his sorrow has discovered his fellow-men and his God as he never did before. When things go well it is possible to live for years on the surface of things; but when sorrow comes a man is driven to the deep things of life, and, if he accepts it aright, a new strength and beauty enter into his soul.

William Barclay, *The Gospel of Matthew*, The Saint Andrew Press, 1987, Volume 1, p.93.

The best remedy for those who are afraid, lonely or unhappy is to go outside, somewhere where they can be quiet alone with the heavens, nature and God. Because only then does one feel that all is as it should be and that God wishes to see people happy, amidst the simple beauty of nature. As long as this exists, and it certainly always will, I know that then there will always be comfort for every sorrow, whatever the circumstances may be. And I firmly believe that nature brings solace in all troubles.

Anne Frank, *The Diary of Anne Frank*, Pan Books Ltd., 1954, p.136.

If it were possible for us to see further than our knowledge extends and out a little over the outworks of our surmising, perhaps we should then bear our sorrows with greater confidence than our joys. For they are the moments when something new, something unknown, has entered into us; our feelings grow dumb with shy confusion, everything in us retires, a stillness supervenes, and the new thing that one knows stands silent there in the midst.

Rainer Maria Rilke, *Letters to a Young Poet*, translated by Reginald Snell, Sidgwick and Jackson Ltd., 1945, p.35.

Give your sorrow all the space and shelter in yourself that is its due, for if everyone bears his grief honestly and courageously, the sorrow that now fills the world will abate. But if you do not clear a decent shelter for your sorrow, and instead reserve most of the space inside you for hatred and thoughts of revenge—for which new sorrows will be born for others—then sorrow will never cease in this world and will multiply. And if you have given sorrow the space its gentle origins demand, then you may truly say: life is beautiful and so rich. So beautiful and so rich that it makes you want to believe in God.

Etty Hillesum, *Etty, A Diary, 1941-43*, translated by Arnold J. Pomerans, Jonathan Cape Ltd., 1983, p.81.

I believe that the wisest plan is sometimes not to try to bear sorrow—as long as one is not crippled for one's everyday duties—but to give way to it utterly and freely. Perhaps sorrow is sent that we *may* give way to it, and in drinking the cup to the dregs, find some medicine in itself, which we should not find if we began doctoring ourselves, or letting others doctor us. If we say simply, "I am wretched—I ought to be wretched;" then we shall perhaps hear a voice, "Who made thee wretched but God? Then what can He mean by thy good?" And if the heart answers impatiently, "My good? I don't wan't it, I want my love;" perhaps the voice may answer, "Then thou shalt have both in time."

Charles Kingsley, *Daily Thoughts*, Macmillan Publishers Ltd\., 1884, p.145.

> When hearts are full of yearning tenderness
> For the loved absent, whom we cannot reach,
> By deed or token, gesture or kind speech,
> The spirit's true affection to express;
> When hearts are full of innermost distress,
> And we are doomed to stand inactive by,
> Watching the soul's or body's agony,
> Which human effort helps not to make less—
> Then like a cup capacious to receive
> The overflowings of the heart, is prayer;
> The longing of the soul is satisfied,
> The keenest darts of anguish blunted are;
> And though we cannot cease to yearn or grieve,

We yet have learned in patience to abide.

Richard Chevenix Trench, *Poems*, Macmillan Publishers Ltd., 1885, Volume 1, *Sonnet*, p.198.

Then a woman said, Speak to us of Joy and Sorrow.
And he answered:
Your joy is your sorrow unmasked.
And the selfsame well from which your laughter rises was oftentimes filled with your tears.
And how else can it be?
The deeper that sorrow carves into your being, the more joy you can contain.
Is not the cup that holds your wine the very cup that was burned in the potter's oven?
And is not the lute that soothes your spirit the very wood that was hollowed with knives?
When you are joyous, look deep into your heart and you shall find it is only that which has given you sorrow that is giving you joy.
When you are sorrowful, look again in your heart, and you shall see that in truth you are weeping for that which has been your delight.
Some of you say, "Joy is greater than sorrow," and others say, "Nay, sorrow is the greater."
But I say unto you, they are inseparable.
Together they come, and when one sits alone with you at your board, remember that the other is asleep upon your bed.
Verily you are suspended like scales between your sorrow and your joy.
Only when you are empty are you at standstill and balanced.
When the treasure-keeper lifts you to weigh his gold and his silver, needs must your joy or your sorrow rise or fall.

Kahlil Gibran, *The Prophet*, William Heinemann Ltd., 1970, p.36.

SYMPATHY

"Sympathy"—"being simultaneously affected with the same feeling, tendency to share or state of sharing another person's or thing's emotion or sensation or condition (with), mental participation in another's trouble, compassion."

There was a knock on my door. A young woman came to see me. Fortunately I was on my own, apart from "Satan"—the jet-black house-cat—fast asleep on the settee. I asked her to come in and offered her a cup of coffee. We began to talk. She had come with a problem.

After about ten minutes she suddenly burst into a flood of tears. There had been a breakdown in a relationship and the full impact of the implications suddenly hit her. Satan's reaction was swift and sure. On hearing her cry, he spontaneously awoke up and shot across the room, straight on to her knee. He immediately began to comfort her. I looked on in amazement. The cat was doing what I ought to be doing—expressing sympathy—but had I ended up on her knee, I would probably have been sent to the Bishop.

Satan and I each did our part to help. The cat's physical presence was an immediate source of comfort. He had acted instinctively and on impulse, according to feelings. I was more cerebral in my approach. I listened carefully, and tried to come out with some words of sympathy. We talked through ways of facing the future, but I suspect she got a better deal from the cat.

And they showed him sympathy and comforted him for all the evil that the Lord had brought upon him.

Job 42.11.

Anxiety in a man's heart weighs him down, but a good word makes him glad.

Proverbs 12.25.

So if there is any encouragement in Christ, any incentive of love, any participation in the Spirit, any affection and sympathy, complete my joy by being of the same mind, having the same love, being in full accord and of one mind.

Philippians 2.1-2.

Have unity of spirit, sympathy, love of the brethren, a tender heart and a humble mind.

1 Peter 3.8.

Sympathy is your pain in my heart.

Anon.

His morality is all sympathy, but what morality should be.

Oscar Wilde, *The Works of Oscar Wilde*, William Collins Sons & Co. Ltd., 1948, *De Profundis*, p.876.

I value kind and perceptive sympathy very much and increasingly.

A.C. Benson, *Extracts from the Letters of Dr. A.C. Benson to M.E.A.*, Jarrold Publishing, 1927, p.22.

Love and sympathy and pity are not less real in God than in man.

Henry Ward Beecher, *Proverbs from Plymouth Pulpit*, Charles Burnet & Co., 1887, p.145.

Sympathy—the one poor word which includes all our best insight and our best love.

George Eliot, *Adam Bede*, Virtue & Co., 1908, Volume II, p.302.

It is sympathy with human life that inspires genial activities and keeps men within suitable restraint.

Henry Ward Beecher, *Proverbs from Plymouth Pulpit*, Charles Burnet & Co., 1887, p.20.

My need for sympathy has often induced me to seek it from people who, instead of strengthening me, unnerved me.

Vincent van Gogh, *Dear Theo: An Autobiography of Vincent van Gogh*, edited by Irving Stone, Constable & Co. Ltd., 1977, p.67.

I think I feel rather differently about sympathy to what seems the normal view. I just like to feel it is there, but not always expressed.

A.C. Benson, *Extracts from the Letters of Dr. A.C. Benson to M.E.A.*, Jarrold Publishing, 1927, p.19.

Many men, by their very culture and refinement, take themselves out of the fundamental element of sympathy and love which is indispensable to Christian life.

Henry Ward Beecher, *Proverbs from Plymouth Pulpit*, Charles Burnet & Co., 1887, p.166.

O the joy of that vast elemental sympathy which only the human soul is capable of generating and emitting in steady and limitless floods.

Walt Whitman, *The Complete Poems*, edited by Francis Murphy, Penguin Books Ltd., 1982, *A Song of Joys*, p.207.

> Unto a broken heart
> No other one may go
> Without the high prerogative
> Itself hath suffered so.

Emily Dickinson, *The Complete Poems of Emily Dickinson*, edited by Thomas H. Johnson, Faber & Faber Ltd., 1977, No.1704, p.693.

Sympathy is derived from two Greek words, *syn* which means *together with*, and *paschein* which means *to experience* or *to suffer*. *Sympathy* means *experiencing things together with the other person*, literally going through what he is going through.

William Barclay, *The Gospel of Matthew*, The Saint Andrew Press, 1987, Volume 1, p.103.

The human capacity to apprehend directly the state of mind and feeling of another person. Empathy involves, in effect, putting oneself in the place of the other, understanding and sharing the other's emotional experience, and seeing the world as he or she sees it. The line between empathy and sympathy cannot be drawn rigidly, but in general terms empathy involves a sharing in quality rather than in quantity, in kind rather than in degree. It is this which makes it possible to enter into the emotional situation even of persons incapacitated by the strength of their feelings without oneself being overwhelmed by those feelings.

Graeme M. Griffin, in *A New Dictionary of Christian Ethics*, edited by James F. Childress and John Macquarrie, SCM Press Ltd., 1986, p.190.

> True love's the gift which God has given
> To man alone beneath the heaven:
> It is not fantasy's hot fire,
> Whose wishes, soon as granted, fly;
> It liveth not in fierce desire,
> With dead desire it doth not die;
> It is the secret sympathy,
> The silver link, the silken tie,
> Which heart to heart and mind to mind
> In body and in soul can bind.

Sir Walter Scott, *The Poetical Works of Sir Walter Scott*, Oxford University Press, 1951, *The Lay of the Last Minstrel*, V, 13, p.34.

> There are ten thousand tones and signs
> We hear and see, but none defines—
> Involuntary sparks of thought,
> Which strike from out the heart o'erwrought,
> And form a strange intelligence,
> Alike mysterious and intense,
> Which link the burning chain that binds,
> Without their will, young hearts and minds;
> Conveying, as the electric wire,
> We know not how, the absorbing fire.

Lord Byron, *The Poetical Works of Lord Byron*, edited by Ernest Hartley Coleridge, John Murray Ltd., 1905, *Mazeppa*, VI. l.234, p.436.

Sympathy relates primarily to the human ability to understand and to share the feelings of other human beings. One common form it may take is the arousal of, for example, compassion and pity in one person by the sufferings of another. By extension, sympathy is also used in a social or political context to describe a sense of approval and support of ideologies or activities in which one is not oneself directly engaged.

Sympathy may also take the form of awareness of the feelings of another in such a way that the person concerned experiences those same feelings within his or her own being. When sympathy in this sense is distinguished from empathy, attention is commonly drawn to the danger of overinvolvement in the feelings of others.

Graeme M. Griffin, in *A New Dictionary of Christian Ethics*, edited by James F. Childress and John Macquarrie, SCM Press Ltd., 1986, p.612.

The fact that human love or sympathy is the guide who conducts us to the heart of life, revealing to us God and Nature and ourselves, is proof that part of our life is bound up with the life of the world, and that if we live in these our true relations we shall not entirely die so long as human beings remain alive upon this earth. The progress of the race, the diminution of sin and misery, the advancing kingdom of Christ on earth,—these are matters in which we have a *personal* interest. The strong desire we feel—and the best of us feel it most strongly—that the human race may be better, wiser, and happier in the future than they are now or have been in the past, is neither due to a false association of ideas, nor to pure unselfishness. There is a sense in which death would not be the end of everything for us, even though in this life only we had hope in Christ.

W.R.Inge, *Christian Mysticism*, Methuen & Co. Ltd., 1899, p.327.

It is one thing to see others suffer, but it is a very different thing to suffer oneself. The arguments and sympathy which we give to others in the hour of trial seem poor and inadequate in our own case. The clearness of vision with which we seemed to understand their meaning and to trace their cause, becomes blurred and obscured when we are ourselves their victims. Their presence, which tradition traces to the dawn of the race, comes to each new sufferer as the presence of a stranger, bewildering, harrowing, and moving his nature to its depths, disclosing every weakness or bringing to light unknown virtues, testing it, probing it, stirring up its dregs. No man really knows himself till he has passed beneath the lash. It is the supreme revealer of character. It is like the Word of God, spoken of in the Epistle to the Hebrews, "living, and effectual, and more piercing than any two-edged sword, and reaching unto the division of the soul and spirit, and of the joints and marrow, and is a discerner of the thoughts and intents of the heart". It is like the fan upon the threshing floor separating the chaff from the wheat. It is the fire that tries every man's work of what sort it is. It tests the foundations of character, whether they be wood, hay, stubble, or gold, silver, precious stones. Under the test of pain or sorrow, the edifice of many an apparently strong character has fallen into ruins, and many who have passed amongst men as weak, have come forth strong and brave.

Basil W. Maturin, *Laws of Spiritual Life*, Longmans, Green & Co. Ltd., 1907, p.94.

I went to see her in the nursing-home. They had pumped her out and she was feeling much better. She came down to meet me in the gothic hall and took me to her room. She was beautifully dressed, and her finger-nails were painted, and she made me feel rather a mess. Her room was full of flowers, my own among them, and the nurse brought in tea, and stayed to chat. We were sorry when she went, because the conversation dragged. I was embarrassed that she had attempted suicide, and did not know whether to refer to it or not. She talked about the viscount in the next room.

When I stood up to go she suddenly broke down and said that now her lover had left her she could not go on. She could not go home if his body was not beside her in the bed. She felt totally down.

I knew what she was asking of me in that moment—to take her in my arms and be her mother. But I was afraid—of making a fool of myself (she had always had an acid tongue), and perhaps of the sexual implications of embracing a woman. And I was in a hurry—I wanted to get away before the rush-hour traffic got too bad—and there were old resentments between us which had never quite healed. So I said something non-committal and went away. A few days later we chatted briefly on the telephone.

A few weeks later she killed herself. I had not stabbed or shot her, nor administered the tablets which poisoned her. But I had let her starve before my eyes.

Monica Furlong, *Travelling In*, Hodder & Stoughton Ltd., 1971, p.28.

TEMPERANCE

*"Temperance"—"moderation, self-restraint, in speech, conduct,
etc., especially in eating and drinking."*

I've recently returned from a chalet reading party in the French Alps. The weather was superb, and we got into the routine of reading one day and walking the next. The walks started off being fairly easy to allow us to get used to the altitude, and then got more difficult as time went on.

There were about a dozen of us in the party, a mixture of post-graduates and undergraduates.

One member of the party in particular personified Temperance. She was Scottish, lean and athletic. In going up and down the mountains she adopted a firm regular rhythm. This meant she could walk for most of the day without getting exhausted. As a vegetarian she was careful in what she ate and made do with small quantities. She drank very little and was practically teetotal. She was quietly spoken and exercised self-discipline in aspects of her way of life out there.

Back in College she was equally temperate. She had worked steadily and got a good degree in Modern Languages. She was now applying herself to her D.Phil. studies and was about to do some research work in Russia. She balanced her academic studies by rowing in our Women's First Eight. In all this she succeeded in making "Temperance" look attractive. Perhaps we would all benefit by taking a leaf out of her book, by being more temperate in our life-styles.

> Put a knife to your throat if you are a man given to appetite.
> Proverbs 23.2.

> If you have found honey, eat only enough for you, lest you be sated with it and vomit it.
> Proverbs 25.16.

But take heed to yourselves lest your hearts be weighed down with dissipation and drunkenness and cares of this life, and that day come upon you suddenly like a snare.
Luke 21.34.

Every athlete exercises self-control in all things. They do it to receive a perishable wreath, but we an imperishable. Well, I do not run aimlessly... but I pommel my body and subdue it, lest after preaching to others I myself should be disqualified.
1 Corinthians 9.25-27.

> We should thank God for beer and Burgundy by not drinking too much of them.
> G.K. Chesterton, *Orthodoxy*, Bodley Head, 1957, p.101.

No man really ever prospers in this world who violates the law of temperance or the law of God in the great matter of purity.

Henry Ward Beecher, *Proverbs from Plymouth Pulpit*, Charles Burnet & Co., 1887, p.184.

Gluttony, intemperance, sluggishness induced by oversleep, and the draining of the system by an inordinate indulgence of the passions, dull the reason, and make a man slow and inefficient.

Henry Ward Beecher, *Proverbs from Plymouth Pulpit*, Charles Burnet & Co., 1887, p.185.

Propound to thyself (if thou beest in a capacity) a constant rule of living, of eating and drinking: which though it may not be fit to observe scrupulously, lest it become a snare to thy conscience, or endanger thy health upon every accidental violence; yet let not thy rule be broken often nor much, but upon great necessity and in small degrees.

Jeremy Taylor, *The Rule and Exercises of Holy Living*, The Langford Press, 1970, p.37.

> Imposter! do not charge most innocent Nature,
> As if she would her children should be riotous
> With her abundance. She, good cateress,
> Means her provision only to the good,
> That live according to her sober laws
> And holy dictate of spare Temperance.

John Milton, *Comus and other Poems*, edited by F.T. Prince, Oxford University Press, 1968, l.762, p.72.

> Learn temperance, friends; and hear without disdain
> The choice of water. Thus the Coan sage
> Opin'd, and thus the learn'd of every School:
> What least of foreign principles partakes
> Is best: the lightest then, what bears the touch
> Of fire the least, and soonest mounts in air;
> The most insipid, the most void of smell.

John Armstrong, *The Art of Preserving Health*, Printed for T. Cadell, Jun. and W. Davies, 1795, p.76.

> If thou well observe
> The rule of "not too much," by temperance taught
> In what thou eat'st and drink'st, seeking from thence
> Due nourishment, not gluttonous delight,
> Till many years over thy head return;
> So mayst thou live, till like ripe fruit, thou drop
> Into thy mother's lap, or be with ease
> Gather'd, not harshly pluck'd, in death mature.

John Milton, *Paradise Lost*, Bk.II, l.530.

What we all want is inward rest; rest of heart and brain; the calm, strong, self-contained, self-denying character, which needs no stimulants, for it has no fits of depression; which needs no narcotics, for it has no fits of excitement; which needs no ascetic restraints, for it is strong enough to use God's gifts without abusing them; the character, in a word, which is truly temperate, not in drink and food merely, but in all desires, thoughts, and actions.

Charles Kingsley, *Daily Thoughts*, Macmillan Publishers Ltd., 1884, p.263.

A man is to be temperate in all things—even in the practice of the virtues and specially in the practice of temperance. Temperance does not lie in not doing too much of anything, but in a general sobriety of living in which a person is controlling what can be controlled and does not attempt to control what cannot be controlled.

Intemperance is evident in one who thinks too much, too quickly, about too many subjects. Temperance is quietness of mind in which concentration makes for profound lucid thinking. The intemperate talk too much to too many people, taking too many into their confidence. Temperance is a readiness to pay attention to what others have to say and only talking about subjects appropriate to the occasion and relationship. The intemperate are too grateful, too sympathetic, too prone to give advice. Temperance is grateful and sympathetic in proportion to the occasion for gratitude or sympathy. To be intemperate is to have too much travelling on account of too many appointments, committees, obligations, commitments and responsibilities. The temperate man knows that a man's life, and usefulness, does not consist in the abundance of his activities; he knows also that the attempt to do too many pieces of work, at the same time, has almost the same result as if no such attempt were made. Temperance entails a ruthless selection of activities on the part of artists, scientists, philosophers, social workers, pastors and all other serious people.

Some take to talking and work in the way others take to alcohol and other drugs as a means of dulling the edges of their fears and keeping themselves from becoming too aware of what is happening to them, within them and through them. All forms of intemperance contain a neurotic element and arise from causes best described as spiritual.

Institutions, societies and the Church itself, through officials, need to be watchful in case the over-willing (the intemperate) be given more work than they can do. In particular the Church is to preserve temperance through maintaining the balance of urgency and tranquillity in all authentic Christian living. In the table of the seven virtues, temperance is placed before fortitude—perhaps to suggest that only the temperate can be brave and that temperance requires bravery. Christian Scripture says: "Let your moderation be known unto all men". That is, let your temperance be known because the truth can only be spoken and done by temperate men.

R.E.C. Browne, in *A Dictionary of Christian Ethics*, edited by John Macquarrie, SCM Press Ltd., 1967, p.338.

UNDERSTANDING

"Understanding"—"comprehend, perceive the meaning of, grasp mentally, perceive the significance or explanation or cause or nature of, know how to deal with, having insight."

One of our undergraduates was reputed to be a very bright geologist. I was curious to know what constituted his brilliance, so asked his tutor about him. He paused for a moment and recalled the experience of a recent tutorial. He had been teaching him a new area of study. The undergraduate was not only able to understand it completely first time round, but was two steps ahead of the tutor in the course of his instruction. It was as if he had an intuitive knowledge of the entire subject, the tutor merely confirming what he already knew. This was one area of his brightness, the ability to assimilate new material quickly. The other was his capacity to understand the significance of what he had learnt and to make imaginative leaps. These two gifts, working together, constituted his brilliance.

Sometimes we come across people who may not be academically bright, but are gifted in their understanding of people. They tend to be quiet, observant and perceptive. They listen rather than speak. Their gifts lie on the feeling side of life, sympathy, compassion and empathy. They are intuitive and imaginative. Sometimes they surprise us with the depth of their insight and wisdom. They are the healers of mankind, and help people by their understanding.

But it is the spirit in a man, the breath of the Almighty, that makes him understand.
Job 32.8.

My son, if you receive my words and treasure up my commandments with you, making your ear attentive to wisdom and inclining your heart to understanding; yes, if you cry out for insight and raise your voice for understanding, if you seek it like silver and search for it as for hidden treasures; then you will understand the fear of the Lord and find the knowledge of God. For the Lord gives wisdom; from his mouth come knowledge and understanding; he stores up sound wisdom for the upright; he is a shield to those who walk in integrity, guarding the paths of justice and preserving the way of his saints.

Then you will understand righteousness and justice and equity, every good path; for wisdom will come into your heart, and knowledge will be pleasant to your soul; discretion will watch over you; understanding will guard you.
Proverbs 2.1-11.

Now I know in part; then I shall understand fully, even as I have been fully understood.
1 Corinthians 13.12.

Think over what I say, for the Lord will grant you understanding in everything.
2 Timothy 2.7.

Such good things as pass man's understanding.
Book of Common Prayer, Collect for the Sixth Sunday after Trinity.

What one has not experienced, one will never understand in print.
Isadora Duncan, *My Life*, Sphere Books Ltd., 1968, p.60.

The highest of all is not to understand the highest but to act upon it.
Søren Kierkegaard, in *The Quaker Contribution*, Harold Loukes, SCM Press Ltd., 1965, p.9.

The real thing is to understand, and love that you may understand.
J.B. Yeats, *Letters to his son, W.B. Yeats and others*, Faber & Faber Ltd., 1944, p.136.

A clear understanding of God makes one want to follow the direction of things, the direction of oneself.
André Gide, *The Journals of André Gide*, 1894, translated by Justin O'Brien, Martin Secker & Warburg Ltd., 1947, p.41.

To understand a matter properly, a man must dominate it, instead of allowing it to dominate him.
Ernest Hello, *Life, Science, and Art*, R. & T. Washbourne Ltd., 1913, p.106.

Understanding a person does not mean condoning; it only means that one does not accuse him as if one were God or a judge placed above him.
Erich Fromm, *Man for Himself*, Routledge & Kegan Paul, 1975, p.237.

We are apt to outgrow our teachers in wisdom, but whoever has helped us to a larger understanding is entitled to our gratitude for all time.
Norman Douglas, *An Almanac*, Chatto & Windus in association with Martin Secker & Warburg Ltd., 1945, p.82.

You never really understand a person until you consider things from his point of view ... until you climb into his skin and walk around in it.
Harper Lee, *To Kill a Mockingbird*, Pan Books Ltd., 1981, p.35.

The language of the mystics cannot, of course, match that of science or reason. Yet, in a world craving for evidence from real life, it will remain one of the means through which our contemporaries can find God.
René Voillaume, *The Need for Contemplation*, translated by Elizabeth Hamilton, Darton, Longman & Todd Ltd., 1972, p.58.

In human life a person can never be fully *understood* but can be fully *loved*, loved to the limit of the lover's capacity to love. This is the principal justification of using the idea of "love" of God; it is why one of the greatest of Christian mystics said of God, "by love he can be caught and held, but by thinking, never".
J. Neville Ward, *The Use of Praying*, Epworth Press, 1967, p.28.

Actually, of course, few people in this world see what is going on about them. Nobody really sees until he understands, until he can create a pattern into which the helter-skelter of passing events fits and makes a significance. And for this sort of vision a personal death is required ... Nobody sees with his eyes alone; we see with our souls.
Henry Miller, *The Cosmological Eye*, New Directions, 1939, p.282.

For the rights of understanding to be valid one must venture out into life, out on the sea and lift up one's voice, even though God hears it not, and not stand on the shore and watch others fighting and struggling—only then does understanding acquire its *official sanction*, for to stand on one leg and prove God's existence is a very different thing from going on one's knees and thanking him.

Søren Kierkegaard, *The Journals of Kierkegaard*, Harper & Row, Publishers, 1959, p.68.

It is perfectly true, as philosophers say, that life must be understood backwards. But they forget the other proposition, that it must be lived forwards. And if one thinks over that proposition it becomes more and more evident that life can never really be understood in time simply because at no particular moment can I find the necessary resting-place from which to understand it—backwards.

Søren Kierkegaard, *The Journals of Kierkegaard*, Harper & Row, Publishers, 1959, p.89.

The outward events of our life cannot be understood, except in their relation to that unseen and intensely living world, the Infinite Charity which penetrates and supports us, the God Whom we resist and yet for Whom we thirst; Who is ever at work, transforming our self-centred desire of the natural creature into the wide-spreading, out-pouring love of the citizen of Heaven.

Evelyn Underhill, in *The Wisdom of Evelyn Underhill*, compiled by John Stobbart, Mowbray, 1951, p.7.

The greatest gift that any human being can give to another is the gift of under-standing and of peace. To have someone to whom we can go at any time, and know that they will not laugh at our dreams, or misunderstand our confidences is a most wonderful thing. To have somewhere to go to where the tensions of life are relaxed in peace is a lovely thing. It is open to us all to make our own homes like that. This is something which does not cost money, and which does not need lavish and costly hospitality. It costs only the understanding heart.

William Barclay, *The Gospel of John*, The Saint Andrew Press, 1974, Volume Two, p.93.

We must learn to *understand*. There is always a reason why a person does some-thing. If he is boorish and impolite and cross-tempered, maybe he is worried or in pain. If he treats us with suspicion and dislike, maybe he has misunderstood, or has been misinformed about something we have said or done. Maybe the man is the victim of his own environment or his own heredity. Maybe his temperament is such that life is difficult and human relations a problem for him. Forgiveness would be very much easier for us, if we tried to understand before we allowed ourselves to condemn.

William Barclay, *The Gospel of Matthew*, The Saint Andrew Press, 1987, Volume 1, p.223.

To understand is to be conscious of the fundamental unity of the thing to be explained—that is to say, to conceive it in its entirety both of life and develop-ment, to be able to remake it by a mental process without making a mistake, without adding or omitting anything. It means, first, complete identification of the object, and then the power of making it clear to others by a full and just interpretation.

To understand is more difficult than to judge, for understanding is the transference of the mind into the conditions of the object, whereas judgment is simply the enunciation of the individual opinion.

Henri Frédéric Amiel, *Amiel's Journal*, translated by Mrs. Humphry Ward, Macmillan Publishers Ltd., 1918, p.188.

The comprehension of life, of its living flow is beyond conceptual thought, which, in the very effort to comprehend, arrests, divides and falsifies it. Life can be understood only by living. To understand any living thing you must, so to say, creep within; and feel the beating of its heart. Every creature knows at least enough about the world to support its own existence there. The intellect seems to stand in its own light, reducing all it contemplates to the shadowiness of its self-chosen concepts, and by its own confession we can know nothing more than these, its peculiar creation. Life lies too deep to be penetrated by them. It is an island fortress. You cannot march into it on your two feet of logic and mathematics.

W. Macneile Dixon, *The Human Situation*, Edward Arnold, 1937, p.64.

UNITY

"Unity"—"oneness, being one or single or individual, being formed of parts that constitute a whole, due interconnexion & coherence of parts."

T he unity of the Christian Church used to concern me. In my teens I was an Anglo-Catholic; in my twenties an Evangelical. In my thirties, I read *The Choice is Always Ours*—an anthology by Dorothy Berkley Phillips—and this led to a fundamental change in outlook. From then onwards I was greatly influenced by the concept of "man made in the image and likeness of God". This radically changed my way of looking at people. I came to see that "the divine inbreathing", fully worked out in the life of Christ, revealed an enormous potential of life to be found in the depths of our being. This could be described as a rebirth of the Father, Son and the Holy Spirit—as in Baptism. In addition—and this is where it gets exciting—it showed divine attributes such as Life, Light, Truth, Joy and Love. From this perspective denominational barriers came tumbling down. The important thing now was to trigger off the "divine" in people, and finds ways and means of stimulating and nurturing growth. This led to the development of Visions of Faith, Hope and Love, and discovering the practice of Reflection.

We now have thirty Reflection Groups in College, each meeting for an hour a week, during the term. Our Groups are made up of Roman Catholics, Church of England, Methodists, URC, Christian Union, the occasional Jew, Hindu, Muslim, Buddhist,—and Atheists and Agnostics. We don't always agree with each other, and from time to time there is conflict and tension, but there is at least an underlying unity and we no longer need to pigeon-hole people and put them in denominations.

Behold, how good and pleasant it is when brothers dwell in unity!
Psalm 133.1.

Come, let us join ourselves to the Lord in an everlasting covenant which will never be forgotten.
Jeremiah 50.5.

I appeal to you, brethren, by the name of our Lord Jesus Christ, that all of you agree and that there be no dissensions among you, but that you be united in the same mind and the same judgment.
1 Corinthians 1.10.

Lead a life worthy of the calling to which you have been called... eager to maintain the unity of the Spirit in the bond of peace.

Ephesians 4.1,3.

Unity is not in government nor in creeds, but in faith, and hope, and love.

Henry Ward Beecher, *Proverbs from Plymouth Pulpit*, Charles Burnet & Co., 1887, p.203.

Plurality which is not reduced to unity is confusion; unity which does not depend on plurality is tyranny.

Blaise Pascal, *Pensées*, translated by W.F. Trotter, Random House, Inc., 1941, p.308.

Here is the unity of blades of grass and bits of wood and stone, together with everything else... all that nature tries to do is to plunge on into that unity, into the Father-nature, so that it may all be one, the one Son.

Meister Eckhart, *Meister Eckhart*, a modern translation by Raymond Bernard Blakney, Harper & Row, Publishers, 1941, p.148.

The needed Copernican revolution in theology involves... a shift from the dogma that Christianity is at the centre to the realisation that it is God who is at the centre, and that all the religions of mankind, including our own, serve and revolve around him.

John Hick, *God and the Universe of Faiths*, Macmillan Publishers Ltd., 1973, p.131.

Above and beyond merely human ends or aims, something is at work in us which is transcendental, spiritual and divine,—something which is the source of every achievement that human life has to its credit, and binds men together in an inner unity.

Rudolf Eucken, *The Spiritual Outlook in Europe To-day*, The Faith Press Ltd., 1922, p.89.

It seems to be quite true that the East is at the bottom of the spiritual change we are passing through today. Only this East is not a Tibetan monastery full of Mahatmas, but in a sense lies within us. It is from the depths of our own psychic life that new spiritual forms will arise.

C.G. Jung, *Modern Man in Search of a Soul*, Routledge & Kegan Paul Ltd., 1973, p.250.

The missions of the higher religions are not competitive; they are complementary. We can believe in our own religion without having to feel that it is the sole repository of truth. We can love it without having to feel that it is the sole means of salvation.

Arnold Toynbee, *An Historian's Approach to Religion*, Oxford University Press, 1956, p.196.

In practice, mystics belonging to nearly all the religious traditions coincide to the extent that they can hardly be distinguished. They represent the truth of each of these traditions.

The contemplation practised in India, Greece, China, etc., is just as super-natural as that of the Christian mystics.

Simone Weil, *Gateway to God*, William Collins Sons & Co. Ltd., 1974, p.125.

It is not enough for the whole *oikoumene*, both Rome and the World Council of Churches, to address fine speeches to the "outer world", to society at large, and "inside", between Churches, merely to set up everlasting mixed commissions, arrange polite mutual visits, indulge in endless academic dialogue without practical consequences. There must be genuine, increasing integration of the different Churches.

Hans Küng, *On Being a Christian*, translated by Edward Quinn, William Collins Sons & Co. Ltd., 1977, p.525.

Christian unity is very important because Christians stand as a light for the world. If we are Christians we must be Christlike. Gandhi once said that if Christians lived their Christian life to the full there would be no Hindus left in India. That is what people expect of us, that we live our Christian life to the full.

The first Christians died for Jesus and they were recognized because they loved one another, and the world has never needed more love than today.

Mother Teresa of Calcutta, in *In the Silence of the Heart*, compiled by Kathryn Spink, SPCK, 1983, p.78.

The purpose of God is manifested in the unity of all He has made. We are called to unity as a vocation. As we seek unity with God, there will come a unity in our own being. But we shall only attain to unity with God as we *keep His word.* When He says, "No," we must not say, "Yes" ...

Our Lord ever sought the perfect unity of His will with the will of His Father, and so, though men slew Him, out of His death came that revelation of love and beauty which does act as a magnet to draw men of goodwill towards one another. Often there are things in others of which we cannot approve, but if we really are in unity with God our relationship with them will have redeeming value, whatever quality of pain there may be in some of the contacts that we must have with them. When things are wrong between other people and ourselves, the real secret of unity lies for us in our own souls. We must first get right with God ourselves. We cannot be in a wrong relationship with others if our wills are in union with the will of God.

The basic unity of the Church depends really on three great principles. The first is unity of vision. Those who see and love the same thing have a unity in that love which is a unity of freedom. They choose to follow the beauty that they see, and as they are all following the same splendour, they are united in their quest. So the unity that follows from the common love of the vision of our Lord is a very real unity.

Again, there is a unity that comes from an essential relationship of life. Those who are sacramentally united to Christ are essentially related to one another. Not only are they the children of the same Father, but by their communion they have claimed their relationship with Him. Their brotherhood is real. They have only got to realize it.

Thirdly, as people through the receiving of Christ attain to likeness with Him, there will come amongst them what may be called a family likeness. All who are like Him must be, to the degree in which they are like Him, like also to one another.

So, following the same vision, receiving the same life, attaining to the same likeness, souls rise above the superficial distinctions of class or nation, and enter into that true unity which is the bond of the children of the kingdom of God. Our unity is in Him, our separations are in ourselves. As we attain to one-ness with Him, so we shall attain to union with one another in Him. This is really the Communion of Saints and that unity of the Church which has never been broken.

Father Andrew SDC, *Meditations for Every Day*, Mowbray, p.348.

VIOLENCE

"Violence"—"quality of being violent; violent conduct or
treatment, injury, unlawful exercise of physical force."

I t was Saturday night. There was a party on the next staircase. It sounded to be
getting out of hand. Someone was being violent. I went to investigate. A gate-crasher
was having problems. He was the worse for wear for drink and was having difficulty in
breathing. His speech was incoherent and he seemed to be in danger of choking.

The Junior Dean arrived on the scene. He made a rapid appreciation of the
situation and wisely stood back. "One for the Chaplain," he thought. I started to
investigate. Suddenly without warning, the young man lashed out. A fist shot out in
the direction of my jaw. Fortunately I used to box and managed a quick feint to avoid
it. The Junior Dean nearly split his sides laughing. He'd never seen the Chaplain
move so fast. We both then got to work, and eventually he was admitted to hospital.

The reasons for violence are complex. This is partly to do with our make-up as
people—we are all rightly creatures of passion, with vast resources of energy. Ideally
this energy should be channelled into something creative and constructive. This is
how we can enjoy life and find fulfilment. Sadly this is not always the case. Many of
us suffer from frustration. When the channels and outlets of energy are blocked, a
subtle transformation takes place. Creative energy turns in destructive power and
finds an outlet in violence.

Such are the ways of all who get gain by violence; it takes away the life of its possessors.
Proverbs 1.19.

Your rich men are full of violence; your inhabitants speak lies, and their tongue is
deceitful in their mouth.
Micah 6.12.

Then Jesus said to him, "Put your sword back into its place; for all who take the
sword will perish by the sword."
Matthew 26.52.

Soldiers also asked him, "And we, what shall we do?" And he said to them, "Rob no
one by violence or by false accusation, and be content with your wages."
Luke 3.14.

The only way to break the chain of violence is to forgive and to love.
Michel Quoist, *With Open Heart,* translated by Colette Copeland, Gill and Macmillan Ltd., 1983, p.47.

We must strive to substitute more and more in this world *effective* non-violence for
violence.
Simone Weil, *Gravity and Grace*, Routledge & Kegan Paul, 1972, p.77.

Why must oppressed people so often be forced to resort to violence to seize power, before those in power realise that their greatness lies in sharing, and even at times giving, this power?

Michel Quoist, *With Open Heart*, translated by Colette Copeland, Gill and Macmillan Ltd., 1983, p.60.

Violence for violence's sake is destructive. Only the violence of love can accomplish anything.

He says (Dom Helder): "To use violence without love is like trying to put out a fire with a blazing torch."

Michel Quoist, *With Open Heart*, translated by Colette Copeland, Gill and Macmillan Ltd., 1983, p.178.

The right to resist oppression by violence is beyond doubt... but one thing can justify its exercise on any large scale,—namely, the denial of free thought, free speech, and a free press. Even then its exercise would be unwise unless suppression were enforced so stringently that all other means of throwing it off had become hopeless.

Benjamin R. Tucker, *Instead of a Book*, Haskell House Publishers Ltd., 1969, p.439.

Non-violence is no good unless it is effective. Hence the young man's question to Gandhi about his sister. The answer should have been: use force unless you are such that you can defend her with as much chance of success without violence. Unless you possess a radiance of which the energy (that is to say the possible effectiveness in the most material sense of the word) is equal to that contained in your muscles.

We should strive to become such that we are able to be non-violent.

Simone Weil, *Gravity and Grace*, Routledge & Kegan Paul, 1972, p.77.

We have heard first hand of the fear of the destructive potential of young people. We have sensed the latent violence as we have walked along the streets; we have seen groups of young people with nothing to do, nowhere to go, and with nothing to lose:

"I wouldn't go out without a pair of scissors to defend me."

"If someone steps on your toe every day, and if they keep on doing it, you might do something drastic."

Faith in the City, Church Publishing House, 1985, p.316.

It is true that Christ is a revolutionary, it is true that He is violent, but not against others, only against Himself.

It is too easy to kill others, it is so difficult to die to oneself.

The violence of Christ is the Cross; it is planted in His heart, not in the hearts of His adversaries.

The violence of Jesus is deep love, not the sword or the prison, which is how we always want to resolve the problems which seem intolerable to us.

Carlo Carretto, *The God Who Comes*, translated by Rose Mary Hancock, Darton, Longman & Todd Ltd., 1974, p.140

I've decided that I'm going to do battle for my philosophy. You ought to believe something in life, believe that thing so fervently that you will stand up with it till the end of your days. I can't make myself believe that God wants me to hate. I'm tired of violence. And I'm not going to let my oppressor dictate to me what method I use. We have a power, power that can't be found in Molotov cocktails, but we do have a power. Power that cannot be found in bullets and guns, but we have a power. It is a power as old as the insights of Jesus of Nazareth and as modern as the techniques of Mahatma Gandhi.

Martin Luther King, *The Words of Martin Luther King*, selected by Coretta Scott King, William Collins Sons & Co. Ltd., 1986, p.71.

Violence as a way of achieving racial justice is both impractical and immoral. It is impractical because it is a descending spiral ending in destruction for all. The old law of an eye for an eye leaves everybody blind. It is immoral because it seeks to humiliate the opponent rather than win his understanding; it seeks to annihilate rather than to convert. Violence is immoral because it thrives on hatred rather than love. It destroys community and makes brotherhood impossible. It leaves society in monologue rather than dialogue. Violence ends by defeating itself. It creates bitterness in the survivors and brutality in the destroyers.

Martin Luther King, *The Words of Martin Luther King*, selected by Coretta Scott King, William Collins Sons & Co. Ltd., 1986, p.73.

To carry through a social reform which... will create so much opposition as to necessitate the use of violence is criminally rash. For the chances are that any reform which requires violence for its imposition will not only fail to produce the good results anticipated, but will actually make matters worse than they were before. Violence... can produce only the effects of violence... where violence has been used for a long period, a habit of violence is formed and it becomes exceedingly difficult for the perpetrators of violence to reverse their policy. Moreover, the results of violence are far-reaching beyond the wildest dreams of the often well-intentioned people who resort to it.

Aldous Huxley, *Ends and Means*, Chatto & Windus, 1965, p.28.

Violence can only be concealed by the lie, and the lie can be maintained only by violence. Anyone who has once proclaimed that violence is his method is inevitably forced to choose the lie as his guiding principle. At its birth violence acts openly, is even proud of itself. But it has scarcely established itself when it feels the air around it becoming more rarefied and it cannot continue to exist without mashing itself with the lie and wrapping itself up in its honeyed rhetoric. Violence does not always necessarily take you physically by the throat and strangle you: more often it merely demands of its subjects that they declare allegiance to the lie, become accomplices in the lie.

And the simple step of a simple, courageous man is not to take part in the lie, not to support deceit. Let the lie come into the world, even dominate the world, but not through me. Moreover, writers and artists can do something more: they can vanquish the lie. Wherever else it fails, Art always has won its fight against lies, and it will always win. Its victory will be obvious, irrevocably obvious to all men. The lie can withstand a great deal in this world but it cannot withstand Art.

Once the lie has been dispersed, the nakedness of violence will be revealed in all its repulsiveness, and then violence, become decrepit, will come crashing down.

Alexander Solzhenitsyn, *One Word of Truth, The Nobel Speech on Literature 1970*, Bodley Head, 1972, p.26.

At the present time when violence, clothed in life, dominates the world more cruelly than it ever has before, I still remain convinced that truth, love, peaceableness, meekness, and kindness are the violence which can master all other violence. The world will be theirs as soon as ever a sufficient number of men with purity of heart, with strength, and with perseverance think and live out the thoughts of love and truth, of meekness and peaceableness.

All ordinary violence produces its own limitations, for it calls forth an answering violence which sooner or later becomes its equal or its superior. But kindness works simply and perseveringly; it produces no strained relations which prejudice its working; strained relations which already exist it relaxes. Mistrust and misunderstanding it puts to flight, and it strengthens itself by calling forth unswerving kindness. Hence it is the furthest-reaching and the most effective of all forces.

All the kindness which a man puts out into the world works on the heart and the thoughts of mankind, but we are so foolishly indifferent that we are never in earnest in the matter of kindness. We want to topple a great load over, and yet will not avail ourselves of a lever which would multiply our power a hundred-fold.

There is an unmeasured depth of truth in that strange saying of Jesus: "Blessed are the meek, for they shall inherit the earth" (St. Matt. v, 5).

Albert Schweitzer, *Memoirs of Childhood and Youth*, George Allen & Unwin Publishers Ltd., 1924, p.102.

WAR

"War"—"quarrel usually between nations, conducted by force, hostility or contention between persons."

Recently I went on a tour of the battlefields of the First World War. Over the years I had read several accounts of the fighting and was familiar with the names and places of battles, such as Ypres and the Somme. I had also taken part in several Remembrance Sunday Services and used those occasions to imagine what it must have been like for those involved in the conflict. The long list of Old Members of the College who fell in the First World War, recorded on memorial tablets in the Ante-Chapel, made sombre reading.

However, going round the battlefields with an expert guide was an entirely different experience. It came close to experiencing the horrors of the First World War itself. We spent several hours in the Ypres Salient, and were taken through the course of the battles. We were deeply moved by the large numbers of war cemeteries we came across, each beautifully kept, with their rows and rows of white crosses. In the evening we heard the Last Post played at the Menin Gate. This huge stone arch is a memorial containing the names of many thousands of those lost in the area without trace.

We moved on to the Somme and Vimy Ridge, and listened intently to the accounts of the battles in these areas. We visited German and Canadian war cemeteries, examined trenches and saw the biggest crater of the War.

The emotional impact of this three-day visit is difficult to put in words. I came back to England with mixed feelings. Sad and despondent on the one hand—yet enormously grateful to be alive on the other hand. Is war ever worthwhile?

War was in his heart.

Psalm 55.21.

Wisdom is better than weapons of war, but one sinner destroys much good.

Ecclesiastes 9.18.

For though we live in the world we are not carrying on a worldly war, for the weapons of our warfare are not worldly but have divine power to destroy strongholds.

2 Corinthians 10.3-4.

What causes wars, and what causes fightings among you? Is it not your passions that are at war in your members? You desire and do not have; so you kill. And you covet and cannot obtain; so you fight and wage war.

James 4.1-2.

Peace is the daughter of war.
French Proverb.

Pride, pomp, and circumstance, of glorious war!
William Shakespeare, *Othello*, Act III. sc.iii. l.356.

War is not an adventure. It is a disease. It is like typhus.
Antoine de Saint-Exupéry, *Flight to Arras*, translated by Lewis Galantière, William Heinemann Ltd., 1942, p.49.

As peace is of all goodness, so war is an emblem, a hieroglyphic, of all misery.
John Donne, *John Donne Selected Prose*, chosen by Evelyn Simpson, Clarendon Press, 1967, 12, p.211.

As long as war is regarded as wicked, it will always have its fascination. When it is looked upon as vulgar, it will cease to be popular.
Oscar Wilde, *The Artist as Critic*, edited by Richard Ellmann, Random House, Inc., 1959, *Intentions*, p.405.

What can a man do more than *die* for his countrymen?
    Live for them. It is a longer work, and therefore a more difficult and a nobler one.
Charles Kingsley, *Daily Thoughts*, Macmillan Publishers Ltd., 1884, p.239.

My voice is still for war.
Gods, can a *Roman* Senate long debate
Which of the two to choose, slavery or death!
Joseph Addison, *Miscellaneous Works*, edited by A.C. Guthkelch, George Bell & Sons, Volume 1, *Cato*, Act II. sc.i. l.23.

I understand well the respect of mankind for war, because (war) breaks up the Chinese stagnation of society, and demonstrates the personal merits of all men.
Ralph Waldo Emerson, *The Works of Ralph Waldo Emerson*, edited by George Sampson, George Bell & Sons, 1906, Volume III, *Society and Solitude, Letters and Social Aims, Addresses, The Conservative*, p.605.

War educates the senses, calls into action the will, perfects the physical constitution, brings men into such swift and close collision in critical moments that man measures man.
Ralph Waldo Emerson, *The Conduct of Life, & Other Essays*, J.M. Dent & Sons Ltd., 1911, p.137.

Animals kill one another only when they're hungry. We kill because we're afraid of our own shadow, afraid that if we used a little common sense we'd have to admit that our glorious principles were wrong.
Henry Miller, *The Wisdom of the Heart*, Editions Poetry London, 1947, p.117.

We forget that Christ could never have thought it possible that men who believe in His doctrine of humility, love, and universal brotherhood would calmly and consciously institute the murder of their brethren.
Leo Tolstoy, *What I Believe*, translated by Constantine Popoff, Elliot Stock, 1885, p.99.

What a country calls its vital economic interests are not the thing which enable its citizens to live, but the things which enable it to make war. Gasoline is much more likely than wheat to be a cause of international conflict.
Simone Weil, in *A Certain World*, W.H.Auden, Faber & Faber Ltd., 1982, p.384.

Oh World!
Oh men! what are ye, and our best designs,
That we must work by crime to punish crime?
And slay as if Death had but this one gate,
When a few years would make the sword superfluous!

Lord Byron, *The Poetical Works of Lord Byron*, edited by Ernest Hartley Coleridge, John Murray Ltd., 1905, *Marino Faliero*, Act IV. sc.ii. l.165.

All great nations learned their truth of word, and strength of thought, in war; that they were nourished in war, and wasted by peace; taught by war, and deceived by peace; trained by war, and betrayed by peace:—in a word, that they were born by war, and expired in peace.

John Ruskin, *The Works of John Ruskin*, George Allen & Sons, 1905, *The Crown of Wild Olive*, p.464.

The most shocking fact about war is that its victims and its instruments are individual human beings, and that these individual human beings are condemned by the monstrous conventions of politics to murder or be murdered in quarrels not their own, to inflict upon the innocent and, innocent themselves of any crime against their enemies, to suffer cruelties of every kind.

Aldous Huxley, *The Olive Tree*, Chatto & Windus, 1936, p.84.

For only love—which means humility—can exorcize the fear which is at the root of all war.
    What is the use of postmarking our mail with exhortations to "pray for peace" and then spending billions of dollars on atomic submarines, thermonuclear weapons, and ballistic missiles? This, I would think, would certainly be what the New Testament calls "mocking God"—and mocking Him far more effectively than the atheists do.

Thomas Merton, *New Seeds of Contemplation*, Burns & Oates Ltd., 1962, p.91.

Waste of Muscle, waste of Brain,
Waste of Patience, waste of Pain,
Waste of Manhood, waste of Health,
Waste of Beauty, waste of Wealth,
Waste of Blood, and waste of Tears,
Waste of Youth's most precious years,
Waste of ways the Saints have trod,
Waste of Glory, waste of God,—
War!

G.A. Studdert Kennedy, *The Unutterable Beauty*, Hodder & Stoughton Ltd., 1964, p.29.

The only comfort I can see in the tragedies of war is that they bring us all face to face with the realities of human life, as it has been in all ages, giving us sterner and yet more loving, more human, and more divine thoughts about ourselves, and our business here, and the fate of those who are gone, and awakening us out of the luxurious, frivolous, and unreal dreams (full nevertheless of hard judgments) in which we have been living so long, to trust in a living Father who is really and practically governing this world and all worlds, and who willeth that none should perish.

Charles Kingsley, *Daily Thoughts*, Macmillan Publishers Ltd., 1884, p.107.

All disasters stem from us. Why is there a war? Perhaps because now and then I might be inclined to snap at my neighbour. Because I and my neighbour and everyone else do not have enough love. Yet we could fight war and all its excrescences by releasing, each day, the love which is shackled inside us, and giving it a chance to live. And I believe that I will never be able to hate any human being for his so-called "wickedness", that I shall only hate the evil that is within me, though hate is perhaps putting it too strongly even then. In any case, we cannot be lax enough in what we demand of others and strict enough in what we demand of ourselves.

Etty Hillesum, *A Diary, 1941-43*, translated by Arnold J. Pomerans, Jonathan Cape Ltd., 1983, p.80.

A true revolution of values will lay hands on the world order and say of war: "This way of settling differences is not just." This business of burning human beings with napalm, of filling our nation's homes with orphans and widows, of injecting poisonous drugs of hate into the veins of peoples normally humane, of sending men home from dark and bloody battlefields physically handicapped and psychologically deranged, cannot be reconciled with wisdom, justice, and love. A nation that continues year after year to spend more money on military defence than on programmes of social uplift is approaching spiritual death.

Martin Luther King, *The Words of Martin Luther King*, selected by Coretta Scott King, William Collins Sons & Co. Ltd., 1986, p.87.

> The hunting tribes of air and earth
> Respect the brethren of their birth;
> Nature, who loves the claim of kind,
> Less cruel chase to each assign'd.
> The falcon, poised on soaring wing,
> Watches the wild-duck by the spring;
> The slow-hound wakes the fox's lair;
> The greyhound presses on the hare;
> The eagle pounces on the lamb;
> The wolf devours the fleecy dam;
> Even tiger fell, and sullen bear,
> Their likeness and their lineage spare:
> Man, only mars kind Nature's plan,
> And turns the fierce pursuit on man;
> Plying war's desultory trade,
> Incursion, flight, and ambuscade.

Sir Walter Scott, *The Poetical Works of Sir Walter Scott*, edited by J. Logie Robertson, Oxford University Press, 1951, *Rokeby*, Canto Third, 1.

I refuse to accept the cynical notion that nation after nation must spiral down a militaristic stairway into the hell of thermonuclear destruction. I believe that unarmed truth and unconditional love will have the final word in reality. This is why right temporarily defeated is stronger than evil triumphant.

I believe that even amid today's mortar bursts and whining bullets, there is still hope for a brighter tomorrow. I believe that wounded justice, lying prostrate on the blood-flowing streets of our nations, can be lifted from this dust of shame to reign supreme among the children of men.

I still believe that one day mankind will bow before the altars of God and be crowned triumphant over war and bloodshed, and nonviolent redemptive good will will proclaim the rule of the land. "And the lion and the lamb shall lie down together and every man shall sit under his own vine and fig tree and none shall be afraid." I still believe that we shall overcome.

Martin Luther King, *The Words of Martin Luther King,* selected by Coretta Scott King, William Collins Sons & Co. Ltd., 1986, p.91.

It is a delusion to think that the nations are becoming too well educated and enlightened for wars. It is the sand in which we are burying our heads. It was observed in the last war that there was a better feeling among the masses of people than among the intellectuals. And this is because our thought is superficial. We do not think, because we are afraid that it may cost us dearly. It may upset our plans and schemes. We simply do what the other man does. The pull of the crowd is irresistible. In the Middle Ages the Church exercised a tyranny over the people; now the jingoes do it. A few demagogues and adventurers with their control over the press and the radio lay down the law, and the masses unthinkingly march to their death. Our wills, our minds are not our own. A machine stronger than ourselves has made tools of us all. We are dressed in uniforms which enter our flesh. The silence of steel suppresses our sense of values. We are unable to look facts in the face. Hatred is made so agreeable and dished up so attractively that we revel in it, though we have no knowledge of the thing we hate. We are called cowards if we do not hate enough to kill. What is called discipline substitutes the certainty of being killed if we do not go to the front for the chance of being killed if we go. We take the risk and gain credit for courage. We wish for the death of brothers in arms, and slay without hatred, like machines, men whom we do not know, against whom we have absolutely no cause of enmity. Held in the terrible vice of wartime discipline, which forbids one to think, we kill by command, not by conviction. We are brave enough to suffer, to accept sorrow, but not brave enough to reject suffering for the sake of superstition. We fight for our symbols, trade, property, empire, symbols which have become stale and petrified. We have not the courage to cast off the old symbols, the outworn traditions, which have become fetters. We cannot shake them off, because the process of false education starts in the nurseries. Tradition and romance and all the unconscious influences of education have been for centuries directed towards the glorification of the independent sovereign State and the suppression of others as the most direct expression of loyalty, to one's own State.

Sir Sarvepalli Radhakrishnan, *East and West in Religion,* George Allen & Unwin Publishers Ltd., 1933, p.87.

WHOLENESS

"Wholeness"—"in good health, in sound condition, intact; thing complete in itself, organic unity, complete system, total made up of parts."

We had a highly intelligent undergraduate reading English in College. Throughout his first term he worked eighteen hours a day. Naturally his tutors were concerned and tried to persuade him to reduce his work-load, and take up other interests. Initially there was no response. The undergraduate was not interested in sport, and bored with university societies in general. Eventually he succumbed to tutorial pressure and became a somewhat reluctant member of the Newman Society.

As time went on he reduced his hours of work, but still remained single-minded in his pursuit of academic excellence. In the end he succeeded in getting a double-First, and left to try his hand at teaching. It was here he came to grief. His lack of charisma and personality meant great difficulty in the classroom. He failed his

Postgraduate Certificate of Education, and eventually ended up a clerk working for the Department of Health and Social Security.

There is still much to be said for the education of the whole person—body, mind and spirit. We are in great danger of turning out "intellectual giants" who are "spiritual and emotional pygmies." I am a great believer in the observation of Aldous Huxley in his book *Island*—that "Holy", "Health", and "Whole" all come from the same root word. It's time we got back to this in our education, and concentrated on producing whole people.

I will give thanks to thee, O Lord my God, with my whole heart, and I will glorify thy name for ever.
Psalm 86.12.

The whole head is sick, and the whole heart faint. From the sole of the foot even to the head, there is no soundness in it.
Isaiah 1.5-6.

Thy faith hath made thee whole.
Matthew 9.22 (A.V.).

And it is my prayer that your love may abound more and more, with knowledge and all discernment, so that you may approve what is excellent, and may be pure and blameless for the day of Christ, filled with the fruits of righteousness which come through Jesus Christ, to the glory and praise of God.
Philippians 1.9-11.

Wholeness demands relationship—with man or with God, and often with both together.
Monica Furlong, *Travelling In*, Hodder & Stoughton Ltd., 1971, p.64.

To be alive, to be man alive, to be whole man alive: that is the point.
D.H. Lawrence, *The Phoenix*, edited by Edward D. McDonald, William Heinemann Ltd., 1936, p.528.

"Holy", "Healthy", "Whole"—they all come from the same root and carry different overtones of the same meaning.
Aldous Huxley, *Island*, Chatto & Windus, 1962, p.92.

Religion is only another word for the right use of a man's whole self, instead of a wrong use of himself.
Henry Ward Beecher, *Proverbs from Plymouth Pulpit*, Charles Burnet & Co., 1887, p.120.

There is no such thing as an immortal work of art. There is one art—the greatest of all, the art of making a complete human being of oneself.
A.R. Orage, *On Love*, The Janus Press, 1957, p.59.

The stuff of the universe, woven in a single piece according to one and the same system, but never repeating itself from one point to another, represents a single figure. Structurally, it forms a Whole.
Pierre Teilhard de Chardin, *The Phenomenon of Man*, William Collins Sons & Co. Ltd., 1982, p.49.

But this work may not be accomplished in one moment of conversion; it is not the work of one day, but of much time, much sweat, much labour, according to the grace of God that pitieth and the zeal of man that willeth and runneth.

William of St Thierry, *The Golden Epistles of Abbot William of St. Thierry*, Sheed & Ward Ltd., 1930, p.45.

In every man there is something of the Universal Spirit, strangely limited by that which is finite and personal, but still there. Occasionally it makes itself known in a word, look, or gesture, and then becomes one with the stars and sea.

Mark Rutherford, *More Pages From a Journal*, Oxford University Press, 1910, p.240.

Science is not enough, religion is not enough, art is not enough, politics and economics are not enough, nor is love, nor is duty, nor is action however disinterested, nor, however sublime, is contemplation. Nothing short of everything will really do.

Aldous Huxley, *Island*, Chatto & Windus, 1962, p.132.

The sense of wholeness! Does one write books in order to give one's fellow-men a sense of wholeness: first, a oneness with all men, then a oneness with all things, then a oneness with our cosmos, and finally a oneness with the vast invisible universe? Is that it? Is that our achievement and our peace?

D.H. Lawrence, *The Phoenix*, edited by Edward D. McDonald, William Heinemann Ltd., 1935, p.740.

Beware of extremes, beware of inhuman efforts, of violent measures, of all that drives you off your balance... Don't attempt the impossible... Take yourself as you are, whole, and do not try to live by one part alone and starve the other. Control, but do not kill...

Janet Erskine Stuart, in *Life and Letters of Janet Erskine Stuart*, Maud Monahan, Longmans, Green and Co. Ltd., 1922, p.59.

The picture of "a universal man" has almost disappeared.

Still, it remains each man's duty to safeguard the notion of the human person as a totality in which predominate values of intellect, will, conscience, and brotherhood since these values were established by the creator and wondrously restored and elevated by Christ.

Second Vatican Council, *The Conciliar and Post Conciliar Documents*, 1981 Edition, general editor, Austin Flannery OP, Fowler Wright Books Ltd, p.965.

Above all, the individual should aim at fullness and wholeness of development. Every human being is confronted with the task of growing up, of building a personality out of the raw materials of his infant self. A rich and full personality, in moral and spiritual harmony with itself and with its destiny, one whose talents are not buried and whose wholeness transcends its conflicts, is the highest creation of which we have knowledge, and in its attainment the individual possibilities of the evolutionary process are brought to supreme fruition.

Sir Julian Huxley, *Religion without Revelation*, C.A. Watts & Co. Ltd., 1967, p.168.

Why do people go for illusory wholeness? Often because they are people with a mania for perfection and to achieve real wholeness involves the difficult struggle to let go of perfection... What is devilish about perfection is that it always seems attainable and it never is... This kills joy.

We need risk, untidiness, chaos in which to refind ourselves. This is what tells us to be forever creating, which means forever denying the perfection which inhibits creation. Wholeness is the only real asceticism, leading us out of the contrivances we know into deserts which we are commanded to make blossom.

Monica Furlong, *Travelling In*, Hodder & Stoughton Ltd., 1971, p.63.

When scientific specialization has almost reached the point where a different surgeon is required to remove each tonsil, a key question hangs in the air of our time. When the specialists have taken Man apart, who is to put him together again? Who will see him steadily and whole as a person who lives, loves, sins and dies? I would contend that it is the preacher and only the preacher who addresses Man in his wholeness, the totality of his being. In this world of specialists, the preacher is an unashamed generalizer. With breathtaking audacity, he states truths which are cosmic in sweep and yet apply to any individual, anywhere at any time.

Colin Morris, *The Word and the Words*, Epworth Press, 1975, p.15.

When a man ignores the existence of the "spiritual life" it means that, however brilliant, well-intentioned, decent, a man may be, he is really only half-alive; his life is incomplete, unfulfilled; for he has not found the clue to the meaning of life. He is unaware of the need for "wholeness" or "integration" which is felt by so many people, even without any reference to what they would call "religion"...

It is our conviction, as Christians, that man was made for "wholeness"—that every part of his nature is so ordered that it cannot find fulfilment unless all is co-ordinated and integrated into a whole; this can only happen—even in a very general and imperfect way—as the whole personality is unified to serve *one* end: "Who keeps one end in view, makes all things serve." In other words: we have been created for God, and we are lost, empty and restless until we come to our senses, and come home to our Father.

Olive Wyon, *On the Way*, SCM Press Ltd., 1958, p.30.

As I draw near to the end of a long active life, I have come to regard a capacity for what I have called Intersection as perhaps the most essential quality of mind and spirit needed by twentieth-century man, placed as he is, in a distracted, divided world, with all its conflicting loyalties, and called upon to assimilate and reconcile within himself so many conflicting truths. Intersection is a way of harmonized and harmonizing life, demanding in a high degree moral and intellectual virtues of charity and humility, and a capacity for selfless seeing. On the Christian—so it seems to me—it is binding, if he is to live to the full the life of charity as described by St Paul in the well-known thirteenth chapter of his first letter to the Christians at Corinth. And for some Christians, who cannot escape from that exclusiveness which has so often sullied the thought of the Christian Church and caused it to commit so many crimes, it is not always easy.

How is it possible for you and me, if we wish to do so, to attain this state of Intersection, so that it becomes a part of us, a pattern of inner life capable of gripping thought and action? It is only by spontaneously throwing ourselves open, humbly and lovingly, to—I can think of no better word to express what I mean than Meister Eckhart's—to Is-ness in all its fulness...

To try to follow the way of Intersection must be primarily an individual adventure; it is something to be sought and cultivated by those who would and can.

F.C. Happold, *Religious Faith and Twentieth-Century Man*, Pelican Books, 1964, p.173.

WONDER

"Wonder"—*"emotion excited by what surpasses expectation or experience or seems inexplicable, surprise mingled with admiration or curiosity or bewilderment."*

O ne morning I went into University College, London, and was hailed excitedly by one of our post-graduates. "Hey, Bill. Have you got a moment? Come and look at this."

I was ushered into his laboratory and invited to look down a microscope. What I saw was a shell of the most perfect dimensions and proportions—something of real beauty. I responded enthusiastically.

"Yes," he said, "it is wonderful, isn't it. But do you know what it is?"

"Well, it's a rather lovely shell."

"Yes, it's a shell all right, but last week we took it to be merely a grain of sand which we've dredged up from the North Sea. Under the microscope, magnified a hundred times, we've discovered it's a shell. That's very significant, isn't it? Maybe there's something to be said for your Creator God after all."

I left his laboratory feeling rather excited. Even in that microscopic shell there was a sense of order and design. Nature still remains a great source of wonder, the sea, the countryside, mountains, even the human figure. I remembered one of our brilliant scientists, delighted at the birth of his daughter. He felt he had come close to the miraculous and his eyes were filled with a sense of wonder.

Seek the Lord and his strength, seek his presence continually! Remember the wonderful works that he has done, the wonders he wrought, the judgments he uttered.

1 Chronicles 16.11-12.

For thou didst form my inward parts, thou didst knit me together in my mother's womb. I praise thee, for thou art fearful and wonderful. Wonderful are thy works! Thou knowest me right well.

Psalm 139.13-14.

And all spoke well of him, and wondered at the gracious words which proceeded out of his mouth.

Luke 4.22.

And all the people saw him walking and praising God, and recognized him as the one who sat for alms at the Beautiful Gate of the temple; and they were filled with wonder and amazement at what had happened to him.

Acts 3.9-10.

Worship is transcendent wonder; wonder for which there is no limit or measure.

Thomas Carlyle, *Heroes and Hero-Worship*, Ward Lock, 1841, p.8.

The idea of God that man has in his being is the wonder of all wonders.

Rabindranath Tagore, *Sadhana*, Macmillan Publishers Ltd., 1930, p.48.

And bid them rise, awake, and walk the way,
The steep white way of wonder, up to God.

G.A. Studdert Kennedy, *The Unutterable Beauty*, Hodder & Stoughton Ltd., 1964, p.102.

Philosophy begins in wonder. And, at the end, when philosophic thought has done its best, the wonder remains.

A.N. Whitehead, *Modes of Thought*, Cambridge University Press, 1938, p.232.

Truth sees God: wisdom gazes on God. And these two produce a third, a holy, wondering delight in God, which is love.

Julian of Norwich, *Revelations of Divine Love*, Penguin Books Ltd., 1976, p.130.

Wonder and love are caught, not taught; and to catch them we must be in an atmosphere where we are sure to find the germs.

Evelyn Underhill, in *The Wisdom of Evelyn Underhill*, edited by John Stobbart, Mowbray, 1951, p.11.

When I dipt into the future far as human eye could see;
Saw the Vision of the world, and all the wonder that would be.

Alfred, Lord Tennyson, *The Works of Alfred Lord Tennyson*, Macmillan Publishers Ltd., 1898, *Locksley Hall*, p.98.

The wonder and curiosity which welcomes what is new and regards it not as threatening but enriching life—that wonder and curiosity is God.

H.A. Williams, C.R., *The True Wilderness*, William Collins Sons & Co. Ltd., 1983, p.111.

There is nothing that is so wonderfully created as the human soul. There is something of God in it. We are infinite in the future, though we are finite in the past.

Henry Ward Beecher, *Proverbs from Plymouth Pulpit*, Charles Burnet & Co., 1887, p.31.

God moves in a mysterious way,
His wonders to perform;
He plants his footsteps in the sea,
And rides upon the storm.

William Cowper, *The Poetical Works of William Cowper*, Oxford University Press, 1950, *Olney Hymns*, XXXV, *Light Shining Out of Darkness*, l.1-4, p.455.

It is wonder that prompts the mind to examine its environment—and at first the elementary wonder how to make the best of it; but the enquiry ends in the wonder of awe, before that which, the more it is understood, by so much the more transcends our understanding.

William Temple, *Nature, Man and God*, Macmillan Publishers Ltd., 1934, p.156.

"All things begin in some wonder, and in some wonder end," said St. Augustine, wisest in his day of mortal men. It is a strange thing, and a mystery, how we ever got into this world, a stranger thing still to me how we shall ever get out of this world again. Yet they are common things enough—birth and death.

Charles Kingsley, *Daily Thoughts*, Macmillan Publishers Ltd., 1884, p.155.

The older I grow the more I find of wonder everywhere, and no explanation: my last gasp will be one of astonishment. To-day an absurd bird sang—on Dec. 31—as if God had already wakened out of his winter snooze; and I was paralysed with a sense, utterly by me inexpressible, of the wonder of the world, the least and biggest thing alike.

Stephen MacKenna, *Journal and Letters*, Constable & Co. Ltd., 1936, p.87.

When the proofs, the figures, were ranged in columns before me...
How soon unaccountable I became tired and sick,
Till rising and gliding out I wander'd off by myself,
In the mystical moist night-air, and from time to time,
Look'd up in perfect silence at the stars.

Walt Whitman, *The Complete Poems*, edited by Frances Murphy, Penguin Books Ltd., 1982, *When I Heard the Learn'd Astronomer*, p.298.

Wonder is the highest thing in man, and if the ultimate phenomenon sets him wondering he should be content: he can be aware of nothing higher and he should seek nothing beyond: here is the limit. But for most men the vision of the ultimate phenomenon is not enough, they insist on going further like children who peep in a mirror and then turn it round to see what is on the other side.

Johann Wolfgang von Goethe, *The Practical Wisdom of Goethe*, chosen by Emil Ludwig, George Allen & Unwin Publishers Ltd., 1933, *To Eckermann*, 1829, p.91.

Then there is the appeal of Jesus to the imagination, to the sense of wonder. How often we read in the gospel story that the people wondered at what Jesus did and said! They marvelled—the wondering imagination.

Jesus evokes that sense of wonder, and isn't it perhaps that sense of wonder which is a large part of what we call worship, and which really makes the difference between what is only an ethical allegiance, and what is religion?

Michael Ramsey, *Through the Year with Michael Ramsey*, edited by Margaret Duggan, Hodder & Stoughton Ltd., 1975, p.24.

No man or woman begins to live a full life until they realise they live in the presence of something greater, outside and beyond themselves. Self-consciousness truly means that you are standing over against that other than yourself and you cannot be living in truth. Wonder is at the base of true living, and wonder leads to worship and after that the great other than self; it is yet kin to you, you are one with it. Then you begin to live more completely and realise the kinship between you and nature, that out of nature you came and are part and parcel with it, this brings nearer faith which is self-conscious life (opposed to birds, trees, etc.), reaching out to perfection.

G.A. Studdert Kennedy, *The New Man in Christ*, Hodder & Stoughton Ltd., 1932, p.132.

Rollers on the beach, wind in the pines, the slow flapping of herons across sand dunes, drown out the hectic rhythms of city and suburb, time tables and schedules. One falls under their spell, relaxes, stretches out prone. One becomes, in fact, like the element on which one lies, flattened by the sea; bare, open, empty as the beach, erased by today's tides of all yesterday's scribblings.

And then, some morning in the second week, the mind wakes, comes to life again... It begins to drift, to play, to turn over in gentle careless rolls like those lazy waves on the beach. One never knows what chance treasures these easy unconscious rollers may toss up, on the smooth white sand of the conscious mind...

Anne Morrow Lindbergh, *Gift From The Sea*, Chatto & Windus, 1974, p.16.

The first and fundamental wonder is existence itself. That I should be alive, conscious, a person, a part of the whole, that I should have emerged out of nothingness, that the Void should have given birth not merely to things, but to me. Among the many millions who throughout the centuries have crossed the stage of time probably not more than a handful have looked about them with astonishment, or found their own presence within the visible scene in any way surprising. Our immediate impressions and requirements, the daily doings, comings and goings of others like ourselves absorb in the years of infancy all our attention. Life steals imperceptibly upon us, without any sudden shock or sense of strangeness. How quietly we accommodate ourselves to the situation! In our early years, when all is fresh and new, we take the miracle for granted, and find abundant occupation and endless variety of interest. We are busy looking about us, and grow accustomed to living, and nothing appears startling to which we are accustomed. Thus it is that in the existence of the world or ourselves there appears for most of us no cause for amazement. So far from asking with Coleridge the unanswerable question, "Why should there be anything at all, any world at all?" we accept life without wonder and without curiosity. One might almost imagine that we were here on well-known ground, and but revisiting a country with which we had a previous acquaintance. Yet let the mind once awake—and distress of mind is the great awakener of mind— and this emergence from the womb of the immeasurable Universe rises to its full significance, to tower above all other thoughts, the wonder of wonders, beyond digestion into speech. To find oneself a member of a particular family and society, among innumerable other families and societies, engaged in a round of activities, to feel, think, love, hate, to eat, drink, sleep, to be involved in all these multitudinous affairs, not knowing in the least why this state of things should be ours, how we came into possession of this peculiar nature, acquired these needs, powers and passions, how or why we were launched upon this most extraordinary adventure— once give way to thoughts like these, and you are a prisoner for life, the prisoner of philosophy. But you will remain one of a negligible minority. And if it be a delusion to suppose that many human beings have been concerned with such musings, it is equally a delusion to suppose they have been spiritually minded, anxious about the state of their souls, eager for communion with God. All but the slenderest of minorities have been immersed in a struggle for existence, for material satisfac-tions, have sought the pleasures of the senses, or followed after power or wealth. Most have died, whatever their pursuits, in the full vigour of their sensuality, and in the full tide of their ignorance. If there has been one God universally acknowledged, universally worshipped, in all ages and countries, it is money.

W. Macneile Dixon, *The Human Situation*, Edward Arnold, 1937, p.75.

WORLDLINESS

"Worldliness"—"temporal, earthly, exclusively or preponderantly concerned with or devoted to the affairs of this life, especially the pursuit of wealth or pleasure, prudence in advancing one's own interests."

I wonder if I am correct in discerning three forms of worldliness in our day and age. Firstly, there is material wealth. "I tell my pupils to go for money," said one of our tutors. Money and what money can buy seem to be crucially important for most people. Secondly, there is success and status. Our sense of identity often comes by having made it to the top.

Thirdly, there are relationships, with sex having a high profile.

I would counter this by regarding women and men as made primarily in the image and likeness of God. Three consequences seem to follow on from this.

Firstly, there is wealth. This is not to be found primarily in cash, but in the human personality, and in realizing one's gifts and talents.

Secondly, there is success and status. Our sense of identity would come primarily in realizing our status as a child of God, and not just in having made it to the top.

Thirdly, there are relationships. First get our inner relatedness with God established, and then our outer relationships will naturally follow, with sex finding its rightful place. There will then be no need to worship it to excess, and exploit people. We shall be in the world, but not of it.

He will judge the world with righteousness, and the peoples with his truth.
Psalm 96.13.

Woe to those who are wise in their own eyes, and shrewd in their own sight!
Isaiah 5.21.

As for what was sown among thorns, this is he who hears the word, but the cares of the world and the delight in riches choke the word, and it proves unfruitful.
Matthew 13.22.

In their case the god of this world has blinded the minds of the unbelievers, to keep them from seeing the light of the gospel of the glory of Christ, who is the likeness of God.
2 Corinthians 4.4.

The kingdom of this world is "human society as it organizers itself apart from God".
Leslie J. Tizard, *Facing Life and Death*, George Allen and Unwin Publishers Ltd., 1959, p.111.

Those who set out to serve both God and Mammon soon discover that there is no God.
Logan Pearsall Smith, *Afterthoughts*, Constable & Co. Ltd., 1931, p.29.

You have too much respect upon the world.
They lose it that do buy it with much care.
William Shakespeare, *The Merchant of Venice*, Act I. sc.i. l.74.

This secular world—formerly regarded as "this" world, the wicked world *par excellence*, a neopagan world—today is not only taken into account in Christendom, but largely consciously approved and assisted in its development.
Hans Küng, *On Being a Christian*, translated by Edward Quinn, William Collins Sons & Co. Ltd., 1977, p.28.

The character of worldly men is shaped by the influence of the love of property, of power, of influence, of praise, and the love of animal indulgence—not by the right, the true, the noble.
Henry Ward Beecher, *Proverbs from Plymouth Pulpit*, Charles Burnet & Co., 1887, p.44.

The so-called "real world"; the world which psychiatrists and social scientists and tycoons in advertising firms want us to adjust to and be at home in. That world saps our integrity and eats up our whole personality, giving us not freedom to do what we really want to do but a whole set of false wants and artificial and quite unnecessary "needs".

Geoffrey Preston, O.P., *Hallowing the Time*, Darton, Longman & Todd Ltd., 1980, p.32.

The world (is) the sum of created being, which belongs to the sphere of human life as an ordered whole, considered apart from God, and in its moral aspect represented by humanity... It is easy to see how the thought of an ordered whole relative to man and considered *apart* from God passes into that of the ordered whole *separated* from God.

B.F. Westcott, *The Gospel according to St. John*, John Murray Ltd., 1908, Volume 1, p.14 & p.64.

> And to thy worst self, sacrifice thyself,
> For with thy worst self hast thou clothed thy God...
> Thy God is far diffused in noble groves
> And princely halls, and farms, and flowing lawns,
> And heaps of living gold that daily grow,
> And title-scrolls and gorgeous heraldries.
> In such a shape dost thou behold thy God.

Alfred, Lord Tennyson, *The Works of Alfred Lord Tennyson*, Macmillan Publishers Ltd., 1898, *Aylmer's Field*, p.152.

The "worldly" man is not necessarily the depraved man. He is the man who is misled into treating the world's goods as absorbing ends in themselves, and so misses the awareness of meaning and purpose beyond them.

The "unworldly" man is not necessarily the devout man, or the man with conscious concern for God or for heaven. He is the man who is not absorbed in the world's goods or dominated by them, for there is in him an imagination or a simplicity or a humility or a care for persons which hints at something beyond. His unworldliness is properly seen not in any neglect of the world, but in the nature of his care for it.

Michael Ramsey, *Through the Year with Michael Ramsey*, edited by Margaret Duggan, Hodder & Stoughton Ltd., 1975, p.123.

There is so much frustration in the world because we have relied on gods rather than God. We have genuflected before the god of science only to find that it has given us the atomic bomb, producing fears and anxieties that science can never mitigate. We have worshipped the god of pleasure only to discover that thrills play out and sensations are short-lived. We have bowed before the god of money only to learn that there are such things as love and friendship that money cannot buy and that in a world of possible depressions, stock market crashes, and bad business investments, money is a rather uncertain deity. These transitory gods are not able to save or bring happiness to the human heart. Only God is able. It is faith in Him that we must rediscover.

Martin Luther King, *The Words of Martin Luther King*, selected by Coretta Scott King, William Collins Sons & Co. Ltd., 1986, p.63.

The world... is a co-operative society with limited liability, existing for purely secular and chiefly for selfish ends, some of which can only be realised by combined action, preying on the weakness of others, and exploiting their moral as well as physical and economic weakness. If its victims are trampled on, or if they are tempted to take part in iniquities the guilt of which is spread and distributed over a large number of persons, the world disclaims all responsibility. Like the Chief Priests to the remorseful Judas, it says, "What is that to us? See thou to that." All who take part in practical work, especially in political or semi-political work, but also in business or commerce, know how extremely difficult it is not to be caught in the toils of this ubiquitous and intricate machinery; they know how difficult it is to win any sort of success without soiling our hands and straining our consciences.

W.R. Inge, *Personal Religion and the Life of Devotion*, Longmans, Green & Co. Ltd., 1924, p.79.

All undisciplined behaviour begins in the *mind*, and springs from three sources. The Bible describes this three-fold desire as the "desire of the flesh", the "desire of the eyes", and the "proud glory of life". (I John 2.16.). This "three-fold desire" is characteristic of the "world"... with its self-indulgence, superficiality, arrogance and conceit.

Now, as then, it is the "life of the world" which dries up the spiritual life at its root.

First, the "*desire of the flesh*": in general this means an excessive love of pleasure. Pleasure itself is not evil, and we are meant to enjoy life to the full. But when the desire for pleasure in any form threatens to absorb us entirely; when it becomes a craving which must be enjoyed at all costs; when we tend to think, "I'm sure I'm not fussy, but *I must have...*" this or that; then we are becoming undisciplined. The initial stages may seem innocent enough, but unless we realize what we are doing we may find that this way is a by-path which leads to spiritual disaster.

Then, the "*desire of the eyes*": this covers a great deal. For instance, it may mean an exaggerated love of *things*, and then the determination to *get* them by fair means or foul. Such a desire, it is clear, will inevitably dry up all desire for anything higher or more worth while, and must lead to the stifling of all desire for God and goodness.

It also includes the vice of excessive curiosity, that prying spirit which makes a person loathsome. Very grave harm is often done by people who overhear scraps of conversation, put their own construction upon them, and then proceed to make untold mischief. This also covers the undue desire to be "in" on everything, to be always "in the know", filling one's mind with trifles or even with sordid and unloving thoughts. Sometimes even to *look* at a certain picture or to go to a play or a film which has lowering suggestions will do infinite harm to the inner life. "Turn away mine eyes from beholding vanity" seems to be the prayer to counteract this tendency.

And finally, the "*proud glory of life*": the Greek word here... has a wealth of meaning: from swaggering and empty display to insolent self-assurance, expressed in love of power and the ruthlessness which tramples on other people's rights. Indeed, it covers most of what we mean by "pride" in the modern sense of the word: pride of family, of birth, of a good name; pride of good health and strength, of physical skill; pride of nation or class or colour; pride of achievement, pride of knowledge; pride of position and the effort to attain it—all of which may appear in some form or another, and often in subtle and disguised forms, within Church circles as well as in "the outside world". For this spirit may infect us all.

Olive Wyon, *On the Way*, SCM Press Ltd., 1958, p.73.

WORRY

"Worry"— "allow no rest or peace of mind to oneself, take needless trouble; full of uneasiness, give way to anxiety—let the mind dwell on troubles."

I n my late teens I went through a bad patch of anxiety. I was burdened with responsibilities, and unable to find a satisfactory way of coping with them. Anxiety deepened into worry and I was going round in circles and getting nowhere.

Almost in despair I got out a pen and paper, and made a list of all the problems facing me. I tackled them one by one and wrote down possible solutions.

I quickly realized it was impossible to write in circles—a waste of time and energy. I then discovered that as soon as I had written down one possible solution, a new insight presented itself for consideration. When this had been committed to paper the mind was cleared and open for a further idea or fresh insight. This I understood to come from the mind, the imagination, or the unconscious.

In the week that followed I was able to work through my responsibilities, and the problems facing me were largely resolved. The period of worry was over, and as a bonus I had found a useful technique for enriching life.

I now believe that the basic answer to worry is faith. A valuable component is this process of writing down possible solutions, and developing this to keep a journal—a "spiritual" diary. This writing process can be regarded as a valuable part of prayer, giving access to a practical way in which we can be guided.

Remove vexation from your mind, and put away pain from your body.
Ecclesiastes 11.10.

And they will look to the earth, but behold, distress and darkness, the gloom of anguish...
Isaiah 8.22.

But the cares of the world, and the delight in riches, and the desires for other things, enter in and choke the word, and it proves unfruitful.
Mark 4.19.

We are afflicted in every way, but not crushed; perplexed, but not driven to despair; persecuted, but not forsaken; struck down, but not destroyed; always carrying in the body the death of Christ, so that the life of Jesus may also be manifested in our bodies.
2 Corinthians 4.8-10.

Cast all your cares on God; that anchor holds.
Alfred, Lord Tennyson, *The Works of Alfred Lord Tennyson*, Macmillan Publishers Ltd., 1898, *Enoch Arden*, p.128.

Every faculty and virtue I possess can be used as an instrument wherewith to worry myself.
Mark Rutherford, *Last Pages From a Journal*, Oxford University Press, 1915, p.292.

I know well the feeling of being all tense with business and worry. The only cure is the old one—"whenever you have too much to do, don't do it."
A.C. Benson, *Extracts from the Letters of Dr. A.C. Benson to M.E.A.*, Jarrold Publishing, 1927, p.60.

We are not worried about our footing when we are about to jump. It is when we have nowhere to jump that we begin to worry about the soundness of our position. They who go places give no thought to security.

Eric Hoffer, *The Passionate State of Mind*, Martin Secker & Warburg Ltd., 1956, p.80.

The peril of certain troubles is that although they prevent consecutive thinking, they stimulate a tumultuous activity round a fixed point. Then ensues rapid, monstrous, diseased growth.

Mark Rutherford, *Last Pages From a Journal*, Oxford University Press, 1915, p.257.

If we are relieved from serious care we are not necessarily relieved from cares. A crowd of small, impertinent worries torment me which I should not notice if I were in real trouble.

Mark Rutherford, *Last Pages From a Journal*, Oxford University Press, 1915, p.308.

Let us put all our worries to God, squarely, and then, having told him everything, so that he should know them from us, we should drop them, leave them to him. Now that he is in the know, it is no longer any of our concern: we can freely think of him.

Anthony Bloom, *The Essence of Prayer*, Darton, Longman & Todd Ltd., 1989, p.116.

While there is always need of wise forethought and due reference to the demands of the future, these have yet nothing in common with mere anxieties and worries which are disintegrating and fret away all the pure gold of life. Worry is simply lack of faith in God. "For your heavenly Father knoweth what things ye have need of before ye ask Him." Only in peace of spirit can any true achievement be won.

Lilian Whiting, *Lilies of Eternal Peace*, Gay and Hancock, Ltd., 1908, p.17.

Annihilation of this swarm of petty invading cares by adoration! They possess and distract, not by their inherent strength but through the absence of a dominant power. The lover is absorbed in the desire to be with his mistress and keeps his appointment with her, breaking all hindrances like threads. Who shall deliver me from the body of this death? The answer was not difficult to St. Paul, but how is it with me?

Mark Rutherford, *Last Pages From a Journal*, Oxford University Press, 1915, p.290.

Each one of us finds himself tormented by worries of one kind or another and because we are in some sense infinite, we are always able to make room for still more. Many of these worries are, to put it simply, mis-directed and consequently have to be eliminated from our lives.

At times, nonetheless, our worries are quite well founded and even noble in their concern for others, but we are too weak to bear them single-handedly. Still less are we able to resolve them. Worry can paralyze, and if we would live a full life we have to give our worries to someone else to carry. But there is Someone who desires to do just that.

Michel Quoist, *The Christian Response*, Gill and Macmillan Ltd., 1965, p.55.

Unless we learn to live care-lessly, we will be fruitlessly wasting our strength on the air. Life's difficulties besiege us from every side and even break through the outer ramparts to keep our interior life in a state of constant confusion.

We can not long keep up the good fight and get the better of the forces arrayed against us unless we can spontaneously and sincerely give all our problems into the

Lord's hands. It takes many long years to learn to exchange our own personal weakness, at each step of our lives, for the strength of God. But once we have achieved this necessary renunciation, we will soon experience the peace of God in our lives.

Michel Quoist, *The Christian Response*, Gill and Macmillan Ltd., 1965, p.58.

Staying in a cottage in Sussex, the home of the widow of a minister, I saw cut into the window "*This is the day.*" The woman explained. "I have had a lot of trouble in my time, and I am a great one to worry. I was always afraid of what was going to happen tomorrow. And each morning, when I woke up, I felt as though I had the weight of the world upon me. Then, one day, when I was very upset about things, I sat down and read my Bible... it happened that I was reading the one hundred and eighteenth Psalm. When I came to the twenty-fourth verse I stopped. '*This is the day that the Lord hath made; we will rejoice and be glad in it.*' I looked again to see what particular day was referred to. But I could not find it. And then it occurred to me that it means any day, every day, *this* day. '*This is the day* that the Lord hath made.' And why should I be afraid of the days if He makes them... Somehow, you don't feel afraid of the day if you feel that *He made it!*"

F.W. Boreham, *The Tide Comes In*, Epworth Press, 1958, p.23.

Worry (Jesus says) is characteristic of a heathen, and not of one who knows what God is like... Worry is essentially distrust of God. Such a distrust may be understandable in a heathen who believes in a jealous, capricious, unpredictable god; but it is beyond comprehension in one who has learned to call God by the name of Father. The Christian cannot worry because he believes in the love of God.

Jesus goes on to advance two ways in which to defeat worry. The first is to seek first, concentrate upon, the Kingdom of God... to be in the Kingdom and to do the will of God is one and the same thing... To concentrate on the doing of, and acceptance of, God's will is the way to defeat worry. We know that in our own lives a great love can drive out every other concern. Such a love can inspire a man's work, intensify his study, purify his life, dominate his whole being. It was Jesus' conviction that worry is banished when God becomes the dominating power of our lives.

Lastly, Jesus says that worry can be defeated when we acquire the art of living one day at a time... If each day is lived as it comes, if each task is done as it appears, then the sum of all the days is bound to be good. It is Jesus' advice that we should handle the demands of each day as it comes, without worrying about the unknown future and the things which may never happen.

William Barclay, *The Gospel of Matthew*, The Saint Andrew Press, 1987, Volume 1, p.258.

Let us now see if we can gather up Jesus's arguments against worry.

(i) *Worry is needless, useless and even actively injurious.* Worry cannot affect the past, for the past is past... It is not that a man can or ought to dissociate himself from his past; but he ought to use his past as a spur and a guide for better action in the future, and not as something about which he broods until he has worried himself into a paralysis of action.

Equally, worry about the future is useless... Worry about the future is wasted effort, and the future of reality is seldom as bad as the future of our fears.

But worry is worse than useless: it is often actively injurious. The two typical diseases of modern life are the stomach ulcer and the coronary thrombosis, and in many cases both are the result of worry. It is a medical fact that he who laughs most lives longest. The worry which wears out the mind wears out the body along with it.

Worry affects a man's judgment, lessens his powers of decision, and renders him progressively incapable of dealing with life. Let a man give his best to every situation—he cannot give more—and let him leave the rest to God.

(ii) *Worry is blind.* Worry refuses to learn the lesson of nature. Jesus bids men look at the birds, and see the bounty which is behind nature, and trust the love that lies behind that bounty. Worry refuses to learn the lesson of *history*... The man who feeds his heart on the record of what God has done in the past will never worry about the future. Worry refuses to learn the lesson of *life*. We are still alive and our heads are still above water; and yet if someone had told us that we would have to go through what we have actually gone through, we would have said it was impossible. The lesson of life is that somehow we have been enable to bear the unbearable and to do the undoable and to pass the breaking-point and not to break. The lesson of life is that worry is unnecessary.

(iii) *Worry is essentially irreligious.* Worry is not caused by external circumstances. In the same circumstances one man can be absolutely serene, and another man can be worried to death. Both worry and serenity come, not from circumstance, but from the heart.

William Barclay, *The Gospel of Matthew*, The Saint Andrew Press, 1987, Volume 1, p.259.

Index

Maugham, W. Somerset, 112, 132, 150

May, Rollo, 68, 90, 139, 148

Melville, Herman, 105, 120, 130, 130

Mencken, H.L., 130

Meredith, George, 59, 93

Merton, Thomas, 16, 38, 47, 53, 53, 54, 68, 69, 100, 119, 127, 128, 141, 221, 226, 226, 226, 226, 233, 247, 251, 276

Miller, Henry, 242, 265, 275

Milton, John, 22, 46, 49, 50, 179, 186, 262, 262

Moberly, Elizabeth R., 245

Moltmann, Jürgen, 23, 23, 102

Monnin, Alfred, 230

Montefiore, Hugh, 75, 76, 86, 219, 219

Morgan, Charles, 150

Moore, George, 93, 167

Moorhouse, Geoffrey, 91

Morris, Colin, 281

Murdoch, Iris, 127, 168

Acknowledgments

We would like to thank all those who have given us permission to reproduce extracts from publications in this book, as indicated on the list below. Every effort has been made to trace and contact copyright owners. If there are any inadvertent omissions in the acknowledgments we apologize to those concerned.

Curtis Brown Ltd: from *The Passionate State of Mind*, Eric Hoffer.

Extracts from the Authorized Version of the Bible (the King James Bible), the rights of which are vested in the Crown, are reproduced by permission of the Crown's patentee, Cambridge University Press.

Harry James Cargos: from *Encountering Myself*, © Harry James Cargos.

The Report of the Archbishop of Canterbury's Commission on Urban Priority Areas (Church House Publishing 1985) by permission of The Central Board of Finance of the Church of England.

Cyril Connolly, Literary Agents: from *The Unquiet Grave*, Cyril Connolly, published by Hamish Hamilton 1945, and now by Pimlico.

Darton Longman & Todd: from *The Heart in Pilgrimage*, Christopher Bryant; from *Seeds of Hope*, Henri J.M. Nouwen.

Margaret Duggan: from *Through the Year with Michael Ramsey*, edited by Margaret Duggan.

Thanks are expressed to Epworth Press for permission to quote from *The Use of Praying*, J. Neville Ward; from *The Pure in Heart*, W.E. Sangster.

Faber & Faber Ltd: from *The Complete Poems and Plays*, T.S. Eliot; from *Collected Shorter Poems*, Louis MacNeice; from *The Whitsun Weddings*, Philip Larkin.

Monica Furlong: from *Travelling In*, © Monica Furlong.

Gill and Macmillan, Dublin: from *With Open Heart*, Michel Quoist.